S0-DVR-728

THE COMMANDER OF THE FAITHFUL

VOLUME 2
THE MODERN MIDDLE EAST SERIES

Sponsored by

The Middle East Institute
Columbia University, New York

Editorial Board

THE COMMANDER
OF THE FAITHFUL

The Moroccan Political Elite —
A Study in Segmented Politics

John Waterbury

Assistant Professor of Political Science,
University of Michigan

Columbia University Press
New York

Published in 1970 by
Columbia University Press, New York

Library of Congress Catalog Card Number: 76–108417

SBN: 231–03326–5

Printed in Great Britain

To
I.N.F. and S.W.W.
E.D.W. and M.F.W.
C.W.

CONTENTS

CONTENTS

TABLES

ILLUSTRATIONS

ABBREVIATIONS USED IN THE TEXT AND NOTES

BEPI	Bureau d'Etudes et de Participation Industrielle
BNDE	Banque Nationale de Développement Economique
BRPM	Bureau des Recherches et de Participation Minière
CGEA	Centres de Gestion et d'Exploitation Agricole
CURS	Centre Universitaire de Recherches Scientifiques
IHEM	Institut des Hautes Etudes Marocaines
INRA	Institut National des Recherches Agronomiques
OCE	Office de Commercialisation et d'Exportation
OCP	Office Chérifien des Phosphates
OMVA	Office de Mise-en-Valeur Agricole
ONI	Office National d'Irrigation
ONMR	Office National de Modernisation Rurale
PTT	Postes, Téléphones, et Télégraphes (Ministry of)
RTM	Radio-Télévision Marocaine
TP	Travaux Publics (Ministry of)

MISCELLANEOUS

CCI	Chambres de Commerce et d'Industrie
FAR	Forces Armées Royales
MAP	Maghreb Arabe Presse

ABBREVIATIONS USED IN THE TEXT AND NOTES

POLITICAL AND ECONOMIC ORGANIZATIONS

FDIC	Front pour la Défense des Institutions Constitutionelles
MP	Mouvement Populaire
PDI/PDC	Parti Démocratique de l'Indépendance/Parti Démocratique Constitutionel
PCM	Parti Communiste Marocain
PSD	Parti Socialiste Démocrate
UGEM	Union Générale des Etudiants Marocains
UGTM	Union Générale des Travailleurs Marocains
UMA	Union Marocaine d'Agriculture
UMCIA	Union Marocaine des Commercants, Industrialistes et Artisans
UMT	Union Marocaine de Travail
UNEM	Union Nationale des Etudiants Marocains
UNFP	Union Nationale des Forces Populaires

PUBLICATIONS

A.A.N.	*Annuaire de l'Afrique du Nord* (Aix-en-Provence)
A.P.S.R.	*American Political Science Review*
A.U.F.S. Report	*American Universities Field Staff Report*
B.E.S.M.	*Bulletin Economique et Social du Maroc*
M.E.J.	*Middle East Journal*
R.F.S.P.	*Revue Française de Science Politique*

A NOTE ON TRANSLITERATION

The English-speaking scholar is faced with peculiar problems in devising a transliteration system for materials dealing with ex-French North Africa. Convenience for the reader, consistency, and phonetic accuracy are three standards probably impossible to honor equally. The puzzle has several levels. First, many place and proper names are Berber, an unwritten language that must be transliterated into some written language. In the case of Morocco, this is almost always French or Arabic, and both commit grave faults in their common transliterations of Berber. Generally, the French bypassed Arabic renderings of Berber words and devised their own which are often sloppy. Arabic versions, while hardly satisfactory, seem to be more faithful to the phonetics of Berber than either the French or the less frequent Spanish.

Beyond this, French transliteration, which over the years has become standardized even in English usage, seeks to reproduce not the classical Arabic pronunciation, but the dialectical. This does not make it easy to adhere to forms common throughout the Arab world.

To complicate matters further, the French consonants, vowels, and diphthongs employed in their transliteration systems may make little sense to the English-speaker. Thus, French transliteration employs the diphthong *ou* to represent either *w* or *u* (pronounced as in *boot*): e.g. *Ouezzan* (Wazzan) or *Boujad* (Būjad). No distinction is made between ﻙ (*kaf*) and ﻕ (*qaf*), and ﻍ (*ghayn*), is often transliterated as *rh*, as in Rharb (Gharb). Any name may embody several sins of this sort: e.g. Boubker Kadiri (Abū Bakr al-Qādirī).

So many French transliterations have become standardized over

xiii

the years that it is difficult to avoid using them. They appear constantly in print, in bibliographies, and indexes, and to alter them would only confuse the reader who might wish to find out more about their objects through other sources. On the other hand, French forms will be ignored for the following terms: bilad al-makhzan (Fr. bled al-makhzen), bilad as-siba (Fr. bled as-siba), murabit (Fr. marabout), shurafa (Fr. chorfa), and shari'a (Fr. chrâa). These will appear in the text as shown here and will not be italicized. The terms guich (jaysh), dahir (zahir), goum/goumi (qawm/qawmi), and douar (duwar) are so prevalent in literature pertaining to Morocco that they will be retained from the French and will likewise remain unitalicized. Finally, the word bled/blad (bilad: countryside), meaning just about all the territory outside Morocco's urban agglomerations, will be used in the text in its dialectical form, blad, without italics.

For all other cases a few simple and convenient guidelines have been chosen. As regards place names, standard French trans-literations will be employed. Thus Salé instead of Slā and Oujda instead of Wajda or Ujda. However, certain exceptions will be made to this general rule. Whenever the ou commences a word and represents a w, a w will be used. As a result, the place names Wazzan and Warzazat will replace Ouezzan and Ouarzazat. If the ou is medial, it will be left unchanged: thus Tetouan. There are, nonetheless, a few words with medial w that the French have often transliterated that way, such as 'Alawi or Chawia, and I shall, of course, do likewise. A minimum of diacritical marks will be employed. Where feasible, an apostrophe will represent the ع ('ayn).

The same procedure will be followed in transliterating proper names. These appear in newspapers and other publications in their French form and are, moreover, generally the preferred spellings of their bearers. It seems unreasonable to tamper with names such as Laghzaoui (al-Aghzawi), Medhi Ben Barka (al-Mahdi ibn Barka) or Boucetta (Abu Sitta). Again, the exception will be such names as Hassan Wazzani or Halima Warzazi in place of Ouezzani and Ouarzazi.

One peculiarity of Moroccan Berber and Arabic needs special note. There is the consonant gaf (ڭ, گ, ڧ) which crops up often in words such as Agadir or Reda Guedira. As a general rule, the gaf will generally be transliterated gu (as in Guedira).

A GLOSSARY OF SPECIAL ARABIC TERMS

'ar	'ār; religious constraint, or obligation through sacrifice.
'azib	'azīb; sharifian landholding.
baraka	baraka; quality of blessedness.
bay'a	bay'a; fealty.
blad/bled	bilād; countryside.
dahir	thahīr; imperial edict.
douar	duwār; small rural village or agglomeration.
goumi	qawmī; soldier.
guish/guiche	Jaysh; army.
khammes/khammas	khammās; a sharecropper who retains a fifth of the crop.
makhzan	makhzan; the central government of Morocco.
makhzani	Makhzani; government soldier or guard.
m'sid	masīd; Quran school: sometimes nationalist free school.
murabit/marabout	murābit; a saint.
pasha	bāsha; city governor.
qadi	qādī; religious judge.
qaid	qā'id; rural administrator.
shari'a/chraâ	sharī'a; Islamic religious law.
shurafa (pl. of sharif)	shurafā'; descendants of the Prophet.
siba	sība; dissidence.
taifa	tā'ifa; a religious order (alt. zawiya).

xv

tertīb	tartīb; an agricultural tax.
'ulema (pl. of 'alim)	'ulamā,; religious savants of Islam.
za'im	za'īm; an inspiring leader.
zawiya	zāwīyya; a religious order (alt. ta'ifa).

ACKNOWLEDGMENTS

This book was made possible through the generous support of the Foreign Area Fellowship Program during two years of research in Morocco. I am also indebted to the Center for Near Eastern and North African Studies at the University of Michigan for having prolonged my stay in Morocco as well as for having provided me a summer in which to revise my manuscript. Of course, neither organization is in any way responsible for, nor to some extent even aware of, the judgments and opinions expressed in the following pages.

A number of people played a direct or indirect role in the writing of my thesis. Foremost among them were unwitting accomplices: David M. Hart, Ernest Gellner, Stuart Schaar, I.W. Zartman, Rémy Leveau, and John Cooley, all of whom freely shared with me their knowledge of Morocco with no assurances as to how I would exploit it. I am also grateful to a congenial band of doctoral candidates with whom I compared notes frequently: Kenneth Brown, Larry Rosen, Edmund Burke, Ross Dunn, and Vincent Crapanzano.

There are many Moroccans who followed my progress with varying degrees of interest and apprehension, but none stinted in their courtesy and aid. They will remain un-named, but my thanks to them are nonetheless sincere.

Finally, I am particularly grateful to J.C. Hurewitz of the Middle East Institute at Columbia University who encouraged me to undertake this study and who saw me through to the end.

The King, Commander of the Faithful (*Amir al-Mu'minin*), symbol of the unity of the Nation, guarantor of the perennity and the continuity of the state, watches over the observance of Islam and the Constitution. He is the protector of the rights and liberties of the citizens, and of social groups and collectivities.

The Moroccan Constitution of 1962, Article 19

INTRODUCTION

... this increase in sociological realism makes it possible to approach the central question in this area – what in fact *are* the relationships between the way in which New State polities behave and the way in which traditional ones behaved – without succumbing to either of two equally misleading (and, at the moment, equally popular) propositions: that contemporary states are the mere captives of their pasts, re-enactments in thinly modern dress of archaic dramas; or that such states have completely escaped their past, are absolute products of an age which owes nothing to anything but itself.[1]

Almost every western political scientist who has written on the developing nations has warned that analytic tools devised for western societies are not suitable for use in this new environment. In recent years, a major effort has been made to re-tool for the complex and enigmatic problems confronted in the comparative politics of the new states. Two trends in this direction are of particular importance. First, there is the structural-functional approach, which seeks to categorize and compare regimes and the structures of their governments according to their response to a common set of developmental problems. Regimes are analyzed in reference to how they cope or fail to cope with the processes of 'social change', 'political transition', 'economic and political modernization', and 'nation-building'; terms that flow perhaps too easily and indiscriminately from the pens of political scientists. Second, one finds a more recent and derivative concern with political culture and the interrelation of contemporary national politics in the new states with the social and historical heritage of indigenous political behavior and attitudes. One may surmise that some of those who have become engaged in the latter endeavor are frequently the same scholars who first ventured into structural-functional analysis and found it not entirely adequate to the task at hand.

In earlier studies, political and social change may have been taken too much for granted. The weight of the analysis was placed upon the response to or administration of change rather than upon the nature of the transition process itself. Structural-functional categories suffered as a result. Various models have indeed had a general validity but in attempting to apply them to specific societies they would seem somewhat askew, like a recognizable melody played out of tune. At least part of the cause of the deficiencies in these first essays at model-building was that social and political change was presented as an amorphous back-drop for the analysis of a given regime's performance in carrying out its functional requisites. The cultural characteristics of societies undergoing the ubiquitous torture of more or less abrupt transition were seldom made explicit. Various political units – governments, elites, parties, classes, etc. – may meet all the objective requirements for classification within a single functional category, but these same units often reveal a disconcerting tendency to behave very differently from one another. These differences may be surface manifestations of variations in political culture and a differential rate of change of social institutions from one society to another.

It is perfectly legitimate, although not always very useful, to construct typologies of political regimes according to the nature of their governmental institutions, the kinds of policies they apply, and their formal arrangements for political participation. But often the categories so constructed either blur meaningful distinctions between regimes in an attempt to be all-inclusive, or are so narrow that each regime in effect becomes a separate category. Moreover, single-minded concern with regime types leads to distortions in our appraisal of any given change in regime.

To refer only to the Middle East, the fact that the Yemen was changed from a theocracy to a republic in 1962 did not alter the social and economic determinants of politics in that country. Nor can one argue that because, in 1924, Reza Khan was compelled to become the shah rather than the president of Iran that some qualitative change had been wrought in the Iranian political process since the growth of the constitutional movement in the early years of the twentieth century.[2] Finally, it does not advance us very far in our understanding of politics in Morocco to say that the regime is a 'modernizing autocracy' or a 'conservative oligarchy'. Morocco is all that, and, as a regime, can be compared with Iran or Jordan. But this approach obscures the social and cultural context for politics, and on this level Morocco can be meaningfully compared with revolutionary Algeria.

The political culture of a society guides the behavior of political actors and contains the catalysts as well as the constraints to political action. A regime may actively seek to change the content of the political culture of the society which it governs. But until the time it actually does so, the regime is to some degree the captive of its culture. This, I would argue, is the situation in Algeria today and would be the situation in Morocco were a revolutionary regime to come to power. The present Moroccan regime is a more-or-less willing captive of its political culture, and the manner in which the regime is influenced by and in turn seeks to sustain certain elements of its political culture will receive extensive analysis in the rest of the book.

Generally, the systematic treatment of political culture has been confined to the analysis of overt value or belief systems, how they came into being, and what mechanisms may exist to impede or punish deviation from them. The elements of these systems form well-known, repeatedly acknowledged guidelines to political action. Sydney Verba states that: 'The political culture of a society consists of the system of empirical beliefs, expressive symbols, and values which defines the situation in which political action takes place.'[3] I have taken a somewhat different approach to the problem of political culture. My primary concern is with political behavior, but it became apparent to me that in Morocco political behavior is not very often governed by any overt belief or value system. There are, however, discernible patterns of political behavior. These are not often recognized as such by the actors themselves, and consequently there are no formal sanctions for deviation from them. But adherence to these patterns is encouraged by the fact that they are 'functional' to survival in the system.

To explain the persistence of these patterns in modern Morocco requires an understanding of both the traditional social structures of the country and its recent history. The influence of Morocco's past in the maintenance of certain behavioral patterns is less conjectural than the role of social structure in their formation.

3

Morocco is unique in that so much of the traditional governmental and political system survived the half century of direct French rule relatively intact. Certain social groups, such as the tribes or the urban bourgeoisie, were in many instances carefully protected by the French, and even the sultan was, in a way, put in mothballs, to be resurrected at the time of independence in 1955. Many habits of political action that had yet to be unlearned seemed peculiarly appropriate in the post-protectorate years.

The predilection to revive these habits was bolstered by the phenomenon of the reanimation, or even exacerbation of primordial sentiments that often follows the granting of independence. Morocco, like many other developing nations, is composed of numerous groups that are conscious of their identity as such, or at least of their animosity for other groups. These may be tribes, cities, regions, sects, and the like. During the colonial period their differences are often sublimated in two ways. First, all of them are obliged to accept what can be called binding arbitration, on the part of the colonial power. No group in this situation is capable of defying the regime's policies, no matter how unjust or discriminatory they may be. The leaders of any group are therefore let off the hook *vis-à-vis* their followers, for they can plead that they have no effective influence over policy decisions. Thus, the central authorities are to some extent 'insulated' from the web of primordial sentiments. Second, the growth of nationalist movements tends to gloss over group animosities in the joint quest for independence. But these animosities are rekindled once the colonial power departs, for it is no longer a question of binding arbitration by an outside power, but a question of one faction or coalition of factions from within the same country trying to rule the others. As leaders of tribal, lingual or religious groupings contest for seats in the government and for the control of policy-making, they seek to discipline their followers by telling them of the duplicity of the rivals. They encourage their followers to demonstrate on the basis of their primary sentiments.[4] In this way some new nations come unstuck, regardless of regime. The rekindling of such sentiments has never become that acute in Morocco, but the process has ramifications there, and these help to explain the continuity in traditional behavior.

Recent history has preserved but it is social structure that gave rise to Morocco's political culture. I would reiterate that I am particularly concerned with that aspect of political culture which relates to patterns of behavior rather than manifest belief systems. In Morocco, political behavior is directly related to the manner in which men compete for power and the control over material wealth within various social groups and to the manner in which these groups compete among themselves. This competition is in turn defined by the internal structuring of the participant units, and there is no necessary correlation between overt belief systems (what people say they do, or should do) and the actual style of the competition. In this sense it is more important to understand what Moroccans really do and why they do it than to understand what they think they are doing. It should also be noted that certain patterns of political behavior persist well after their structural underpinnings have begun to decompose. There is thus a behavioral lag that develops (like cultural lag in value systems) and continues until the social context for politics has so changed that further adherence to the old patterns becomes clearly ill-advised and politically non-productive. It is difficult to know when that moment has arrived, but Morocco has not yet reached it. The patterns of political behavior that characterize this period in Morocco's political development are the focal point of the book. Although a full analysis of them will be presented in chapter 3, a few preliminary remarks are necessary here.

Since its independence in 1956, Morocco has managed to sustain a high degree of political tension without provoking any noticeable movement in any direction. Political groupings are ever on the verge of waging war amongst themselves or against the palace, but hostilities seldom actually occur. The imminence of crucial political decisions at the governmental level is constantly bruited about, but the decisions are not often made. Almost daily, disparate politicians proclaim the urgent need for action to end corruption, reform agriculture, purge the administration of Zionist elements, nationalize all basic industries, encourage foreign private investment, to cite but a few popular themes. Yet in the end almost nothing happens. Tension goes hand in hand with stalemate, and the recognized need for action is paired with a pervasive lack of initiative. It is my contention that this state of affairs can be explained by a common Moroccan attitude towards power and authority.

When a Moroccan succeeds in amassing a certain amount of

5

political power, i.e., is capable of controlling or influencing the actions of others, if necessary against their will, he will use such power to protect a patrimony of some sort. His use of power is essentially defensive, and the idea of bold initiatives is repugnant to him. This judgment, I believe, is valid for all levels of the social hierarchy. While the Moroccan may wish to extend the scope of his power in order better to protect or expand his patrimony, he goes about this with great caution. His major concern is conservation rather than expansion. His preoccupation with defense renders him hypersensitive to the encroachments of others upon his power base. But he is aware of his sensibilities in this regard and rightly assumes that any untoward aggrandizement on his part will activate the defense mechanisms of his rivals. He may make jabs and thrusts in various directions to determine just how far he can move; he may try to bluff his rivals into submission, or slip around their flanks. But outright conflict is avoided for it could spell defeat for one side or the other with the victor swallowing the patrimony of the vanquished. Defeat, then, may bring about disequilibrium, a state that Moroccans generally seek to avoid. As a result, what one finds in Moroccan politics is a constant jostling and rubbing of various political units, accompanied by an atmosphere of tension and crisis, that usually continues the maintenance of balance, or, if it is upset, tends towards its restoration.

This conception of power, as I mentioned above, is contingent upon the traditional forms of social organization in Morocco, forms which are by no means moribund today. First of all, the great majority of Moroccans were tribesmen and continue to identify themselves as such at the present time. At the risk of a gross generalization, Moroccan tribes were commonly internally segmented, the component segments being in a state of balance and opposition. I shall discuss the concept of segmentation at greater length in chapter 3, but I wish to stress here the role of tension in this system. Tension and the ever-present threat of conflict served to re-enforce the structure and identity of participant units. Tension, then, played a positive role in the maintenance of group identity and cohesion. The group in turn, putative common ancestors notwithstanding, had as its primary task the defense of a patrimony: in tribal areas this almost always consisted of land, flocks, water, and pasturage. If the group were to lose its cohesion, it would be incapable of protecting its patrimony, which would be

6

seized by a rival. Thus the system worked to guarantee tension in order to invigorate the group and ultimately to maintain equilibrium among the groups. Moreover, traditional Moroccan cities were organized along segmentary lines also, and consisted of various groups juxtaposed to one another in a limited area but hardly forming a homogeneous whole. These groups formed self-contained quarters with special economic interests often differentiated according to trade and the regional origins of the inhabitants. The family and the quarter of the city would go about defending its interests in the same manner as the family and the lineage in the tribe.

The primacy of defense leads to a basic trait of Moroccan political behavior: that is, the remarkable flexibility of political actors and groups. To protect his flanks the Moroccan must be prepared to enter into all sorts of improbable alliances. Today's enemy may be tomorrow's ally, and it is essential to the politician to communicate with all groups and to avoid dogmatic stances that might lead to his isolation. Further, this instinct to cover his flanks makes the Moroccan a very cautious man indeed in times of crisis, and he will balk at having to make a choice between two rival factions. His usual course of action is to pull out of the dispute, try not to offend either side irretrievably, and then make his peace with the winner, if one ever emerges. An amusing anecdote related by Colonel Justinard captures the essence of this attitude. In 1917, when the French had begun the pacification of the Anti-Atlas, the military situation was as follows. The French held Tiznit and the surrounding coastal plain while the upper valleys of the Anti-Atlas were under the sway of al-Hiba, pretender to the throne and implacable enemy of the French. The tribes lying between the two contending forces were under constant pressure to join one side or the other. The tribes, however, refused to be stampeded into any sort of compromising decision. As Justinard notes:[5] 'At Tiznit, the prayer was said in the name of Sultan Moulay Yussef; at Kerdous and on the mountain, in the name of the *aguellid* Ahmed al-Hiba; at Ouijjan, between the two, in the name of "he whom God has chosen".'

As a result of this attitude it becomes hazardous for a political leader to provoke a crisis, for he cannot rely on his allies or the members of his immediate group to follow him through to its logical conclusion. Tension is tolerable, or even desirable, for it

7

reaffirms the identity of the group, but conflict is reprehensible, for it may lead to the attrition or destruction of the group. To return to the contemporary situation, the tension and friction among groups is manifested in the appeals for action, the polemics, threats, and machinations of various groups, while the defense of group interests and the maintenance of equilibrium is reflected in the flexibility of political actors, their abhorrence of bold initiatives, and the overall stalemate that characterizes Moroccan politics.

This brief and schematic presentation of the interrelation between social structure, political culture, and political behavior in Morocco greatly oversimplifies a much more complex situation. The rest of the thesis should supply ample evidence of this complexity. The above remarks were felt to be necessary to illustrate the perspective with which I have approached the core of this study: the analysis of the behavior of the Moroccan political elite* and the course of politics since independence.

The group of men with whom I am dealing has monopolized national politics in Morocco during the last decade and has become adept in the use of paraphernalia – parties, unions, interest groups, and the like – that are common to most modern political systems. The style with which elite members perform their political roles is founded upon a shared cultural tradition, a high degree of social homogeneity, and the smallness of the elite itself. The contours of the elite correspond fairly closely to the privileged Moroccan minority that benefited from advanced educations under the protectorate. The lawyers, doctors, engineers, educators, army officers, skilled technicians, and political hacks who occupy the most prestigious and rewarding career posts in mid-century Morocco, are the sons of men raised in the color and chaos of the old sultanate. When members of the elite act according to traditional norms, they do not always do so out of nostalgia for a bygone era or out of studied emulation of revered ancestors. Rather, because of the immediacy of the past to contemporary Morocco, current adherence to older modes of social and political behavior, whether or not suited to the tasks at hand, comes naturally and spontaneously to members of the elite. This is the essence of Morocco's peculiar and fascinating version of new traditionalism, and the leitmotif of the Moroccan political elite.

*What is meant by 'political elite' in these pages is set forth in detail in chapter 4.

It may be stated at the outset that politically active Moroccans would probably not accept this analysis of their comportment and would resent the suggestion that they are influenced by anachronistic holdovers from the past. One is forced as a result to speculate on the latent functions of Moroccan political behavior, and in so speculating refer back to an historical situation that no longer applies. This is an awkward and risky approach, for it relies upon a subjective and selective interpretation of research data. However, the stubborn adherence to a certain value orientation may endure well beyond its functional *raison d'être*, and it has been demonstrated in other contexts that such adherence 'may be unwitting and below the threshold of awareness of many of those involved in it'.[6]

The second risk in this approach, emphasized by Geertz in the citation at the beginning of this chapter, is to fall victim to conservative analysis which implicitly denies the significance and scope of political change. Indeed, in the introduction I have underlined the elements of historical continuity in Morocco, particularly insofar as they serve to maintain widespread patterns of political behavior. But implicit in the discussion of behavioral lag is the acknowledgment of the profound changes that have been wrought in Morocco's political and social structures in recent decades. These changes will be made explicit in future chapters, but it seemed necessary at the outset to define the anomaly of Moroccan political behavior as sharply as possible.

Despite the risks involved, my tentative analysis of elite behavior may be of considerable use in comparative studies of societies that share common social institutions and roughly similar historical backgrounds. Douglas Ashford, in his masterly study of Moroccan politics, warned that:[7]

The scholar interested in systematic study cannot become so fixed on the unique characteristics of the situation at hand that he renders himself incapable of drawing more general conclusions. The cultural idiosyncrasy or the political quirk may seem obviously suited to explaining a particularly difficult problem in the analysis of politics, but the explanation is itself nullified by the impossibility of comparing or testing what is claimed.

But phenomena that at first glance appear to be freakish or idiosyncratic, may in fact be manifestations of anomalous, but nonetheless generalized, patterns of behavior that may find echoes in the ramifications of the same cross-national political culture and may thus be susceptible to comparative testing.

On a more modest scale, this essay has as its primary objective an elucidation of the dynamics of national politics in Morocco since that country's independence in 1956. In a sense this is a case study of the immobilism inherent in prolonged transition and the seemingly permanent integrative revolution. Accompanying the immobilism, if not guaranteeing its existence, is a pervasive state of political tension and conflict among elite factions that does not, however, bring about any significant realignment of political forces. In the final analysis, intra-elite conflict prevents any one elite faction from attacking the problems of social transition about which all of them polemicize at inordinate length. In Morocco, the vitality of the monarchy has been founded upon the factional stalemate within the elite, and the king has been an active factor in the prolongation of elite immobilism. It follows that the role of the king within the elite in a general sense, and more specifically his techniques and instruments of elite manipulation, will be of particular importance to this study.

Before launching into the main body of the study, it is probably advisable to make a few remarks regarding the composition of the Moroccan population.

It can be safely assumed that the total population of Morocco in 1967 was about 13,500,000. The most recent hard figures date from the end of 1964. At that time the population revealed the following age distribution.

0–14	5,842,300
15–59	6,374,100
60–75	412,600
Total	12,629,000

The last national census took place in 1960 at which time the national population was calculated to be 11,626,232. It is generally believed that the annual rate of population increase is about 3·2 per cent.

It is a young population, with over half of its members under the age of twenty. Despite rapid urbanization, two thirds of all Moroccans still live in rural areas or in communities of less than ten thousand inhabitants. Again using figures for 1960, one finds that 3,411,671 Moroccans lived in cities and 8,214,561 in rural areas. Casablanca alone groups almost a million inhabitants, followed by Marrakesh (242,000), Rabat (225,000), Fez (216,000), Meknes (177,000), Tangier (142,000), Oujda (127,000) and Tetouan (101,000). Coastal cities, such as Casablanca, Kenitra, and Safi, have been expanding rapidly in past decades, while interior cities such as Fez and Marrakesh have remained stable or have increased only slightly in size.

It is not very productive to speculate on the Berber-Arab composition of the country. There are, for example, 'Berber' tribes that now speak only Arabic (the Za'ir) and 'Arab' tribes that speak Berber (the Arab tribes of the Suss Valley). Suffice it to say that there are three main Berber groups, each with its own dialect: the Rifis of the Rif mountain range in the north-east of the country; the Middle Atlas, Central High Atlas and some Saharan groups that speak Tamazight; and the High and Anti-Atlas groups speaking Tashilhit. Perhaps 40 per cent of the population speaks one or another of these dialects, but most adult males, and certainly their children, also speak some Arabic. However, it is often true that women in Berber areas speak only the local Berber dialect. The political problems posed by the existence of self-conscious Berber groups is discussed in future chapters.

There is only one important religious minority among native Moroccans, the Jews. There is no indigenous Christian community. Jewish communities were, and to some degree still are, scattered throughout Morocco. Most cities had special quarters reserved for Jewish habitation, and there were pockets of Jews strewn through southern mountain hamlets and desert oases. In the nineteenth and twentieth centuries, the rural Jewish populations gradually migrated to the cities, and there was a general movement of Jews, both urban and rural, to the coastal cities, particularly Casablanca. At the time of the creation of the state of Israel in 1948, there may have been some 255,000 Jews in Morocco. Steady emigration to Canada, Europe, and Israel has reduced that number to about 60,000 in 1966. The war between Israel and the Arab states of June 1967 may lead to the emigration of half the remaining community.

Reliable figures on the current size of the European community in Morocco are not readily available. In 1954 there may have been as many as 600,000 Europeans in the country, including almost 300,000 Spaniards concentrated in the northern zone but represented elsewhere as well. If one takes the evolution of the French population as indicative of the general trend, one discovers that between 1953 and 1965 it steadily dwindled from 385,000 to 111,554. The diplomatic tension between France and Morocco resulting from the Ben Barka affair has accelerated the exodus since 1965.

With the attrition of both the European and Jewish communities, it is probable that in the next few decades Morocco will become religiously and ethnically homogeneous. I am expressly avoiding the problem of the ethnic origins of Berbers and Arabs, and I am inclined to accept the view that most of Morocco's Arabs are simply Berbers that have, over the centuries, adopted the Arabic language or intermarried with the numerically small tribes of the original Arab invaders of the eleventh century. At any rate the population that I have briefly described above is, to borrow an image cherished by the followers of Mao, the sea in which the Moroccan elite swims, from which it came, and from which will emerge those who would join it or replace it.

PART ONE

MOROCCO'S
TWO LEGACIES

CHAPTER ONE

THE MAKHZAN:
A STABLE SYSTEM OF VIOLENCE

It will frequently be suggested in future chapters that contemporary political behavior in Morocco has been historically conditioned, or is at least derivative to a substantial degree from the country's past and its traditional social institutions. At present, I shall consider Morocco's governmental legacy from the pre-protectorate sultanate and its rudimentary administration, the makhzan. Behavioral patterns and political roles that typified Morocco before the coming of the French are of great relevance to present-day Morocco now that the French have left. In 1912, the organization of the 'Alawite dynasty bore a close resemblance to that established in the seventeenth century by the first great 'Alawite sultan, Moulay Isma'il.[1] There was surprisingly little change in the organization because there had been only minimal change in the internal problems with which it was faced. These remained the collection of taxes, the maintenance of an army, and the suppression of tribes. The brief forty-four years of protectorate administration transformed these tasks, without, however, destroying the country's continuity with its past. The makhzan is still a vivid memory for a fair number of living Moroccans. It should be recalled that the first king of independent Morocco, Muhammed Ben Yussuf, was but the grandson of Morocco's last great sultan, Moulay Hassan (d. 1894). King Muhammed's father, Moulay Yussuf (d. 1927) was the brother of both Moulay 'Abd al-'Aziz and Moulay Hafidh, the last two sultans before the establishment of the protectorate.

Having insisted upon the organizational continuity of the makhzan and the internal tasks with which it dealt, it must be noted that Morocco's relations with foreign powers changed drastically during the nineteenth century. The traditional trade patterns of the country were disrupted as a result of the increasing emphasis on sea trade and the French occupation of large parts of West Africa and Algeria. Simultaneously, a number of European powers and private interests were eager to open up new markets for manufactured goods in Morocco, and to tap the Moroccan hinterland for its natural resources and agricultural produce. Such endeavors led to the rapid growth of hitherto somnolent coastal fishing ports (Casablanca, Mazagan/al-Jadida, Safi, Mogador/Essaouira) and the displacement of significant portions of the native population from the interior to the coast. The introduction of new products and materials led to a revolution in consumption habits and stimulated the development of a market economy. The European entry into the Moroccan economy also brought about the first elements of class stratification (see pp. 159–65).

The European economic presence was sustained by its military presence. The defeat of the Moroccan army at Isly in 1844 at the hands of French troops from Algeria, and the seizure of Tetouan by the Spanish in 1860, revealed to the makhzan its military inferiority and led to plans for the reform of the sultan's armed forces. At the same time, tribes were able to procure relatively modern arms from willing European suppliers, thereby increasing their capacity to resist the fiscal visits of the makhzan.

Nonetheless, despite the undeniable significance of these changes, despite the growing awareness of the makhzan that renovation would be the price of survival, little was done to change the essence of the system. The essential task of the makhzan remained the collection of taxes and the maintenance of an army to extract them. Putting a few thousand Moroccans in Ottoman uniforms, importing a handful of foreign military instructors, and announcing the creation of a modern infantry, did not fundamentally alter the nature of the game.

In general, Moroccan dynasties based themselves upon the large towns, such as Fez, Marrakesh, Meknes, and Rabat, which were the military, commercial, and administrative centers of the empire. Tax-exempt tribes provided troops and garrisons for the dynasties. Other tribes swore allegiance to the sultan and were administered in his name by notables issued from their ranks. Finally there were the dissident and semi-dissident tribes that might recognize the religious authority of the sultan but refuse to accept his fiscal authority. Each sultan would have to construct anew, with more or less success, tribal alliances like those of his predecessor. Throughout his life, a sultan who wished to expand or maintain his territorial control and the level of his revenues, would have to engage in constant military ventures against dissident tribes, buy off others, re-settle others, reconcile yet others, in a never-ending process. Ibn Khaldun cogently analyzed this system, describing the tribe rallied to its leader sweeping in from the mountains or desert to rid the country of a degenerate regime, quashing all other contenders, re-establishing the territorial authority of the makhzan, but often, in a matter of one or two generations, losing its solidarity (*'aṣabiya*)* and in turn degenerating into military and moral flabbiness. The essence of Ibn Khaldun's theory is a doctrine of the circulation of elites where the circulating units are neither classes nor individuals, but tribes, rotating within a fundamentally stable structure. This process transformed socially-cohesive and militarily-formidable tribes into incohesive and militarily-feeble city-dwellers.[2]

It is significant that the sultan's government was known as the makhzan (literally storehouse), for its rudimentary administrative and military apparatus was devoted to the extraction of taxes in specie and in kind. The principal justification of the sultan to collect taxes was his role as 'defender of the faith', and in order to carry out his duty adequately he needed the wherewithal to equip and maintain an army. Seldom, however, was his right to collect taxes accepted without contest. Alliances of tribes, murabitin, and shurafa (plural of sharif)† would often form in varying combinations to deny the sultan his revenues, or, occasionally, to put forth a contender for his title of *amir al-muminin* (Prince of the Faithful). Thus the army of the sultan seldom engaged the enemies of the faith, for its time was taken in asserting the sultan's authority among the believers. A stable system of continuous violence was the result: collect taxes to pay the army to crush the tribes to

*One anthropologist, D.M.Hart, eschews the term spirit, preferring 'unifying structural cohesion' or 'agnation in action' (personal communication, 19 September 1966).
†The murabit is a saint whose sanctity (*al-baraka*) can be passed onto a follower or descendant. Various murabitin (referred to by the French as marabouts) headed or inspired the several brotherhoods (zawiya or *taifa*) that played an important role in North African history. A sharif is a descendant of the Prophet. One may find sharif and murabit joined in one person, such as the sharif of Wazzan.

collect still more taxes.[3] One of Sultan 'Abd al-'Aziz' vizirs, Si Faddoul Gharnit, neatly summed up the makhzan's philosophy on fiscal policy: 'One must pluck the tax-payer as one would a chicken. If the tax-payer becomes wealthy, he revolts.'[4] Despite wild fluctuations in the participating personnel and a high mortality rate among the occupants of the throne, the primitive rules of the game were never fundamentally altered until the coming of the French.[5] Gellner attributes this surprising stability to the inability of the urban centers to perform the same role as had their European counterparts. Moroccan cities required constant protection from the ever-menacing tribes and consequently were never in a position to challenge the rule of the makhzan.[6] The tribes in turn were too internally divided to concert their actions against the government, but they were strong enough to resist permanent subjugation to the would-be central authorities.

Challenges to the sultan usually came from members of the dynastic family itself, who would ally with disgruntled tribes to storm the makhzan. Moulay Hafidh, who later signed the protectorate treaty, deposed his brother Moulay 'Abd al-'Aziz, ironically, for having been too accommodating to European encroachments on Moroccan sovereignty. He first proclaimed himself sultan in Marrakesh in August 1907, touching off a sporadic civil war. It was not until June 1908 that the 'ulema (plural of 'alim; the religious savants of Islam who, through their pronouncements, theoretically have the power to 'bind and loose' the allegiance of ruled to ruler) of Fez, sensing the course of events, recognized Moulay Hafidh's sultanate.

More frequently, however, the throne was challenged upon the death of its occupant.

The most common signal of revolt is given by the death of the sultan since everyone assumes – thanks to age-old experience – that several claimants [will] dispute the succession through combat, enlisting the tribes behind them, and that chaos will prevail until the strongest or most skilled carries the day. The longest periods of anarchy that southern Morocco has experienced in the last century and a half were the great seven-year siba [see below] after the death of Sidi Ben 'Abdullah (1790–97); that occurring after the death of Moulay 'Abdarrahman (1859–64); and that after the death of Moulay Hassan (1894–97).[7]

To avoid this recurrent threat to the dynasty, the reigning sultan would commonly try to associate one of his sons as closely as possible to the levers of power during his own lifetime. The chosen son would be put in command of a significant body of troops and made *khalifa* (governor) of one of the major regions that included one of the four principal cities of the sultanate. On occasions the son, during his father's lifetime, would be permitted to carry the parasol, symbol of the sultan's office. 'In fact, the more the son lived in the intimacy of the dead sultan, the more ready are the people to believe that his father's *baraka* has descended to him.'[8] If *baraka* did not suffice, and it seldom did, the designated successor had troops at his command ready to deter all other pretenders as soon as the news of the sovereign's death had been announced. Muhammed v, first king of independent Morocco, followed this procedure precisely and perhaps instinctively. In 1957 he proclaimed his son, Hassan, heir apparent, having already entrusted him with the organization of the Royal Armed Forces (FAR), Morocco's post-1956 army.

After a change of reign the grand vizir (*wazir as-sadr al-a'zam*) would consult with the 'ulema and notables of the makhzan. He would then send a letter to all *qadis* (judges in matters of personal status) and *'amils* (local governors) notifying them of the sultan's death and inviting them to convoke an assembly of the population under their jurisdiction to proclaim the new sultan. Then would come the ceremony of the proclamation itself. All the notables would gather in the largest mosque of the area to discuss the terms for the *bay'a* (the swearing of fealty). Typical conditions would be that the sultan suppress certain taxes or that he honor the word given by his predecessor regarding some local matter.[9] The *bay'a*, or its lack, determined the fronticr between the bilad al-makhzan, that area in which the sultan had military control and taxing powers, and the bilad as-siba, the area of dissidence which refused to recognize the makhzan's authority.

It is unlikely that many grand vizirs sent letters to their local deputies in areas of chronic restiveness with any great hopes that they would be taken seriously. Qaids (local officials) there, who were often members of the tribal grouping they administered supposedly in the name of the sultan, would almost automatically adopt an *attentiste* or even defiant attitude vis à vis the new sultan. In general, bi-lateral agreements were arrived at only after the new sovereign had demonstrated his military superiority. Sometimes a show of force would suffice, while at others full combat was required. The makhzan's degree of success or failure ranging, obviously, from total victory to total defeat, would determine the nature of the pact that was to follow. The bilad al-makhzan was never clearly delineated from the bilad as-siba; the one blended into the other according to relative degrees of submissiveness or defiance on the part of the tribes. It was not uncommon to find islands of submissiveness in seas of defiance (for example Sijilmassa) and vice versa.[10]

These pacts, which made up Morocco's own unique form of *bay'a*, were considered binding only so long as the sultan continued to make a show of force. Once the sultan's armies had left a region, the local tribes habitually seized the opportunity to defy the orders of the qaid or governor which the makhzan had left behind. This would require a return military engagement and the drawing-up of a new pact. This interminable process determined the very nature of the makhzan, which was never fixed in one place but wandered continuously along the perimeters of a triangle described by the major garrison cities of Fez, Meknes, Rabat, and Marrakesh. According to Moroccan lore, the ideal sultan was one whose throne was a saddle and whose baldaquin was the sky. Few sultans, however mediocre their other attributes, could avoid living up to this ideal to some extent.

The initial years of the reign of Moulay Hassan amply demonstrate both the itinerant nature of the court and the peculiarities of Moroccan *bay'a*. Upon the death of his father in 1873, Moulay Hassan was, as *khalifa* of Marrakesh and the Suss, in command of a significant number of troops. He immediately subdued the Sussi tribes and received *bay'a* at Marrakesh, after which he proceeded to Rabat to receive *bay'a* there. He then set out for Meknes, crushing the Beni Hassan on the way, and was proclaimed sultan in Meknes. Next he departed for Fez and engaged the Beni Mtir. In Fez for a year, he fought the Ghiyyata twice near Taza. More engagements followed as he moved about the country, subduing the Beni Moussa and the Ait Attab and once again the Beni Mtir in 1879. In 1880, his uncle, Moulay al-Amin, was dispatched to crush the Qal'aya tribe, and in the same year tribal revolts were put down between Tangier and Wazzan. The north momentarily in hand, Moulay Hassan returned to the south to bring the Suss under control once again. At Taroudant the sultan, in 1882, appointed forty-three qaids among the Sussi tribes, almost all of whom were sons of local tribal shaykhs or the shaykhs themselves.[11]

The threat of force underlay almost all forms of interaction between the sultan and those he would govern, but he enjoyed only a relative monopoly of coercive means. The extent of his monopoly varied, sometimes daily, and his rivals continually gauged the ebb and flow of his power. Thus, at those moments when the makhzan was between campaigns, it engaged in alliance-building, for its strength was reckoned as the sum-total of the strengths of its allies. Alliance-building is one face of the general policy of divide and rule, picking sides in local disputes, pitting rivals against one another, favoring some factions with special dispensations and punishing others by heavy impositions. Force was the commodity with which the makhzan could attract allies or threaten the dissident, but it was employed only when less costly and when more pacific tactics had failed.[12]

The sultan's army, over the centuries, varied in composition. It was not large and in no way professional. Because the tribes could seldom coordinate their individual acts of defiance, a major force was not required to put down their rebellions. Moreover, it was not until the disaster of the battle of Isly in 1844 that thought was given to the formation of a professional infantry.

At the death of Moulay Isma'il in 1727 one can discern the major elements of the military organization of the ʿAlawite dynasty. The previous dynasty, the Saʿadis, formed garrisons of several eastern tribes (known as the Charagui from *sharq*: east) that had fled the Tlemsen region to escape the Turks. These makhzan or guish (from *jaysh*: army) tribes were settled in garrisons around Fez. The Saʿadis also formed the guish al-Wadayya, composed of the Ahl as-Suss, Mughafra, and Wadayya tribes. The guish tribes developed an organization unlike that of the other submissive tribes. They were in fact military settlements, all of whose members served the makhzan. In exchange for life service to the sultan, they received the usufruct of land granted them by the sultan and were exempt from taxes (except *zakat* and *'ushur*). Frequently, members of guish tribes had access to important civilian, as well as military posts, although there was never a clear distinction between the two.[13]

These tribes, and most submissive tribes for that matter, were subjected to considerable internal restructuring. The makhzan destroyed old organizational patterns founded on the *jama'a* (an annually renewable council of elders), replacing all that went before by arbitrary divisions of thirds, quarters, and fifths, which commonly had no other purpose than to facilitate the gathering of taxes (in non-guish tribes) and the recruitment of troops.[14]

The makhzan tribes were frequently rebellious, and Moulay Isma'il sought to counter their influence by the formation of a corps of Negro slaves brought together from the southern oases. This corps, which may have reached 150,000 men under Moulay Isma'il, became known as the *'abid al-Bukhari*, or simply the Buwakhir.[15]

While all able-bodied men of the Buwakhir bore arms, each guish tribe supplied one or more *rha*, a cavalry unit of five hundred men. Each *rha* was under the command of a *qaid ar-rha* (roughly equivalent to colonel) assisted by an *'allaf* in charge of pay. The *rha* itself was subdivided into companies of one hundred men led by a *qaid al-mia* (captain) assisted by several *muqaddims* (sergeants). In general all officers were appointed by the sultan and the *wazir al-harb* (minister of war), subject to the approval of the tribe.[16] The troops furnished by the guish tribes seldom exceeded nine or ten thousand. This number was divided between sedentary garrisons in the major towns and a mobile contingent that moved with the court which, when *en route*, was known as the *mahalla*.[17]

In times of serious internal crisis or external attack, when there would be a general call-up, known as the *harka*, the makhzan received the services of the *nuwaib* tribes (auxiliaries). These supplied contingents of cavalry, armed and maintained at tribal expense and under the command of a local qaid.

After the battle of Isly, the makhzan became aware of the deficiencies of an army based solely on cavalry. Sultan Moulay 'Abdarrahman set about to remedy the situation, forming an infantry of roughly seven thousand men drawn haphazardly from the entire population on a nominally voluntary basis. The men, known as *'askars*, were grouped in units (*tabur*) of battalion size, often under the command of a European officer. In addition, artillery units, both mobile and fixed, were introduced. This last effort to modernize the army, however, came too late and was uniformly ineffectual. The infantry proved useless against the siba in the Taza region in 1904, and there was never any question of its ability to engage French forces.

Under Moulay Hassan the army totalled about twenty-five thousand men, *nuwaib* included. Nonetheless, in the face of a serious external threat, it is conceivable that the sultan could have levied a *harka* of forty thousand infantry and again as many mounted troops. Whatever its size, the army suffered from a chronic lack of discipline. At all ranks the pay was derisory, and the normal relation between an officer and a recruit was one of mutual hostility. At harvest time each year there would be massive desertion which largely went unpunished.[18]

Complementing the military organization, and seldom distinct from it, was the civil administration itself, the makhzan and its local agents. Administrative personnel, as mentioned above, was to some degree provided by the tribes, although posts requiring special skills, such as those treating legal and financial matters, were reserved for relatively well-educated city bourgeois. Writing just before the establishment of the protectorate, Aubin described the makhzan as follows:[19]

Previously authority came into the hands of men at once of the camp and the country, occupying, along with their fellow tribesmen, a position superior to that of the Arab or Arabized people of the plain . . . [and who are] possessed of a limited culture and disposed to regard force as the real basis of the state. It was military government in which the influence of a sort of rural aristocracy was predominant. With the secretaries, who are scholars, and the Oumana [see below], who are rich merchants, begins the regime of learning and wealth. . . . The majority of these secretaries and all these Oumana belong to the Moorish population, whose chief center is Fez, but which abounds at Rabat, Salé and Tetouan as well.

The makhzan consisted of two sections, the first being the sultan's court and retinue and the second the administration proper. The sultan maintained a numerous following, financed from a personal budget and private revenue (*bayt al-mal ad-dakhiliyy*). The *hajib* (chamberlain) directed the internal organization of the court, while the *qaid al-meshwar* handled external contacts, arranged audiences, and acted as master of ceremonies on public occasions. Under his command were the sultan's personal mounted guard and foot soldiers. The *hajib* was in charge of food and bedding, the upkeep of the palace stables, and the setting up of the camp while the *mahalla* moved about the country.[20]

Pre-eminent among the sultan's ministers was the grand vizir.

As was the case with all ministers, his functions were never clearly defined, but basically he was responsible for internal affairs. The *amin al-umana* (minister of finance) directed the public treasury, the *bayt al-mal al-muslimin*, which received tax revenues both Islamic (*zakat, kharaj*,[21] *ushur, juzya*) and non-Islamic market dues (*maks*), port taxes, *qnatar* (extraordinary levies) and revenues from makhzan property.[22]

The wazirs of foreign affairs and war were late additions to the makhzan's ministerial entourage. Foreign affairs was under the surveillance of the *wazir al-bahr* (lit. minister of the sea), for Morocco could, until 1830, have relations with non-Islamic states only by sea. As European merchants took an interest in Morocco, the *wazir al-bahr* became more and more a buffer between these commercial interests, concentrated in Tangier, and the sultan. The *wazir al-harb* (minister of war) was unknown before the French occupation of Algeria in 1830. Formerly there had been an official, the *'allaf al-kabir* (loosely: paymaster general), who was chiefly concerned with the pay and upkeep of the troops. Gradually the sultan ceded his place at the head of the army to the *'allaf* who took on more and more responsibility for the entire military organization of the country. Finally, there was the somewhat lesser figure of the *wazir ash-shikayat* (the minister of claims), whose major function was to receive throngs of plaintiffs who were permitted to besiege his office at certain designated hours.[23]

The ministers of the makhzan were badly paid. Perforce they handled only matters which involved a commission (*sukhra*), without which they could not survive. Moreover, their functions and responsibilities were ill-defined: the minister of claims might conduct a military expedition or the minister of war regulate a matter with a qaid. All positions in the makhzan tended to become hereditary. Increasingly the official caste became urbanized, its members losing their direct tribal links.[24]

The internal administration of the country was based on three or four regions, at whose head was a *khalifa* appointed by the sultan and generally of the royal family. The *khalifa* maintained a court which was often a replica of that of the sultan. As was noted in reference to Moulay Hassan, who was *khalifa* in Marrakesh before his father's death, these regional chiefs had important contingents of guish at their disposal. In addition, all the qaids in a region were, in theory, responsible to the *khalifa*.

The obedience of the qaids varied greatly. Some were appointed for the sake of form only, such as those appointed by Moulay Hassan in the Suss. In fact, their execution of a central directive was entirely problematic. The qaids of submitted tribes generally were selected thus: when the post of qaid became vacant, the notables of the tribe would go to the makhzan to give their advice on a replacement and to do all in their power to have their choice sustained. In short, the candidate who paid the most money was appointed, and he would return to the tribe with the notables as escort.

The qaid's lot was seldom pleasant. His major, if not sole task was to raise money and men for the sultan, for which service he received no remuneration. But in collecting taxes in the sultan's name he was able to retain a percentage for himself. Also, in organizing the *hadiya*, the tribal tribute presented thrice annually to the sultan, the qaid commonly extracted considerable sums for his own use.[25] Some of the large southern tribes nurtured qaids, subordinate to the makhzan in name only, who presided as lords over territories defended by their own armies, and lived near fortified grain storehouses which allowed them to withstand most threats from the makhzan. Principal among these qaids were the Glaoui, Goundafi, and M'touggi. Their power was enhanced under the reign of Moulay Hassan. After his death they asserted themselves, and during the protectorate years the Glaoui in particular played an important role.[26]

The counterpart in the cities of the tribal qaid was the pasha, assisted by a corps of *muqaddims* in charge of the various quarters of a given town.

Special note should be given to the judicial organization of the country. Those responsible for the application of the shari'a were the *qadis*, judges in matters of personal status: marriage, divorce, and inheritance. Only this judicial corps, through the issuance of *fatwas* and the interpretation of law, could introduce new legislation. The dahirs (*thahīr*), the imperial edicts of the sultan, were, in theory, simply administrative orders outside the sphere of religious law. A certain measure of independence and autonomy was attached to the office of *qadi*, for appointment to it was for life. Thus were the sultan to die, the *qadis* which he had appointed could not be revoked by his successor. Just how much autonomy the *qadis* actually enjoyed is moot. In addition their competence in penal affairs tended to devolve upon the pashas and qaids, who meted out justice in all criminal cases.[27]

The foregoing description of the makhzan, its habitual mode of action and its structure, has neglected the context in which the makhzan existed. Mention has been made of tribes and siba, both of which require more attention. Likewise two groups which not unfrequently played a decisive role in the quest for power have yet to be described: the shurafa and murabitin.

The murabitin, around whom were formed the zawiyas or *taifas* in which were grouped the followers of the saint in question, became influential in Morocco particularly after the beginning of the sixteenth century. At that time the Portuguese, who had seized various coastal positions in southern Morocco after 1458, pushed into the interior through the Doukkala plains, reaching the gates of Marrakesh in 1515. The intrusion of the infidel required the resistance of the faithful, and the inspiration and organization of this resistance fell to a large extent into the hands of the murabitin. At one point, the great religious figure of the Anti-Atlas, Al-Jazouli, and the Idrissi shurafa of the western Rif, both rallied to the sultan's banners. A degree of religious unity restored, the makhzan went on to defeat the Portuguese at the battle of Wad Makhazan in 1578. After this date the zawiyas proliferated throughout Morocco and found a ready response among the Berber tribes. Not many years ago a French scholar felt warranted to state, 'The marabouts are the greatest political power in Morocco; the people revere them infinitely more than the sultan, despite the religious character of the latter.'[28]

Although the murabitin may have helped spread Islam among semi-pagan tribes, they also served to re-enforce tribal organization and beliefs. Berbers had long attributed magical powers to trees, stones and other objects. The saintly figure of the murabit, imbued with *al-baraka* and able thereby to intercede between God and His mortal following, fits in nicely with Berber notions that predated Islam. From another aspect, that of constant feuding between tribes or tribal factions, the murabit again tended to bolster old patterns through his ability to transform the feud, perhaps against a rival murabit, into a holy war (*jihad*). Thus the murabit did not induce change in Berber institutions, but rather encouraged their continued vitality.[29] In areas of siba, where there was no supreme authority over the tribes and where tribes were as hostile towards one another as they were towards the makhzan, a primary function of the murabit was to act as arbiter and conciliator of tribal disputes, and guarantor of tribal pacts and accords.

Given the fact that the political and social role of the murabit depended considerably on the continued existence of tribal siba, it is only natural that the murabitin in general, in the face of an expanding makhzan, encouraged Berber autonomy. If ever they were to support the makhzan, the *ziyara* (alms offered by the followers to the saint and his descendants) would be paid to some other murabit who did not cooperate with the sultan. Perhaps the attitude of the murabitin vis à vis the makhzan is best summed up by the motto attributed to the Wazzani zawiya: 'No sultan over us; no sultan without us.'[30]

The ruling dynasty of Morocco today, the 'Alawis, came to power in the middle of the seventeenth century only after crushing the Dila'is, a powerful zawiya that had carved out an extensive domain for itself. From then on the 'Alawis remained on uneasy terms with the murabitin.[31] Despite the dynasty's efforts to control and diminish the influence of the zawiyas, their functional *raison d'être* was not fully undermined until the French ended the siba during the 1930s. Although it is hazardous to attempt to estimate the membership of the orders, it is possible that in 1939 there were 500,000 brothers with some 225,000 grouped in the twenty-three major brotherhoods.[32]

Intermingled with the zawiyas yet distinct from them were the shurafa, composed of several families divided into two great branches based on descent from either Moulay Idriss, founder of Fez, or the Filali shurafa (from which is issued the 'Alawite dynasty) who established themselves in the date oases of Sijilmassa some time in the fifteenth century.

Many of these families had founded brotherhoods of their own, the most important of these being the Wazzani order. In addition, many families were able to build up economic fiefs through feudal estates, known as *'azibs*, ceded to them by the makhzan. These would take the form of . . .

a village or a part of a village, whose inhabitants are, from father to son, granted by the sultan to a sharif and his descendants who then receive all legal alms and taxes normally accorded the sovereign power. In short the sharif is substituted for the sultan *vis-à-vis* those individuals who are conceded to him.[33]

At the time of the Portuguese encroachments mentioned above, the Merinid dynasty, accused by the shurafa and murabitin of laxity in repulsing the Christian invader, mollified their animosity by accepting the tax-free status of their 'azibs. Later the Sa'adian dynasty tried to withdraw these privileges (they were shurafa themselves) thereby provoking a long series of internecine struggles among the shurafa from which the 'Alawis emerged victorious.[34]

The grist for the mill of pre-protectorate politics was furnished by the tribes. The guish tribes, generally Arabic-speaking, have already been considered. The Berber-speaking tribes determined the contours of the bilad al-makhzan and the bilad as-siba. These areas expanded and contracted at the expense of each other, but there was always a territorial core that was permanently makhzan and one that was permanently siba. The mountains of Morocco harbored tribes which were chronically dissident, while the coastal plains usually submitted to the makhzan. The plains are entirely surrounded by mountains: the Rif chain running west-east in the north of the country, and the Middle, High, and Anti-Atlas mountains running from the north-east to the south-west (roughly Oujda to Agadir). These mountains contain a spectrum of tribal types. In the desert areas south of the High and Anti-Atlas were to be found oasis dwellers, date cultivators, and camel herdsmen. In the mountains themselves, and the steppe regions, tribes specializing in arboriculture, sheep and goat herding, and rudimentary agriculture lived side by side.

The coastal, watered plains (Gharb, Doukkala, Chawia, Haouz) were inhabited by sedentary Arabized tribes, some of which were guish tribes, which could not easily defy the makhzan and in fact sought its protection from marauding steppe and mountain tribes. Morocco's major urban centers were located in or on the edges of the coastal plains: thus the four imperial cities of Rabat, Meknes, Fez and Marrakesh. Certain areas of the coastal plains enjoyed only marginal security. The region lying between Fez and Rabat, and including Meknes, was subject to constant harassment, particularly by the large tribal confederations of the Zayan, the Zemmour, the Beni Mtir, and the Za'ir.

The siba was predominantly a phenomenon of the deserts and the mountains. Here were to be found the tribal pockets of resistance, sometimes grouped about a murabit, which had simply opted out. Opting out was necessarily temporary, for economically the tribes were not autarkic units and could afford to cut off vital economic exchanges with cities and markets only on a short-term basis. Seldom was their objective to attack the makhzan or to overthrow the sultan; rather it was to escape his secular arm, and to avoid his taxes and his qaids. The tribes often distinguished between sultan and makhzan, regarding the former with religious veneration and the latter with contempt. The sultan would sometimes take the field against dissident tribes. In one such incident, the Ait Oumalu routed the forces of Moulay Sliman, killed, mutilated and exhibited his closest companions, but greeted the sultan himself with warmth and respect.[35]

Periodically, however, great agglomerations of tribes would rally to a leader, a sharif, or a murabit, sweeping out the vestiges of a decadent and divided dynasty to replace it with one whose fate was unlikely to be any better. The urban populations, as noted above, were passive spectators to the constant manoeuvres among tribes, makhzan, shurafa and murabitin. The life of the cities was built on trade, and trade depended on a minimal degree of stability and security. To assure these luxuries, the city bourgeois contributed their skills to the management of the financial and diplomatic affairs of the makhzan. They were obliged to tolerate the presence in the cities of unruly garrisons of makhzan soldiers, whose nuisance value was far preferable to the horrors of tribal pillaging.

At this point I would like to emphasize certain characteristics of the political process under the makhzan: those, in effect, that influenced political behavior and general attitudes towards power and authority. It will be useful to have these traits in mind when I undertake the analysis of contemporary Moroccan political behavior in terms of the country's political culture.

As mentioned earlier, the makhzan had only a relative monopoly of coercive means within the country. Moreover, what power it did have was not institutionalized and varied from one sultan to another. It was delegated, contingent power. Groups which were its retainers of first instance, tribes, *shurafa'*, local big men, 'ulema, accepted that the power that they and their followers represented be used towards generally specific ends on the basis of generally specific pacts. The power of the sultan consisted of the sum total of the power of his momentary allies at any one time. The sultan provided a convenient rallying point and a widely accepted religious authority, around which various interests could form in the light of their own, rapidly changing interests. The particular con-figuration of makhzan allies was often transformed more than once even during the sultan's lifetime: enemies became allies, became enemies again, and so on. Most political actors were fully aware of the inevitability of these fluctuations, and thus avoided placing exclusive moral judgments on rival groups and personalities. The definition of local, immediate interest determined the choice of a faction's allies. 'Tensions were institutionalized in such a way that enemies could not destroy one another without ruining themselves. The result was the role of "live and let live" which defined relations among antagonists.'[36]

Historically the political process was one of constant and con-fusing flux, no less so for the participant than the observer. To survive and certainly to prosper, one had to assess all the possibili-ties for alliance with others as well as all the possibilities of counter-alliances. A sort of defensive maintenance of the status quo often revealed itself as the sole feasible guideline in political manoeuvring. Subgroups, interested in obtaining enough auto-nomy to play out their own internal rivalries free from interference, would seek to balance off rivals, and more powerful out-groups that sought to control them. Thus, one of the early 'Alawi sharifs, Moulay Muhammed, was invited by the citizens of Fez to help rid the city of the Dila'i rulers. In his initial attempt Moulay Muhammed failed, but in 1662, at a time when the Dila'is were in decline, he tried again. This time the Fassis judged him to be a greater threat than the Dila'is and appealed to the latter to protect them from the sharif.[37] Probably each sultan entertained the thought that he could master all the political forces in the country, but because his power was delegated and not institutionalized in the makhzan, what mastery of the situation he achieved seldom outlived him. Moulay Isma'il tried to bring about the military occupation of his own kingdom, as did Moulay Hassan, and latterly Hassan II. Upon the deaths of Moulay Isma'il and Moulay Hassan, power reverted to its primary retainers. Today, however, because of the reorganization of the army and administration, the throne may finally have institutionalized and hierarchized under its authority the use of coercion (see chapter 14).

In the light of the above, Gellner's remark on the inability of urban centers to challenge the makhzan, may be refined. No single group was able to challenge the makhzan on a long term basis, but, equally important, no sultan was able to maintain his own authority on a long term basis. The retention of power by any group was precarious and ephemeral. Few groups could ever build up a solid economic base to sustain their challenge. Sultans confiscated the goods of rebels, dissidents, and officials whom they dismissed. Successful claimants to the throne destroyed the goods of rivals. Trade was no refuge, as internal conditions were too unsafe, the potential market too reduced, and the sanctity of contracts too problematic to encourage anything but short term speculation. The vagaries of nature and the depredations of tribes discouraged Moroccans from the acquisition of land. But if material wealth was not easily hoarded and transferred, it was sometimes possible to transfer positions of access to wealth and authority, i.e., hereditary access to local and central positions within the makhzan.

It is revealing to consider elite politics under the traditional makhzan, for there, as elsewhere, there is a remarkable continuity between past and present political behaviour. The same game of manipulation, cajolery and force that was played out within the empire as a whole was reflected in microcosm among the jostling factions of the makhzan elite. Terrasse's neat description of makhzan politics is as applicable today as it was before 1912.

. . . the makhzan constituted but a coalition of interests and represented neither constructive thought nor a common positive will. Its ideal consisted in its continued existence for the greater profit of the collectivities and individuals who composed it.

Finally, it suffered simultaneously from the selfishness of its members and their instability. Within the 'beneficiary collectivity', where the mere whim of the sultan could bring about the most astonishing fortunes and the most irrevocable disgrace, each member had to advance and defend his own cause ruthlessly. Rivalries among individuals and clans, beneath a facade of seeming politeness, was constant and pitiless. The incertitude of the future rendered more ardent their ambitions, and more delicious the satisfactions of the moment.[38]

The heritage of the makhzan which has been handed down to the new kingdom of Morocco is a defensive preoccupation with survival. This attitude stems from the single-minded concern for the maintenance of the sultan's authority within the territorial core of the bilad al-makhzan. Few sultans ever entertained more ambitious objectives, and few Moroccans expected any more from their government. Neither today's monarchy nor today's Moroccan have fully divested themselves of these anachronistic attitudes and expectations.

The coming of the French put an abrupt halt to this stable system of violence. Between 1912 and 1934, the siba was ended, and between 1912 and 1955 the entire political context was altered dramatically. The administrative structure of Morocco was greatly strengthened and extended, at the expense of the zawiyas and the tribes. The economy was totally transformed, and while the traditional commercial class was for some years eclipsed, a new class of industrial workers was rapidly formed. These constitute some of the outstanding aspects of Morocco's French legacy, to which we shall now turn.

CHAPTER TWO

THE PROTECTORATE

At the time of the establishment of the protectorate, the sultanate which had partly governed Morocco prior to 1912 had undergone almost no significant changes in its traditional apparatus. Morocco had not even been subjected to the relative modernization afforded her North African neighbors through Ottoman administration. There were, to be sure, the first indications of significant social change following the French conquest of Algeria in 1830, and a growing commercial interest in Morocco on the part of Europeans. Coastal hamlets underwent the first stages of rapid urbanization.[1] Added to this were the numerous Moroccan merchants living abroad, especially in Manchester, Lyons, Genoa, Cairo and Dakar. During the nineteenth century there was a trickle of foreign technicians to the makhzan, such as the Italians who supervised Moulay Hassan's arms factory at Fez. Although these contacts were important, they were never sufficient to reorient traditional methods of government. The French brusquely intruded into this closed, archaic, and picturesque little sultanate, and, forty-four years later, departed.

During their brief sojourn in Morocco, the French set up a modern administrative apparatus geared to an expanding economy based on commercial agriculture, mining, industry and trade. However, Moroccans were at best marginal participants in this endeavor. While some Moroccans were able to grasp abstractly the rationale of French administrative and economic practices, comparatively few ever gained the practical experience of direct contact with them.

In the next chapter, I shall discuss certain basic characteristics of contemporary Moroccan political behavior and the roots of these characteristics in the traditional political culture of the country. While the French totally disrupted the governmental and administrative continuity of Morocco, they brought about no correspondingly profound changes in the political style of Moroccans. The administrative and economic infrastructure introduced by the French remained, throughout the protectorate period, an exogenous and basically exotic creation imposed upon an uncomprehending population. There was practically no sustained attempt made by the French to familiarize or, more important, to associate Moroccans with the new structures. The transformations wrought by the protectorate were resented by Moroccans without being fully understood. They led to a feeling of confusion and doubt among the local populations and their leaders without stimulating any meaningful process of adaptation to the new situation. If this phenomenon is kept in mind, then it becomes easier to understand that in post-protectorate Morocco, despite the 'rationality' and the sophistication of the administrative apparatus, those who utilize it often do so in a manner that smacks of the old makhzan.

In 1912 the Moroccan economy was stagnant, had few foreign trade outlets, and had developed nothing approaching a national market system. The single most important causal factor of this economic stagnation was the instability of the makhzan and its inability, for lack of the technical means available in Europe, to exert its authority, constantly and effectively, over the entire territory nominally within its jurisdiction. But what Morocco lacked the French possessed. By its military conquest of Morocco (known euphemistically as 'pacification') France provided that degree of security and predictability which enabled the protectorate government to undertake, for whatever motives, the development of the economic infrastructure of the country and some basic steps towards a modern economy.

The pacification of Morocco, 1912–34, totally transformed the system described in the previous chapter. The makhzan became a decorative appendage of a modern and for the most part non-Moroccan administration. The tribes, having lost military parity with the central authorities, lost also their ability to challenge or evade these same authorities. Because the protectorate was able to administer areas formerly in the bilad as-siba, the importance of the murabit as an accepted mediator in local disputes was greatly diminished. Thus the central elements of the traditional system –

tribes, murabitin, and the makhzan – were reduced to a role of secondary importance under the protectorate.

But as the pacification process was coming to an end, new elements, heretofore muted, gradually took on increased weight in protectorate politics. A nationalist movement which had its origins in a revival of religious orthodoxy, under the guidance of the educated bourgeoisie, principally of Fez, remained a strictly elitist movement until after the Second World War when it placed emphasis on numerical size. Its task of mass recruitment was facilitated by the emergence of a sizeable urban working class which proved susceptible to political organization. This mass of laborers, crowded into the industrial centers developed by French capital, was a product of the economic policies of the protectorate. The growth of the working class was particularly marked after 1945, and was complemented by the entrance into the nationalist movement of intellectuals of varied backgrounds, moulded by secular French educations, received either in France or in Morocco. Pacification, the setting up of the administration, and the implantation of the French colony, elicited their 'dialectical opposite',[2] the nationalist movement. These are the two aspects of the French *oeuvre* in Morocco which will be treated in this chapter.

The absorption of the bilad as-siba into the bilad al-makhzan represents a revolution whose consequences are as far-reaching as those of the signing of the protectorate treaty, or of the gaining of independence, or of all the changes, taken singly or collectively, which have taken place in Morocco since 1956. This revolution was some twenty-two years in the making (1912–34), but its net result was to render anomalous the traditional patterns of government. The makhzan no longer needed an army to collect taxes, and, in any case, it was not permitted one under the terms of the protectorate agreement. The formerly nomadic court took up fixed residence in Rabat, and there grew up about it a sophisticated administrative apparatus whose heart was the Direction of Interior and Political Affairs. At the other end of the scale, the tribes could no longer attack one another with impunity, nor could they feasibly challenge the central authorities. In essence, pacification made the administrative authority of the sultan coextensive with that of his *baraka*.

The military presence of France was felt well before the signing of the protectorate treaty of 1912. A French national, murdered in

Marrakesh in 1907, instigated the seizure of Oujda and the occupation of the Beni Iznassen region. A similar event in Casablanca in the summer of 1907 resulted in the landing of French troops there and the occupation of the Chawia agricultural plain. When the first resident-general, Lyautey, arrived in April 1912, he found part of the task of pacification already completed. The Gharb and Chawia were under control, as was the upper Moulouya, Oujda, and the south-eastern oases of the Tafilalt. However, the Fez region was in revolt, and in the south at Taroudant, Al-Hiba, the fourth son of Ma al-Aynayn, laid claim to the throne. The French quickly subdued the tribes around Fez and then turned to the threat of Al-Hiba. To thwart his drive northwards from the Suss valley, the French encouraged the *grands caids* of the High Atlas to oppose him. But all these qaids (Madani al-Glaoui and his younger brother Tihami, 'Abd al-Malik Mtouggi, and Tayyib Goundafi, and with the exception of 'Aissa Ben 'Omar al-'Abdi) acquiesced to Al-Hiba's seizure of Marrakesh. Al-Hiba's downfall was brought about by the almost fortuitous victory of Colonel Mangin's troops over those of Al-Hiba outside Marrakesh. Although the *grands caids* had done nothing to aid the French against Al-Hiba, Lyautey, militarily and administratively undermanned, felt obliged to seek their aid in holding down the southern portions of Morocco. Thus was born the policy of the *grands caids*.[3] This *ad hoc* arrangement became firm policy over the ensuing years and was later justified as conforming with official desires to preserve indigenous institutions. In fact the arrangement was based on the judgment that 'it is more economical and easier for the protectorate to control, by means of a limited number of local chiefs, all the country, than to assume directly its administration'.[4]

By the end of 1914 the coastal plains had been made safe for colonization. With the subduing of the regions around Taza and Khenifra, road communication between Fez and Oujda and Fez and Marrakesh by way of the Middle Atlas was opened up. The capture of Tiznit in 1917 led to the pacification of much of the Suss by 1919. During the same years the route from Meknes to the Tafilalt, through the heart of the old siba, was made secure.

Still there remained about one-third of the country outside French control. In twelve years after the first world war France finally managed to bring to heel all of the Middle Atlas (1931), the Tafilalt (1932), the Jabal Saghro (1933–4), and the Anti-Atlas and deep south (1934).[5] In the course of these operations Lyautey was replaced as resident-general in 1926, but lip-service continued to be paid to his theories of pacification: to wit, show force in order not to use it. Occasionally this maxim was observed, but the general practice was not only to show force but to use it as well. General Guillaume, writing in 1946, stated, 'No tribe ever came to us spontaneously. None ever surrendered without a fight, and some only after having exhausted all means of resistance.'[6] Some indication of the intensity of the fighting is given by the French casualty figures for the period 1907–35: twenty-seven thousand dead and fifteen thousand wounded.[7]

Of course, the most renowned contact between French troops and Moroccan tribes came when 'Abdulkrim al-Khattabi's rebellion (1921–6) in the Rif (Spanish protectorate zone) spilled over into the French zone. Its suppression required an enormous Franco-Spanish force and the presence of no less a figure than Marshal Pétain.

Singled out by many as simply another in a long line of Berber dissident leaders, 'Abdulkrim was rather a portent of things to come. He has been depicted as ignorant, but he had occupied posts in the Spanish administration, had edited an Arabic section of a Spanish newspaper, and was at one time chief *qadi* at Melilla. His association with heterodox brotherhoods, his reliance on tribes, and his indifference to the 'Alawite dynasty (an indifference shared by most educated Moroccans at that time), earned him the reputation of being a throwback to an earlier era.[8] But 'Abdulkrim had been forced to work with the materials at hand.

One of the most important causes of my ['Abdulkrim's] failure, if not the most important, was religious fanaticism. This is so because the influence exerted by the heads of the religious orders in the Rif surpassed that in other parts of Morocco and the Islamic world. I was powerless to do anything without them and had to ask their help at every turn.[9]

'Abdulkrim was all things to all men; to the nationalists he was and is the first nationalist; to the Rifian tribes he was and is a leader cast in the old mould. He is an appealing figure in that he incarnates at an early date Morocco's attempt to capture what is new while relying on what is old.

After the completion of pacification, while it remained possible for given areas to resort to violence in order to protest the actions of the central government, no longer was there the possibility of opting out for any extended length of time. Certain isolated mountain hamlets, cut off from the plains by the winter snows, escaped briefly each year the impositions of the makhzan. But, aside from these seasonal sibas, after 1934 it was widely recognized that regional and local autonomy was a function of the indulgence of the protectorate power and a privilege that could be withdrawn almost at will.

At the same time as the military operations were being carried out, the protectorate administration was being set up and the way prepared for an influx of French colonists and capital. The authority behind this administration was vested in the resident-general. His powers were considerably broader than those indicated in the protectorate treaty itself.[10] The latter authorized the resident-general, acting as representative of the sultan, to undertake reforms necessary for the well-being of the sultan's subjects. Specifically foreign affairs, defense, and finance were to be controlled by the residency. The sultan did not delegate his authority directly to the resident-general, for this act would have compromised his sovereignty. Instead, by a decree of 31 October 1912, regulatory power was delegated to the grand vizir in accord with article 4 of the Treaty of Fez. It was simply a matter of time before the grand vizir in turn ceded his powers to various members of the French administration.[11]

Although the Spanish zone in the north is not of direct concern to us here, it is worth noting that a roughly similar process took place there. It was not in fact a protectorate, but a zone of occupation which had been ceded to the Spanish by the French through a secret accord of 1904. The boundaries of the zone were traced by the Franco-Spanish treaty of 27 November 1912. The two enclaves of Ceuta and Melilla were considered to be Spanish territory, while the rest of the northern zone remained under the nominal sovereignty of the sultan. It was administered by a Spanish high commissioner and by a *Khalifa* appointed by the sultan upon the recommendation of the Spanish government. From 1923 on, Tangier was under international administration, but the sultan was represented there by a *Mandoub*.

Efforts to erect some sort of legal facade for the protectorate seem irrelevant, for it was inevitable that the technocratic invasion which Morocco witnessed after 1912 would reduce the outmoded makhzan to a subservient role. With a monopoly of arms, capital, and brains the protectorate was an irresistible force. Lyautey's plans for indirect administration and the revivification of traditional institutions were pipe-dreams. All factors made for direct administration. The campaigns to pacify the country, provide security for the colonists, fight famine and epidemics, and establish a transportation network, all dictated direct administration. Moreover, most Moroccans were ill-trained, if not totally incapable, of undertaking these sophisticated administrative tasks. Once the administration was staffed by the French, it tended to stay that way.[12]

For many years the makhzan was thoroughly effaced by the French implosion, although the French were there nominally to protect the sultan's authority. In fact, all the tangible aspects of the sultan's power were done away with, while certain ludicrous trappings were conscientiously maintained. In conformity with the protectorate treaty, the *wazir al-bahr*, the *amin al-umana*, and the *'allaf al-kabir* were suppressed. Two new ministries, Habous (to administer religious mortmain property) and Justice, were created, as well as a Delegate of the Grand Vizir for Education. The grand vizir stayed on, as mentioned above, ostensibly with broad powers but in fact fully subordinate to the residency, which appointed all ministers.[13] In 1928, the Service des Etudes Législatives, attached to the Secrétariat-Général, was created, succeeding the Comité de Législation, established in 1913. Both organizations were French-staffed and were empowered to process, edit, and present to His Majesty for signature all measures drawn up by the various residential services. Finally, to coordinate the Sharifian and French administrations and to watch over the former's activities, there was established the Direction of Sharifian Affairs, headed by the (French) Counsellor of the Sharifian Government, authorized to supervise the sultan's judicial, administrative and educational services.[14]

The clause in the protectorate treaty stipulating the 'safeguard ... of the respect for and traditional prestige of the sultan ...' was generally honored in trivial ways or used as a justification for the exclusion from Morocco of French parliamentary institutions. Great care was taken to maintain the physical appearance of the old makhzan. The traditional *baniqas* (a kind of office and reception

39

room) of the wazirs was continued, their occupants seated on the floor in traditional garb, surrounded by their secretaries and scribes. All this, it is alleged, so that the qaids and religious officials would not feel that the 'ancient makhzan had disappeared, and that they were face to face with an entirely new organism in which their co-religionists played but a subordinate role'.[15] At the same time, in its concern for the purity of the sultanic institution, the notion of the separation of powers was muted by the protectorate authorities. In this vein, Lyautey forbade in 1924 the public display of the Declaration of the Rights of Man, for, it was claimed, certain of its clauses, such as the law being the expression of the general will, were incompatible with the theocratic nature of the throne.[16]

The administrative apparatus established by the French after 1912 was elaborate and subject to frequent change in detail though not in essence. Divided into the Technical (Neo-Sharifian) and Residential Services, coordinated by the secretary-general, the real heart of the administration lay in the three *Grandes Directions*: Interior and Political Affairs, Finance, and Public Works. The importance of the first department is fairly obvious, being responsible for internal security and regional control. The Department of Finance took on the character of a control point for protectorate financial policy as shaped by powerful banking institutions which funnelled capital into Morocco. Because there was such a massive program of public works, this aspect of economic development became the focal point of a lucrative system of spoils, with the Service of Public Works and Transport acting as a clearing house for the award of contracts and the distribution of a considerable amount of public funds.[17] In turn these *Grandes Directions* were often but the facade for the 'trois grands' of the French colony, without whose support no resident-general could long hope to survive: the President of the Federation of the Chambers of Agriculture, the President of the Chamber of Commerce and Industry (CCI) of Casablanca, and the independent banker, Yves Mas, owner of two daily newspapers.[18]

Under the protectorate Morocco was divided into seven regions. Three of the regions, Casablanca, Rabat, and Oujda, having been brought under control in the early years of the protectorate, were administered by civilian authorities headed by a *chef de région* appointed by the resident-general. All qaids and pashas in these regions were supervised by *contrôleurs civils*, and, after 1947, there was established the 'urban control' to keep the burgeoning *madinas* and *bidonvilles* (shanty towns) in line. The three military regions, Fez, Meknes, and Agadir, were also directed by *chefs de région*. However, the equivalent to the *contrôleur civil* in these areas, which were largely tribal, was the *officier des affaires indigènes*, dispatched upon the recommendation of the resident-general by the French Ministry of War. Finally, there was the region of Marrakesh, which presented a mixture of these two systems. The *chefs de région* were responsible for all that went on in their areas. The *contrôleurs civils* and the *officiers des affaires indigènes** were responsible to them. After 1940 the administration of public health, mail, telephone and telegraph, and the collection of taxes, were organized on a regional basis, thus providing the *chef de région* with many of the powers of the French *préfet*. The almost total subordination of native officials to the local civilian or military supervisors completed a system which made of each region a semi-autonomous administrative unit, staffed at all key posts by French personnel who made no attempt to obfuscate their direct role by 'makhzani camouflage'.[19]

Under the control of each *chef de région*, but appointed by the sultan, was a corps of qaids and pashas, assisted by *muqaddims* (for each tribal douar) and *khalifas* (for city quarters). In both Arabic-speaking and Berber-speaking areas the qaid presided over tribal *jama'as*, selected from among tribal elders on a rotational basis, whose membership had to be renewed every three years. Reforms of 1951 and 1954 introduced the elective principle into the selection of the members of the *jama'as*. These assemblies had real life only in the Berber-speaking areas, where the French systematically undermined or excluded the presence of the makhzan. A dahir of 11 September 1914 stated: 'The tribes of Berber custom are and remain regulated and administered according to their own laws and customs under the control of the authorities'[20]. This principle was made more precise in dahirs of 1916 and 1921, before, however, there were any committed nationalists to contest their portent. What had been a relatively discreet policy of excluding *qadis* and the shari'a from tribal areas, was blatantly – and with poor timing – made public in the notorious 'Berber dahir' of 16 May 1930. It reaffirmed the principle of the judicial competence of the *jama'as* to administer *'urf* (customary) law. In addition, the geographic area

*The equivalents to the *officiers* in the Spanish zone were the *interventores*.

roughly corresponding to the old siba became subject to French penal law. From the above it can be seen that the French maintained the bilad as-siba as a distinct administrative (military regions controlled by *officiers des affaires indigènes*) and judicial (application of tribal customary and French penal law) entity.[21]

Brief mention should be made here of French attempts to associate some elements of the Moroccan educated elite with its *oeuvre* in Morocco. One aspect of this was Lyautey's schools for the sons of notables who were to be Morocco's *evolués*. While this minority was relatively pampered, the rest of the Moroccan population was neglected as regards education. Feeling alarming pressure from the nationalists in 1944, a series of reforms was announced. The protectorate promised, in the decade 1945–55, to construct two hundred new classrooms a year and to expand the schoolgoing population by ten thousand annually. As the nationalists pointed out, this gesture was almost farcical. In 1944, of two million Moroccans of school age, only thirty-six thousand were in school. If the French reforms were implemented, in twenty-five years there would be four million Moroccans of school age, of whom only two hundred and fifty to three hundred thousand would be in school.[22] But even the French policy of educating a picked elite backfired. Many of those Moroccans who were able to go on to institutions of higher learning were systematically excluded from posts of real responsibility in the protectorate services. They generally became fodder for the nationalist movement.

There were also some efforts to associate Moroccan commercial and financial interests with the protectorate. This policy was, to a degree, successful, for pacification opened up opportunities for trade which had previously not been available to the city bourgeoisie. But this budding native capitalism was always underfinanced and overly-speculative, and was choked off by the massive influx of French capital after 1945. Contracts and licenses were automatically awarded to French investors, and it was at that time that the slighted Moroccan bourgeoisie gave its unstinting financial support to the nationalist movement.[23]

One of the tactics employed by the French to give native Moroccan businessmen and landowners some feeling of responsibility under the protectorate was the creation in 1919 of Consultative Chambers of Agriculture, Commerce and Industry (counterparts for the European community had been created in 1913), surmounted by a Council of Government composed of a French and a Moroccan section (created in 1923), which met separately and had a purely consultative role. The two sections were emanations of the Chambers of Commerce, Industry and Agriculture, and while members of the French section were elected, all members of the Moroccan section, until 1947, were appointed. A reform of that year introduced restricted suffrage in the election of the Moroccan sections of the chambers. In any case the Council of Government was authorized to examine only economic questions and its recommendations had no binding effect.[24] It was never intended to be the forerunner of a parliament, and demands for steps in that direction fell before the old argument that such institutions would compromise the protectorate's efforts to uphold the sovereignty of the sultan:

> Doubtless the idea of political representation, tending to introduce the democratic system at the governmental level, was formally excluded as being conspicuously incompatible with the theocratic principle of the sovereignty of the sultan. . . .[25]

All that has been described above, pacification, the administrative apparatus, and the creation of the local chambers, was geared toward serving the needs of the European colony and toward the exploitation of the mineral and agricultural wealth of the country.[26] For the purposes of this study, the most significant aspect of the French economic effort in Morocco was its shattering, in many areas of the country, of the former stagnant, subsistence economy. Although the economic benefits derived from the construction of port facilities along the coast, the building of dams and the extension of irrigated acreage, the construction of roads and railroads, the institution of modern farming methods on *colon* land, and the development of public health services, may have accrued largely to the European community, the general effect was to shock, challenge, and upset the educated members of the native population. The social and economic change initiated under the protectorate stimulated the emergence of a nationalist movement which, no matter how it phrased its grievances, was faced with a situation without historical precedent.[27]

The Moroccan nationalist movement, as was common elsewhere in the Middle East, had its origins in a revival of Islamic orthodoxy 'best understood as yet another example of a classical historical pattern – a puritanical movement appealing to a threatened or déclassé people, urban and rural, during a period of social breakdown, a time of troubles'.[28] Known as Salafism, this Islamic reformism called for a return to the tradition of the founders of the religion, the pious ancestors (*as-salaf as-salih*). The major standard-bearers of the movement were Jamal ad-Din al-Afghani, Muhammed 'Abduh, and later Rashid Rida, and it was through contact with these men and their writings that their ideas began to circulate in North Africa.

The first Moroccan Salafists, 'Abdullah Ben Driss Senoussi and Boucha'ib ad-Doukkali, were not preoccupied with nationalism, but their cause, soon after the First World War, became inextricably bound up with nationalist objectives.[29]

Unorthodox religious practices, saint worship, and other forms of *bid'a* (unacceptable innovations) were widespread in Morocco, their major protagonists being the murabitin and zawiyas. The Salafists, in their concern for orthodox religious practice, set out to purge Morocco of the influence of the brotherhoods. Some of the most fervid enemies of the orders (such as Doukkali himself) were former *khwan* (brothers). At the same time, the presence of a Christian power in Morocco, there to administer a Muslim population, could not fail to arouse the opposition of the Salafists. The transition to nationalism came as a result of the tacit alliance worked out between the protectorate authorities and the zawiyas, an arrangement basically similar to that arrived at between the protectorate and the *grands caids* of the south: some degree of autonomous activity in return for loyalty to the residency. Under this arrangement, 'Abd al-Hay al-Kittani, head of the Order of Moroccan Marabouts, played tweedle-dum to Thami al-Glaoui's tweedle-dee. In view of the 'Alawite dynasty's long-standing enmity toward the brotherhoods, the bargain offered by the protectorate was particularly advantageous. As for France, 'She saw in the marabout nothing but complacency, and in the ulema nothing but independence.'[30]

The link between the original Salafist movement and the first nationalist groups was Moulay al-'Arabi al-'Alawi, student of ad-Doukkali and tutor of 'Allal al-Fassi.[31] Besides the latter, Shaykh al-'Alawi aroused the interest of Bel Hassan Wazzani, Brahim al-Kittani, and Rashid Darqawi, all clearly descendants of families ranking high in Moroccan hagiology. The funeral of

Boucha'ib ad-Doukkali in 1928 was the occasion for some of the first guarded criticisms of the regime erected by the protectorate.[32] From then on the twin objectives of the purification of the Muslim community and the expulsion of the foreign intruder became clearly linked. The Salafist movement proved to be a syncretic device for a small group of bourgeois adolescents to blend their sentiments of religious anxiety and national bitterness.[33] Not only did religion and nationalism find common ground within Morocco, but, because much the same phenomenon was taking place in the rest of the Arab world, Moroccan nationalists received a certain measure of international support at strategic moments. A prime example of this is the propaganda campaign mounted at the time of the Berber dahir in 1930, with international coordination provided by Shakib Arslan, the friend and biographer of Rashid Rida. It was the protest stirred up over this event that got the nationalist movement off the ground.

As mentioned above, the Berber dahir of May 1930 made public at an indelicate moment a policy which had long been in practice. The maintenance of tribal areas as separate judicial units was a manifestation of a belief, long cherished by many protectorate officials, that the Berbers, for many reasons, were potentially assimilable. A sometimes-Christian or Judaic past that predated Islam, a disdain for the plain- and city-dwellers (who were the fomenters of most oppositional sentiment), a simple combative spirit that endeared Berbers to the French military, their ignorance of Arabic and their reluctance to take Islamic ritual very seriously; all these factors led a school of officials to encourage separatism. Robert Montagne evokes the outlook of this school when he speaks of vast natural regions, inhabited by the tribes, which could, with French support, become free of the despotic and decadent influence of the makhzan.

> In these provinces, far from the cities, whose boundaries history has traced fairly exactly, the Berbers will become more immediately aware, under an administrative regime adapted to their existence, of the links, so firm, that unite them to their soil.[34]

The Berber dahir was issued in just this spirit and provided excellent material for the young nationalists who had been casting about for some way to capture the imagination of their coreligionists. The ensuing polemics raised the spectre of creeping Catholicism and accused the authorities of having violated their pledge to protect the throne and the Islamic institutions of the country. It is indicative of the character of the early nationalist movement that some of its most effective protests were delivered in mosques. By using a prayer form known as *latif*, employed in times of trouble or sorrow, 'Abdallatif Sbihi, in the great mosque in Salé, emphasized the gravity of the situation caused by the dahir. Several mosques in other cities followed suit.[35]

The protest elicited by the promulgation of the Berber dahir forced the residency to retreat. A dahir of 8 April 1934 reunified the penal system of Morocco, suppressing the jurisdiction of the customary and French tribunals in penal matters. However, in the High Sharifian Tribunal a penal section was created in which two Berber notables, with consultative voices, were seated.[36]

The close interrelation of religious reform and nationalist protest was manifested throughout the protectorate period in the form of the *écoles libres*, privately founded schools emphasizing religious instruction in Arabic within a modern curriculum, and aimed at countering the type of education given in the French *lycées*. The first such school was founded in Fez in 1921 and by 1932-3 almost all of them came under nationalist control. Schools were founded in all major cities and towns, and by 1937 there were twenty in Fez alone. Several were founded in rural areas and provided thereby the first contacts of the city-based nationalists with the rural population.[37]

The founders of the nationalist movement had no fixed methods, and, until 1944, independence was not one of their declared objectives. The early attempts to organize, to formulate political demands, and to choose allies, were eclectic and *ad hoc*. From its inception until 1937, the movement was that in name only. It consisted of a small coterie of young educated Moroccans in Fez and Rabat who enunciated certain demands for the reform of the protectorate regime. This phase culminated in the Plan of Reforms drawn up in 1934, and continued until the fall of the Blum government in 1936 at which time the illusions of liberation engendered by the Popular Front were dispelled. In 1936-7 some first steps were taken toward organizing a mass following, but this was brought to nothing by the Meknes riots of 1937. From then on until 1945 all nationalist activity had to be carried on semi-clandestinely, with 'Allal al-Fassi in exile for the entire period.

After the war and the founding of the Istiqlal Party in 1944, the original nucleus, re-enforced by some younger elements, managed to rally a considerable following among the urban workers, rural peasantry, and Moroccan commercial class. During this period the king (then still referred to as sultan) openly revealed his sympathies for the Istiqlal, a stance which brought about his exile in 1953. This event coincided with the imprisonment or exile of many prominent Istiqlalis who had been held responsible for the protest demonstrations held after the murder of the Tunisian labor leader, Farhat Hachad, in 1952. A vacuum was thus created in which the protectorate authorities were left face to face with urban terrorist groups, and, in 1955, a rural Liberation Army, both devoid of the potentially moderating influence of their missing leaders. This sequence of events is well known, but as regards this study certain aspects of the nationalist movement require further attention.

The Istiqlal has, since independence, found itself the victim of its own success during the period before 1956. For years the nationalists allied themselves and gave unconditional support to the king, thereby creating a public image of devotion to the throne, embodied in the nationalist slogan 'revolution of the throne and the people'. This popular image served the Istiqlal and its predecessor organizations in good stead before independence but has embarrassed the Istiqlal now that it is in opposition, albeit loyal. The character of the nationalist movement was significantly altered by the events of the years 1952-5, but the special relationship between the palace and the party, at least as conceived by the party rank-and-file, survived these years to plague the Istiqlal thereafter. To understand the predicament of the Istiqlal in the post-1956 setting, one must understand the nature of the party's ties to the throne.

For the young, educated Moroccan entertaining his first nationalist thoughts during the 1920s, the continuance of the sultanate was not taken as a necessity. It seemed to many that the sultanate was, in fact, responsible for Morocco's present state, that it was the sultanate which had reduced Morocco to financial insolvency and military impotence, that it was a sultan who signed away Morocco's sovereignty in 1912.[38] In 1927, Muhammed Ben Yussuf was chosen for his youth and docility by the resident-general, Steeg, to succeed the deceased sultan.[39] By 1930 Sultan Muhammed Ben Yussuf was still an unknown quantity for most

Moroccans. Since 1912 the sultanate had apparently become the willing plaything of the residency, and for the nationalists it was hard to conceive of the sultan having a primordial role in their plans. It was, moreover, Muhammed Ben Yussuf who signed the Berber dahir, an act which seemed to confirm the impression that the sultan was unable to protect Moroccan sovereignty and defend the faith.

After 1931, the original nationalist nucleus decided to increase the size of its organization. The inner core, terming itself the zawiya, set up a receiver body known as the *taifa* (both terms borrowed from the nomenclature of the brotherhoods) to screen unknown sympathizers. The *taifa* was also used to spread cells in the cities which in turn reported back to the Fez zawiya.[40] This exploitation of existing forms of religious organization, essentially antipathetic to nationalist-cum-Salafist objectives, was simply a case of pouring new wine in old bottles (reminiscent of 'Abdulkrim). The Salafists and nationalists were able in this way both to denounce the zawiyas and to make use of their organizational forms. Nationalism made no real and important progress until it took the form of a religious brotherhood, the 'nationalist zawiya', and until Allal al-Fassi became Shaykh Allal.[41]

It was at this juncture, in 1933 and 1934, that the French began to be alarmed at the extent of the nationalist movement. It was suggested to Sultan Muhammed Ben Yussuf that the nationalists were all republicans, a danger to the throne, and hence deserving of the sultan's condemnation. Apparently the sultan came close to accepting this interpretation. In fact, there was probably only one confirmed republican among the nine principal leaders: Bel Hassan Wazzani.* Nonetheless, the nationalists felt compelled to counter the French propaganda by running a series of articles in their journal, *La Voix du Peuple*, which were favorable to the sultan. On Throne Day, 18 November 1933, peaceful demonstrations of loyalty to the sultan were held, and on 8 May 1934, in Fez, the nationalists organized a large loyalty demonstration on the occasion of the sultan's visit. This was an important moment for an alliance which none had foreseen was born and was to endure

*The other eight were 'Allal al-Fassi, 'Omar 'Abdjellil, Muhammed Ghazi, Ahmad Mekwar, Hassan Bou'ayyad, Muhammed Diouri, Ahmad Balafrej, Muhammed Lyazidi. This nucleus formed the Comité d'Action Marocaine (CAM) in 1934 and the National Party in 1936. In 1937 Wazzani broke away from the latter to found the Popular Party (al-Hizb al-Qawmi).

until 1955. A sultan physically isolated from his subjects and lacking the means to halt the whittling away of his powers suddenly found that the nationalists were a potential source of support in his efforts to protect the integrity of the throne. As for the nationalists, they found in the sultan not only the symbol of Morocco's threatened sovereignty but also a personage whose position evoked a mass response which the nationalists could not hope to generate alone. This alliance, entered into by both parties for partly tactical reasons, proved to be a trap for the nationalists. Although it may be true that much of the sultan's prestige depended on the Istiqlali agitation in his favor and the counsel of the party's leaders, what these same leaders failed to realize was that in successfully building the image of the sultan as the most prominent symbol of the struggle for independence, they were, at the same time, giving him the ability to act autonomously, to rise above what would later be termed 'partial interests' (i.e. the Istiqlal) and 'political factions'.

Between the years 1937 and 1944, contacts between the palace and the nationalists were infrequent. But after the Allies' landing in Morocco, and the sultan's conversations with President Roosevelt, those nationalist leaders remaining in the country felt the moment was ripe to demand complete independence from France.* It was obviously important to have the neutrality, if not the backing, of the sultan in the event of the presentation of the demand. Towards this end, Muhammed al-Fassi, one of the tutors of Prince Hassan, acted as liaison between the sultan and three leaders of the National Party: 'Omar 'Abdjellil, Ahmad Balafrej, and Muhammed Lyazidi. During clandestine conversations with these men Muhammed Ben Yussuf agreed that there was no further point in calling for reforms within the context of the protectorate and that independence had become the sole valid solution. But he felt that he could not publicly support the nationalist demand, for that would, in all likelihood, lead to his deposition, in which case he would be lost as a symbol and shield of the movement. At the same time he vowed that he would act in such a manner as to make it impossible for the protectorate authorities to prosecute the nationalists other than through illegal means.

---

* Roosevelt met privately with the sultan in January 1943 at Casablanca at the time of his meeting with Churchill and De Gaulle. He led the sultan to believe that he would use his good offices to promote Moroccan independence following the war.

Also discussed at this time was the question of the future regime of independent Morocco and of constitutional monarchy. While the sultan declared himself in favor of democratization of the monarchical regime, he judged it unwise at the time to introduce the term 'constitutional monarchy' into any public demands. What was needed, he contended, was maximum unity among all Moroccans in the struggle ahead, and the notion of constitutionalism might be too radical for some of the more traditional personalities of the makhzan to swallow.

These conversations concluded, and the sultan's passive sympathy guaranteed, the leaders of the National Party announced on 11 January 1944, the founding of a new party, the Istiqlal, 'which includes the members of the ex-National Party and independent personalities ... to ask for the independence and territorial integrity of Morocco under the leadership and guidance of H.M. Sidi Mohammed Ben Youssef. . .'. In compliance with the sultan's request, there was no mention of constitutional monarchy:[42]

The Istiqlal leaves to H.M. the task of establishing a democratic regime similar to the form of government adopted in the Moslem countries of the Orient, safeguarding the rights of all elements and all classes of Moroccan society, and defining the obligations of each.

The declaration was signed by sixty-one Moroccans, revealing a general rallying of the Moroccan bourgeoisie to the movement as well as the first appearance of what were to become the 'young Turks' of the party: Mehdi Ben Barka and 'Abdarrahim Bou'abid. Al-Fassi summed up the significance of the declaration in his statement that it represented 'the transition from the notion of obtaining independence through reform to the notion of obtaining reform through independence'.[43]

After the war the sultan identified himself much more closely with the Istiqlal. In February 1945 the party prepared the sultan's entry into Marrakesh, the French-protected fief of Thami al-Glaoui.[44] In April 1947 Muhammed Ben Yussuf visited another area where the authority of the makhzan was minimal :Tangier. In a speech there, in the presence of Resident-General Labonne, the sultan spoke of Morocco's future, Islam, and the Arab League, but failed to make the customary obeisances to the French 'mission' in Morocco.[45] In early 1951 his identification with the Istiqlal became almost complete. Resident-General Juin, in the Moroccan section of the Council of Government, had bitterly denounced critical reports of the budget submitted by Muhammed Laghzaoui and Ahmad Lyazidi, brother of Muhammad Lyazidi of the Istiqlal Executive Committee. After the altercation, all those present who sympathized with or were members of the Istiqlal left the session and went to present their grievances to the sultan, who received them immediately.[46] Soon after this episode, al-Glaoui, whose domain was increasingly riddled with Istiqlal cells, rebuked the sultan at a public reception, saying, 'You are no longer the Sultan of Morocco, you are the Sultan of the Istiqlal. . . .'[47]

The French continually pressed Muhammad Ben Yussuf to disown the Istiqlal, while the latter encouraged him to go on strike and sign no decrees which would compromise Morocco's sovereignty. Having become sincerely devoted to the nationalist cause, the sultan followed the advice of the Istiqlal. The 'strike of the dahirs' eventually led to his deposition and exile, in August 1953. All these years of unceasing nationalist and residential demands, counsel, and cajolery, had left their marks on the sultan in a way which was to manifest itself after independence. As one Istiqlali remarked, 'It was inevitable that King Muhammad developed certain despotic tendencies despite his fundamental good will. For years we had been telling him that he was all-powerful, and that only he could stand up to the French, while the French told him that he, being all-powerful, alone was capable of standing up to the Istiqlal. After all this he came to believe in his own power.'

In the five years after 1944, the Istiqlal began to construct an impressive organization that took on mass proportions. On the eve of the repression of 1937, the old National Party may have had five to six thousand adherents. This figure was greatly diminished in the ensuing war years, and by 1944 had sunk to approximately three thousand. After the return of many exiled leaders, such as 'Allal al-Fassi, and with the first sincere attempts to rally the masses, the Istiqlal grew from ten thousand in 1947 to some one hundred thousand in 1951.[48] Much of this expansion was due to the efforts of some of the younger members to organize urban labor and the teeming *bidonvilles*, which acted as more-or-less temporary way stations for the rural unemployed.[49]

Al-Glaoui and Shaykh al-Kittani were to have their day in the sun, first in January 1951, when al-Glaoui's tribal cohorts demonstrated in and around Rabat in order to aid General Juin's show of force to compel the sultan to sign certain decrees and to keep his distance from the Istiqlal. The sultan gave in to Juin's threats at that time, but a new crisis developed in September 1952 when the sultan refused to sign decrees authorizing the election, by both French and Moroccans, of municipal councils, and the formation of a mixed Council of Ministers. At issue was the notion of co-sovereignty, by which French citizens, having in principle neither the rights nor duties of Moroccan citizens, would be allowed to elect representatives, equal in number to the representatives of the Moroccan community, in seventeen cities. [50] The sultan's intransigence in this matter led to the gradual mustering of all the forces in Morocco well disposed toward the protectorate and hostile to the sultan and the party. The objectives of the European community and protectorate administration, increasingly beyond the resident-general's control, coincided nicely with those of al-Glaoui and al-Kittani. All were agreed on the desirability of replacing Muhammed Ben Yussuf by someone more amenable. With the support of local French administrators, al-Glaoui set about instigating a protest movement of qaids and tribes who were to proclaim their distaste for the sultan.[51] All these processes culminated in the deposition of the sultan on 18 August 1953, and his replacement by Muhammed Ben Moulay 'Arafa of the 'Alawite family.

The exile of the sultan took place at a time when it was difficult for the nationalists to react in a coordinated fashion. As mentioned above, the Istiqlal had been decapitated in 1952. Not only were most of the party's leaders in prison or exile but also two lesser members of the party, Mahjoub Ben Seddiq and Tayyib Bou'azza, who had had some success in wresting the Union Générale des Syndicats Confederés Marocains from its French leadership. In 1951 Bou'azza was elected secretary-general of that body, the first Moroccan ever to hold this position. The Istiqlal leaders and cadre had been victims once again of their own success. They were too powerful not to disturb the regime, but too weak to overturn it by simple mass movements. They were neither capable of nor eager to pass on to armed opposition. In the end they were put out of harm's way by the same police repression against which they had so long protested. The brutal change in outlook and tactics needed to conduct resistance necessitated a new organizational apparatus and new personnel.[52]

Juin had obliged the sultan, in February 1951, to curtail his contacts with the Istiqlal. By way of riposte the Istiqlal joined with the two nationalist parties of the Spanish zone and Wazzani's Parti Démocratique de l'Indépendance (PDI) to form in Tangier, on 9 April 1951, the Moroccan National Front. Among some of the resolutions adopted at that time were two stating that there would be no negotiations before the proclamation of independence nor would there be any talks with the 'occupying power' concerning minor problems within the existing situation.[53]

This briefly-achieved unity came to nothing after the arrests of 1952. The following summer, as it became clear that the French wished to engineer the sultan's departure, there was a brief flurry of activity by what remained of the Istiqlal and the PDI. On 13 August 1953 there was formed a Committee of National Awakening for Defense of King and Throne.* It futilely denounced the qaids who at that time proclaimed Ben 'Arafa sultan.[54] This was, in effect, the last gasp of peaceful protest.

In 1954, a patchwork of urban terrorist groups had developed in some of the major cities. The attitude of the Istiqlal toward these groups was ambivalent. The Provisional Executive Committee, set up after 1952, contained only two members who had strong ties with the terrorist groups: Bashir Bel'Abbas and 'Abd al-Kabir al-Fassi.[55] The party was so concerned by violence that disciplinary committees were instituted to deal with any members suspected of terrorism. The distance and hostility existing between the party's leadership and the urban resistance groups was not overcome before independence. Immediately after that event, the returning Istiqlali leaders were faced by unfriendly armed bands which were not in any way beholden to the party. This situation gravely weakened the Istiqlal's bargaining position *vis-à-vis* Muhammed v, who had returned a national hero from his exile, and in whose name the terrorist campaign had been launched in the first place. In addition resistance elements had taken the most uncompromising stance on the necessity of the return of the exiled sultan.[56]

Complementing these urban groups were disparate bands of

* Muhammed Ben Yussuf's title had officially remained 'Sultan', but the nationalists, since 1934, had rejected that term as lacking in modernity, replacing it in their slogans by the title of 'King' (*malik*).

rural resistants. In the fall of 1953 isolated and numerically insignificant groups in the mountainous areas undertook sporadic acts of sabotage. The northern groups took on more importance a year later when there were attempts to coordinate the Moroccan resistance with the Algerian uprising of 1 November 1954. At that moment there was no formal organization in Morocco known as the Liberation Army. Rural resistance operations were under the *nominal* control of the Istiqlal, and the center of operations was in the Spanish zone. There was an official representative of 'Allal al-Fassi, who, at that time, was in Cairo, who acted as liaison between the Istiqlal, rural resistance, and the Spanish high commissioner, Rafael Garcìa Valiño.* The links of the rural bands with the Istiqlal were symbolic and did not entail a close working relationship. Eventually, in the fall of 1955, as fighting in the Rif spread, the rural resistants announced the formation of the Liberation Army. It too contributed directly to the return of Muhammed v, a contribution for which the Istiqlal could take little credit. With relatively few men the Liberation Army was able to tie down large numbers of French troops and Moroccan goums that France could ill-afford due to her preoccupations in Algeria. It soon became a question of a major military build-up or acceptance of some Moroccan demands. The French chose the latter course.[57]

Like its urban counterpart, the Liberation Army demanded the return of Muhammed v and favored continued military operations against the French until Algeria had in turn won its independence. Thus one finds the Liberation Army refusing to lay down its arms even after the return of the king to Morocco on 16 November 1955, and the formal granting of independence on 3 March 1956.

The situation facing Muhammed v in 1955 was not unlike many another interregnum in Moroccan history. There was the common element of unknown political power, who could muster what strength, who would ally with what faction. Like Moulay Isma'il, Muhammed v set about the pacification of his own country. The units involved were, of course, somewhat new to Morocco, although in the case of the Glawi and his supporters among the notables we find a group cast in the old mould: would-be backers and beneficiaries of a pretender to the throne. At the same time,

* Immediately after independence, Valiño was decorated by the Liberation Army for services rendered prior to 1956.

one finds small bands of urban and rural terrorists, a rural army, and a lame-duck colonial power. Moving cautiously among these were a king and a party without arms, both trying to win over those that had them in order to gain the upper hand. Ultimately the game was being played for higher stakes than in any previous interregnum, and the participants were manoeuvring for control of the administrative apparatus introduced by the French. This, in effect, was the embodiment of the new Moroccan state, and it had to some degree habituated Moroccans, probably for the first time, to regular and thorough control, both fiscal and military.

Although the Liberation Army was never numerically impressive, in the winter of 1955–6 it was of considerable importance, as no regular Moroccan army had yet been organized. It represented yet another lever of control, a sort of threat, which the newly-returned king could wield against the Istiqlal. The party claimed to have master-minded much of the resistance, both urban and rural, but in the National Council of the Moroccan Resistance, which met in the summer of 1956, there was among its fifty-odd members only one from the Istiqlal executive committee, 'Allal al-Fassi himself.

The new alignment of forces that developed in the three years after 1952 was completed by the formation of an autonomous Moroccan labor union. In September 1954, Ben Seddiq and Bou'azza were released from prison, and on 5 January 1955 they founded, illegally, the Committee of Organization and Development of Free Syndicalism in Morocco, and on 20 March the Moroccan Union of Labor (UMT). Six months later, the protectorate authorities, which had heretofore prohibited the formation of Moroccan unions organizationally distinct from the French locals, recognized the *fait accompli* and officially allowed the creation of Moroccan unions. Although the UMT was for most purposes an auxiliary of the Istiqlal, it represented a faction of the party leadership and rank-and-file that was not entirely in accord with the 'old guard' leaders, who had never paid much heed to labor problems.

The growth of groups outside the control of the Istiqlal, and the development of a body of opinion within the party which did not take for granted the political sagacity of the party's leadership, left the king in an enviable bargaining position. Although it would try, the Istiqlal could no longer maintain that it was the sole legitimate nationalist force in the nation, nor could the leaders, who had been in prison or abroad for three years, claim that through their efforts alone was independence achieved. Most significantly, no longer, in discussions with the king, could the Istiqlal insinuate that the monarchy would crumble without the party's support and that the king's authority was coextensive with that of the party apparatus. Muhammed v, who, for all his political naiveté, had an instinctive grasp of how best to protect his throne, did not waste this opportunity. Proclaiming himself above all parties, he called for a government of 'national union'. The clear implication was that the Istiqlal no longer embodied all elements of the population, that it was no longer capable of doing so, and that the monarchy, the true symbol of national unity, would arbitrate the differences which had arisen among the various political factions in the country.

It is probably true, as many Istiqlalis have complained, that the French and the PDI pushed the king toward this way of thinking. The influence of the PDI allegedly took root when 'Abdalhadi Boutaleb and 'Abd al-Qader Benjelloun spent some time with the king in his exile in Madagascar, warning him of the evils of the Istiqlal. After his return, it is reliably reported that the king cautioned the Istiqlal: 'We were allies to break the French enslavement of my people; I can no longer be your ally to enslave my people once again.' The French, for their part, were understandably apprehensive as to the future of French interests in Morocco were the Istiqlal to gain entire control of the government.

The PDI had suggested that the first government of independent Morocco be divided equally among members of the PDI, Istiqlal, and independents.[58] As it turned out, the new government was formed by five independents, including M'barrek Bekkai as prime minister, nine Istiqlalis, six members of the PDI, and one representative of the Jewish community. Naturally the Istiqlal was not very pleased by this government, in which it saw itself as unjustifiably underrepresented. The king, however, in his speech of investiture, dubbed it 'as representative a government as possible',[59] publicly revealing thereby what he thought to be the Istiqlal's political strength. By this act King Muhammed established the throne as an independent political force, beholden to no political organization. It represented the first step in a policy which has been maintained skilfully, and even ruthlessly, ever since. That policy has, over the years, become more sophisticated, and, with the growth of a well organized army and police force, more determined. Its diverse aspects will be examined in detail in the following chapters, but it should be kept in mind that what manoeuvrability the monarchy has enjoyed in the years since 1956 is rooted in the king's manipulation of the political groups that confronted one another on the eve of independence.

The preceding chapter has been highly selective in its presentation of persons and events. It has treated only the bare bones of the nationalist movement and the protectorate administration. Certain aspects have been emphasized, for they bear directly on the politics after independence, and can be recapitulated as follows. During the twenty-two years after 1912, pacification and colonization were the two sides of the coin of the setting-up of the protectorate administration. Of the major actors in the pre-protectorate system, only the tribes had a significant role to play in this period, and theirs was largely negative. After 1934, the tribes variously accepted to cooperate with the protectorate. The deposition of Muhammed v brought this cooperation to an end, and the tribesmen became 'nationalists', although somewhat aloof from the Istiqlal. Many Berbers had joined the Istiqlal more out of antipathy to the French than out of loyalty to the party. Likewise, after 1956, many abandoned the party, often joining the PDI more out of hostility to the Istiqlal than admiration for Hassan Wazzani.

The monarchy was shunted off to one side by the residency and was allowed to wallow in its medieval customs. No major reforms were made in its structure, nor was any attempt made to associate it with or give it experience in the modern administrative apparatus put in place by the French. Almost forgotten until 1934, the monarchy came to life with borrowed warmth from the nascent nationalist movement. The nationalists themselves had been carefully excluded from administrative positions of responsibility so that they, like the king, greeted independence with only minimal knowledge of the tasks which faced them.*

The origins of the nationalist movement in the Salafi revival have been noted, for the old guard of the Istiqlal always bore the traces of its religious orientation. Despite the political flexibility of 'Allal al-Fassi, the party outgrew these leaders after 1944 with

---

* There is an apocryphal but nonetheless indicative story of the first Moroccan minister of finance asking his departing French predecessor, 'Où est le coffre?'

the influx of younger members educated in the secular French system, and the increasing importance among the party rank-and-file of the less religiously-motivated urban masses.

With the granting of independence, Morocco found itself endowed with a colorful makhzan, overflowing with an abundant court of royal officials and 'ulema juxtaposed to a modern administration that no one, except the remaining French technical advisors, really knew how to run. A basically rational administrative set-up and the physical means to control the country, all at the disposal of an often-Byzantine governing elite, has probably been the determining factor of the style and content of the wielding of influence in independent Morocco.

Thus Morocco in 1956 was heir to two legacies, that of the pre-protectorate past with its centuries-old customs and attitudes toward power, and that of the protectorate itself, embodied in an elaborate infrastructure which was neither wholly understood by its heirs nor adapted to their habits. Much of the political history of Morocco since 1956 has consisted in the welding together of these two legacies, of bending the Moroccan personality to modern institutions, the market economy, and political parties, and the no-less significant bending of all the above to the Moroccan personality.

PART TWO

AN EXPLANATION OF THE NATURE AND BEHAVIOR OF THE MOROCCAN POLITICAL ELITE

CHAPTER THREE

THE SOCIAL CONTEXT OF MOROCCAN POLITICS

All seek to maintain in the midst of the group that tension which is life, that variety that is solidarity.[1]

For centuries Moroccan society has been characterized by constant tension and varying degrees of violence, but at any given point in history, with a few rare but notable exceptions, the most salient product of this tension has been stalemate. Moroccan society appears to be ever on the verge of an explosion that never occurs. Despite the indisputable upheaval in Moroccan social institutions caused by forty-four years of the protectorate and eleven years of independence, Moroccan society is still characterized by stalemate. This is all the more peculiar because the political atmosphere has been so heavily charged since the founding of the nationalist movement in the 1930s. Moreover, independence in Morocco has been accompanied, as elsewhere, with the acceptance, often seemingly fervent, of predigested political ideologies introduced to audiences of illiterate, poor, and, if we are to believe one of the catch-words of contemporary sociology and political science, 'uprooted' individuals seeking a new religion or frame of reference. However, it is all too easy to miss the stalemate for the tension, to discern a high degree of politicization and deduce therefrom a not quite so obvious process of rapid political and social change. In the last eleven years, and probably for some years to come, stalemate has been and will continue to be the dominant trait of Moroccan politics, and it is upon an explanation of this stalemate that I shall concentrate. In so doing, I shall be primarily concerned with Moroccan attitudes towards power and authority, and patterns of political behavior derived therefrom, upon which I touched briefly in the Introduction.

Morocco as a geographic entity has muddled along for hundreds of years partially shut off from the rest of the Near and Middle East, but the functions performed by the basic social institutions of Moroccan society – family, clan, tribe, village, and city – are generally similar to those performed by corresponding institutions throughout the area.

Broadly speaking, this society is sprung from the tribe, and, with the possible exception of the great river valleys, norms and modes of social and political behavior have their origins in the tribe. Analytic frameworks applied by western scholars to Middle Eastern tribes can, in a more general sense, be highly useful in understanding the social and political conduct of the society as a whole. There is a striking resemblance between the internal stalemate common to many Middle Eastern tribes and that manifested in the contemporary Moroccan political process. As we shall see, the resemblance is not coincidental. The major concept that will interest us here is that of 'segmental opposition', developed by E.E.Evans-Pritchard in his study of the Nuer and in his later study of the Sanusi.[2] In political systems where a central authority is either weak or non-existent, 'maintenance of tribal structure must rather be attributed to opposition between its minor segments than to any outside pressure'.[3] The tribe was not held together by some common purpose, nor devotion to a single leader, nor even common ancestorship, although that was frequently invoked, but paradoxically, to the tension, friction, and hostility among its component parts. This tension resulted in feuding, occasionally intertribal warfare and a considerable display of hostility, but the net result was the maintenance of tribal structure.

Tribal segmentation may take place according to diverse criteria such as age-sets, territory, sex, and the like. In the Middle East, however, the most common form of segmentation, in fact one which is characteristic of the entire area, is the division of tribes into agnatic lineages all claiming descent from a common ancestor. These lineages are continually re-enforced, at least in theory, through the practice of parallel cousin marriage,[4] and they form the active units of a hierarchy of ascendant internal segments (for example: patrilinear descent group, sub-clan, clan, tribe, confederation) which provide for the escalation and response to disputes arising either among the component units or with rival tribes. Rival units at the base level of the tribe, when confronted by a threat from other units at the same level, or from without, will unite to meet the challenge. Referring to the diagram in figure 1 (below), let us suppose that at level I, A, the rival of E, is threatened by C. At that moment A and E will cease their hostilities and coalesce to meet the challenge, obliging, in all likelihood, C to call upon the aid of F. The dispute will then have escalated to level II where A confronts C – escalation simply being the recasting of the dispute in terms of larger aggregates. This process can be continued until, in some instances, all the base groups that constitute the tribe are split into two hostile factions. These in turn will unite when threatened by another tribe.

Segmentary Diagram*

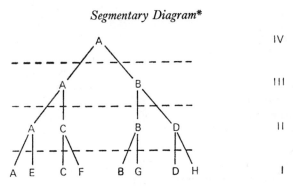

That, in brief, is the essence of the segmentary process for treating disputes, but the system is a good deal more than that, and its dynamics are applicable to situations of political conflict far removed from the tribal context. Here I shall attempt to single out the basic aspects of group interaction in the segmentary tribal system so that further on I can reintroduce them with reference to the Moroccan political process. These aspects are the functions of tension and hostility, the locus of hostility, the objectification of conflict, the process of overlapping alliances, and the nature of group interests.

The tribe† (maximal grouping A in figure 1) is defined negatively.

---

* From Murphy and Kasdan, *op. cit.*, note 4.
† The term 'tribe' has been used loosely and for the sake of convenience in the above text. Strictly speaking, it does not refer to the same level of social organization in every situation, and in Moroccan tribes the term *taqbilt* (Arabic: *qabila*) is used by tribesmen to refer to a number of levels in the structural hierarchy. Its definition is relative to the other units with which it interacts. In general, tribes shape their identity through reference to a common ancestor and

It exists as such only in opposition to some external force. In turn, it is but an ephemeral collage of microgroups which are similarly defined. Were any group's rivals to disappear, the group itself would lose its corporate nature and cohesion, common descent notwithstanding. It can be argued that patrilinear descent serves to re-enforce and explain group cohesion at any given level, but it is alone insufficient to hold the group together.

Thus, tension and hostility serve as catalysts to group cohesion. Their manifestations may take the form of outward expansion at the expense of other groups,[5] or of intratribal conflict, most commonly embodied in the feud.[6] In fact, hostility and conflict within tribes, particularly sedentary tribes, is just about universal in the Middle East, and such conflict tends to be more intense among close agnates than among distant tribal cousins.[7] Members of extended families or subclans are intimately involved in the exploitation of whatever material patrimony they may have, and the just distribution of scarce resources such as water, fields, or a father's inheritance, inevitably leads to friction. Moreover, close agnates are responsible for the family's honor in the feud, the collective swearing of oaths, the payment of blood money, and the protection of their women (not least of all from one another), all factors for intense friction and hostility.

But this is essentially what Coser calls realistic conflict, for it is involved in the attainment of defined ends.[8] At higher levels of tribal organization, however, one suspects that there is a certain amount of ritual conflict or hostility mixed into the pursuit of objective goals. It is seldom possible to separate out these two elements,[9] as they are inextricably mixed in tribal activities at all levels. But we may postulate that intensity of conflict is greatest when material interests are involved and that this sort of conflict arises most often within closely related groups. When confronted by blood feuds, defense of the chastity of tribeswomen, invocations of illustrious ancestors, wars over breaches of honor, one must not be led astray. These are the trappings for the defense of a patrimony, and a tribe is above all a mechanism by which a number of segments collectively exploit a sector of strategic resources.[10] In

---

a shared territorial base with transhumant tribes emphasizing the element of common descent and sedentary tribes shared territory. I cannot do justice in a footnote to the many insights upon segmentation in Morocco provided me by the articles and personal communications of David M. Hart and Ernest Gellner.

many tribes in Morocco the acquisition of land in a tribal area is equivalent to the acquisition of political rights, and, inasmuch as political rights are reserved to agnatic descendants of the putative common ancestor, the new proprietor acquires new blood.

Often, segmentary systems develop mechanisms for group coalition and alliance which cut across the hierarchy of descent groups. An individual may find himself caught up in several overlapping dual divisions which exert countervailing influences upon him to the point that he is immobilized. For instance, in some Moroccan tribes a tribesman, as we have seen, is a member of a lineage group in rivalry with other such groups. At the same time he and his clan may be members of a *liff* alliance which tends to polarize conflict among groups on a territorial basis. The clans allied through *liff* may be rivals in the first situation. Again, a tribesman may participate in a more narrowly defined local alliance for the protection of grazing rights, distribution of water, and so forth. In this instance his lines of alliance may cut across both agnatic ties and *liff*.[11]

It should be clear from the above that such systems of overlapping alliances are designed to stifle or restrain actual conflict which might lead to the disruption of the entire system or at least to the redistribution of scarce resources among its parts. On the other hand, it encourages the pervasive tension, and hostility, that is so essential to the maintenance of group cohesion and boundaries. As E.A. Ross has remarked, such a society is 'sewn together by its inner conflicts'.[12] Segmentary systems tend toward an internal equilibrium, which, it cannot be too strongly stated, is seldom achieved nor long maintained. However, neither are gross imbalances in the power of given units within the system long tolerated. Other units will regroup and coalesce to offset or wear down any undue power accumulation on the part of others. This is so well known to participants that units that have gained a slight power advantage will not try to increase it unduly, preferring modest gains to a total reversal of fortunes. Actors in segmentary systems have a zero-sum conception of power. There is a fixed quantity, and one man's loss is another man's gain. Participants are able to weight and assess power factors and are very sensitive to shifts in power increments. Slight shifts in the balance of power do not go undetected, and before they can be consolidated counterpressures will be put in motion.[13]

While the overall tendency of segmentary systems is toward the maintenance of the status quo, they are not static. Component parts are in almost constant motion moving along the lines of shifting alliance patterns, probing, repulsing, regrouping like so many particles bound together by their own friction. The fact that today's ally could be tomorrow's enemy leads to a certain moral relativism. There are very seldom any sworn enemies nor any friends for life. Particularly among the agnatic descent groups common to the Middle East there is little inclination towards intense and durable antipathy towards out-groups. Members of this system must remain ambivalent both towards out-groups and towards their own; their enemies and allies being chosen according to their own advantage in a particular situation. This makes for (although of course never achieves) value neutrality regarding group membership, with an often-ignored ease of movement of individuals among groups (through demanding refuge, acquiring land, marrying-in) and the possibility of their reintegration into their original lineage – all this without there being *necessarily* any severe or material sanctions.[14] Part and parcel of the above is the flexibility of alliance arrangements, which, it seems to me, predisposes actors to defensive manoeuvres. They must protect all flanks against friends who may be enemies and maintain communications with enemies who some day may be friends.

Despite this value relativity, segmentary systems in the Middle East have developed a nomenclature to identify endemic conflict. As suggested above, although material interests are almost always involved, there is also a considerable element of ritual hostility added in. The social structure depends on the existence of tension and, in a circular fashion, must generate it.[15] Yet to give such contrived conflict meaning, labels are applied and over the years, perhaps some moral content is accreted to these labels. One finds local groups identifying their particular cleavages in terms of sweeping territorial alignments, such as Adnan and Qahtan in the Middle East proper,[16] or Tahuggwa and Tagazzoult in southern Morocco.[17] These giant alliances of several tribes (has there historically ever been an instance in which any one of them acted corporately?) provide a rationale for local conflict, and give it some sort of supra-local, historical, even mythical justification. But reference to these super-alliances is probably a nomenclatural device to identify and explain pervasive tension. What in fact caused the tension in any instance is not of immense importance for I would argue that it is inherent to the system. If a cause did not exist, it would have to be invented.

In the preceding paragraphs I have exposed some of the elements of group interaction within segmentary lineage systems, but these are by no means the only type of segmentary systems. Indeed, segmentation and complimentary opposition are universal phenomena.[18] In his cogent analysis of segmentary lineages, M. G. Smith has treated them as parts of a system of political relations, and has postulated the inseparability of political action from segmentary organization.

> Political action is . . . that aspect or form of social action which seeks to influence decisions of policy by competition in power. That is to say, political action is always and inherently segmentary, expressed through the contraposition of competing groups or persons.[19]

For analytic purposes, Smith proposes that we distinguish clearly between power and authority. 'Authority is the right to order certain actions, power is the ability to secure their performance.'[20] Power is segmentary, conditional, relativistic and cannot be centralized. The centralization of power proceeds by its transformation into authority, which is expressed through a specific administrative hierarchy.[21] Of course, as Smith himself notes, power and authority are not easily separated in practice, but the distinction is valid. Thus, the competition for power (with a view to its conversion into authority) is segmentary and wellnigh universal. What distinguishes one system from another are the kinds of segments involved, the degree of segmentation, the intensity of the competition, and, I would suggest, the style of the competition.

It is with all the above in mind, that we now consider the nature of political competition in Morocco, its characteristic patterns of political behavior, and its relation to lineage theory. First, it will be postulated that the 'segmental-faction' is the principal instrument involved in the competition for the control and allocation of scarce resources. The term 'segmental-faction', while cumbersome, calls our attention to the dynamic interaction of various units whose cohesion and identity are sustained through competition with other similar units. They are not mere particles, so many unrelated potatoes in a sack. They have goals that, as seen by the actors themselves, are to varying degrees incompatible, and it is believed that those successful in the competition will redistribute a fixed quantity of power at the expense of the other participants. Were the competition to cease, or were certain groups to be excluded from it, those affected would dissolve and lose their identity.[22]

The aspects of group behavior within segmentary lineage systems which I presented earlier in this chapter may serve as a model for group behavior among segmental-factions. I shall elaborate this suggestion throughout the rest of the chapter. Much of the discussion will revolve about the notion of faction and its manifestations, historic and contemporary, in Morocco. Competition and conflict in lineage systems takes place among corporate segments. Competition in other segmentary systems takes place among factions which *tend* to be noncorporate, ephemeral, founded on self-interest, and leader-oriented.[23] So stated, the distinction between the two types of group has been unduly dichotomized. Corporate segments are often ephemeral (disappearing through fission or fusion), and oriented toward material interests, while factions may be literally a mixture of corporate groups and interest groups (a union local whose members happen to be of the same tribe: a modern farm managed and owned by a religious sect).[24] Consequently, the segmental faction is generally bound at once by affective links and common material interests, and engages in both ritualistic and objective conflict. Let us return to the hypothesis that the segmental faction is the principal instrument involved in the competition for the control and allocation of scarce resources. This is so in Morocco, and probably in many developing societies, for the following reasons. First, much of all adult activity is political, that is, involved in acute competition at all levels of society for relatively scarce goods. There are relatively few opportunities for individuals to find gratification and rewards through other forms of social activity, nor is it often materially feasible to avoid political activity. Further, the cultural context of many such societies, and the political values and style derived therefrom, lend themselves to the primacy of the segmental faction. We have already seen that segmentary lineage systems are common to all the Middle East. Moreover, the cities and villages of the area are subject to segmentation, or what Patai has analyzed, a bit simplistically, as 'dualism'.[25] Morocco is a segmentary state both in its most general sense and by the fact that for centuries a large part of its population was organized in segmentary lineages. As a result, the behavior of political actors today is formed at once by the factional system in which they operate and by the legacy of their traditional political culture. Finally, the proclivity toward and the intensity of factional politics in these societies is to some extent a function of the contemporary period of political uncertainty and rapid social change. The dissolution of colonial regimes has enormously increased the scope of political competition for indigenous factions as well as the amount of resources they can seek to control. Factions seldom know their own strength or weakness nor that of any of the others, but all are determined not to be excluded from the spoils. To impress others, leaders and followers alike, however their interests may be defined, call attention to their solidarity and spirit, engage in shows of strength, and in a circular manner, egg one another on. Whether the end result is a wild scramble for the sought-after prizes or a bristling stand-off (somewhat the Moroccan case), there is no denying the intensity and pervasiveness of the competition.[26]

In Morocco, what are the principal types of segmental-faction? To answer this question I shall group my examples about the following categories: factions founded on primordial attachments; those displaying a blend of objective interests and primordial attachments; and those defined exclusively according to objective interests. All this with the routine but necessary caveat that reality seldom if ever produces pure types. Also, one should not read into the order in which I present the categories any necessary implication on my part of an evolutionary sequence.

Primordial Factions

In Morocco, primordial sentiments have revolved about tribes, religion, sometimes regions (Anti and High Atlas and the founding of the Almohades dynasty), cities and city quarters, and families. These are the overlapping pieces of a vast segmentary mosaic which made up traditional Morocco. An individual might identify himself as a member of any combination of these categories and would consider his welfare to be intimately linked to their fate.

One of the most profound, yet most flexible political divisions in Morocco over the centuries has been the blad al-Makhzen vs. the blad as-siba (see chapter 1). But dissidence in Morocco was never a coordinated venture; the blad as-siba never seceded as a bloc. Rather, the blad as-siba was a congeries of uncoordinated tribes whose defiance was facilitated by their location, and who did not opt out in the name of a cause but rather because a given power situation indicated to them that it was feasible to do so. They were fully capable, once the balance of power had shifted, to reverse ground and join their enemies to put down their allies.

Tribes had patrons at court who used the claimed strength of their tribal followers to augment their prestige within the makhzen. In turn their influence at court was used to lighten the government's imposition upon their tribes, thus consolidating their power among their clients. Herein tribe becomes interest group, tribal notable becomes political manipulator, and, as was inevitable, the pure type is debased. Even in independent Morocco, tribes have acted as political factions, at the behest of ambitious politicians, but in these instances the patron at court has used his prestige to demand that the government become more, not less, active in tribal areas. Today tribes opt in not out.[27]

Blad al-makhzen and blad as-siba lived on together for centuries in that symbiosis of interdependence and mutual hostility which is typical of segmentary societies. They reflect on a national scale the sorts of frictions that arise at all levels of society in the bitter exploitation of a shared patrimony to which no partner is willing nor able to abandon his claim. Their differences might be expressed ethnically, politically, religiously and geographically. In some instances all these facets neatly correspond, and an individual is simultaneously Berber, dissident, saint worshipper, and mountain dweller. Among the inhabitants of the western High Atlas, their patron Saint, Lalla 'Aziza, long served as symbol of the mountains' (Berber, dissident) resistance to the plain (Arab, submitted).[28] But it is more common to find an overlap in roles, for individuals circulated with some ease among segments. By no means all Arabic-speaking tribes were subjugated by the makhzen, nor were all Berber-speaking tribes dissident.* Tribesmen shuttled back and forth between city and country, and Qarawiyin of Fez, Morocco's bastion of orthodox Islamic learning, always had a strong rural contingent of students. These exchanges mitigated the hostility between blad al-makhzen and blad as-siba, but the most important

* In 1895, for instance, the Mtouggi (Berber mountain dwellers) helped the sultan put an end to the dissidence of the Rehamna (Arab plain-dwellers).

element of interdependency was provided by commercial exchange. For the city, the rural world was a potential market and to some extent a source of labor, raw materials and food products; for the tribesmen the city was a source of processed and imported goods (sugar, tea, cloth), a place to sell raw produce (wood, grain, eggs, milk),* and a place of refuge during economic and political crisis in a given locale.

Morocco is an overwhelmingly Muslim country, but when people participate in political competition, with religion as their cause or justification, Islam reveals itself in many forms. Groups of 'ulema have intrigued in the investiture of a new sultan, pronounced upon the legality of new taxes, or, recently, insisted that ritual prayers be performed in the schools. Again, zawiyas have thrived upon and encouraged rural dissidence, their shrines sometimes becoming the centers of religio-commercial networks and the nucleii of petty states. Shurafa, as we have seen, have constituted small feudal patrimonies which they have defended and sought to expand over the centuries. At times tribal feeling has been converted into religious zealotry and the quest for reform (again the Almohades). At others religion and tribalism have made a fruitful alliance to depose a sultan: Thami al-Glawi and Abdulhay al-Kittani (see chapter 2).

Moroccan cities have entered into the competition for the allocation of scarce resources. The incorrigible rivalry between Rabat and Salé is still to be reckoned with, but over the centuries they have had to share the same outlet to the sea, the Bouregreg river, and there have always been extensive commercial relations between them. Fez and Marrakesh chipped away at one another when they were the great emporiums of trans-Saharan trade.† Furthermore, Moroccan cities are internally segmented into rival subcities (Fez al-Jadid vs. Fez al-Bali), districts (Qarawiyin vs. Andalous), and rival quarters which sometimes correspond to sectarian divisions (the Jewish *Mellahs*).[29] The quarter is to some extent a self-contained unit with its own ovens, baths, and mosque. Each quarter might specialize in a particular trade (tanning, weaving, etc.) and where these trades are exercised by inhabitants of certain

---

* One reason why the Rehamna abandoned their siege of Marrakesh 1895 was that they were besieging their principal market and denying themselves access to it.

† Similar rivalries exist elsewhere in the Middle East, such as between Aleppo and Damascus, Mosul and Baghdad.

regions or practitioners of certain religions, one may speak of regional and sectarian division of labor, in turn re-enforcing the identity of the quarter.

This social framework, larger than the family but less extensive than the city, is for the city dweller, what the clan or tribe is for the country dweller; corporate fraternity, more or less intense according to city and trade, reveals itself by self-help and assistance, by reciprocal invitations on the occasion of family celebrations and for all communal rejoicing.[30]

There is a good deal of friction between quarters, expressed sometimes in religious terms – Jew v. Muslim – or according to one's region and antecedents. Rivalry between quarters may take the form of ritual mock battles between the children of the quarters concerned.[31]

Intense rivalry between families occurs frequently, and in recent times (1936–7) the hostility between the al-Fassis and al-Wazzanis may have caused the first split in the nationalist movement.[32] The family (there can be thousands bearing the same patronym) is not immune to rivalry between its parts. In the legislative elections of 1963, Hassan al-Wazzani of the Fez branch of that family ran as a candidate at Wazzan where his opponent was Shahid Husni al-Wazzani, a native of Wazzan and secretary of the Wazzan branch of the Istiqlal. Only after a bitter campaign, and a contested election in which Hassan al-Wazzani's accusations of rigging were upheld, did the latter gain his seat. It is thus not uncommon for great urban families to have several internal divisions. In this vein, the Tazi family is divided into three major branches: Tazi-M'zallak, Tazi-Shaykh, and Tazi-Mukha'. In the early 1930s a member of the Tazi-Shaykh branch, a firm collaborator of the French, was pasha of Fez and gladly threw nationalist members of the other branches into jail. The latter blamed his behavior on the habitual perfidity of the Tazi-Shaykh.[33]

Mixed Factions

Practically all the segmental factions described above embody a blend of primordial sentiments and objective interests, with, however, the former outweighing the latter. I shall now treat those factions where objective goals define the group to a greater extent than affective ties. The first example is a borderline case, that of the

Sussi-Fassi rivalry. This very important rivalry, which has significant consequences in contemporary Moroccan politics, will be discussed at greater length in chapter 6, but some mention of it is necessary here. The Fassi merchant has generally symbolized economic well-being, and over the years has been one of the few Moroccans capable of accumulating liquid wealth. In contrast the 'Sussi' petty tradesman (from the region now in Agadir province watered by the Wad Suss) traditionally has never had any financial leeway, or disposable funds for speculation. Throughout Morocco the Swasa (plural of Sussi) dominate the grocery trade, generally family enterprises that are self-financed. An old saw has it that when two Sussi brothers run a grocery store, they take turns using a single pair of slippers, a lone plate, and one bed, in order to economize. What the Sussi retails in his little shop is often what the Fassi imports. The Sussi generally feels beholden to the wealthy Fassi from whom he must buy his goods and, less often, obtain short-term credit. It is also the Fassi who runs the governmental services dealing with taxation, licensing, construction authorizations, import permits; in short all those regulations to which the Swasa are habitually submitted. In turn the Fassi is condescending toward the struggling Sussi even though the petty tradesman is a convenient and necessary outlet for Fassi goods.

The principal form of the mixed segmental-faction is the clientele group. Often it borrows from or modifies the nature of groups founded on primordial sentiments. However, its objectives are almost exclusively material. It may take the form of village or clan factions jockeying for control of water, pasturage, and land, a Sussi lineage setting-up a corner on the grocery trade in a given city, or a factory recruiter whose source of recruits and hence his clientele is his own tribal faction. The clients will buy into the group through gifts and favors to the patron and in return expect protection from physical reprisals and a share in the spoils. The groups are generally small and manoeuvrable and are ultimately bound together by material rewards rather than blood or devotion. They seek to create or corner a patrimony and then defend it. Clientele factions have a long recorded history in Morocco, particularly with regard to intrigues within Makhzen, the appointments of governors and Qaids, and so forth. A graphic analysis of clientele-building has been provided us by Arnaud in his account of the rivalry between Mahdi al-Menehbi, minister of war under Moulay

'Abdulaziz, and Si Feddoul Gharnit, the man Menehbi had hand-picked to be grand vizir. Both spent years seeking reliable clientele within the Makhzen while the sultan toyed with both, and the bulk of his court refused to join either one.[34]

Interest-Oriented Factions

Because much of the rest of the book is devoted to groups falling into the third category of factional segments defined almost exclusively by objective interests, I shall not go into much detail here. This category consists largely of political parties, labor unions, economic interest groups, officers corps, and the like. To no small extent these groups themselves are agglomerations of groups from the mixed category. They are reflections of the impact of European culture and were created and adopted by Moroccans both to demonstrate their modernity and to fight the foreign culture with its own weapons. Since independence they have become the major competitors for governmental spoils. As mentioned earlier, their behavior and the behavior of their components is shaped both by the nature of segmental competition and by the traditional political culture of the country.

At the present time in Morocco, it is difficult to discern any faction or group of factions whose major interests and objectives are phrased purely in class terms. Most factions, regardless of their nature, are recruited from the materially well-off. There are of course labor unions, and while these employ a good deal of proletarian verbiage, they are, in the Moroccan context, a favored group (see chapter 9). There are no significant organizations to represent the interests of the lower strata of the artisans, merchants, and bureaucrats. Nonetheless, I would argue that there are important forces at work that will lead to a gradual regrouping of factions in a more conventional class framework. I shall return to this point in the conclusion of Part Two.

It remains to consider the patterns of political behavior in Morocco, the distillations of the makhzan and tribal tradition and the contemporary political process. Central to all aspects of Moroccan political behavior is the defensive use of power and authority. In essence, most of a Moroccan's political actions are defensive, and are consciously or instinctively intended to be so. The political actor will judiciously try to augment his wealth, whether it is measured monetarily, or according to his local prestige, or the number of his sons. But to do so he realizes that someone else may proportionately decline in wealth or prestige, and that he is likewise vulnerable to another's aggrandizement. As a result, the primacy of defense is re-enforced; keep what one has from falling into the hands of others and avoid arousing the envy and fear of others by an ostentatious increase in the patrimony.* For the Moroccan, power over others is not a means whereby he can act positively, create, destroy, or strike out in new directions: rather power is to protect, maintain, and conserve – it is the parry without the thrust. This attitude towards power, which seems prevalent among Moroccans, goes a long way toward explaining the peculiarities of Moroccan politics and the paradoxical stale-mate that has manifested itself since 1956. The rest of the thesis should furnish ample evidence of its relevance and importance to national politics. Derived from this attitude are a number of congruent patterns of political behavior and tactics.

First of all, one assures one's defenses through an infinite variety of alliances, perhaps commencing with the members of one's own family.[35] The object is to keep open the maximum number of alternate ways of action (or inaction). It is not necessary that the actor have any purpose in mind when he forms an alliance, but it is comforting to know that it is there if he needs it. For want of a better term, this behavioral pattern will be referred to as 'bet-hedging', and, as such, it often goes beyond the formation of alliances.[36] It is rooted in the ambivalent attitudes one has towards enemies and allies and in the acute sense of the temporary nature of victory. Practically all social and political activity is permeated by this attitude.

It is a grave political error to lose an option, or to be forced into a position where one must make a choice. Situations where a man must choose are rare, but the Moroccan instinctively avoids them. If forced to choose between two rival groups or factions, the Moroccan will do all in his power to maintain some sort of contact with the group he has ostensibly excluded from his range of action. This is so because in a system of segmented politics defeat is seldom total, and the vanquished group is only temporarily so. In order to

---

* It may be asked, how do those who have nothing ever get started? They become clients of those who have until they accumulate enough rewards to start on their own. For many that day never comes.

restore equilibrium, those who suffered defeat will make a come-back, perhaps in a different form, and the momentarily victorious will want to have a door open to them. Recent Moroccan history is rife with examples. When al-Hiba was moving on Marrakesh, the Glaoui family did nothing to stop him but was sending off messages to Colonel Mangin assuring him of the Glaouis' covert sympathy. Muhammed v in 1944 told the nationalists that he privately sym-pathized with their views but could not publicly say so. The found-ing of the Mouvement Populaire in 1957 (see chapter 12) was quietly encouraged by the king, but he made sure that if it were to fail, he would be in no way involved. Again in 1963, with the launching of the royalist Front for the Defense for Constitutional Institutions (FDIC), King Hassan gave it his private blessing but saw to it that he would not be tarnished if it fizzled, which it did.

In any given alliance system there may be an individual or group of individuals who consider it desirable to bind the alliance as closely to themselves as possible. In so doing they may upset the balance of the constituent parts of the alliance and thereby provoke its dissolution. Two or more groups may claim title to leadership of the alliance and oblige the rank-and-file to choose sides. The man in the middle may do one of three things: 1. Choose one side and break contact with the other; 2. Choose one side and tell the other that he did so under duress; 3. Withdraw from the conflict but maintain contacts with both sides. The split of the Istiqlal party in 1959, which will be discussed at length in chapter 8, and the more recent split of the Mouvement-Populaire, illustrate these alternatives. In both instances the number of drop-outs has been impressive.

Moroccans conceive of themselves or others acting autonomously with difficulty, and they feel comfortable only when integrated into a group. Group orientation is ancient in Morocco, and individuals, as such, (except for murabitin and itinerant scholars and magicians) could not play any significant role in society. If, for instance, a man killed a kinsman, and was forced to flee his clan or tribe, he could not simply move on to another region but was obliged to seek refuge in another group, most likely another tribe. It has also been noted that an essential function of the clientele group is the protection of the individual.

A man must have a group, for otherwise he is without defenses, and no man is willingly defenseless. It is in relation to the group that the Moroccan defines himself, and without the group he loses his identity.[37] If for Aristotle the man without a *polis* was either an animal or a god, for the Moroccan a man without a group is either mad or very cleverly dissimulating his true allegiance. The role of lone wolf in Moroccan politics is, by nature, temporary, and the individual is sooner or later forced to integrate himself into an alliance system or undergo political death.

On the other hand, while the group is of paramount importance, the individual within it is remarkably free to do as he pleases. Shifting from one group to another is not harshly judged, and, as with all units in the segmented system, exchanges are frequent and fully accepted.[38] Simultaneous membership in several groups is not unusual, and the resultant multiplicity of roles is another side of the competing allegiances engendered by the overlap of segments.

Much of a Moroccan's time is spent in alliance-building and alliance-maintenance. He assumes, and rightly so, that most other Moroccans are doing the same thing, and that therefore he must always be on his guard lest he be out-manoeuvred. Covert machinations, dissimulation and trickery are accepted as the facts of political life, and a man's ostensible motives for a given action cannot be trusted. One must try to find out what he *really* wants, what scheme he is cleverly masking. In his dealings with others, and this is true on a national and international scale, the Moroccan takes for granted an element of conspiracy. Such an attitude is not one of paranoia; because conspiracy is automatically assumed, the Moroccan tends to be quite relaxed in his political actions and takes an expert's delight in playing the game.

There are many ways to build and particularly maintain alliances, but running like a thread through all of them is the device of moral and financial debt, the cement, so-to-speak, of the alliance system. A man who is obligated or indebted to you, for whatever reason, cannot easily become your enemy, and, more positively, may necessarily become your ally. Debt relations in Morocco are complex and pervasive. A man is automatically obligated to stand by the immediate members of his family and his agnates. Likewise he is indebted to all those who may have rendered him a service- Probably only a native Moroccan could ever know all the intricate and tacitly understood rules which determine the level of one's

indebtedness, as well as the undeniable social and political sanctions which are applied when the rules are violated. One often
hears Moroccans justifying their actions by pointing out 'I couldn't
possibly have done what you asked me, because X is my wife's
cousin, or Y got a scholarship for my son . . .'.

Equally widespread is monetary debt, and a Moroccan accepts
being indebted to others as long as others are indebted to him.[39]
The following example indicates one of the ways in which debt
relations may have political applicability. Hajj 'Abbid is a well-
known Sussi merchant in Casablanca who has become, by Sussi
standards, quite wealthy. Being one of their own, Sussi grocers and
petty tradesmen, over the years, have gone to him for credit.
Typically, the amount of the loan is casually noted down and its
duration unspecified. The 'contracting' parties will retain all this
by memory. No interest is charged. A few hundred petty tradesmen
have come to rely on Hajj 'Abbid for their credit needs, but what
benefit does the Hajj derive from all this? First, he has the comfort
– the 'just in case' assurance – of knowing that a few hundred men
and their families are obligated to him. He can, when he wants,
demand and receive all sorts of small services from his 'allies'.
Without being able to specify the nature of the actual arrangement,
we find that in the 1963 legislative elections, when Ahmad Reda
Guedira (at that time director-general of the Royal Cabinet) ran as
a candidate from a district which included the *bidonville* of Ben
M'sik, Hajj 'Abbid mobilized his cohorts, whose shops were
located in the same district, in favor of Guedira. It is safe to assume
that Hajj 'Abbid's reward made up for years of lost interest. A
freak example?* Probably not, for in Morocco there are alliances
that lie about waiting to be used, and sooner or later they will be.

Hostility and conflict are most intense within groups or alliances,
for it is there that the ultimate control and distribution of the patrimony is debated. Feelings towards rival groups are less intense and
more formalistic. Perfectly realistic and attainable objectives may
become impossible of realization through the enmity and paralysis
bred by the close contact of the allies. In 1963, three parties formed
a coalition (FDIC) to win a parliamentary majority in the name of
the king, but the disputes arising from the selection of candidates
so poisoned the atmosphere that the coalition, as an effective

* Larry Rosen found that in Sefrou such a debt alliance played a key role in
the elections to the local Chamber of Agriculture in September 1966.

alliance, was foredoomed. The relative majority in the parliament that FDIC won was a pyrrhic victory.

One final characteristic of alliance-building and, in general, all social activity, is imitative behavior, a direct result of group orientation. Imitative behavior acts as a catalyst in the conversion of traditional alliances and groups to modern political functions. Internal rural migration patterns may provide (and do) ready-made networks for nascent political organizations. Thus, the 1955 resistance groups and the UNFP after 1959 all relied to some extent on the close-knit Sussi communities of Casablanca, Agadir and other Moroccan cities. If a tribal qaid or an *amghar* joins a given party, the entire tribe will join. Or one may make a political choice simply because a father or brother did so first. A choice of this kind is seldom taken with regard to program or ideology, but rather because X says it is a good thing.

In sum, there is scant pressure in Moroccan society to open new paths, and individual initiative, while not discouraged, is not rewarded.

Similar patterns of behavior are to be found wherever political competition is actively engaged. The frequency and style with which they are performed and the extent of their grip on all social activity will vary according to the cultural and institutional context. In Morocco, culture and social institutions have re-enforced one another to a great degree. In this sense, Morocco offers a strongly highlighted statement of segmented politics and one that has ramifications throughout the Middle East.

As a type of political and social system, Morocco, and more generally the culture area of which it is a part, raises important questions about our notions of political pluralism. It has become widely accepted among western social scientists that the friction generated among groups competing with one another is conducive to their integration into the wider society, to their ultimate loyalty to the political system, and to the attainment of broadly accepted goals. While the conflict that results serves to sustain group identity, it also fosters the ability to compromise in the quest of particularist goals, and to recognize the legitimacy of other like groups within the system. Of course, the crucial element here is consensus, the acceptance on the part of all or most political actors of a set of rules and general beliefs that provide a framework within which it is not only safe but productive to disagree.[40]

No amount of wishful thinking can convert the plural systems of the Middle East and many other transitional societies into competitive systems within a democratic and tolerant framework. It is within the realm of possibility that such systems may emerge, but we must not assume that there is anything inherently fruitful and healthy in plural systems *per se*.[41] Extrapolating from the Moroccan example, there seem to be negative plural systems whose members, if they share in any consensual agreement at all, accept only to seek a stagnant equilibrium in which any group's efforts for good or ill are paralyzed by those of its rivals. In Morocco not even the monarchy provides a force for the development of a consensus capable of accepting and dealing with change. The monarchy is accepted, *faute de mieux*, by almost all political actors, without anyone having any clear ideas as to what would in fact be better.

The segmental factions which compete in the Moroccan political arena today vary in their attitudes towards the system from contempt to embarrassment. Yet, it is a comfortable, familiar, and for the elite, a profitable system. What political actors partake of it, and why they do so will concern us in the following chapters.

CHAPTER FOUR

THE MOROCCAN POLITICAL ELITE:
SIZE AND STYLE

I realized that this generation that they had educated was a generation of rotten apples; if necessary it could produce cider, bitter cider. The first westernized generation, it dreamt of reforms, purges, shaking the world – but no! You understand nothing. You'll be bricklayers for the old-guard. . . .[1]

Morocco offers an example of a country experiencing a pronounced breakdown in communications between two consecutive generations, more pronounced than in most of the rest of the Arab world. This has seldom led to the rejection of the elders by their offspring, but it has made young Moroccans uneasy, if acquiescent, successors to the pre-protectorate generation. Other Arab nations have had at least three or four generations of contact with the industrialized nations (Egypt and Algeria have each had well over a century of such contact), in addition to which almost the entire region was at one time or another under the suzerainty of the relatively advanced Ottoman Empire. Thus, in these countries the ineluctable spread of 'westernism', largely a product of revised educational systems, has been phased over a number of generations. In Morocco, however, contacts with the outside world were minimal before 1912, and Morocco leapt from a traditional regime to one imported from Europe overnight. Added to the administrative revolution was the full impact of the French concern for its 'mission' and its cultural values. As a result, one can legitimately speak of *a* pivotal generation rather than generations.*

* If the traditional past of the Arabian peninsula is as near in time as Morocco's, that region has yet to undergo the cultural shock that Morocco received with the influx of French ideas, bureaucrats, and *colons*.

81

Only a tiny percentage of the Moroccan population bore the brunt of the French educational and cultural effort. Another group knew the French through military service and a few administrative posts. The first group was largely urban and the second rural, with little overlap. The two taken together inherited administrative and military power after 1956, and constitute Morocco's political elite, as well as the subject of this book.

The term 'political elite' has been adopted in this thesis for the sake of convenience. While few political scientists can concur in any universally valid definition of what constitutes a political elite, at least the term has certain general connotations that are familiar to all. What I have in mind are Raymond Aron's stylistically awkward 'strategic minorities'. Aron describes these minorities as existing at strategic points in society, and they 'not only retain power in their own domain but also in public affairs'.[2] It is my judgment that the Moroccan political elite is itself an agglomeration of such strategic minorities. Thus, the term 'political elite' will be employed here to denote a group of Moroccans who, for diverse reasons, have an actual or potential influence on decision-making and the distribution of spoils and patronage, and who articulate, occasionally or persistently, their demands. Their influence results from their clientele or 'alliance-mates', who may or may not be formally organized. Such clientele groups may include parties, unions, student groups, regional interests, prominent families, tribes, the officer corps, 'ulema, and shurafa. Often leading members of these groups will be high-ranking government employees and ministers, but the elite is broader than the government and contains the government's opposition. Neither education nor wealth are criteria for membership in the elite, although most members tend to be educated or wealthy or both. Access to the elite is through co-optation.

In the previous chapter, the political importance of tribes, families, and regions was alluded to, and future chapters will spell this out more clearly. The claims to elite status of the leaders of parties, unions, and the officer corps are reasonably evident. As regards the 'ulema and the shurafa, some further explanation is in order. The leading members of the 'ulema are included, for as long as the monarchy maintains its theocratic veneer, the sanction of the 'ulema will be requisite to sustain the throne's claims to Islamic legitimacy. The 'ulema enjoy no direct authority in the decision-making process (except nominally in the investiture of a new king, and even that role, since the constitution of 1962 established the dynastic principle for Morocco, is ambiguous) but they are capable of harassing or vetoing various policies.* Moreover, because the king relies to some extent on the bedrock of Moroccan religious sentiment, it is not in his interests to offend the 'ulema. On the contrary, it suits his purposes to assure their prestige.

The monarchy also seeks to maintain the influence and prestige of the shurafa and to a lesser extent the murabitin. They form part of what may be called Morocco's 'holy family', one of the many clientele groups the palace manipulates. With the exception of those who have been appointed to a government post (like Hassan al-Wazzani), the shurafa and murabitin have no formal political power but do have considerable prestige. Like the 'ulema, their authority is not sufficient to enable them, in the present circumstances, to criticize or challenge the throne, and were the palace to campaign actively against them, their prestige would suffer greatly. But the fact is that the palace is not likely to do so as their influence can be useful.

It should be evident from the foregoing that one cannot be content to conceive of the Moroccan political elite as those who have attained the topmost level of *formal* power in Moroccan society.[3] This definition is overly-restrictive, for a man's political power and influence in Morocco are not always proportionate to his office, be it in or out of the government. For instance, the office of qaid, in itself, is today of modest importance, and all qaids have the same civil service ranking and salary. But if the qaid happens to be an 'Alawi or a brother of a minister, he can expect to be able to influence, occasionally, decisions taken at the governmental level. His alliance group and not his administrative position confer elite status upon him. Moreover, it is his alliance group that won him the administrative post in the first place. Looked at from another vantage, a high formal position is not necessarily an indication of political power. The office of prime minister has no institutionalized political attributes. When he occupied that post, Si Mbarrek Bekkai was able to exercise a certain amount of political

* In neighboring Tunisia, President Bourguiba's battles with the 'ulema over the question of fasting during Ramadan reveal the kind of influence they can still exert.

authority, while Ahmad Bahnini in the same position was at best a front man for the royal cabinet.*

The above holds true for non-governmental organizations. One of the Istiqlal's principal pre-independence financiers, Muhammed Laghzaoui, and Ahmad Nejjai, President of the Union Marocaine des Agriculteurs (UMA), an Istiqlali auxiliary organization, were never members of the party executive committee, despite their importance to the organization.

Nonetheless, in a more or less arbitrary manner, I have decided that certain administrative posts confer elite status upon their occupants: members of the royal cabinet, ministers and their personal cabinets, the secretary-general of each Ministry, the heads of all national offices and public and semi-public banks, all governors, super-qaids, pashas, and qaids, and all ambassadors and members of overseas missions. One must also consider the chief representatives of Morocco's major political parties and economic organizations. Thus, the executive committees of all political parties, labor unions, Chambers of Commerce and Agriculture, are included in the political elite. Finally, all army officers of the rank of commandant and above are members of the political elite. The guardians of the state's coercive power, they are of incalculable political significance simply because they are there, semi-unknown, in the back of all civilian minds, a sort of lurking threat (or hope?) forming an inescapable back-drop against which all political decisions are taken.[4]

In the remainder of Part Two we shall examine in some detail the background of the present elite, which reveals significant regional and social biases. Above all else, the elite is characterized by its high level of education relative to the rest of the population (c. 80 per cent of the Moroccan population is illiterate). A minority by the fact that they are educated at all, the members of the elite are doubly confirmed in that status by the fact that they were almost all educated prior to 1956 under a system which deliberately cultivated an elite complex by highly selective education. More details concerning French educational policy will be given in chapter 16. Suffice it to say for the moment that between 1912 and 1954, only 530 Moroccan Muslims passed both sections of the *baccalauréat* examination, the final hurdle to entry into a French university.

* Bekkai was prime minister from December 1955 to May 1958. Bahnini occupied that office from November 1963 to June 1965.

Before the protectorate, literacy and advanced religious instruction were for the most part privileges of the urban bourgeoisie and tended to remain so after 1912. France established in the major cities secondary schools known as the *Collèges Franco-Musulmans* that led to the first half of the *baccalauréat* examination. Certain gifted Moroccans, having passed the first half, would be permitted to transfer to a French *lycée*, set up for the local French population, in order to take the second half. If successful this second time, the Moroccan student might then go on to university-level studies in France. Needless to say, the number of Moroccans that achieved this level was extremely small, and in it the proportion of students of urban bourgeois background was very high. This was only natural because the urban bourgeoisie had a long tradition of learning, and this motivated its members, more than those of any other segment of the Moroccan population, to seek places for their children in the new educational system that was set up by the French. Parallel to the French system were the *écoles-libres*, run by the nationalists and offering a modern curriculum in Arabic combined with religious instruction. But here too the student body was mainly urban, perhaps more open to children of lower social standing, but perforce elitist in that operating expenses never permitted massive enrolment.[5] However, the graduate of an *école-libre* could not go on to advanced studies unless he spoke French well or unless he was able to attend a university in the Middle East.

The social composition of the educated elite is probably not much different than it would have been had the protectorate never been established. Young men from Fez, Rabat, Salé, and Marrakesh, whose families had long known one another and to some extent intermarried, became class mates in the various *collèges*. A certain feeling of social superiority was compounded by the 'old school tie' sentiment. Later they went on to found the nationalist movement, confounding French hopes that these students would eventually become the faithful defenders of the French presence in Morocco. In the first tentative nationalist activities, alumni organizations were converted to new purposes, to be followed by similar groups founded among university students in Paris. All these observations are intended to bring out a notable introversion that permeates the Moroccan political elite of today, an introversion whose origins are to be found in the protectorate period. It should be added that the intimacy of this elite was heightened by two other factors: the increasing tendency for members to marry into one another's families, and the fact that many were placed in long and close contact during frequent periods of imprisonment immediately prior to independence.

What must be emphasized in all this is the astonishing extent to which the members of the Moroccan political elite personally know one another. Whether in any given instance the relationship is one of friendship or hostility is of secondary importance to the fact that a relationship exists. Once established, a personal link, whatever its nature, carries with it all sorts of social obligations and taboos. These may not guarantee cooperation when politics are involved but often do prevent political stances from being developed to a point of breaking off the personal relationship. In countries where the political community is much broader politicians may have no personal relations with one another to trouble the purity of their political positions. But in Morocco we may be dealing with an elite of about one thousand men at the most.* Within this small band we encounter once again political stalemate.

Over and above all the conflicts, there exists a sort of spirit of comradery among the major participants in political life which sets the tone for effective relations. The same factor also makes difficult attempts at political union, for personal rivalries soon outweigh programmatic reconciliation.[6]

It can be contended that one of the principal causes of this stalemate is the reduced size of the elite, which makes it perfectly possible, and, in fact, probable that all members are mutually acquainted. If we consider the Moroccan elite as a percentage of the total population, it may not vary greatly from those of other countries. But taken in terms of absolute numerical size, the Moroccan elite offers a setting for modes of behavior and for a political style which is denied larger elites such as that of Egypt.

---

* I have arrived at this estimate out of curiosity and do not feel that it is altogether requisite to the analysis to think in terms of absolute numbers. But for whatever it is worth, the elite breaks down somewhat as follows: 100 army officers; 450 administrators of the Ministry of the Interior; 300 high-ranking officials in the rest of the administration; 130 prominent politicians and union leaders; 100 important members of economic organizations, independents, and 'ulema; for a total of 1,080. This figure is too generous as there is a high degree of overlap between categories.

When the numerical size of the Moroccan elite increases significantly, and it will, we may expect as a necessary consequence that the elite will have to readapt its style and behavior to fit the new circumstances or risk bursting apart at the seams. Relatively intimate personal relations sustained by an underlying social homogeneity will become increasingly difficult to maintain with a massive influx of elite aspirants of widely varied educational and social backgrounds. The Moroccans have made a great effort in opening up educational opportunities since independence, and the consequences of this policy for the elite are just now beginning to be felt. The new initiates are mostly too young to have acted in the nationalist movement or to know well the spider web of family and economic ties linking members of the protectorate elite, or the personal rivalries that developed before 1956. This is why the elite that grew up under the protectorate is in every sense a pivotal generation. In conflict with the generation of undefiled traditionalists which preceded it, this 'first westernized generation' will be in no less conflict with that which is to follow. While there has been a divorce in mental habits between the present elite and the generation that sired it, the conflict has not been pushed to the point of rupture. Few educated Moroccans have renounced their families, and many have become the willing or reluctant accomplices to family interests despite a superficial scorn for filial piety. It is to these Moroccans, who may have peddled *Humanité* as students in Paris but who later use their French educations to defend the family patrimony just as their fathers intended, that Chraibi refers in the passage quoted at the beginning of this chapter.

The political elite that dominated politics after 1956 is pivotal in its political style also, blending and exploiting old forms of behavior and social organization to fit new purposes. Sometimes this has been a calculated tactic, at others a spontaneous and genuine reaction to a given set of circumstances.

In the Moroccan political process there are the same ingredients that one finds in other newly independent nations: a competition for power and patronage among political parties, pressure groups, and regional interests. Meaningful differences in the political process from one country to another may emerge from significant variations in political style. Sidney Verba has written that political style stems from those beliefs and norms which are the product of a given society's political culture, and that beliefs tend to fall into explicit (ideological, inflexible) and implicit (pragmatic, flexible) belief systems.[7] What is puzzling in Morocco is that the political style of the elite is related to no discernible belief system *per se*. Perhaps it is more accurate to speak of implicit preferences and tacitly accepted norms that are not backed by a defined system of sanctions and whose abuse may not be sanctioned at all. These preferences and norms do emerge from Morocco's political culture, and while neither sanctioned nor rewarded in a formal way, evidently have proved useful in regulating the internal and external relations of the small, ingrown elite.

An organization, the clientele party; a political function, arbitration; and a political role, *za'im*; are recurrent themes of Moroccan political style. All three have a long history in Morocco and have been adapted for use in the present political setting.

The clientele party can be any sort of alliance group or combination of alliance groups that deems itself a political party.[8] Shared background, interests, and mutual obligations may be the catalyst to the formation of the alliance and the party. Seldom in Morocco does one come across as frank an avowal of the real nature of such an organization as that of the founders of the Liberal Independents Party. In 1937, when the nationalist movement split between partisans of Hassan al-Wazzani and 'Allal al-Fassi, a group of young Rabatis refused to choose sides in what they regarded as a sterile dispute. After 1945 this original group of dropouts formed an organization that was modestly known at the time as the Friends of Rashid Mouline. Many other political groupings in Morocco were, at their inception, no more than 'The Friends of . . .' a prominent personality or personalities. While some groups have subsequently accreted a number of new alliances around the old nucleus, most have retained the character of clientele groupings.

At the national level political stalemate has resulted from a balance of hostile clientele groups, parties and unions. If any one segment of the elite seems to have gained the upper hand, disparate elite elements coalesce to counterbalance the threat. The Istiqlal between 1956 and 1958 evoked the founding of the Mouvement Populaire.* Each large political grouping tends to be a more or less uneasy coalition of suballiances, and the cohesion of the wider

* See below, chapter 12.

organization may depend upon the maintenance of balance among the component units. Thus, both within and among these organizations there is a situation of tension and balance. To regulate differences which arise in such a situation, short of groups entering into some sort of direct conflict, one has recourse to arbitration. Once again this is an old and respected political function held over from the pre-protectorate period. In tribal areas the arbiter was traditionally a holy figure of the shurafa or murabitin, known in Berber as the *agurram* (pl. *igurramen*). He lived apart from the tribal segments, was never armed and therefore could never impose any of his judgments. Besides arbitrating conflicts, he would preside at all oath-takings and at the periodic election of the tribal leader (*amghar*). One of his most important functions was to provide an element of continuity in a system of discontinuous political leadership.[9] Transposed to the contemporary political setting, the arbiter function is performed on a semi-constant basis within political organizations, and among them by the king (see chapter 7). Arbitration commissions crop up constantly in political parties, notably in the Istiqlal in 1958–9, the UNFP in 1962, and the Mouvement Populaire in 1963–4–5.*

Throughout history, Moroccans have been aware that their society tended toward a static balance of its subunits. It was found that about the only way to upset this balance was to rally a preponderant force around a great leader (*za'im*) and some sort of ideology. The prototype for both may be the Prophet Muhammed and the Quran. In Morocco the tribal deadlock was occasionally destroyed, and successive Berber dynasties (the Almoravids and Almohades) were founded by charismatic leaders with a reformist creed. The same type of figure reappears periodically in Morocco, and there is a predilection among Moroccans for this kind of leadership, although they seldom find it. Ambitious politicians may try to exploit this potential market by attributing to themselves the desired characteristics and hoping that the population will accept the package as presented. At the present time in Morocco the man who comes closest to meeting all the requirements of the *za'im* is 'Allal al-Fassi, who reminds the author of William Jennings Bryan in a Moroccan context. The Istiqlali press often drops all mention of al-Fassi's name, substituting for it the grandiose *al-za'im*.

* The conflicts that they were to arbitrate will be explained in Part Three.

The *za'im* and would-be *za'im* is the mainstay of various alliance groups and clientele parties; the two go hand in hand. One of the more ironic examples of this is Mehdi Ben Barka and the UNFP. In breaking away from the Istiqlal in 1959, Ben Barka claimed that the founders of the UNFP had introduced to Morocco

. . . a more modern conception of political parties. Whereas before parties saw themselves much more as an assemblage or in relation to a leader than in relation to a program – that is somewhat like the Middle East in the 1930s – one can now say that increasingly clientele parties will be clearly differentiated from parties based on a program and an ideology.[10]

But, as we shall see, the UNFP, despite the intellectual brilliance of its organizers and their strong commitment to modern forms of political organization, followed closely the old patterns of clientele politics that it was designed to escape. And Ben Barka, despite himself, was built up by his followers as a super leader and eventually began to act like a *za'im*.

The Moroccan politician, in forming, holding, and augmenting his clientele is not reluctant to profit from old habits of social behavior, and this fact represents one of the most interesting elements of political style. In chapter 2 we saw how prayer forms were put to political use to protest the Berber dahir. The Istiqlal also developed a technique to supplement its finances which consisted of asking all Muslim nationalists to turn over to the party at the time of the feast of *'Id al-Kabir* all the skins of the sheep they had slaughtered (in commemoration of the sacrifice of Abraham) so that the party could in turn pocket the proceeds of the sale of the skins. Examples of this sort are abundant, and a few taken at random may give some idea of the style of Moroccan politics.

The following story about Mahjoubi Ahardan may be apocryphal, but the fact that it is widely accepted by Moroccans is in itself significant. In the 1963 legislative elections, Ahardan, as secretary-general of the Mouvement Populaire and minister of defense, chose as his constituency Khenifra, center of the Zayan tribal confederation and symbolic capital of the Middle Atlas Berbers. Ahardan did so despite the fact that he was born in a rival confederation, the Ait Sgougou. He felt that this could safely be overlooked in view of his importance in the Mouvement Populaire. His opponent, Hammadi Bou Mssis, an obscure but home-bred

Zayani, was the Istiqlali candidate, and he campaigned against the outsider. As election day neared, Ahardan suddenly realized that he was in danger of losing and resorted to a manoeuvre to force his opponent into a position of obligation. By sacrificing a sheep on his opponent's threshold, Ahardan activated a form of social constraint known as 'ar which, originally, was a religious act of supplication. The person to whom the sacrifice is made is absolutely obliged to aid the petitioner. All Ahardan asked of the ensnared Bou Mssis was that he order all his followers to vote for Ahardan. But Bou Mssis knew the rules of 'ar better than his rival and replied that he would vote for Ahardan, but if the latter wished all the 'Istiqlalis' to vote for him, he would have to sacrifice a sheep on each and every one of their thresholds. Obviously Ahardan could not do this, and on election day Bou Mssis, faithful to the obligation of 'ar, cast his vote for the losing candidate.

Ahardan's defeat reveals at the same time the perils involved in leaping tribal boundaries. He comes from a small tribe, the Ait 'Ammar, of the Ait Sgougou confederation that falls between the two great confederations of the Zemmour and the Zayan and is looked down upon by both. As Berque pointed out with regard to the Seksawa, old tribal antipathies and rivalries lend themselves to political polarization: tribe A adopting one party label and rival tribe B adopting another out of spite.[11] Ahardan, it would seem, was trapped in just such a bind.

Hard times and natural disasters have often been linked in the popular mind with the misdeeds of those in power. A Moroccan proverb states: 'If you see dearth in the world, know that there is much oppression and evil.'[12] The periodically-elected tribal *amghar* could be relieved of his duties in mid-term if the harvests were poor, or if other misfortunes befell the tribe during his incumbency. On 29 February 1960, when 'Abdullah Ibrahim was prime minister, a severe earthquake destroyed most of Agadir. Ibrahim was known to be friendly towards the newly founded UNFP, some of whose members had been arrested a few months earlier for having plotted against the life of the crown prince. The prime minister was from Marrakesh and had a significant following in the High and Anti-Atlas and the Suss where the UNFP had put down roots. The Agadir disaster was popularly conceived in some quarters as retribution for Ibrahim's bad faith towards the monarchy and a sure sign that he and the UNFP had lost their *baraka.* When in May the king dismissed the Ibrahim government for reasons that had nothing to do with the earthquake, many Moroccans regarded this action as fully justified in view of the tragedy.

Reactions such as these are common in Morocco, and the politician must take them into account. Those who are impatient with non-rational patterns of behavior are sooner or later forced to recognize their tenacity. Ben Barka, for all his protestations to the contrary, was too shrewd a political operator to make light of this phenomenon. It was indeed curious to find the UNFP at the time of the constitutional referendum in 1962 giving a prominent place in its press to the religious pronouncements of Shaykh al-Islam, Moulay al-'Arabi al-'Alawi. He condemned the new constitution as being incompatible with the shari'a in that it provided for primogeniture in dynastic succession and a legislative assembly. The shaykh pointed out that in Islam only the 'ulema were empowered to pronounce on the fitness to rule of each sultan, and that there was no need for a legislative body, inasmuch as the shari'a is the supreme and final corpus of Islamic legislation, requiring only application and interpretation. Needless to say the majority of the leaders of the UNFP must have found these arguments irrelevant,* but because the shaykh was widely venerated throughout Morocco, and because their objectives coincided, the UNFP did not hesitate to exploit his religious prestige.

For over a decade the elite described in this chapter has controlled the Moroccan political process. It is a small, socially homogeneous, and educated group of men whose political style is marked by superficial westernism and impregnated with a willing resort to folklore and traditional modes of behavior.† For external consumption, they strive to present the facade of westernism, and they have, in fact, cut themselves off from traditional Morocco enough to make effective communication with the older generation almost impossible. Yet one finds elite members instinctively using power for defense, seeking to establish debt relations, manoeuvring alliance systems, and always feeling most comfortable in a situation of equilibrium, and in this respect there has been no clean break

* The major complaint of the UNFP was that the constitution had been drawn up in secret rather than by a popularly elected constituent assembly, although certain UNFP leaders did have advance knowledge of the text.

† To what extent the political elite is an aspect of an economic class will be discussed in the conclusion to Part Two.

with the past. To a large extent the style of the elite is predicated upon its small size and the concomitant intimacy of its members. It is only a question of time before the Moroccan elite outgrows its style and intimacy, but that time has not yet come.

CHAPTER FIVE

COMPONENTS OF THE ELITE

1 The Urban Bourgeoisie

Moreover, the very notion of Fassi, is it not a frame of mind?[1]

If to be Fassi is to have a certain frame of mind rather than to be born in the city of Fez, then it can be said that the Moroccan elite is basically Fassi. While Fez is by no means the only historical urban center in Morocco, it has, until recently, been the uncontested pace setter in culture, intellectualism, and social behavior, influencing to some degree the educated elites of all other Moroccan cities. In recent years this role has been assumed by Casablanca, and to a lesser extent Rabat, but in the case of Casablanca, leaving aside the European and Jewish communities, its elite is largely formed of transplanted Fassis. It has never been necessary to live in Fez to be Fassi; one's family, not one's birthplace, determines one's origins. Just as the Fassis of Casablanca are known as such, so were those who, over more than a century, settled in various commercial centers of the Sharifian empire, particularly the seaports, where they might intermarry with the local elite. In a very general way, the bourgeois elites of Moroccan cities enjoyed a similar style of life and shared similar attitudes toward authority and power. They all exhibited two important characteristics: they were bourgeois by the fact that their livelihood depended on commerce and real estate; and they lived in cities that were to varying degrees harassed by surrounding tribes. As was noted in chapter 1, they never played in Morocco the positive, innovating role of their European counterparts and never made a concerted effort to alter the makhzan system, which they regarded as their sole, if inconstant, means of protection for their commercial network.[2]

In writing of the *grandes familles* of Fez a certain amount of circumspection is required. The motor force of political life in countries as widely varied as France, Lebanon, and Ecuador has been attributed to X number of ruling families (two hundred seems to be the popular favorite), and this approach seemingly explains much that is otherwise obscure. Morocco is susceptible to a similar analysis, but, while this chapter will concentrate on the families of Fez as prototypes of the Moroccan bourgeoisie in general, the author does not wish to imply that Morocco is run by an oligarchy of Fassis.

The prestigious families of Fez fall into three broad categories with considerable overlap: the makhzan families, the sharifian families, and the commercial families. This categorization is not artificially contrived for the purposes of analysis, for the members of each category identify themselves, admittedly in a flexible manner, with their respective groupings. In addition, there is a group of Fassi families which does not fall conveniently into these three categories. They have more or less shunned government service and commerce and pride themselves on their profound knowledge of Islam. Yet they are not shurafa.[3] Each has furnished the present elite with their offspring, and there are significant differences in the proportions of each source of supply which warrant a tentative explanation.

Of these categories the makhzan families have fared the worst in independent Morocco. As we saw in the first chapter, these families served the makhzan over long periods of time, sometimes centuries, and on an increasingly hereditary basis. The Ben Slimans for instance date their service to the 'Alawite dynasty from the reign of Moulay Isma'il.

The makhzan families themselves are of two sorts: those who served in the central administration as *wizirs*, *amils*, etc., and were thereby often highly literate,* and those who were local representatives of the makhzan, mostly tribal qaids.† Very seldom did members of the second category achieve recognition in the first, Madani al-Glaoui being one of the exceptions. It is true, however,

* Some principal families of this category are the Gharnit, 'Ababou, Ben Sliman, Moqri, Jama'i, and Bargach.

† These families varied with the dynasty and the contours of the bilad al-makhzan; in recent times some of the more notable examples have been the families of the Glaoua, 'Ayyadi, Ou Sa'id, Ou Hammou, Mesfiwi, al-'Ayyashi, and al-Mernissi.

that some families in the first category, the Jama'i for example, were issued from guish tribes but had lost their contacts with the blad through generations of sharifian service. Also, there were a number of families that represented the makhzan locally, but could, at the same time, lay claim to a certain culture and erudition. These latter often passed on the office of pasha in various cities from father to son.[4]

In the waning years of the old system a few families that had previously been associated primarily with commerce began to play an increasingly important role in the central apparatus of the makhzan (a branch of the Tazi family and to a lesser extent the Bennanis), and one finds that the only makhzan families able to sustain their social and political prestige through both the protectorate years and the early years of independence were precisely those families which had an autonomous economic base that did not depend on their administrative post. Thus the Tazis, the Ben Slimans, and the Bargach are still of considerable economic and political importance, while the Gharnit, Moqri, Ben Ghabrit, Jama'i and others have greatly diminished in stature. The same observation holds true for the makhzan families on the local level. Two factors seem to be at work here. First, under the pre-protectorate system there were several families that were very powerful so long as they retained their high posts in the makhzan, by which they could buy and sell administrative favors and build clientele through patronage, be it on a local or central level. Their patrimony, clientele, and alliance systems were all basically derived from and dependent upon their continued tenure in office. Deprived of any significant amount of patronage by a French administration, which kept them on as shadows of their former selves, they saw their power and patrimony gradually dissipate. Added to this is the second factor: almost all of the old makhzan families chose the wrong man in 1953 when Muhammed v was exiled, and some had actively connived at his deposition in favor of Ben 'Arafa. As a result, those families that had lost their clientele during the protectorate years cut themselves off from a comeback after 1956 by discrediting themselves in 1953.* Nonetheless it should not be concluded that they will never again regain their

---

* Their sins were often mitigated by a son conveniently placed in the nationalist movement, such as Tihami al-Glaoui's son, Abdessadiq, in the Istiqlal.

former importance. It has become clear in recent years that those Moroccans who have little popular support of their own are, from the point of view of the palace, highly desirable allies (see chapter 13). As for those makhzan families that have come through the last sixty years relatively unscathed, the major ingredient of their success was an economic autonomy that weathered the vagaries and convolutions of the regime. Their patrimony provided them with the privilege of not having to choose sides in 1953 and thereby not having to jeopardize their status.* Since 1956, the Bargach, Tazi and Ben Sliman have continued to make an important contribution to the elite while the rest have slipped into semi-obscurity.

The patrimony of a sharif is, in many ways, his name. His is one of the easiest patrimonies to defend, for his name is heritable, cannot be stolen, nor does its value depend on the personal comportment of its bearer. As long as religious spirit flows strongly in Moroccan society, the sharif will surely be entitled to a certain amount of deference. But having said this, one must add that if all descendants of the Prophet are shurafa, some are more sharif than others. The complicated problem of the transferral of baraka[5] in sharifian lineages from one generation to another explains to some extent, at least as far as Morocco is concerned, the variations in prestige of sharifian families. However, in Fez the problems of baraka were not as important in determining the social prestige of sharifian families as was cumulative respect owed certain family branches, perhaps according to their wealth and learning.

There were wide differentiations in wealth among shurafa; some lived in absolute poverty, receiving from time to time doles from the gifts that shurafa as a group regularly received.[6] The wealthier shurafa became so through marriages with merchant families or through economic ventures of their own. Few, it would seem (leaving aside the 'Alawis), undertook service in the makhzan administration. At the present time, however, one finds sharifian families which have successfully engaged in both commerce and government service (for instance, Lamrani, 'Alami, Laraqi and

---

* I hasten to add that all the preceding passage consists of generalizations and should not be taken to mean that *no* makhzan families joined the nationalist movement. Given branches and members of practically all these families *did* aid the nationalist cause, but the overall tendency was one of hostility toward Muhammed v or *attentisme*.

Wazzani).* Many shurafa have employed their major asset, their name, to good advantage, and non-sharifian families have always sought to ally with sharifian families both to manifest publicly their piety and to imbue their mundane affairs with the sharif's saintly *baraka*.[7]

The commercial families of Fez epitomize the Fassi frame of mind, for Fez was, above all else, a great center of trade, and those Fassis that were known in other regions of Morocco and abroad inevitably were the merchants. They represent the nucleus of the Fassi bourgeoisie, and certain families among them have been engaged in trade with the interior of Morocco, sub-Saharan Africa, the rest of the Maghrib, the Middle East, and Europe, for hundreds of years. The importance of Fez as an emporium was founded over the centuries on its location at the juncture of various trade routes, and the mercantile elite which gradually developed to handle the goods that moved along the arteries of this far-flung network resemble in most respects the pre-industrial bourgeoisie of Europe. The commercial ebullience of the nineteenth century in Morocco led to the expansion of the original nucleus of merchants and to the development of counterparts in other cities; a process that was accentuated during the protectorate. But it would be erroneous to view the commercial elite, despite the sometimes spectacular rise and fall of certain of its component units, as a product of the programs of industrialization and the growth of a national market economy encouraged by the French. The trading families, their commercial practices, interests, and outlook, all have their roots in a far more distant past.

The offspring of the commercial families were largely responsible for the founding of the nationalist movement, and, since 1956, have made a singularly important numerical contribution to the political elite. The political style of the elite reflects in no small way the behavioral norms of these families. It should be added that it would be unfortunate to read into this observation that the elite, in recruiting members for any given position, does so on a purely ascriptive basis – that is, as a result of their being members of certain families or groups of families – regardless of more rational qualifications. Actually, the progeny of the commercial families of

* A few other important sharifian families of the urban bourgeoisie are; the Guennoun of Tetouan, the Tahiri, Sqalli, and Kittani of Fez, the Debbagh of Marrakesh, and the Naciri of Salé.

Fez happen to be those Moroccans with the highest levels of education and technical capacity and thereby merit their importance according to technical as well as ascriptive criteria. In the following lines we shall consider their marriage habits, educational patterns, economic interests, and political affiliation. In so doing we shall be resorting to examples drawn mostly from the behavior of the commercial families, but the observations are probably valid for makhzan and sharifian families too.

The absolute wealth of the Fassi bourgeoisie has been exaggerated over the years, particularly in recent times, by Moroccan critics of the Left who seek to discredit what they regard as an exploitative class. In 1948, a French inspector of finances ranked according to income the three hundred wealthiest Fassis. Of these only three had incomes of over five hundred million old francs (c. one million dollars). At the other end of the scale two hundred family fortunes fell into the ten to thirty million old franc range (i.e. twenty to sixty thousand dollars).[8] But there is no gainsaying the fact that these fortunes, modest though they may be by U.S. standards, were very large indeed in the Moroccan context. The families that had accumulated them are our principal object of concern. Known as tajirin or maswaqin in Arabic, that is wholesalers and importers, they played a far more important role than the hawantin or petty shopkeepers.[9] The former group was more enterprising, traveling and living abroad, and establishing branches of their families and interests in the major seaports of Morocco. Through a highly developed family and commercial 'grapevine', imported goods would be directed upon arrival to that part of Morocco where they would fetch the best price.[10] The adaptability that these Fassis developed over years of trade experience, their contacts with Europe and the Middle East, and their own innate sense of how best to defend their interests, made of them the first indigenous source of modernization in Morocco and that group most eager to learn the new methods introduced by the French.

In 1905, René Leclerc drew up a list of the sixty-eight leading merchants of Fez according to their commercial importance.[11] and it is striking the extent to which these same families continue to dominate the import-export trade of Morocco (that part of it that is in Moroccan hands), and also to some extent its political life. There we find the mainstays of the Fassi commercial community: Benjelloun, Tazi, Lazraq, Lahlou, Bennis, Bennani, Berrada,

Guessous, Ben Chekroun, Sqalli, Chraibi, Ben Milih, etc.* Like the makhzan families, there have been significant fluctuations in the importance of certain of these families, but unlike the makhzan families there is no general explanation for these fluctuations other than luck. The Benjellouns, Bennanis, Bennis, and Bou'ayyads were all quite successful in the lucrative cloth trade with Manchester, but the latter two families have lost almost all commercial standing in recent years. The Bou'ayyad have maintained a fragile link to great wealth through the marriage of a daughter to Muhammed Laghzaoui. With Laghzaoui we observe the other side of the coin, the sometimes spectacular growth in the wealth of a few families since the establishment of the protectorate. It is significant that René Leclerc's list of outstanding Fassi merchants did not include the names of Laghzaoui, Sebti, Mekwar, or Laraqi, which are synonymous today with great wealth. They represent the closest thing Morocco has to risk-taking entrepreneurs, and they amassed their fortunes by exploiting fields dependent upon a modern economy-motorized transport, grain storage, food processing, mass-produced cooking oils, etc. – as opposed to the more customary importation of sugar, tea, and cloth combined with speculation in real estate.†

The commercial elite of Fez has developed the technique of bet-hedging and alliance building to a high art, always with the ultimate objective of protecting the family patrimony. Toward this end the Fassis manipulated such devices as schooling for their children, marriage alliances, strategic political affiliation, and their own trade expertise and savvy. The hard-headed economic and political acumen of the Fassi confronted with the intrusion of the modern market economy after 1912 is forcefully depicted in Driss Chraibi's *Le Passé Simple*, albeit with little sympathy. At one point in the

---

* It should be noted once again that at the turn of the century great fortunes were not all made through commerce. Actually some of the biggest fortunes were built up by makhzan families. If we take those families who, *c.* 1900, had large houses on the outskirts of the *madina* of Fez as a rough index of family wealth, we find the following to be the most obviously endowed: Benjelloun (Jbina), Tazi (Haj Madani), Gharnit (Si Feddoul), Qadi Laraqi, Moqri, Ben Sliman, Glaoui, Jama'i, Bennis, al-Fassi, Ben Souda, Berrada (Khami). See Le Tourneau, *Fès avant . . .*, p. 222.

† Many of the new fortunes were made during the war years. For instance the Sebti brothers may have been the beneficiaries of a windfall in 1939, having, by chance, large stocks of food and cloth on hand which they sold at enormous profit during the war years. However, Le Tourneau judges this to be yet another example of Fassi commercial foresight. *Ibid.*, p. 439.

narrative the father informs his son who has just passed the *baccalauréat*:

Until now I had no need for you in my business, but henceforth I shall. My era and your era; the patrimony that is handed on from father to son like a recipe for a fine vintage, like a torch, but because of the change in eras, it is improved. My era; hew in the name of Allah, speculate in the name of Muhammed, buy sell without pity, without scruples, money. And alone, and here I touch the real essence, alone the Moroccan capitalists are taken seriously, they alone resist. There are no negotiations with utopians but with cooking oil, Sebti, the Sebti brothers; doubtless you've heard of them. Not nationalists, just millionaires. They don't give a damn about politics, Islam, or France. They alone – there are three of them – have done more for the good of the country than the whole mass of nationalists. They are feared, respected, why? Rubies on the finger, they have the means to buy all the Sharifian territory. Your era: it will be an era of consolidation, wrangling, legal disputes. It was for this that I educated you – you will succeed in protecting the patrimony where I would have failed.[12]

How many Fassis, sensing their own imminent failure in a situation for which their skills no longer fitted them, sent their sons off to be educated in the methods of the new world? One can only speculate, but it is a motivation that many Moroccans, mostly the educated sons, acknowledge. The sons that benefited from this education, those who formed the alumni associations of the *Collèges Franco-Musulmans*, became the core of the early nationalist movement and the voice of the nationalists in their dialogue with the French. The *Collège* Moulay Idris at Fez, is, without too much exaggeration, the Eton of the Moroccan political elite. The list of important Moroccans that have gone to the *Collège* Moulay Idris and its counterpart in Rabat, the *Collège* Moulay Yussef, would be too long to reproduce here. But if we consider the group that founded the nationalist movement, we discover that the following attended one or the other of the above-mentioned institutions: Hassan al-Wazzani, 'Omar 'Abdjellil, Muhammed Diouri, Muhammed al-Fassi, Muhammed al-Sebti, 'Abd al-Kabir al-Fassi, Tihami Wazzani, 'Abd al-Qader Benjelloun, 'Abd al-Qader Tazi, Muhammed al-Kholti, Muhammed Lyazidi, Ahmad Lyazidi, Mas'ud Chiguer, Muhammed Hassar, and 'Abdallatif Sbihi.[13] Supplementing the inner circle of Rabat and Fez were graduates from the *Collèges* of Casablanca and Marrakesh. From there the most gifted would proceed to a *lycée* (the Lycée Gouraud at Rabat was the most important of these) to take the *baccalauréat* examinations. Higher education might be received in Morocco (principally the Institut des Hautes Etudes Marocaines – THFM), in France in diverse faculties (law, political science and medicine predominated), with a smattering traveling to the Middle East (somewhat a Spanish zone phenomenon with the likes of the Bennouna brothers, 'Abd al-Khaleq Torres, Mekki Naciri, originally from Salé). It should come as no surprise then that the preferred language of the Moroccan elite is French, and that this language is one of the keys to the inner club.[14] There are important members of the elite who speak no or very little French (for instance Fqih Basri of the UNFP and 'Abdulkrim Ghallab, editor of the Istiqlal's *al-'Alam*), but some elite members, such as 'Allal al-Fassi and 'Abdalhadi Bouteleb, having been educated entirely in Arabic, have felt obliged to learn French as adults.

If the strategic education of bourgeois progeny was designed to protect the family fortune, so too were the marriage alliances concluded within and among families. In principle, endogamy was the ideal formula for marriage among all families: the shurafa married their cousins to preserve the purity of the blood, the wealthy commercial families to protect their nest egg, and the makhzan families to re-enforce the hereditary principle in obtaining administrative sinecures. Endogamy serves a number of interrelated purposes. The upkeep of the family fortune is embodied in the proverb 'Our patrimony for us only' (*ma nahadushi khayrna li ghayrna*). In addition, cousin marriage helps maintain family unity, provides the convenience of having a daughter-in-law who knows the internal relations of the family and her place within them, and acquires a person whose feeling of responsibility for the economic welfare of the family is more acute than that of an outsider.[15] The tacit approbation and desirability of endogamous marriages is so prevalent that in politely refusing an unwanted suitor, a mother or father need only reply that the daughter has been promised to her cousin.[16]

However the endogamous ideal was no more than that, and, as often as not, was violated. Those families without a prestigious name, great wealth or high administrative post naturally sought to marry into better endowed families. Further, among the commercial families there was considerable intermarriage for the benefit of family enterprises and likewise alliances with shurafa and makhzan families. In general the shurafa avoided 'mixed' marriages, and, until recently, there were sorts of boarding houses in Fez where old-maid daughters of the shurafa were allowed to bide their time, often futilely, until one of their own came along to seek their hand. Frequently, however, financial need would compel alliances between sharifian families and the merchants. For their part, the commercial families were eager for such alliances, which added to their respectability, served to manifest their piety, and brought good luck to their business. They would often literally give an expendable daughter (generally an old maid) to a sharif, and the maxim encompassing this practice recommends, 'If she is ugly, give her to a sharif'.[17]

Besides arranging alliances with shurafa, the commercial families married into makhzan families to assure administrative benevolence, and into other commercial families to consolidate their financial positions. The readiness of these families to disregard endogamous alliances in the interest of economic betterment manifested itself under the protectorate with an increasing number of 'political' marriages.

With the growth of the nationalist movement, the protectorate authorities made it proportionately difficult to organize nationalist activities openly. But there was already extant a significant network of marriage alliances, and the young nationalists who were the products of these marriages found that an innocent family reunion could easily substitute for a political meeting. Moreover, one could add to the inner core by 'marrying-in' new families in Fez and other cities. The marriages themselves, like Mayor Curley's Irish wakes, became the scene for a good deal of politics, and because of the nature of the affair police surveillance was extremely difficult.[18]

The resort to political marriage alliances became more pronounced after 1944 when the bourgeoisie lent its unreserved support to the nationalist movement, specifically to the Istiqlal, and since 1956 it has become almost a rule of thumb. One is confronted today with an enormous web of marriage alliances involving the bourgeoisie of all the major cities. There has even been an (as yet) limited effort to tie into this network some of the rural families. Naturally, the father who arranges such a marriage has no real assurance that it will last, and he can almost assume that his son or daughter will have little respect for his motives. Nonetheless, it is striking that the fathers persist and the marriages continue to take place at a rapid rate.*

Marriage, schooling, commerce and political affiliation are thus all closely intertwined for the urban bourgeoisie. The Istiqlal Party is generally regarded as the Fassi Party, and there is a good deal of truth in this. The direction of the party has always been in the hands of bourgeois families of a number of urban centers with the Fassi element predominating. Not long ago 'Allal al-Fassi reported that prior to 1934 the original nationalist nucleus consisted of himself, Ahmad Mekwar, Hamza al-Tahiri (d.), Muhammed Bin Taleb Bennani, Ahmad Bou'ayyad (d.), al-'Arabi Bou'ayyad, Hassan Bou'ayyad, 'Omar Sebti, 'Abd al-Qader Tazi (d.), and Hassan Wazzani. These men constituted the *zawiya* of Fez, and later 'Omar 'Abdjellil, Ahmad Balafrej, Muhammed Diouri, Muhammed Lyazidi, 'Abdassalem Bennouna, Muhammed Daoud, Ahmad Ghilan, Fqih Tanana, Muhammed Ghazi, Muhammed Belkura were asked to join.[19] In 1944 began a trend that has yet to be entirely reversed. In that year the Istiqlal Party was founded, and the nationalists demanded for the first time complete independence for Morocco. The party leaders set their sights on mass enlistment in party ranks, and this desire happily coincided with the growing willingness of the commercial bourgeoisie to finance party activities. The war years had brought wealth to the likes of Sebti and Laghzaoui, and they threw their weight behind the nationalists.

They, and others like them, did so for a number of reasons. The postwar years were marked by an accelerated expansion of the French community and French economic interests. As a result Moroccan capitalists, whose financial capacity was greatly inferior to that of their French competitors, felt that they would be inexorably pushed out of the capital market. Still more important was the fact that the protectorate administration awarded contracts, favors, and all forms of patronage to French contractors at the expense of the Moroccans. The Moroccan bourgeoisie came to the

* To trace all these alliances would warrant a thesis in itself, but in recent years all the following have established marital links: Tazi, Laraqi, Boutaleb, Bargach, Sebti, 'Alami, Benjelloun, Lahlou, Guessous, Bennani. In the summer of 1966 there were marriages between: Lahlou-Oufir, Bennouna-Mekwar, Bennouna-Ben Chekroun, Bouqa'a-Bennani, BelKahya-al-'Ayyashi, Lazraq-Kittani.

conclusion that its financial salvation lay in the dismantling of the protectorate apparatus and the gradual expulsion of French economic interests. The son educated in French schools was expected to play a key role in this confrontation with French capital. Strategic alliances occasionally led to a combination of family fortunes that put the allies in a more favorable bargaining position *vis-à-vis* their French competitors. The whole system (the word is perhaps not too strong) was cemented by the nationalist cause and the Istiqlal Party.

The system described in the preceding paragraph has perpetuated itself into the independence period with, however, some important modifications. The Moroccan capitalist, like most of his compatriots, wants to keep as many economic options open as possible. Thus we find him maintaining relations by diverse means with most of the political and economic groupings which have emerged since 1956. The Istiqlal no longer holds the practical appeal for the commercial class that it once did, for it has accomplished its task, the protectorate regime has been sent packing, and the Europeans are gradually liquidating their enterprises voluntarily. Nonetheless, the Istiqlal is subsidized on a reduced scale by its traditional benefactors (except for Laghzaoui), to wit, Sebti, Mekwar (probably the only important Fassi merchant still living in Fez), and 'Abd al-'Aziz 'Alami (director of the Volvo assembly plant, whose brother married the daughter of Muhammed Sebti).*
The general trend, however, evidenced by 'Allal al-Fassi's periodic bemoanings of party finances, is for the commercial interests to take their distances from all political organizations while breaking off contact with none.

The Union Marocaine des Commercants, Industrialistes et Artisans (UMCIA) created in 1956 was closely associated with the Istiqlal. The secretary-general of the organization was the well-known Istiqlali Muhammed Laraqi, and the chief organizer was Muhammed Bin Jilali Bennani (whose sister is married to Ahmad Balafrej), brother of the one-time director of both the Compagnie Marocaine de Navigation (COMANAV) and of the Société Marocaine de Constructions Automobiles (SOMACA). As so often happened

---

* It has been suggested, but I cannot confirm this, that 'Omar 'Abdjellil, president of the Banque de Crédit Populaire and member of the Istiqlal executive committee, is responsible for collecting big donations on an agreed upon periodic basis. If a given donor is short of cash when his donation falls due, Crédit Populaire will put up the cash for him until he can pay it back.

at the time of the Istiqlal Party split in 1958–9, the political ardor of the members of the UMCIA was cooled, and they began to avoid overt political affiliation thenceforth.[20] In 1962 the UMCIA quietly went out of existence. It should be added that the palace, by various means, let it be known to the commercial elite that apoliticism is a desirable trait.

The reluctance to be too closely identified with any particular political group is bolstered by the important place the urban bourgeoisie occupies in the administration of independent Morocco, and to avoid placing this position in jeopardy great pains are taken not to incur the wrath of a monarch who prefers political independents. The commercial families, under the makhzan, had never left government service to the exclusive care of the makhzan families. The sultan had often called upon their expertise in finance and their familiarity with the outside world to handle the finances of the empire and to staff diplomatic missions abroad.[21] Since independence the bourgeoisie has continued to dominate these two administrative spheres. But the Moroccan administration, constantly expanding its authority and activities, has, since 1956, needed a great deal of trained personnel in all areas, a need which the bourgeoisie was particularly suited to fill. While other sectors of the society may be closing the gap in education that was opened during the protectorate period, the urban elites are as yet the major beneficiaries of high government status.

It is in the realm of public and semi-public finance that the commercial elite is most prominent. The state has assumed since 1956 an ever-growing part in the economy of Morocco and is responsible for a number of enterprises, banks, credit institutions, currency controls, import and export licensing, and has recently taken over the export of several commodities (citrus fruits, vegetables, and artisanal products). It is obviously important for commercial interests to be assured of administrative neutrality, if not partiality, in the conduct of their businesses. In fact, probably no project or transaction of significant size can be undertaken without the approval and aid of the state. Thus, whether by design or by default, such interests have succeeded in placing many of their own in positions that count. The following are a few examples of this placement, based on a tally as of summer 1966.

TABLE I. *Strategic Placement of the Urban Elite*

Banque du Maroc	President: Driss Slaoui
Banque Marocaine pour le Commerce Extérieur	President: 'Abdelmajid Benjelloun (PEC)*
Banque Nationale de Développement Economique	President: Ahmad Lyazidi Dir-Gen: Amin Benjelloun (Muhammed)†
Banque du Crédit Populaire	President: 'Omar' Abdjellil (PEC)
Bureau des Etudes et de Participation Industrielle	Dir-Gen: 'Abdelqader Bensliman
Bureau des Recherches et de Participation Minière	Dir-Gen: Sir Naceur Bel 'Arbi
Caisse de Dépot et de Gestion	Dir: Ahmad Benkiran (PEC)
Caisse de Crédit Agricole	Dir: Muhammed Brik‡
Caisse des Prets Immobiliers du Maroc	Dir: M. Lazraq
Commission Nationale des Comptes	President: Amin Benjelloun
Crédit du Maroc (Crédit Lyonnais)	Dir-Gen: Karim Lamrani (PEC) (Made Director of OCP in Spring, 1967)
Customs	Dir: Hassan al'Alami
Minister of Development	Muhammed Bargach§
Minister of Finance	Mamoun Tahiri ‖
Office des Changes	Dir: 'Abdalkrim Lazraq¶
Office de Contrôle d'Exportation	Dir: 'Abdalwahab Laraqi
Vice-Premier	Muhammed Zeghari ** (PEC)

* PEC. This designates members of the king's Private Economic Council, formed in the summer of 1967. Other members are Prince Moulay al-Hassan Ben al-Mehdi, president of the Administrative Council of the BNDE; Muhammed Benkirane, who had succeeded Benjelloun at the post of director-general of the BNDE, Muhammed ben Larbi, director of SOMACA; 'Abd al'Aziz 'Alami, who succeeded Brik as director of Credit Agricole.

† Amin Benjelloun is from that branch of the family that made its fortune in the cloth trade. He was born in Manchester in 1930.

‡ Brik is a member of the executive committee of the Istiqlal.

§ Bargach was preceded by Muhammed Zeghari, Muhammed Cherkaoui, Driss Slaoui, Muhammed Douiri, and 'Abdarrahim Bou'abid in this Ministry.

‖ Tahiri was preceded in his post by Driss Slaoui, Muhammed Douiri, 'Abdullah Chefchaouni, and 'Abdalqader Benjelloun.

¶ Lazraq is the son of Tihami Lazraq, a wealthy cooking oil manufacturer, and married the daughter of the wealthy Casablanca entrepreneur, Moulay 'Ali Kittani.

** Zeghari was preceded by Prince Moulay Hassan, 'Abdarrahim Bou'abid, and Zeghari himself. Zeghari is a wealthy Fassi, graduate of Moulay Idris, one time director at Fez of the Compagnie Algérienne and the Idrissia Mills, and, after 1956, director of the Banque du Maroc.

The well-being of the commercial elite is a function of both its privileged position in the administration, which can be lucrative in itself, and of its commercial ventures, which have enjoyed a sort of governmental umbrella. However, with the education explosion of the post-1956 years, its monopolization of expertise will dwindle. The commercial elite will do all that it can not to offend the powers that be, namely the palace, in order to protect its increasingly shaky position. At the same time, all elite members are aware that alliance arrangements can fluctuate in a disconcerting manner and that possible combinations are almost infinite. No member dares predict who will ally with whom or who will be the palace favorite tomorrow. Lines of contact with all groups must be kept open – just in case. Some elite members favor one group more than another (Karim Lamrani and the UNFP or the Sebtis and the Istiqlal), for it is reassuring to know that there is an organization to fall back on.

The commercial, marital, and social ties of the urban bourgeoisie cut across all political boundaries. Any given member of the group is a member of several alliance systems that may contradict one another. It could be that we have here a process peculiar to transitional societies, but whose net result is similar to that of multiple-membership in voluntary organizations in western society: i.e., the near impossibility of following a dogmatic stance to its logical end because of conflicting allegiances, and thereby the preservation of group cohesion.

Since marriage alliances have been referred to constantly in this chapter, it would not be amiss to recapitulate one whose contours slice through all sorts of conventional political groups. The alliance in question encompasses members of the Ben Sliman, Khatib, Boucetta, Boujibar, and Hassar families. Captain Housni Ben Sliman, head of the Forces Auxilliaires* of the Ministry of Interior, is the brother of 'Abdulkrim Ben Sliman, member of the executive committee of the UMT.† Both are nephews of Si Fatmi Ben Sliman, former head of the throne council in 1955 and recently ambassador to Saudi Arabia. He in turn is the father of Yahya Ben Sliman, former governor, minister, and director-general of the royal

* The Forces Auxilliaires are uniformed soldiers under the orders of local administrators of the Ministry of the Interior and are used to deal with any local disturbances.

† The grandfather of 'Abdulkrim and Housni was 'Abdulkrim Ben Sliman, Vizir of Foreign Affairs under Sultan Moulay Hafidh.

cabinet. One of Si Fatmi's daughters married Muhammed Boucetta of the executive committee of the Istiqlal. To complicate matters further, Si Fatmi's wife was of the Guebbas family (a makhzan family like the Ben Slimans), and his sister-in-law married 'Omar Khatib, father of Dr 'Abdulkrim Khatib, president (until November 1966) of the Mouvement Populaire. Dr Khatib's wife is a Boujibar, a family originally from the Aith Waryaghar, whose head had served 'Abdulkrim Khattabi as a sort of minister of foreign affairs. One of Dr Khatib's sisters married into the Hassar family, prominent in the Istiqlal. Finally, there is Dr Khatib's brother, 'Abdarrahman, a lawyer once close to the UMT, a firm supporter of FDIC and the PSD, and a former minister of the interior. Need it be pointed out that this sprawling complex has doors open to practically every important organization in Morocco, including the army and the palace? Various members of the participant families hasten to make clear that this interlocked group seldom functions as an alliance, at least in a political sense, with a concerted plan of action. One member remarked that when they are all together on family occasions, they never talk politics. This takes nothing away from the fact that they *do* get together frequently, and all feel the pressure of family obligations at least to the extent of not permitting political differences to rip the whole nexus apart. Moreover, there seems to be a good deal of reciprocal back scratching in economic affairs. These two observations could be applied as easily to the Moroccan political elite as a whole.

The offspring of the urban bourgeoisie constitute the dominant element of the political elite. They form a compact group whose style and mannerisms have been identified by other Moroccans, rightly or wrongly, as Fassi, and when they came to the fore after 1956 in the government and parties, there was much talk of 'Fassi colonization'. Each stage of their individual lives seemed to re-enforce their group consciousness: being born into a system of closely linked families, being educated together at all levels,* being of the chosen few to receive advanced educations and on that basis alone constituting an elite, militating together in the nationalist

* Acquaintances that developed in the course of education often make hash of political boundaries. For about three years the following lived together in Paris: Muhammed Lahbabi (UNFP), Tihami Wazzani (PDI-UNFP-PSD), Muhammed Boucetta (Istiqlal), Driss Slaoui (independent-FDIC), Muhammed Tahiri (UNFP, now in voluntary exile). All are Fassis except for Boucetta who is from Marrakesh.

movement, going into prison or exile together, finally running the country together. Many, if not all, revolted against the 'old turbans', their fathers and the archaic system that they embodied. In their youthful élan they refused to be used by the older generation for crass economic motives, and many chose Marxism to symbolize their revolt.* But, despite themselves, they came back to the fold in their own peculiar manner. They have taken up the old defense of the patrimony, not for their fathers but for their own account. Yet the result is the same. With a modern veneer they have adopted the tried and true techniques of building clientele groups and alliances with patronage, encouraging far-reaching systems of mutual obligation, and utilizing their power for defensive purposes. Their years of unity of purpose in the nationalist movement was brought about by a defensive reaction to the French economic juggernaut, but with the French retreat, the unity of the urban bourgeoisie has dissipated, and they have nothing to defend against but one another.

2 The Rural Notability

The protectorate's policy was purely and simply inspired by the model of a national park. These tribes were to be our sequoias. *Our* Berbers would remain good savages, worthy of love and respect, but whose ultimate advancement would consist of the rank of junior officer in the goums.[22]

The rural populations of Morocco were traditionally marginal actors in the politics of the Sharifian empire. They were linked to the urban centers by the exigencies of trade, and, through their acceptance of the spiritual authority of the sultan, were aware of belonging, however vaguely, to some supra-tribal, supra-regional community.[23] But most often the rural populations were mere objects of makhzan policies: those whom the sultan had to suppress in order to extract his revenues. Of course the guish tribes of the plains were more positively involved in the makhzan admini-

---

* The flirtation with Marxism is almost a general rule among Moroccan students in Paris. Some of those who have ostensibly repented are Hassan 'Ababou, Mamoun Tahiri, Driss Slaoui, 'Abdalhafidh Boutaleb, 'Abdarrahman Khatib, 'Ali Benjelloun, all ministers at some point. Those who have not repented are the actual leaders of the PCM: 'Ali Ya'ata, Hadi Messouak, 'Aziz Belal. In all events they live up to the Marxist prediction that the initial leadership of the proletariate will come from disaffected elements of the bourgeoisie.

stration, particularly through the chosen few from their midst who assumed high-ranking positions in the government. However, it was only with the establishment of the protectorate that the inhabitants of the old bilad as-siba gradually realized that it was to their advantage to participate actively in a system that for the first time included an all-embracing administration, an educational network in embryo, and the beginnings of a national market economy. After 1956, the state became even more committed to the distribution of the benefits of social welfare programs on a nation-wide basis, and the rural populations have become acutely conscious of the fact that they are relatively ill-equipped to administer policies that are ostensibly designed to help them. They have struggled on in the shadow of their wealthier, better educated, more sophisticated, urban compatriots, to overcome the gap in expertise and to take up their rightful place in the elite.

The rural elite has experienced a conflict of generations that may not be as pronounced as among the urban bourgeoisie but which is nonetheless significant. It amounts to the disparity in mentality between a group we shall refer to as the 'notability' and their off-spring. The rural notables are, in part, a creation of the French administration of the bilad as-siba; it was, moreover, the French who insisted upon the word *notables* to designate this group. There were, of course, prior to 1912 and all through the period of pacification, local chiefs who had carved out small domains for themselves, often with the help or encouragement of the makhzan. These were the *grands caids*, whom we considered in chapter 2. The French, using these men as a nucleus, stimulated the formation of a far broader group of notables in each tribal faction, douar, or market site. Their choice sometimes fell upon a man respected by his lineage and faction mates; sometimes a complete unknown was selected. The choice was that of the local *officier des affaires indigènes*, and the criteria were the selectee's presumed reliability and faithfulness to France. Often the local sinecure was awarded to those who had aided the French in pacification. The *officiers* were given great latitude in their selections, and many entered into the game of local king-making with gusto.[24]

According to Ayache, the notability constituted 10 per cent of the rural population in 1950, or 500–600,000 individuals. One must assume that he includes in this figure both the individual notables and their dependents. As a group, they owned about four million hectares (1 hectare = 2·471 acres), the bulk of which consisted of plots of twelve to fifty hectares. Despite their modest holdings they are distinguished from simple peasants in that they usually employed sharecroppers to till their land. Among this group Ayache discerns 7,500 'great feudalists' (including the *grands caids*) who own some 1,800,000 hectares farmed by traditional methods. Their agricultural endeavors, however, only served to supplement their major source of revenue: the profits and spoils gained from their administrative posts.[25]

As a general rule, and with the exception of the *grands caids*, political leadership in the siba areas was discontinuous, with a certain amount of rotation of tribal chiefs (*amghars*) who had a specific delegation of authority (distribution of water and pasturage rights, leadership in war). The French altered this system fundamentally, first by bringing the bilad as-siba under the authority of the makhzan, and second by attributing permanent competence to the local notables (shaykhs, *muqaddims*, qaids), albeit under the strict supervision of the local *officiers*. The position of the notables was bolstered by augmenting their property holdings, and property in Berber society is the major index of a man's political power.[26]

One tends to forget that the notables – the title is misleading in this respect – lived on a modest scale and are in a way Morocco's *kulak* class. They could never hope to rival the financial wealth of the urban bourgeoisie, nor was there any tradition of learning among them that would have permitted them to meet the city elites on an even footing. Many could not even communicate in Arabic, not to mention French, and thus were condemned to their marginal position on the fringe of the national political and economic system.

For the offspring of the notables the prospects were somewhat different. Once again extrapolating from policies first laid down by Lyautey, the French sought to educate a group of Moroccans completely loyal to France, who would act as intermediaries between the protectorate administration and the rural populations, and who would serve in subordinate posts in the protectorate bureaucracy. Perhaps the French placed even greater hopes in this new rural elite than in its urban equivalent, and it is certain that French military personnel and the *officiers des affairs indigènes* found the simple, pugnacious Berbers an appealing lot. Everything possible was done to seal the rural areas off from the 'corrupt' influence of the city Arabs and their 'religious fanaticism', a policy that was considered more and more judicious with the spread of nationalism from the urban centers.

During the process of pacification the French military became convinced of the great fighting capacity of the Berbers, particularly of those of the Middle Atlas, and with an eye toward the future in Europe, saw in the Berbers a source of military manpower. The *officiers* had little difficulty in convincing local warriors that their sons should consider a career in the French army, and a military academy was founded in Meknes to receive the young Berbers funnelled in from all over Morocco.[27]

The French, however, were interested in more than just military personnel from the rural areas. Firmly committed to the maintenance of spoken Berber, the containment of Arabic, and the spread of French, they needed Berberophones, trained in French, to serve as school teachers, court clerks, interpreters in the Ministry of the Interior, telephone operators, and assistants of all kinds. To build this corps of junior army officers and petty bureaucrats, a system of schools for the sons of notables was set up in the rural areas, whose best students would then be forwarded to the *Collège* at Azrou. What Moulay Idris is to the urban bourgeoisie, Azrou is to the rural elite.

The *Collège* at Azrou, founded in 1924, was the keystone of France's Berber policy. The system that it symbolized was, on paper, artfully conceived. Once a Berber youth had achieved his primary school certificate at an *Ecole des Fils de Notables* in his region, it became possible for him to go on to secondary school at Azrou, but only Azrou. If he were from Khemisset he would not go to Rabat or Meknes, or if he were from Taroudant most often he would not go to Marrakesh. All roads lead to Azrou in what amounted to a closed French-Berber circuit, free from all contacts with 'Arabs' and Arabic.

At the school all courses were given in French, with one to one and one-half hours of Arabic instruction per week (prior to 1944, on Sunday mornings). The students were required to wear their regional *jellabas*, and once when a student wrote his name Ahmad *bin* Lahsan, he was reprimanded for not having employed the Berber *ou* rather than the Arabic *bin*. The atmosphere thus created was designed to 'tear [the students] away from Arabization, to channel them towards French culture, in a setting of local color'.[28]

Unlike Moulay Idris and Moulay Yussuf, the *Collège* at Azrou did not lead to the first half of the *baccalauréat*, but stopped at the *brevet*, a diploma representing four years of secondary school studies.* The Berber student who wished to continue further was doubly handicapped. First, very few students came from families wealthy enough to pay for additional education for their sons. Second, having been trained entirely in French, they found themselves at a serious disadvantage at either Moulay Yussuf or Moulay Idris, where a good deal of course work was in Arabic and where they would have to prepare for the first leg of the *baccalauréat*. The overall result was that very few students ever went beyond the *brevet*, and this was precisely what the French wanted. Young and impressionable, the graduate of the *Collège* would be given a modest position in the administration and sent back to the blad from whence he came. His education would entitle him to some respect, his elders would be proud of his administrative status, and he would toil on happily in the service of France, ignorant of the evils and enticements of the 'big city'.

What in fact happened did not correspond very closely to what the French had planned. Knowledge of the cities, and more particularly of the nationalist movement, filtered not only into the student ranks of Azrou but into the rural world in general. The French apparently chose to ignore the highly developed commercial relations of the cities and the countryside as well as the constant seasonal migration between them. The old myth of tribal autarky haunted the French long after they knew better. Fez, Meknes, and Marrakesh, situated along the edges of Berberdom, sent feelers out into the countryside, and the early nationalists found willing recruits in the areas adjacent to these cities. Of incalculable importance in this endeavor was Driss M'hammedi, who was responsible for Istiqlal activities in the Meknes region which included most of the Middle Atlas and extended all the way to the Tafilalt. His efforts during and after the war years contributed greatly to foiling the French design to keep the Berbers free from nationalist contagion. It is significant in this respect that many of the oldest graduates of Azrou have remained steadfastly loyal to the Istiqlal over the years, despite the general rural hostility to the party that developed after 1956.

* Towards the end of the protectorate, students were able to prepare the *bachot* at Azrou.

The *Association des Anciens Elèves d'Azrou* was founded in 1942. It is likely that its establishment had the tacit approval of the residency, which perhaps viewed it as a potential mouthpiece of anti-nationalist sentiment. 'Abdulhamid Zemmouri,* its president, soon revealed the organization's sympathies for the nationalist movement by demanding a substantial increase in the hours of Arabic instruction. In 1944 the students of Azrou struck in solidarity with Moulay Yussuf and Moulay Idris and to symbolize the failure of the French attempts to cordon off Berber youth from the urban nationalists. All the leaders were arrested, and the association was obliged to remain quiescent until 1952. Nonetheless, its determination in 1944 won for Azrou a few concessions, such as increased Arabic instruction, the admission of Arabic-speaking students, and access to better administrative posts. At its 1954 congress the association issued a mild protest over the deposition of Muhammed v and in 1955 called for complete independence for Morocco.†

In independent Morocco a few of the old-guard notables have national or regional prominence: Addi ou Bihi, governor of Tafilalt province and Lahsan Lyoussi, first minister of the interior, being prime examples. But these men were exceptional, and most of the rural notables installed by the French enjoy only local authority today, if they have any authority at all. National politics was and is a mystery to them. Canny political operators on the local level, they were at a loss when it came to the issues of nationalism and colonialism. The French had bolstered the status of the notables, and in some cases had created it out of nothing. Most were reluctant to alienate their benefactors by taking up with nationalists whom they regarded as outsiders anyway. Moreover, when al-Glaoui called for the deposition of the sultan in 1953, many old Berbers happily joined in what they instinctively felt to be another round in makhzan-siba conflict, and they had the added incentive of tacit French approval of the venture. In 1954 they were the victims of their own inexperience in supra-regional politics, of their inability to think beyond the confines of their parochial spheres of action. Thus one finds that only seventeen qaids

---

* Abdulhamid Zemmouri was appointed minister of commerce in 1965.

† Hassan Zemmouri and Muhammed Chafiq, both ex-presidents of the association, were very helpful in supplying me with information pertaining to that organization.

THE COMMANDER OF THE FAITHFUL

opposed the deposition of Muhammed v in 1953 (including Mbarrek Bekkai, Mahjoubi Ahardan, and Lahsan Lyoussi), while the overwhelming majority condoned the move. In the immediate years after independence the rural notables paid dearly for their misjudgment, although since 1963, when most of them were amnestied, they have made something of a comeback.[29]

If we consider the notability as a group, the sins of the fathers were not visited upon the sons. The Moroccan political elite has a significant dosage of the offspring of the rural notability, and the *Collège* at Azrou was the seed-bed for this group. Its political importance is derived almost solely from its position in the administration, although a number of its members have become big land-owners in the course of exercising their official functions. The rural elite is concentrated in the Ministries of Interior, Education and Justice, and the officer corps. In 1956, when the most pressing administrative problem was to bring the countryside under control, scores of Azrou graduates were detached from Justice and Education, and even some from the army, and reassigned to Interior. Thus it is that Interior today is in no small way the preserve of the rural elite (see chapter 14), and in reference to the year 1960, Hassan Zemmouri, who was at that time under-secretary of state for the interior, estimates that approximately 250 of the total corps of qaids of 320 were graduates of Azrou. If we shift our gaze to the pinnacle of the administrative apparatus, five former students of Azrou are presently (summer 1966) ministers: Muhammed Tadli, Mahjoubi Ahardan,* 'Abdalhamid Zemmouri, General Oufqir, and Haddou Chiguer.

The rural world was always far more compartmentalized than the cities. Commercial interests, merchant mobility, and inter-city bourgeois marriages, combined over the years to provide the skeleton of national politics for the urban elite. But the countryside did not enjoy a sophisticated system of interregional relations. There were of course relations between rival tribes within a common confederation, including occasional interfactional or intertribal marriages, and there were also relations with the urban agglomeration nearest the tribe or tribes, be it a full-fledged city or merely a market town. The Berber would build his alliances and obligation systems within a relatively confined geographic area and seldom

* Ahardan attended the *Collège* for only three months, but after a special dispensation is nonetheless considered an *ancien*.

thought beyond his particular locale. Marriage alliances were restricted to one tribal area where the fixed property of the contracting parties was located. However, local big-wigs might seek to curry the favor of the makhzan through the offering of 'concubines . . . sent by qaids who are accustomed to supply the soverain with that which is good in their tribes in the way of girls, horses, and mules.'[30] The qaid Amharoq's gift of a daughter to Muhammed v in 1958 is in this tradition.[31]

Bet-hedging, at which the notables are quite adept, is also primarily a local art, and they have only begun to transfer their skills to national politics. The strategic placement of their children was a matter largely taken out of their hands by the French, but since independence some of the more prominent notables have encouraged a judicious political and administrative distribution of their progeny.

In sum, the notable's patrimony, almost always his property holdings sometimes complemented by his reputation as a fighter, was also locally defined. Thus in the fractured world of tribal Morocco we find nothing of the outer-directedness of the urban bourgeoisie that stemmed primarily from its commercial interests. It has only been since 1956 that a few politicians have sought to bring these myriad local alliances into some sort of political harmony, like so many beads on a string.

Before considering the nature of the rural elite's political affiliation, we should take note of a peculiar conception of political organization which is reflected to some degree in all sectors of Moroccan society but which is particularly prevalent in the rural areas. Politics for the typical rural notable is devoid of ideological content. He reduces everything to the simplest acts of power, and this is hardly surprising, for his local well-being and prestige have always depended upon his coercive potential. At the risk of making gross and unfair generalizations, it may be said that he conceives of political organizations as neutral receptacles which can be filled, occupied and vacated by any imaginable combination of compatriots. A political party, a resistance group, or a union are but enlarged alliance systems, ready-made so to speak, membership in which implies no commitment to a program, ideology or set of goals, but rather furnishes the adherent with allies to whom he is obligated and who are in turn obligated to him. He sees the organization as a possible means for protecting his local interests and prestige, and also as a potential opening for patronage from the central government. If the organization cannot provide what he expects of it, he will lose interest in it. Looked at from the point of view of rural politicians, this attitude makes it well-nigh impossible for them to maintain their clientele if they are in 'opposition' to the government, and, even if so inclined, they will avoid cutting themselves off from patronage sources merely for the sake of some party ideal. This mechanism has long functioned in rural areas. The oft-cited respect of the Berbers for the local murabitin in the bilad as-siba, which was to all appearances divinely inspired, could not be stretched to the point of paying *ziyara* to a murabit who ceased to resist the incursions of the makhzan. In so doing, the murabit had neglected his duties of protecting local interests, and *ziyara* could be directed to one whose sense of local responsibility was greater. The political parties of Morocco have experienced this rural hard-headedness and to some extent have begun to resemble the image Berbers had always had of them: open-ended receptacles devoid of ideological content.

The attitudes described above may be more characteristic of the old rural notability than of their sons, but the latter are by no means free of them. The Alumni Association of Azrou has had a political history since 1956 that is indicative both of the similarities and the differences. In 1957 the association held its first congress since 1955, and Mehdi Ben Barka was there to ensure the association's loyalty to the Istiqlal. In 1959 the group ostensibly sided with the progressive faction of the Istiqlal when it split, but some members suggest that what determined this stance was more the formation of the Ibrahim government, identified with the progressives, than ideological considerations. Tihami 'Ammar and Hassan Zemmouri, successive presidents of the association, were both members of Ibrahim's government. Moreover, it is suggested that because so many of the association members were government employees, they wanted to demonstrate their loyalty to the new prime minister.

During the early years of independence the newly-founded Mouvement Populaire made a bid to rally the support of the association in competition with the Ben Barka wing of the Istiqlal.*

---

* The old-guard of the Istiqlal may have been working at cross purposes with its younger members. In the first years after independence the Ministry of Education was controlled by Muhammed al-Fassi, 'Omar 'Abdjellil, and

In this competition certain factors came to light that make it inaccurate to depict the offspring of the notability in quite the same terms as their fathers. Two broad political tendencies – they are no more than that – became apparent. On the one hand were the 'agents of authority' and the group of army officers, and on the other those graduates of Azrou who had received an advanced or technical education.

The first group, perhaps feeling somewhat inferior because of a generally lower level of education and having more limited political horizons, identified much more closely with the 'Berber' politics of the MP. This identification became more open when the MP leaders entered the government in 1961. The second group had shared with the urban elite the experience of advanced education in France and Morocco and rejected the obscurantism and anachronism of the MP. This group, represented by Tihami 'Ammar and Hassan and 'Abdulhamid Zemmouri, was associated with the UNFP. In 1960, Muhammed Chafiq, who, while sharing many of its views, was not a member of the UNFP, was elected president of the association to act as a neutral between the two factions, a post which he occupied for five years.

At the time of the 1962 constitutional referendum, the bureau of the association abandoned momentarily its careful avoidance of taking stands on political issues and recommended that association members boycott the referendum. A subsequent congress approved this motion, although the 'agents of authority' group did not attend in strength. This motion earned the association the displeasure of the palace and it was demoted from the legal status of a group of 'national utility' to that of a simple regional cultural organization. This incident damped down the fires of radical ardor among the members of the association, and the arrests of hundreds of UNFP members in 1963 in connection with a plot against the king reduced that party's appeal drastically. In 1966, a rump congress* of the association, engineered by a former UNFP militant turned conservative, saw a sparse turnout of 'agents of authority' who all but

---

'Abdulkrim Benjelloun, all of the old-guard, who saw in Azrou a source of recruits for the Mouvement Populaire or any other groups opposed to the Istiqlal. Financial allocations to the *Collège* were allegedly cut and students diverted to other institutions.

* Since 1959 the congresses have had steadily diminishing turnouts proportionate to the general political lassitude that has spread through Morocco since then. At the 1966 rump congress about seventy delegates attended.

declared the association an auxiliary organization of the Mouvement Populaire and Mahjoubi Ahardan.

Between the two broad tendencies that have been described, of which one is momentarily dominant, there has always been a grey area from which various individuals move off in all directions. Simply because a man is a qaid or an army officer does not enable us to predict any necessary political alignment on his part, any more than we could on the basis of his being a school teacher or an agricultural engineer. The fact of being a Berber[32] is never wholly absent from a Berber's mind, no matter how highly educated he may be, and he seems to feel more at ease with his own kind. There is also a certain predisposition to draconian measures in politics, a facile resort to violence, and an impatience with the conventions of politics that confuses all attempts at classification according to conservativism or radicalism. The Berber politicos are at once conservatives and radicals, and, if we follow their own recommendations, these terms are best left unused. They have their own style, for which there is no adequate nomenclature. As a result, one finds the most extraordinary gyrations and reversals in their political behavior which have no programmatic or ideological consistency, and the reason is that programmatic and ideological considerations were not foremost in their minds at the time of acting. For all their lack of sophistication, rural politicians have always been masters at protecting their interests and have pioneered in the art of bet-hedging. Referring to the struggle between Bou Hamara and Sultans Moulay 'Abdulaziz and Moulay Hafidh, Salim al-'Abdi explained the behavior of certain tribes by the query 'Was it not politic for a tent that wished to prosper in the given circumstances to have a father with the sultan and a son with Bou Hamara?'[33]

The douar of Tashawit, about a mile from the small urban center of Midelt which lies at the junction of the Middle and High Atlas ranges, offers a composite political history mirroring that of the bilad as-siba as a whole. When Moulay Hassan set out to invade the Tafilalt, he pacified the area around Midelt, and there are still a few old men from Tashawit who recall as boys working all night to pack holes in the walls of the douar, caused by the sultan's artillery barrages, with fresh mud and straw. Each morning the sultan would be confronted with the unimpaired walls of the douar, and the old men remember with pride that this trick permitted Tashawit to resist Moulay Hassan even after Midelt had capitulated. The French began to bring the same area under control only after 1917. Thus the turbulent epoch of siba is still very much alive for the inhabitants of Tashawit, and even for those who are too young to have lived in siba, the period is universally regarded as the 'good old days', perhaps as Americans regard the 'wild west'.

If we move closer to the present we find that in 1946 the French-appointed *muqaddim* of Tashawit was the douar's principal notable and landowner. His four sons have all gone to Azrou, the oldest returning to the Midelt region as a qaid after 1957. Another will start teaching soon in the secondary school system. The father takes great pride in his eldest son's accomplishments, which reenforce his local prestige. As Tashawit's most important landowner, he is the possessor of fifteen to twenty hectares of poorly irrigated land in scattered plots. Before independence he had used sharecroppers, *khammas*,* to till his land, but after 1956 wage labor became more prevalent, and he often hired Negroes to do the work. A major threat to his seigneurial status has come from an unexpected quarter: the Promotion Nationale, a program designed to alleviate rural underemployment, offers per diem wages (four dirhams in specie or in kind) superior to those normally paid agricultural laborers. They have abandoned the notable's farm to work for Promotion Nationale, and the patriarch has had to plow some of his fields himself. As a result Promotion Nationale, without, in this instance, mitigating rural underemployment, is contributing to the breakdown of the land tenure system upon which the notability based its status. The sons of the douar have all left to work in the administration, and there will be no one left to till the land. Perhaps one of the sons, with administrative connivance, or perhaps a wealthy merchant of Midelt, will buy up the scattered plots that constitute the patrimony of Tashawit's inhabitants, and farm them commercially,† but subsistence agriculture within a tribal framework is becoming a thing of the past.

---

* From the Arabic word for five (*khams*): i.e. one who receives one-fifth of the crop off the land he has tilled. The landowner furnishes the land, the seed, the plow animals, and the plowing instruments, while the *khammas* furnishes his labor. It is thus in a sense a form of wage-labor with this peculiarity: the remuneration of the laborer consists essentially in one-fifth of the harvested grain after the chaff has been removed.

† New landownership patterns will be discussed in more detail in chapter 6.

The politics of Tashawit show the irrelevance of ideological labels on the local level. Midelt and environs evidenced considerable sympathy for the PDI after 1956, largely because it was the only well known party opposed to the Istiqlal, and was favored by Governor Addi ou Bihi who was disturbed at the incursion of Istiqlali government employees in his domain.* Ou Bihi raised the standard of revolt against the government in 1957, and with the smell of siba in the air, the former *muqaddim* of Tashawit and most other notables brought their rifles and knives out of storage to defend the Ait Izdeg and Berberdom as a whole. Tashawit has subsequently become firmly loyal to the Ahardan branch of the Mouvement Populaire.

Another son of Tashawit who became a qaid in the region after independence was Muhammed Barrou. It was he who encouraged the sons of the former *muqaddim* to undertake university-level studies, and he procured them scholarships in Rabat. Barrou was widely respected in Tashawit and Midelt, and his prestige was not in the least tarnished when, after he was transferred to Salé, he became associated with the UNFP. But as the UNFP became stigmatized as an anti-monarchical party, Barrou's reputation began to suffer, and when he ran for parliament from Midelt in 1963 he was able to win only 3,000 votes out of 28,000 cast. Later that year he was arrested on suspicion of plotting against the king's life, and he is now in voluntary exile in Algeria. While he is secretly admired by his age peers, he has been condemned by his elders, not because he is a 'socialist', but because he gambled and lost.

The essence of rural politics in Morocco is extremely hard to grasp, and the observations made in the preceding pages are presented with considerable trepidation. Some general conclusions may be drawn from these observations nonetheless. Of the two major components of the rural elite, the notability and their sons, the latter has made the most important contribution to the national elite. A few of the notables (such as Amharoq and Lyoussi) have preserved some political authority locally and nationally, but their power is fading with the breakdown of tribal society. Their offspring, however, through their education and military training, are solidly entrenched in the administration and army, and the personnel of the Ministry of Interior reveals an undeniable rural bias. Their political attitudes resemble those of the older generation

* More will be said of the Addi ou Bihi revolt in chapter 11.

in their authoritarian use of power, their contempt for political niceties, and their preference for direct, radical measures. They differ from their fathers in that their education has, willy-nilly, given some political or programmatic coloring to their actions, and one can discern a vague bifurcation of the younger elite along progressive v. conservative lines.

The element common to both the urban and rural contingents of the national elite is education, and this factor alone has led to numerous examples of complete assimilation of rural elite members into the dominant urban group. At the same time, there is a good deal of jostling and friction at the apex of the Moroccan political system between the two elite components. Indicative of this is the unpublicized battle of Mahjoubi Ahardan and General Oufqir to keep the officer corps a Berber club; this in the face of the un-relenting attempts of the urban bourgeoisie to place sons in an organization that could determine Morocco's political future.

Yet there is one very important attitude that members of both the urban and rural elites share: the consciousness of belonging to an elite. The consequences of this attitude are manifold, but it predisposes elite members to think in terms of personalities rather than organizations. When one does think in terms of political organizations, they are often conceived of as manoeuvrable alliances which can be broken down and reconstituted with a totally new political orientation if need be. A member of the Mouvement Populaire once told the author:

We are all members of a big family; perhaps there are two hundred of us. Some call themselves progressives, UNFPistes, others Istiqlalis, others monarchists. But we all know one another, and one shouldn't take our public name-calling very seriously. Today we need support from the US, so the monarchists are in power. But if our relations with France sour even more, and the US does not aid us, all we have to do is bring in a UNFP or UMT government and start knocking on the door of Russia or China.

Or consider the remark of a political independent speculating on future political alignments:

Right now [spring, 1966] the Istiqlal is in opposition and demanding all sorts of radical measures and trying to ally with the UMT. At the same time the Mouvement Populaire may begin to move away from its blind pro-monarchism, egged on by some UNFP cast-offs. Now, if the King forms a government of the Istiqlal-UMT, we may find a new radical opposition of the MP, the remnants of the UNFP, and disgruntled members of the UMT. The roles will be reversed: the Istiqlal-UMT will become the conservatives and the MP the progressives. On the other hand, Dr Khatib may ally with Reda Guedira along with some UMTistes, and form a radical party of his own . . . etc.

All is possible in the little world of the Moroccan political elite, and elite factions are so many interchangeable parts without any fixed political connotations. Common social origins, combined with similar educational backgrounds blur and soften the political divisions of much of the elite. A more general phenomenon, which encompasses both urban and rural elite members, is an increasing identity of economic interests among all elite members: having inherited the political kingdom in 1956, the elite has moved on to the kingdom of goods and property.

3 Notable for their Absence: Women and Jews

The overt role of women in the political elite can be treated quickly, for it practically does not exist. Like the murabit, a woman is respected by Moroccan males so long as she does not go beyond those few spheres of social activity in which she is held to be competent. Politics (despite their right to vote) is not judged to be a legitimate field for female endeavor.

Yet women do have a significant, though poorly understood, indirect influence on the course of politics in Morocco. Considered in its broadest sense, their influence has traditionally been manifested in the performance of important social functions: the upbringing and socialization of children, involving instruction, even immersion, in the mother's primitive religious concepts during childhood years; the initial selection, subject to paternal approval, of marriage mates; generally accepted and unobtrusive mediation between patriarchal families. Advice from spouse or mother is seldom rejected out of hand and is often voluntarily sought. Women may fan or damp down the fires of interfamilial disputes both by their frequent contacts with the women of other families (at weddings, circumcisions, the hammam, and the like) and their influence over the males in their own. They have found it

relatively easy to transpose this role to the sphere of contemporary
local and national politics which have remained, to a certain extent,
but the extension of older patterns of familial politics. Elite members may find it convenient to resort to the women of their families
to act as contacts or negotiators with rivals, as a source of political
intelligence and information in their own right, and as respected
counsel on policy. Up to the present time, however, the influence
of women on the elite has been exercised within the confines of the
family, and their overt participation in national politics has
generally been under male guidance.

There is in Morocco no autonomous feminist movement led by
women. There have been sporadic attempts at such a movement,
beginning with those of Princess Lalla 'Aisha during the nationalist
period, but most have been half-hearted. Every political party and
labor union maintains for show purposes a feminist branch
organization, but overall responsibility is always vested in a male.
A woman like Malika al-Fassi, head of the Istiqlal's feminist wing,
and wife of Muhammed al-Fassi of the party's executive committee, may have had hopes of creating a viable organization, but,
like the Istiqlal itself, her group has atrophied. So far Moroccan
women have made little effort to assert themselves, and, unlike
American Negroes, have accepted the leadership of those who are
their alleged oppressors. One is hard put to find more than a
handful of women who act as politicians, build alliances, and seek
to influence the award of favors. One of the rare exceptions is
Halima Warzazi, who has had a colorful political career and is now
a Moroccan representative to the United Nations. The king's
appointment of his sister, Lalla 'Aisha, as ambassadress to the
Court of St James, is negated for all symbolic purposes by his
refusal to allow his wife ever to appear in public.

Women play no part in private commerce and cannot gain elite
status through independent wealth. Under the protectorate only a
tiny minority received an advanced education, and the French
acquiesced thereby to Muslim preconceptions as to the benefits of
female education.[34] From this point of view few women ever
gained the expertise necessary to qualify for elite membership.
For all these reasons women do not now occupy an important place
in the elite, nor are they likely to do so for some time.

The Jews, at one time, were undeniably represented in the elite, but the basis for this representation – the talented, well-educated, wealthy members of the Jewish community – is gradually being liquidated through emigration and death.

The Jews in Morocco were given privileged positions in the country's expanding international trade in the nineteenth century, especially with the advent of Sultan Moulay 'Abdarhahman. French commercial interests spread from Algeria to Morocco, and the British were not far behind. Consequently, small coastal harbors such as Al-Jadida, Casablanca, Safi, and Essaouira began to grow rapidly with the influx of import-export firms. Jews who had lived for centuries in the Suss and High Atlas[35] were attracted to the cities where coreligionists, many from Algeria, were serving as representatives of European concerns. One Jewish family, the Corcos, some of whose members were naturalized French citizens, served the 'Alawite dynasty for close to eighty years in the capacity of *tajir as-sultan* (merchant of the sultan), acting as go-betweens for the makhzan and the European merchants (the Bitbols of Rabat still carry out some of the same functions for the palace today). Some members of the Corcos family (centered in Marrakesh and Essaouira) performed similar services for the Glaouis.[36]

Whether resident in the cities or in the blad, Jewish families would have a local Muslim patron and protector. This did not spare them harassment, discrimination, and periodic pillage on an individual and communal basis, but it did provide them with a voice in their disputes and difficulties with other Muslims. In Fez, wealthy Jews, to protect their trade and affairs, would occasionally be able to marry a financially well-endowed daughter into a Muslim commercial family, contingent upon her adopting the Islamic faith. It is not altogether surprising then that well-off urban Jews varied little from their Muslim counterparts except in religion, and that they have gone about defending their patrimony along similar lines. Many Fassi commercial families, in fact the core of the commercial elite, are themselves of Jewish origin, having converted to Islam in the course of several centuries. Of these the most important are: Lahlou, Berrada, Guessous, Bennis, Benjelloun, Ben Chekroun, Ben Kiran, and Kohen.[37] Two factors, the trade expansion of the nineteenth century and the facility with which Jews could become *protégés* of various European consulates, reversed the patron-client relationship of many Jews and Muslims. The former became the favorite intermediaries of European interests, and

Muslims competed for access to various Jewish *protégés*, contractors and consular agents.[38]

The Jewish role in Moroccan society was thus of some importance, and their predilection as a group for modern education, and their favorable response to the establishment of the protectorate, enhanced their position in trade and the colonial administration. Their avidity for modern education, promoted since 1862 by the activities of the *Alliance Israélite*, produced a Jewish elite singularly versed in those fields most important to the protectorate's undertakings. In 1952, Ayache notes, 67 per cent of all school-age Jewish children were actually in school as opposed to 10 per cent of the Muslim children.[39] On the basis of wealth and education many Jews were qualified for membership in the post-1956 political elite.[40]

In fact, at the time of independence, there was a small group of young Jews who had militated in the Istiqlal and who encouraged an active participation of Jews in the politics of independent Morocco.* They encouraged Jews to join all political parties in the interests of a 'Judéo-Muslim entente'. Beginning in July 1956, under the presidency of Dr Hassar (Muslim), the mixed *Comité de l'Entente* started publication of a quarterly review entitled *El-Wifaq* (Entente) to attract an audience and give publicity to their endeavors. But the indifference and lack of urgency on the part of Muslim elite members and the hesitation and fear on the part of the bulk of the Jewish community brought these plans to nothing.

The creation of the state of Israel in 1948 induced the emigration of some 70,000 of Morocco's 255,000 Jews to that state by 1955. Following the granting of independence to Morocco, Zionist organizations campaigned for increased emigration, warning that Muslim rule would be disastrous for the Jewish community. This steady emigration to what was regarded by the Moroccan government as an enemy state did little to promote the sought-after entente. In addition, several members of the Jewish elite insisted on calling attention to their distinctiveness as a group. When it became known that Muhammed v would appoint a Jew as minister

---

* These young Jews were especially close to Mehdi Ben Barka, who was sympathetic to their projects, and today feel more at ease with members of the UNFP than with those of any other political party. Albert Aflalo, a member of the *Comité de l'Entente*, has furnished the author with many details on this ill-fated venture.

in his first government (in the event Léon Benzaquen, minister of PTT), certain Jews demanded that this man be elected by the Jewish community. Thus one group was trying to play down Jewish interests *per se*, emphasizing instead their paramount identity as Moroccan citizens, while another group saw Moroccan citizenship as secondary in importance to community solidarity. The latter tendency eventually won.

The Jewish population of Morocco has dwindled to about 55,000 (1966). The bulk, consisting of the elderly, the uneducated, and the poor have emigrated to Israel. The more wealthy tend to leave for Europe. Emigration has continued without any very stringent measures having been taken to stop it, and many Moroccans have made fortunes in the traffic of passports, transferring funds abroad and buying up abandoned property from departing Jews.[41] The community that is left is relatively well educated and relatively well endowed. Many are bureaucrats and technicians with long administrative experience, and their services are particularly important to the Ministries of Industry, Finance, and Public Works.* In a private capacity they are to be found as doctors, lawyers, insurance brokers, independent businessmen, and representatives of foreign firms. There is for this group no longer any question of political integration into the dominant elite.[42] An active politician like Meyer Toledano, an important member of the UNFP, is increasingly hard to find. The majority prefers to make the most of its economic position and to avoid rankling their Muslim compatriots by ostentatious politicking. For their part, the Muslim elite has been content to make occasional symbolic gestures toward some sort of political integration but has never seemed interested in a concerted effort.

Morocco's Jewish 'problem' is in the process of self-liquidation, and despite their importance in the past and their present qualifications, Morocco's Jews will never in the future occupy an important place in the political elite. Morocco's women, with no tradition of elite status but with a growing expertise through education, almost surely will.

* In 1965 the *Chef de Cabinet* of the minister of defense was a Jew, and Morocco must have been unique among Arab states in this respect.

CHAPTER SIX

THE SPOILS OF VICTORY: ECONOMIC ORIENTATIONS OF THE ELITE

The Fassi and the Sussi are always after money: they never sleep.[1]

Harsh as this judgment may sound, the entire Moroccan elite, not just Fassis and Sussis, has taken up the quest for wealth with the gusto of children playing with a new toy. The penury of the nationalist era is a thing of the past, the administration, with its immense potential for spoils, the economic infrastructure and enterprises set up by the French, and the cash-crop farms of the *colons*, have been abandoned or sold at bargain rates to eager Moroccans. A new commercial and industrial bourgeoisie is taking shape, just as is a new rural notability of landowners that utilizes modern farming methods. We have already noted (chapter 4) that the present political elite is issued from a pivotal generation, significantly different from the preceding generation in its social attitudes and behavior, yet significantly the same. The same holds true for the economic attitudes and behavior of the new money-making elite, whose contours differ very little from those of the political elite. The elite homogeneity, bred by common social backgrounds and similar educational experiences, is backed up today by pervasive, shared economic interests. This view would come as no surprise to most members of the elite, and the political consequences of this situation are occasionally publicized.

The frontiers separating political parties do not express rigorously and objectively the frontiers separating dominant economic interests and different social positions. This results in the difficulty of the parties to define clear and durable political demarcations, and to avoid on the political level contradictory positions.[2]

1 The Urban Bourgeoisie

The new commercial elite has its roots in Casablanca, and, while there has been a growing community of Fassis at Casablanca since the 1830s, the post-1956 period has opened up to this group opportunities it never had before. Nonetheless, we can not yet speak of an entrepreneurial bourgeoisie in Casablanca, and the commercial elite there has not broken with its traditional outlook on investment and speculation.

Two forms of investment are typical of the Moroccan bourgeoisie: non-productive commercial ventures (import-export), and speculation in urban and rural real estate. It was the prospect of foreign trade that attracted Fassis to Casablanca in the first place, and by the time the French arrived, there may have been some twenty Fassi commercial families already settled there. The major concern of the Fassi community of Casablanca was the importation of cloth, tea, sugar, tobacco, and manufactured articles, and the exportation of wool, skins, cloth, handicraft and agricultural produce.[3]

With the coming of independence, however, some very timid steps were taken to break away from the old patterns. Few business-men have shown the entrepreneurial zeal of Muhammed Laghzaoui, but there has been some productive, as opposed to speculative, investment in those sectors of the economy in which the urban bourgeoisie has had some experience and which can be most readily converted to new foreign and domestic markets. The most note-worthy effort along these lines has come in textiles. There had been some investment in the manufacture of textiles prior to 1956, but it was after 1957 that the industry became particularly attractive. In 1957, a protective tariff on all imported goods, raw and finished, was enacted,[4] giving a particular fillip to the textile industry. The Banque Nationale de Développement Economique (BNDE), created in 1959, advanced credit to textile manufacturers on favorable terms. It is estimated that an initial investment in the setting-up of a textile plant can be amortized in five years on the basis of local sales, and because of this quick return Moroccans have invested so heavily in textiles that this sector is probably the only one in which Moroccan private capital is dominant. Other industries that have attracted some Moroccan capital are food processing, construction, and transport. But it is undeniable that the Moroccan capitalist is still wary of long-term investments. One aspect of this is his readiness to buy industries and enterprises that have been established by Europeans (bakeries, breweries, auto repair shops, etc.) and that are going concerns requiring only maintenance, and his extreme reluctance to start a productive enterprise from the ground up. Many of the younger elite members, the sons who were educated to keep the old family patrimony intact, have been more attracted by acting as representatives for foreign firms than by founding or investing in strictly Moroccan endeavors. A handful of Moroccans in Casablanca, more or less sympathetic to the Moroccan left,* have backed a limited number of productive ventures, but they are a distinct minority. It would be illusory to expect the emergence out of the midst of the urban commercial families of a group of risk-taking entrepreneurs sincerely interested in the long-range development of Morocco.[5] Too often the Moroccan businessman will utilize his profits to build or add to his private home, to acquire urban real estate, but seldom will he plow back his earnings into his enterprise. His behavior is fully in keeping with that described by Fred Riggs as being typical of transitional societies. In highly industrialized nations economic considerations guide economic transactions, but in transitional societies such attitudes might result in loss of future earnings. Surplus income as a result is directed toward 'strategic spending', with the individual entrepreneur paying out tributes and gifts to safeguard his power base and his ability to extract in turn gifts and tributes from others. Wealth, within such societies, contributes to the loss of productivity and hence 'negative development'.[6]

Perhaps, as occurs in so many fields that require a high degree of skill and expertise, the Moroccan lacks the confidence and self-assurance necessary to undertake complex economic projects.

The European is rational in his research and efficient in his procedures; added to which is his willing and lucid acceptance of risk which excludes, however, fantasy and blind luck. The Moroccan bourgeois entrepreneur does not possess these qualities . . . and has behind him an

---

* One may cite in this vein Karim Lamraani, director-general of Crédit du Maroc (Crédit Lyonnais); Moulay 'Ali Kittani, textile manufacturer; and Ahmad Benkirane, director of the Caisse de Dépôt et de Gestion. There is on the local level a certain affluence developing among local contractors who may have a more enterprising spirit, but unfortunately less disposable income, than their city colleagues.

education and habits of thought and action that only with difficulty can be reconciled with the definition of the European entrepreneur.[7]

One recent example of the Moroccan bourgeoisie's inability to respond to the economic needs of the country was the nationalization of a large portion of Morocco's export trade in July 1965. Despite the professed 'liberalism' (i.e. the state's desire to limit its direct participation in the economy) of the regime, no group of Moroccan entrepreneurs was forthcoming to take over the organization of the export of citrus fruit, artisanal products, and vegetables, from the French interests that had been nationalized. The state was obliged, as a result, to undertake this task itself through the Office de Commercialisation et d'Exportation (OCE).

Ineluctably the administration's role in the economy has grown,* and it has been used by elite members as a device to protect their economic interests, as a source of profits and spoils in its own right, and, politically, as a means to build alliances, attract clientele, and create obligation systems through patronage.

Far from becoming a source of competition for the private sector, the state has become for the latter a support for hazardous initiatives. The principal beneficiaries of this policy are the Fassi bourgeoisie of Casablanca and certain businessmen who belonged formerly to the UNFP. All are ready to buy back to good advantage foreign enterprises and to create new ones with the help of the state. But, as yet, there is no private bank nor large Moroccan industrial concerns. The economic power of the bourgeoisie is still too thoroughly linked to exportation and speculation to be able to reorient itself over night towards those investments whose risk it cedes to the state.[8]

The government is a source of spending and a source of business. Not a few enterprises depend wholly or mostly on governmental contracts, and this economic leverage can and is used by the regime as a method of elite control. A number of high-ranking officials, making liberal use of their posts, have cushioned themselves against evil days by setting up, joining, or sponsoring private firms that

* Under the protectorate the major public enterprise was the mining and export of phosphates through the Office Cherifien des Phosphates (OCP). Since 1956, and especially between 1959 and 1961, the government has greatly expanded its economic role. An office to develop irrigated land, the above-mentioned BNDE, and several mixed companies such as General Tire, SOMACA, etc., have all been started since independence. In 1969 the state acquired a 50 per cent interest in COSUMA, a French owned sugar refinery that is Morocco's largest producer.

owe their welfare to governmental beneficence and benevolence. Thus Ahmad Lyazidi, President of the BNDE, is also the representative of the Royal Maroc d'Assurances which does a good deal of its business with the palace. 'Abdulhadi Boutaleb, minister of justice,* has an interest in a printing house in Casablanca which prints and sells text books to the Ministry of Education. Variations on the same theme are far too numerous to discuss in detail, but it should be fairly clear just how broad are the horizons of administrative protection and spoils. The fact that everyone is playing the same game, sometimes even cooperating on a given scheme, leads to a convivial silence with minimum public revelation of anything smacking of scandal. The elite's access to the levers of administrative control nicely complement its privileged position in the commercial affairs of Morocco. The design of the old guard merchants has been executed, and, although few of their sons probably ever foresaw that they would fall into the trap, the patrimony of the urban bourgeoisie has been defended and even augmented.[9]

2 The Sussis

In the discussion of the rural notability and its contribution to the political elite no mention was made of the petty tradesmen from the Suss valley, and for good cause. The Sussis are distinguished neither by their wealth, their learning, nor their place in the administration: according to all three indices they are as underprivileged as any group in Morocco. At the same time, their group cohesion and mutual economic defense is such that they have obtained a foothold in the economic, and hence potentially the political, elite. The brunt of their commercial effort has been felt in Casablanca.

Petty trade is of great importance in Morocco, and the Sussis control its most important branch, wholesale and retail trade in foodstuffs, including tea, sugar, and tobacco, and household articles. There are now throughout Morocco elaborate networks of small shops run on a rotational basis by members of the same extended families or tribal fractions. Often the Sussi who was the first from his tribe to open a shop in a northern city has gone on to become a wholesaler and to run a chain of retail shops managed by agnates who rely on him for goods and protection. In this

* Made minister of education in May 1967.

manner the Sussis have been able to make life in their valleys economically feasible and have transferred their internecine struggles for local prestige to the commercial arena in northern cities. The frugal Sussi of the cities salts away his cash to acquire land and to build impressive houses back in the 'valley'. There is at the same time an increasing tendency among the wholesalers to diversify into modern industry and the purchase of productive agricultural land outside their tribal area.[10]

Sussi commercial habits are illustrative of the imitativeness of Moroccan political, economic, and social behavior (see page 79). The four tribal groupings that supply the bulk of the Sussi merchants, Ida ou Gnidif, Ammeln, Ait Swab, Ait Mzal, all have maintained over the years specific trade specializations. The Ammeln are almost always tobacconists and grocers, while some Ida ou Gnidif have challenged the Fassis in leather and textile trade. One almost never finds a member of the Ammeln in Meknes or Fez which seem reserved to Ida ou Gnidif, and tribal fractions around Igherm are noted for waiters and café boys.[11] André Adam attributes this phenomenon to almost irreversible or unalterable patterns of trade and residence maintained over decades by strongly patrilinear Sussi families (i.e. where father goes so goes the family).[12] The young Sussi who starts off as delivery boy in the shop of his father, uncle, brother, or cousin integrates himself into a given family and trade sub-alliance, and when he matures he automatically takes up his place within it. Because the Sussi enterprises rely on a system of family financing with little or no resort to outside sources of credit,* the economic and familial pressure on any given member to maintain his place within the old alliance is great.

Despite the weight of tradition, there are some Sussis who have begun to break away from the old patterns, for the most part in Casablanca. A number of them have been eager to purchase hotels, cafés, and retail shops from departing Europeans. Over and above the Hajj 'Abbids of Casablanca, who while rich are classic Sussi figures, there is a growing group of wealthy Sussi merchants. Some have dearly paid for the privilege of marrying the daughter of a Fassi in order to gain entrance to the inner sanctum of the city's economic elite.[13]

* When a Sussi does look beyond his family for credit, it is to someone from the 'the valley' like Hajj 'Abbid.

In 1957, there was one petty tradesman for every thirty Moroccans for a total of 295,420 licensed small retail businesses.[14] Of course the Sussis are by no means a numerical majority of this group, but because of their long experience in the field and their highly developed commercial networks, they are, in a way, its vanguard. Petty trade has become a tenuous alternative to total inactivity in a situation of acute unemployment in Moroccan cities. A cardboard shack or a peddler's suitcase is all that is needed to set up 'shop', and merchandise may consist of a few razor blades, tea, and sugar. If work becomes available, or if the 'tradesman' has to return to his blad for the harvest, the enterprise is easily and quickly liquidated. But there is a more positive pull towards this sort of retail trade: the laborers in the cities, the field hands and sharecroppers, the migrant workers in Europe, not unfrequently put aside their earnings in order to open their own small trade one day somewhere in Morocco. Many of these men eke out a meagre existence as shop owner, transporter, taxi driver, etc., preferable to that of wage laborer. Consequently Morocco gives the appearance of being oversupplied with retail businesses that are fortunate to break even. Of Morocco's three hundred thousand petty tradesmen, only thirty-two thousand, or about 10 per cent, were subject to profits tax.[15] The marginality of most petty trade is undeniable, but there seem to be growing opportunities for more of the same. In the countryside consumption habits are undergoing a far-reaching change. The peasant or tribesman had always made his purchases at the weekly *suq* (market), often selling his own produce to buy goods from the city. Against this there is a growing body of salaried agricultural laborers, who may have their families elsewhere, who have or expect to have cash in their pockets and who buy items (such as bread) whose purchase the peasant would never consider. These men shun the local *suq* for the grocer, and the latter have been pushing out into the douars (villages), where, until recently, there would not have been a local clientele capable of sustaining much trade. The agricultural laborers who utilize these stores almost all maintain short-term debts with the grocers.[16]

Because of the foregoing, one would have to assume that the Sussis will continue to find outlets for their talents. They are, as a vaguely defined interest group, politically significant in themselves, but because they occupy an important place *vis-à-vis* the rest of the society,* and because of their broad geographic distribution and intermediate position in the social and economic hierarchy (between the poor, consuming masses and the wealthy capitalist elite), they could, if so inclined, assume a far more active political role in the country.

The Sussis have tested their political wings, making their debut under the auspices of the UNFP in 1959. The UNFP has fallen upon hard times, but characteristically the Sussis have been able to adjust to the new situation. The Sussis who joined the Istiqlal before independence chafed under the leadership of the urban bourgeoisie, and when the Ben Barka faction, very much a non-Fassi group and including 'southerners' such as 'Abdullah Ibrahim, Fqih Basri, and Oulhaj, broke away from the old guard, the Sussis followed. Some suggest that this was sheer political opportunism, for 'Abdullah Ibrahim was prime minister at the time. There may be some truth in the charge as the Sussis, particularly those of Casablanca, have demonstrated a remarkable degree of political flexibility. But they also have an old and well-founded reputation as political malcontents and sometimes resemble a sort of grocery store *jacquerie*. The truculence and aggressiveness of the UNFP toward the exploitative bourgeoisie probably struck a responsive chord among the Sussis.

The extent of Sussi-Fassi rivalry tends to be exaggerated, and there is no hard and fast rule that the two groups are incapable of cooperating in a given situation. The Sussis long accepted Fassi leadership in the Istiqlal and elected Fassis to the Chambers of Commerce and Industry (Moroccan section) before 1956. They have acknowledged the political role in the UNFP of 'Abbas Kebbaj, a modern farmer in the Agadir region and a Fassi from Tangier, who was elected to the parliament from Biougra (Agadir Province) in 1963. But having said all this, there has been an undeniable and inevitable friction between the Fassi and Sussi communities, again most noticeably in Casablanca.

On 8 May 1960, Morocco held its first public elections since independence for places in thirteen local chambers of commerce and industry. To the surprise of everyone at the time, the newly

---

* Along these lines, the Sussi grocers of the *bidonvilles* are a source of contraband goods, credit buying, how to handle the police, social advice – in short the Sussi is the man who knows the system and is sought out by the confused, ignorant, harassed, penniless initiates of the 'big city'.

founded UNFP made an exceptionally strong showing, carrying a majority of seats in Casablanca, Rabat, Tangier, Kenitra, Meknes, Sidi Slimane, Settat, al-Jadida, Ksar al-Kebir, and conceded Fez where it presented no candidates.* It seemed odd, to say the least, that a party that publicly espoused a socialistic and revolutionary doctrine should find such massive support in the world of private capital and commerce. The UNFP had indeed attracted the sympathies of 'enlightened' businessmen tired of the anachronistic commercial attitudes of many of their colleagues, but the fundamental explanation probably lies with the Sussis. They made use of their great numerical superiority in an electorate composed only of businessmen and merchants of one sort or another. The UNFP provided them with an organizational framework for their latent hostility to the commercial elite of Casablanca. The latter, through its control of the import and distribution of wholesale goods necessary for the retailers, combined with the relatively awesome financial means at their disposal, had bred a feeling of frustration and oppression (not wholly unlike that bred among the Fassi commercial elite by French capitalists before 1956) among the Sussi tradesmen. The fact that a large number of Casablanca merchants were also of the Istiqlali old guard served to sharpen the coincidence of goals of the leadership of the UNFP and the Sussis. The upshot was a UNFP sweep of all twenty-four seats in the Casablanca Chamber of Commerce and Industry (CCI).

The Sussi domination of the CCI of Casablanca was continued in the summer elections of 1963 : this time however they had, under the presidency of 'Abdullah Souiri, aligned themselves with the royalist front, the FDIC. An election for the renewal of one-third of the members of all CCIs was held in August 1966. Coming after fourteen months of political torpor stemming from the king's announcement of the dissolution of Parliament and his assumption of 'emergency powers', no one seemed able to take these elections very seriously. In 1963, the Istiqlal and UNFP (minus their erstwhile Sussi allies) had boycotted the CCI elections, claiming that they would undoubtedly be rigged by FDIC, and after the elections

---

* An interesting twist on this political alignment is the fact that in Fez the UNFP has rallied some support among *hwantin* of Fez al-Bali, the real hard core of Fez, while the Sussi shopkeepers of Fez al-Jadid, dependent upon palace business, have avoided contact with the UNFP. I owe this observation to Muhammed Lahbabi. On the elections see D.E.Ashford, 'Elections in Morocco; Progress or Confusion?', *M.E.J.*, Winter 1961, pp. 1–15.

both parties denounced the resultant chambers as being totally unrepresentative. Thus it must have come as something of a surprise to the members of the chambers when, almost on the eve of the 1966 elections, the Istiqlal mounted an all-out campaign to elect 'national' candidates to the CCIs. These candidates, the party pointed out, were not strictly speaking Istiqlals, and while the party maintained its stand on the unrepresentativeness of the chambers, it nonetheless recommended the election of certain 'sincere patriots'.[17] The Sussis were unprepared for the Istiqlali offensive, and the Istiqlal picked up twelve seats in the Casablanca CCI. It was a pyrrhic victory in that only 15 per cent of the electorate voted, reflecting the Istiqlal's inability to get out the vote, and in Rabat the party made no gains at all. Nevertheless, when it came time to elect the new bureau of the Casablanca CCI, 'Abdullah Souiri was ousted from the presidency by Muhammed Lamraani by a vote of twenty-one to seventeen.[18] Lest one would assume that this vote represents the Sussi-Fassi split in the CCI, it should be noted that a number of the successful Istiqlali candidates were themselves Sussis. Morocco is seldom simple and perhaps least of all the Sussi-Fassi rivalry.

3 The Lure of the Land

As was noted in chapter 1, political instability and the arbitrary use of confiscation impeded the accumulation of landed wealth and certainly frightened off any who might have contemplated long-term development of their land to increase its productive capacity. Nonetheless, there was always a tendency, common to most of the Middle East, to acquire land as one of the least unstable elements – along with jewelry – of a material patrimony. This attitude continues today to orient the Moroccan elite towards the acquisition of land, both urban and rural, and is another factor tending to obfuscate political boundaries. The desirability of accumulating land and the possibility of keeping it was greatly bolstered all during the last century under the influence of European powers who took a keen interest in the stability of property holdings.

During the nineteenth century in Morocco, real estate values in most cities rose appreciably, and the urban bourgeoisie took advantage of this situation.[19] In the present century, the astounding growth of Casablanca and the proportionate inflation of real estate prices was the source of huge profits to many Moroccans, not least among whom were family branches of the Bennanis, Benjellouns, and Sebtis. The profitability of real estate speculation has not diminished with independence and has taken on such proportions in Casablanca that the king recently felt obliged to condemn the machinations of unnamed speculators.[20]

Most of the Fassis of Casablanca maintain a family house at Fez, and before the migration of the commercial elite to the coast, Fassi land purchases had been concentrated in the tribal areas surrounding Fez. Georges Pallez offers the following figures:[21]

Tribe	Surface	% owned by Fassis
Lemta	90km^2	90
Oulad al-Haj del-Wad	250	65
Humaya'a	200	40
Chararda	90	40
Seja'a Ait Ayyach	200	2
Bani Sadden	260	20
Sais Udayya	90	1
Oulad Jema'a	530	70

In the area of the Haya'ina north of Fez much of the best land is owned by the merchants of Fez al-Bali and the Wazzani and 'Alawi shurafa. The merchants were able to make large purchases in the region at favorable prices at the time of the Rif War and after the famine of 1945. One of the most famous land owners of the region was the (ex-) Sultan Ben 'Arafa, whose property has subsequently been sequestered. The land owned by the urban bourgeoisie was not exploited any differently than that of the rural notability, and high yields were sacrificed to nonintensive methods of cultivation and the use of *khammas* to do the farming.[22]

One may state that in general it was only after the influx of the *colons* that some Moroccans began to appreciate land for its productive capacity and to understand that its chief value might lie therein. Most cultivable land had been farmed with rudimentary means, sporadically and inefficiently, and the notion of cash crops and agricultural specialization was not widespread. The great 'feudal' notables of the protectorate period, men like al-'Ayyadi with forty-five thousand hectares, Amharoq with fifty-six thousand and Al-Glaoui with fifteen thousand,[23] allowed much of their land to lie fallow or used it for pasturage. City and rural proprietors alike viewed their property as a symbol of prestige having a relatively stable monetary value regardless of what it could produce in any one year. As long as basic food needs were met, there was little incentive to invest in improving soil fertility and farming techniques.

These attitudes have begun to change, and a new group of cash-crop farmers is developing, either by following the example set by French *colons* or by directly purchasing their farms. A good many of these Moroccan *colons* are the sons of important rural land-owners who have started to up-date cultivation of the family holdings. Others are from the commercial families of the cities who own rural property, and they too, while maintaining residence in the city, are improving their land and acquiring more. Finally, there are those who have used administrative privilege to arrange for the purchase of choice land from departing *colons*. To a certain degree all three categories have been able to count on adminis-trative support – an elite member, if he himself does not occupy a governmental post, is seldom without friends or relations who do – but the practice is particularly noticeable among officials of the Ministry of the Interior and the officers' corps.

About 20 per cent of Morocco's cultivated acreage is farmed by modern methods, and in 1963 two-thirds of that land was still exploited by foreigners.[24] Under the protectorate, a total of 5,903 *colons* farmed 1,017,000 hectares, divided into 289,000 hectares of land of 'official colonization' (i.e. land acquired and sold by the protectorate administration) and 728,000 hectares of land of 'private colonization'.[25] The *colons*, private and official, were con-centrated in the well-watered coastal plains, and the major river valleys where most of Morocco's irrigated land is located (see map on page 285): the valleys of the Sebou, Beth, and Wergha which water the Gharb plain; the Haouz plain around Marrekesh; the whole area watered by the Oum ar-Rabi'a, beginning with the irrigated region (Beni Moussa, Beni 'Ammar) lying in the triangle of Kasba Tadla, Beni Mellal, Kala'a Saraghna, and Fqih Ben Saleh and running through the Chawia and Doukkala plains; the Berkane region (Triffas) of the lower Moulouya; and the Suss and Massa river valleys near Agadir. It is above all in these irrigated areas that the new Moroccan 'rural bourgeoisie' has established itself.

Estimates of the number of hectares of *colon* land bought by Moroccans since 1955 range from three hundred thousand to five hundred thousand.[26] Most of the transactions have been purchases of land of private colonization. In principle all acreage of official colonization was to be subject to recuperation by the Moroccan state, and this long-awaited agrarian reform was made official by the dahir of 26 September 1963. Over 120,000 hectares have been taken over by the state, and gradually all 250,000 hectares will be recuperated. It is alleged that some land of official colonization was acquired illegally by Moroccans, but such acquisitions are of little importance compared with those of land of private colonization. Here too, at the time of independence, there had been good intentions to control strictly all transactions involving this land, and any sale required the approval of three ministers (finance, interior, agriculture). As it turned out such approval was not too difficult to obtain. Moreover certain sales required no administrative approval at all. Private joint stock companies had cultivated extensive landholdings under the protectorate,[27] and sales of their land involved the transfer of stock rights and were not subject to official authorization. All these sales, from the point of view of the elite, the *colons*, and the regime, are highly desirable. The *colon*, knowing that sooner or later he will probably have to leave, and with the threat of expropriation hanging over his head, is content to sell his land at bargain rates to elite members, often government officials who can arrange the transfer of all or part of his capital out of Morocco. If these transactions continue to take place at a rapid rate, the regime may be spared the necessity of coming to grips with the problem of recuperating the land of private colonization and of undertaking its management. Concomitantly, the growth of a rural bourgeoisie with a vested interest in the status quo is in itself a good thing for the regime.

The new Moroccan commercial farmers are as diverse or as homogeneous as the political elite itself. They have acted within the rural context in exactly the same manner as their urban compatriots, filling the economic vacuum created by the gradual repatriation of European interests,[28] and in many instances cash-crop farmer, city merchant, and government official are one and the same person. In the Gharb for example, after 1956, most acquisitions of *colon* land were made by Moroccans who already had large holdings: the Nejjai family of Souk al-Arba',* the Gueddaris, and some branches of the Dlimi family. Since 1960, however, there has been an upsurge in sales to government officials. At Berkane, in the irrigated region of the Triffas, Muhammed Bekkai, son of Si M'Barrek Bekkai, a notable of the Beni Iznassen and a member of the Mouvement Populaire, has become like the Istiqlali Ahmad Nejjai, a successful citrus grower. 'Abbas Kebbaj at Biougra south of Agadir is likewise a citrus grower but a member of the UNFP. Important families of the Marrakesh area and the Haouz have all added to their properties in recent years, particularly in irrigated acreage. It would be hazardous to read too much into this trend, but it seems clear that in the blad, as in the cities, the elite, regardless of its political tendencies, has created a shared interest and a market-oriented patrimony. In addition it is in the realm of landownership and the adoption of modern farming techniques that one finds the closest intermixture of the urban and rural elements of the elite.†

The style of the political elite has been marked by its economic good fortune. Whether in or out of the government, whether urban or rural, all elite members have experienced the manifold financial blessings of independence, which in turn have generated real and potential alliances that cut across or simply nullify for all practical purposes nominal political boundaries. The elite is comfortable and it is aging. While most of its members vaguely desire economic growth and an equitable distribution of national income, few are willing to sacrifice their own well-being to achieve these distant goals. The palace is always there to remind the elite how well off it is, and to sanction any members who may object too strenuously to current policies. The monarchy is the major distributor of spoils and patronage in Morocco, and it considers

---

* Ahmad Mansour Nejjai was Morocco's first minister of agriculture, is president of the Union Marocaine d'Agriculteurs, an important member of the Istiqlal, and a citrus-grower. His father was one of the most powerful qaids of the Gharb.

† I have not cited any sources for much of what has been said regarding the rural bourgeoisie. Without attributing specific remarks to specific individuals, the following were consulted: Muhammed Tahiri (former director of the ONI), Paul Pascon (director of the Tassaout Barrage Project), 'Abdulwahad Radi (UNFP representative from Sidi Sliman), Rémy Leveau (former attaché in the Ministry of the Interior), Hadi Messouak (member of the executive committee of the PCM). I take full responsibility for the choice of interviewees and the interpretation given their remarks.

the entire elite as its clientele group. To maintain its following, to protect the faithful, to attract new recruits, and to chastise the recalcitrant, the palace manipulates its system of rewards, political, economic, and spiritual, to great advantage. Every elite faction is constantly trying to anticipate the king's next move, and all of their actions are calculated with regard to his likely reaction.

CHAPTER SEVEN

THE KING: SUPREME ARBITER AND POTENTIAL ZA'IM

Ce régime ne tranche ni les têtes ni les problèmes.[1]

Only passing reference has been made in the preceding chapters to the most important member of the political elite, the king. He enjoys this status not only because he is head of state, nor simply because he is descended from the Prophet, but because socially and educationally his experience has been similar to that of other members of the elite of his generation. One should note however that this remark is more pertinent to the experience of Hassan II than to that of his father Muhammed V. The latter's upbringing and education were divorced from all that went on beyond the palace walls, and he was given little training for the tasks that would face him as head of state. His political know-how and grasp of national and international politics were gained pragmatically over a number of years, beginning with his first contacts with the nationalists in 1934. His elite status was more or less thrust upon him by the Istiqlali nationalists. Had he rebuffed their overtures, Morocco might well be a republic today, and the 'Alawis no more important to the elite than the Kittanis. On the other hand, Hassan II, a privileged but not cloistered youth, was the beneficiary of his father's pragmatic insight into Moroccan politics, was educated with other Moroccans outside the royal family, and eventually went on to receive a law degree from the University of Bordeaux. Despite great disparities in political style, both kings have employed basically the same tactics to protect the throne.

The king (or in the past, the sultan) is a sharif, he is viewed as a dispenser of *baraka*, and he is venerated. But Moroccans have always had an insouciant ability to distinguish between the personal sanctity of the sultan and the political authority of his government, submitting to the one but often rejecting the other. Try as they might, the pre-protectorate sultans could not impose unpopular decisions, except on a temporary basis, and at the cost of provoking all sorts of counterforces that might ignore the decision or use it as a springboard to act against the sultan. Certainly it cannot be said that former sultans lacked means of physical coercion. On the other hand, seldom did they monopolize coercive means, and other groups in Morocco, solely or in combination, could thwart, neutralize, or even turn against the sultan any unpopular initiative he might undertake.[2]

Sultans did indeed take advantage of the divisions of Moroccan society to keep themselves in power, but these divisons facilitated, or made less difficult, the physical control and taxation of varying proportions of the population. It has only been in recent years that Moroccan monarchs have attempted to set themselves up as the arbiters of social and political conflicts and to create an image of credible neutrality.

It has already been postulated that Moroccan society consisted, and to a lesser degree still consists, of numerous segments related to one another by tension and conflict. Because this was a constant factor of Moroccan politics, one of the most consistently reward-ing political roles in Morocco was that of arbiter among conflicting groups, and to the extent that Moroccan politics remain segmented and imbued with tension that role continues to be important. The function of arbiter has been consciously and publicly adopted by independent Morocco's two monarchs. In essence Article 3 of the 1962 constitution is designed to guarantee and give permanence to a political process that would constantly be in need of a nationally-recognized arbiter.

While the political parties shall participate in the organization and representation of the citizens, there shall be no single-party regime in Morocco.[3]

In Morocco this article is often referred to as the 'Guedira clause', and M. Guedira does take credit for it. He sees in it the culmina-tion of his efforts (and those of the palace) to guard against the total takeover of national politics by the Istiqlal. More positively, he feels that only through the maintenance of several political groupings can the king avoid falling victim to any one of them.[4]

On 13 December 1962, the king in a press conference openly adopted the thesis of his trusted advisor.

> The constitution makes of Us an arbiter . . . I am certain that many have said 'The powers of the King are enormous'. . . . I would say to them, to take a very simple example: 'Imagine two football teams on a field, take away from the referee the power to whistle out and expulse a player, and then gentlemen, play.' The problem is very simple, and thus is it posed.[5]

Guedira would substitute for the dictum 'divide and rule', 'divide and survive'. Muhammed v needed no urging to put this policy into effect as soon as he returned from exile, and his weighting of political groupings in the first government corresponded more closely to a hoped for situation than the actual fact of Istiqlali predominance.

The king in 1955 was closely identified with the Istiqlal, and in order to be acceptable as arbiter among all sectors of Moroccan society, he had to hold himself aloof from any single party. Further he had to *create* and *encourage* the formal organization of rival groupings to the Istiqlal, groupings that would give tangible structure to heretofore latent interests. Once this was accomplished Muhammed v could claim the function of honest broker among the groups he had encouraged (Mouvement Populaire) or disparaged (Istiqlal) without being identified with or indebted to any of them. In fact most elite members acknowledge, and even welcome, the king's arbitration* in intergroup contests for the shreds of power the palace is prepared to distribute. So far the imaginative manipulation of rewards and privations by the king has been sufficient to maintain elite segmentation and to prevent his becoming superfluous to the political process. A sort of circular strategy is thereby put into effect: by encouraging intergroup rivalry, the necessary conditions for discontinuous political leadership are maintained, and the need for a symbol of political continuity is accentuated.

At the same time as Muhammed v was closely linked to the Istiqlal, he was without any significant means of physical coercion. There was no Moroccan army or police until the late spring of

---

* A recent example was 'Allal al-Fassi's invitation to King Hassan in the fall of 1964 to arbitrate unresolved differences between the parliamentary majority and minority as to the agenda of an extraordinary session of Parliament.

1956, but when finally they came into existence, the king saw to it that they were entirely loyal to the throne. It is this quasi-monopoly of force on the part of the monarchy that is at the heart of the elite's discontent, particularly that of the leftist opposition. The utility of his arbitration is uncontested, but most elite members would like to force him into the traditional mould of the unarmed *agurram* who is the last resort for warring factions, the master of ceremonies at important functions, the presiding officer at the time of selection of leaders, but above all a man powerless to enforce an unpopular decision. The throne for its part needed immediate physical protection until rival groups could dispute the Istiqlal's pretensions of being the sole valid spokesman, in conjunction with the king of course, of the Moroccan masses. Once the monolithic facade of the Istiqlal had been cracked, and once the bulk of the Liberation Army and resistance had been disarmed and integrated into the army and police, the threat of the violent overthrow of the monarchy or its subservience to the Istiqlal became more remote. The king was then able to use the army as a pawn in the maintenance of division and balance among elite segments. The army, while still loyal to the monarchy, has become aware of itself as a political force in its own right. In some ways this is an ominous development for the palace, but at the same time it enables the king to curb civilian elements of the elite and to present himself as the most feasible alternative to military rule.

The Istiqlal never contested the personal primacy of Muhammed v as Morocco's national hero, the 'first resistant', and the symbol of the nation's sovereignty. His exile had made of him an extraordinarily and universally revered and admired personnage. Need he really have feared the Istiqlal? Was he not capable of dominating the Istiqlal and using it for his own purposes? Some observers have contended that the personal prestige of Muhammed v was so great in the early years of independence that he could have initiated dynamic and necessarily stringent programs of economic development, exploiting the popular enthusiasm that he aroused toward this end. Any political group that opposed his will would almost have been guilty of sacrilege. Some of these same observers have been puzzled by the role Muhammed v chose to play; the 'temporisateur par excellence',[6] a man willing 'to arbitrate, suggest, restrain, but not to lead'.[7]

If the general interpretation of Moroccan politics presented in this study is correct, then it would seem unlikely that Muhammed v, even had he realized his enormous potential, would have acted differently. Seen from the standpoint of the dynasty, stability – even at the cost of economic stagnation and the segmentation of political forces – are the *sine qua non* of the monarchy's survival. To activate a program, to strike out energetically, and to do so meaningfully, would require nation-wide support, mobilized into some sort of organizational form. But it is precisely the creation of such a force that the monarchy wished to avoid. Momentarily its master, the throne could quickly become its slave or victim. It is far preferable to act as arbiter, to use power for defense only, to shun the potential role of political *za'im* with its undeniable appeal but also its inherent dangers.

Once having assumed the arbiter function, a few simple principles have guided monarchical conduct. First, no group may be permitted to become too strong, and to counter hegemonic tendencies life is breathed into rival groups. On the other hand no group (and this includes the opposition parties) may be permitted to die utterly. Attrition, feebleness, quiescence are all acceptable, but at least the skeleton of the group must be maintained so that, when needed, flesh can be put on its bones. Because political groupings in Morocco are generally composed of a patron and his clientele, the surest method to keep a group alive is to see to it that the patron does not waste all his prestige. Prestige is often measured in terms of a patron's degree of access to the chief dispenser of spoils, the king. By token or symbolic gestures toward various leaders, ceremonial consultations, missions abroad, etc., the palace is able to maintain their prestige at a critical minimum level so that they can quickly reconstitute their clientele when needed.*

An additional self-imposed rule followed by the monarchy is to avoid becoming closely identified with any group it may summon into existence (FDIC, Mouvement Populaire) or any project it may support. This rule is an example of royal bet-hedging, allowing the king to bask in the warmth generated by a

* Under the state of emergency since June 1965 all political groups have tended to languish. While not unhappy with this situation, King Hassan has nonetheless sent Guedira, Al-Fassi and Khatib off on a number of foreign missions, has consulted with Ben Seddiq and Ibrahim, has asked all political parties for advice on educational policy, and has received various leaders at the time of national celebrations.

successful political movement or project launched in his name, but at the same time keeping open the option of disassociation in the event of its failure. Some of his advisors feel that he has unwisely deviated from this rule in becoming prime minister and thereby accepting direct responsibility for governmental actions.*

The entire political elite is the field of action for the alliance-building of the king, and he maintains a number of clientele groups of which he is the patron. Although certain segments of the elite identify their interests more closely than others with those of the throne, the king consistently tries to promote the notion that all segments of the elite constitute a large family, subject to political differences, but essentially united in approval of the direct role of the monarchy in politics. If there is any one discernible rule to the game of politics in Morocco whose violation is followed by immediate sanctions, it is this: the person of the king, the monarchical institution, and the powers it has arrogated for itself are in no way to be attacked or criticized directly and in public. All questions of sovereignty are carefully avoided, and despite the referendum of 1962 and Article 1 of the constitution, it is ill-advised to talk of popular sovereignty in Morocco. In February 1965, the Istiqlal's French daily, *La Nation Africaine*, published a saying of Jamal ad-Din al-Afghani to the effect that 'A people can live without a king, but a king cannot live without a people'. The editor, Driss al-Fellah, was sentenced to ten months in prison and publication of the paper was suspended for six months.[8] 'Abdarrahman Yussufi and Muhammed Basri of the UNFP had met the same fate in the winter of 1959–60 after publishing in the pages of *Al-Tahrir* (Liberation) what were judged to be articles calling into question the sovereignty of the throne.

The king has been very stubborn in delegating any of his authority, and he has refused to relinquish in any way his control of the armed forces. Those who question his right to maintain these prerogatives are severely chastised, and, if they push their opposition hard enough, are ostracized from the family. Mehdi Ben Barka *may* be an example of ostracism carried to its logical end.

King Hassan has been careful never to compromise or make concessions under pressure. He insists on unilateral grants or

* The office of prime minister reverted to Muhammed Benhima in July 1967 following the June 1967 war between the Arab states and Israel.

gifts that are held up as examples of his munificence. In effect he is creating thereby links of obligation with various groups, rendering as many people as possible beholden and grateful to his generosity. Criminals, political or others, are more often pardoned than amnestied; their sins are not expunged, just magnanimously overlooked by the sovereign. The UNFP demanded a complete amnesty for Ben Barka after his condemnation for treason *in absentia* in 1964. The amnesty demanded was to be a legal act, printed in the *Official Bulletin*, like that of the former collaborators amnestied in 1963, absolving Ben Barka of all crimes for which he had been condemned. However, in April 1965, King Hassan would do no more than suggest obliquely that Ben Barka *might* be pardoned if he were to return to Morocco.[9] On this same occasion, the *'Id al-Kabir*, Hassan II emphasized the dynasty's quality of supreme dispenser of justice in Morocco. Speaking of those he had pardoned for past crimes, the king said,

I offer to those whom I have pardoned a precious opportunity that they may reintegrate themselves into the national family and that they may work in the context of its constitutional institutions and political organizations. If they miss this opportunity, if they persist in error and believe that clemency is a door open widely to them at all moments, I warn them against the unfortunate consequences of their poor intentions and manoeuvres, and I call their attention to the fact that Our clemency is equalled only by Our firmness.

This clemency is proof of the innate nature of Our family, characterized by its profound wisdom, its great nobility, and the solid communion which unites Us intimately to Our people. Moreover if We have adopted this attitude impregnated with wisdom and clemency, it is because We have answered to the humanitarian mission handed on to Us by the Savior of the Nation and the Liberator of the citizens, Our late Father Muhammed V, may God bless his memory.[10]

Dispenser of justice, the king is likewise the nation's most prominent dispenser of patronage with which he sustains his secular clientele and builds his secular alliances. The palace has a very real command over Moroccan commercial activities as well as over the distribution of patronage. These are the king's two most effective levers of elite control. Both levers have traditionally been manipulated by Moroccan sultans, but independence has brought with it an amplification of the economic means and the amounts of patronage at the king's disposal.

The sultans created relations of economic obligation with the commercial bourgeoisie, particularly with the expansion of international trade in the nineteenth century, by building warehouses and casbahs for them, protecting their trade centers from marauding tribes, and favoring some with the title of *tajir as-sultan*, empowered to carry out the commercial transactions of the ruler. The granting of monopolies of export and import of given products, and exemptions from customs duties were devices of commercial control designed to tie economic interests to the regime. It is estimated that in Mogador (Essaouira) in 1846 there was not a single merchant indebted to the sultan for less than 60,000 piastres, or 325,000 francs.[11]

Both kings of independent Morocco have worked hard to guarantee the economic prosperity of the elite, and neither has hesitated to take economic reprisals against those not sufficiently appreciative of this fact. Members of the royal family, such as Prince Moulay 'Ali, have taken an active part in the commercial affairs of the kingdom, and the palace has substantial investments in banks and enterprises in Morocco and abroad. Female members of the royal family have married outsiders, and the king's brothers-in-law, Hassan Ya'coubi, Ahmad 'Osman, and Muhammed Cherkaoui, have all received a substantial boost in the business and social world from the palace. They are new members of an economic family whose limits the sovereign tries continually to expand. Toward this end, the king can direct the flow of government business to favor some elite members at the expense of others, or to threaten the unruly. Ironically, the new enlightened Moroccan capitalists are the most vulnerable to these tactics, for in launching a venture they must depend upon the state for credit and protection.*

In this vein, the royal family has increased its landholdings in Morocco, and Prince Moulay 'Abdullah has become one of Morocco's most important landowners. The royal holdings are

---

* Ahmad Benkirane, former director of *Maroc-Informations*, an important businessman of Casablanca, had publication of his newspaper suspended in May 1966 for undisclosed reasons, but probably because of a series of interviews he planned to publish, one of which dealt critically with the Ben Barka affair. In a manoeuvre typical of royal politics, Benkirane having been slapped down in May was appointed director of the Caisse de Depôt et de Gestion the following September. He probably had no choice but to accept the post, for his business position could otherwise have been made untenable.

well managed and efficiently farmed, and the royal family is in the forefront of the new rural bourgeoisie. Some wags have suggested that the king is accumulating all this land only to give it away according to the land reform technique pioneered by the Shah of Iran. The king, would thus, through his generosity, render masses of peasants beholden to the throne. The explanation is far-fetched, but the end that it would serve is fully in keeping with the monarchy's objectives. The more probable reason is that this property offers a regular income, can be obtained cheaply, and re-enforces the throne's economic bargaining position. The lure of the land acts as powerfully upon members of the 'Alawite dynasty as upon any other elite members.

In the previous chapter it was stated that the administration has been a source of wealth to its high-ranking employees. I need not repeat here what has already been said in this respect. Let it suffice to note that the king appoints all officials who are not Civil Service employees and approves all commissions and promotions in the armed forces. He may choose to delegate this authority to a given minister, but there is never any doubt concerning its origin. Consequently the king controls the most desirable administrative posts, and he manipulates appointments in the same manner that he distributes economic sanctions and rewards: to hold his secular clientele in line, attract new recruits, and keep opponents off balance. Few elite members dare turn down a royal appointment,* and most men dread being relieved of their functions. In addition, elite subgroups and clientele alliances, whatever the patrimony they seek to defend, constantly strive to place as many of their allies as possible in high-ranking positions so that the group as a whole may benefit from administrative protection. This facilitates the king's task, who, in orienting the flow of patronage, can inflate some groups, deflate others, and sustain a minimum level of suspense among elite members as to his next move.

The king is the spiritual patriarch of a holy family some of whose members belong to the elite but which is significantly broader than the elite. Within this family there are several alliance systems, and the king seeks to add to them just as he tries to add to his secular alliances. The two families, the secular and the holy,

---

* Hadi Messouak refused the post of minister of agriculture twice, but he is somewhat out of harm's way thanks to a steady private medical practice. Other Marxists, such as Hassan 'Ababou, were unable to reject the bait.

are animated by two personages, the Moroccan head of state and the Sharifian *Amir al-Muminin*. Both personnages are embodied in a single man, the king, and he frequently calls attention to the two fundamental parts he plays in Morocco. On a given morning, dressed in Cardin's latest, he may confer with Edward Kennedy, and in the evening, clad in a white *jellaba*, deliver a Ramadan lecture seated in the midst of mumbling 'ulema in the palace mosque. Lest members of his secular family take him too lightly, he need only hint at the pious legions that would defend his cause. Both Muhammed v and Hassan ii have in this way emphasized that their prestige is dependent on no single group, and that their audience is limited only by the religious faith of Moroccans. As I.W.Zartman rightly pointed out: 'Allal al-Fassi probably has more religious stature than Hassan al-Alawi as a person, but the latter, as Hassan ii, is by his office the dominant religious figure in Morocco.'[12]

The core of the king's religious clientele is the rambling 'Alawite family itself. This is not to say that individual 'Alawis venerate the king; this may not be the case at all. However, the family's *raison d'être* is its descent from the Prophet, and to the extent that there is group identification among 'Alawis, it must be attributed to this fact. The king is simply the most successful member of the family, and, in the same way as a newly-elected president becomes titular head of his party, he is the family leader until defeated from without or successfully challenged from within. Hundreds of 'Alawis come each year to Rabat on the great Muslim feast days to pay their respects to the king and to renew their fealty. The palace reciprocates in various ways such as doles to the *naqib** of the family, distributions of food to the 'Alawis of Tafilalt, and gifts and food handed out during Ramadan. The upper crust of the family is kept happy with administrative appointments, and one finds, for example, a disproportionate number of 'Alawi pashas. In 1961 four of the fifteen provincial governors were 'Alawis, Moulay Ahmad 'Alawi has frequently been a minister, and the Director of Protocol is General Moulay Hafidh al-'Alawi. Outsiders who have become allied to the family through marriage and who may have been indifferent to the

---

* An official traditionally selected by the members of the family in various locales to represent it in its relations with the dynasty. All sharifian families generally have a *naqib*.

qualities of royal sanctity, are made to feel the weight and prestige of descent from the Prophet. The son of Muhammed Cherkaoui, and the nephew of King Hassan, was named by the latter Moulay Sliman, in memory of the last sultan to have sojourned in Boujad, the birthplace of M. Cherkaoui. In conferring upon the child the title 'Moulay', which only agnatic descendants from the Prophet may bear, the king violated the principle of agnation, making all the more striking the honor bestowed upon the child's father.

The 'Alawi family is only one sector of the far larger, but also more diffuse, religious audience of the king. Other sharifian lineages, 'ulema, the uneducated and superstitious female half of society, and even some of the zawiyas have responded in varying degrees to the saintly attributes of the monarchy. In recent years Hassan II has conscientiously encouraged the delegations to the annual *moussems* (anniversaries) of local saints, and most recently, in insisting that all Moroccan students receive religious instruction and perform ritual prayers during school hours.[13] The king is aware that youths of school age are less susceptible to religious pressures than their fathers and grandfathers. The palace cannot afford to lose a constituency that has served it well in the past as a source of support and as a balance to its secular constituency. At those times that the king has directly participated in the political arena – as prime minister 1961–3 and again in 1965, at the time of the constitutional referendum, and as tacit sponsor of FDIC – he has used his religious prestige to render difficult any opposition to his purely political stances.

Despite the special powers and position that are the king's, he has resorted to the same methods used by other members of the elite. Having gone to school with many of them, having been taught by others, having aided yet others in the nationalist movement, Hassan II shares their style and behavior. He is singular in the power at his disposal, but he uses it to carry out the same well-worn political functions that his less privileged compatriots perform according to their means. At the same time, he has more or less written the rules of national politics, decided what the rewards and sanctions will be, and has used his patronage and economic leverage to bring about elite acceptance of the game. These same devices have been wielded to promote elite consciousness of itself as a group, the awareness that as a group it is very well off, and that it has only the palace to thank for this. Under the rules elite factions may vie for whatever the regime has to offer, and for those who would dispute the king's handling of the competition, the army is kept in reserve. Finally, the entire elite is constantly reminded of the fact that the king's religious status opens to him a national audience far more extensive than that of any single elite faction.

The monarchy has used its power and authority for defense and has avoided bold initiatives. All the elements are present, however, to enable the king to adopt the role of *za'im*. He could crusade for economic development, usurped Moroccan territory, or almost any cause he might wish. An illiterate and gullible population is at his disposal, as are the technical means with which to reach it. The army, scouts, and sympathetic politicians could organize the populace for civic action. But the king has rejected the role of national leader and has never exploited the immense demagogic potential that he retains. Arbiter is the more familiar role, the more desirable option, but in order to prevent the arbiter from becoming irrelevant to Moroccan politics, an equilibrium of forces must be maintained. To achieve this end, the king has been obliged to devote most of his energies and thought to the manipulation of elite units. At times it appears that he loses sight of the ultimate goal of balance and arbitration as he immerses himself in the minutiae of day-to-day manoeuvres. The net result is that initiative and growth fall victim to an unevolving situation of tension and conflict.

One is thus left with the impression that the king has no other long-term strategy than to hope that his short-term tactics continue to pay off. This is not far from the mark, but one can nonetheless discern a few elements that constitute a more far-sighted policy.

There is, for instance, a concerted effort made to treat potentially critical problems of economic development and social change in purely technical terms. Thus, the problems of urbanization, unemployment, agricultural production, and the like are not discussed in terms of land reform and the nationalization of industries, but in terms of fertilizers, housing, and local initiative. Increasingly the king has turned to the Ministry of the Interior and the army to attack the economic problems of the country, and to apply governmental policies ranging from the management of state owned land and the building of schools to returning the urban unemployed to the blad. Both organizations have clearly delineated command structures, and, more important, special ties to the throne. They represent the king's answer to the opposition's demands for making hard political choices, as well as the king's fervent hope that, without any change in the political *status quo* progress can be registered in all fields through the efficient and determined execution of existent policies.

However, King Hassan is willing to maintain a semblance of political life and discussion within the elite in order to keep up his liberal image. In so doing he has developed a number of strategies for holding political passions at a low ebb and for curbing the access of elite members to new sources of mass recruits.

The coastal cities, and above all Casablanca, are considered to be the most fertile ground for opposition politicians. Casablanca is Morocco's most important city, not only in terms of port activity, industrial production, and commerce, but also in terms of the number of unemployed and the number of unionized workers. The political climate of the entire country is to no small extent determined by that of Casablanca, and all elite members are acutely aware of that fact.

The king would like to reverse this imbalance between the urban and rural world. In recent years he has emphasized rural problems, and has encouraged the formation of rural elites by giving local and regional assemblies some control over the allocation of local patronage. Great publicity is given to his turning the first spade in the construction of dams, but he no longer observes the habit of his father in attending the labor parade on 1 May in Casablanca. The Ministry of the Interior has entered directly into this policy, and in 1967 initiated programs to repatriate from the cities to their villages all those in the city slums who could not show proof of employment: this in order to scatter concentrations of the unemployed in the cities. Even the Mouvement Populaire, the staunchly royalist Berber party, may have been drawn into the strategy. Since November 1966 it has tried to find recruits in the slums of Casablanca, and, by implanting itself in the countryside seeks to deny access to these areas on the part of city-based parties and unions.

Morocco's one attempt at parliamentary democracy in 1963 to 1965 (to be discussed in Part Three) did not please the king. The king was not able to achieve a workable majority within the Parliament and he soon tired of the sterile factional disputes among the deputies. Throughout the short life of Parliament, and ever since, the king has consistently belittled the notion of formal democracy, describing it as an impediment to the struggle against need and misery. He has unequivocally stated the incompatibility between Parliament and true democracy. When he suspended Parliament in June 1965, he said that if he had allowed the empty debates to continue, Morocco's democracy, moral values, dignity and will to create would have been shaken.[14]

Instead King Hassan has reverted to the more familiar form of a consultative assembly whose members are appointed by royal decree. Muhammed v had experimented with this format between 1957 and 1959 with fair success, and Hassan II revived it in the winter of 1968. Such bodies emphasize the king's judgment of who is important in Morocco, they can only offer advice, they can be convoked and dismissed at will, but despite all this, they have a certain propaganda value. Such an assembly may provide an opportunity for the controlled ritualistic dissipation of elite frustrations without its polemics affecting government policies. The body that met in March 1968 was called to deliberate the new five year plan. It was addressed by the king, it considered and approved the plan as presented in four days, and then went home with the promise of future convocations.[15] Finally, the relation between this council and the throne confirms the king in his role of father figure among elite members. As he put it himself in a circular to all political parties following the Casablanca riots of March 1965: 'My hand is open to all my subjects for they are all my children.'[16]

One of the monarchy's most pressing problems is to devise some sort of credible ideology to satisfy the cravings of Morocco's youth. So far King Hassan has relied upon 'civisme', a blend of civic spirit and religious values, through which he hopes to form future citizens and subjects. He has exhorted the young to sacrifice and work for the country as they did under his father in 1957 in building the Unity Road to link the French and Spanish zones. After the floods of 1965 in the Ziz Valley, King Hassan launched an appeal for massive voluntary labor to build a dam across the Ziz as a symbol of national concern. In June of 1966, he announced the institution of obligatory military service, supplemented in the summer of 1968 by plans for a compulsory youth corps to undertake community projects. During the same period an order was issued for the observance of ritual prayers in all the schools of the kingdom, and, again in the summer of 1968, it was decided to establish a network of 'Houses of Thought' to teach civic values to young Moroccans.

To light the flame of *civisme* and to keep it burning may be possible, if at all, only through contrived means. National disasters or border conflicts may evoke such spirit, but it will be at best temporary, and the contrivance will lose its effectiveness through repetition. Conscription of youth into a work corps will certainly generate more resentment than pride. For the young it seems all too clear that the same devotion and self-sacrifice is not required of the elite.

In sum, these broader concerns for the future have generally fallen victim to the king's concern for elite control. Since his accession to the throne in 1961 Hassan II has been led, through the very success of his manipulation of elite elements, to strive for absolute negative control of its activities; negative control in the sense that each group is ground down to the merest shadow of itself to maximize royal control and surveillance of even its most trivial undertakings. The one force the king cannot afford to sap is that represented by the army and police. But here he must exercise his referee functions with the utmost skill. He is engaged in a dangerous game of juggling and balancing personalities who control the forces of order lest they turn against the throne.

Elite members have docilely accepted their reduced scope for action for they have found in it a certain satisfaction. They are able both to criticize the regime and to partake of it. Following independence, most nationalist politicians genuinely wanted and sought real collective responsibility for national policy. As the throne held them off and coaxed them into the royal stables one by one, they tacitly came to accept a total lack of individual or collective responsibility for national affairs, all the while protesting the contrary. They are too disillusioned to fight the regime themselves and too attached to its benefits to renounce it. Yet they hope that the memory of their rhetoric may tide them over the regime's possible demise.

CHAPTER EIGHT

CONCLUSION OF PART TWO

Instruct your children for they have been created for a generation other than your own.[1]

Having sketched out the political and economic relations that link the king and his clients, I will make a few tentative remarks on class aspects of the Moroccan political elite. I can provide no conclusive answer to the question of whether or not elite members represent an economic class in the sense that that term has been applied in Europe. The bulk of the Moroccan political elite is recruited from a broader social elite, the prestige and rank of whose members are defined by actual political power, locally or nationally, or by religious and cultural criteria, or by a combination of the above. The elite is not (yet) recruited, except secondarily, from a class whose power is rooted in material wealth, except insofar as any elite, in any political system, tends to be distinguished from the rest of society by a high standard of living.

It seems certain, nonetheless, that there is occurring a process of class development, a process that started with the broad commercial contacts with Europe in the nineteenth century and which gained momentum during the protectorate period and above all since independence. The phenomenon is particularly interesting in that it has been duplicated to some extent throughout the Middle East. It is a problem difficult to treat with regard to Morocco, for want of data, but class analysis will be of increasing relevance to an understanding of that country.

In the past, and to a considerable degree today, the transfer of material goods from one generation to another was an extremely precarious process. The political system, common to most Muslim empires, was predatory. The goods of court officials, administrators, retainers, protegés, and challengers were confiscated usually upon a subject's death but not infrequently during his lifetime also.[2] Beyond this, political instability, regional dissidence, drought, and the like, left but a circumscribed and fluctuating market for urban merchants. Only a few were ever able to participate in foreign trade and this only at the whim of the sultan. Thus, what stability there was in the personnel of the traditional elite was founded upon hereditary access to political office, the ability of a father to will to his sons the possibility to build their own patrimony.

With the development of widespread European commercial influence upon Morocco and the rest of the area, there came a new emphasis upon purely economic pursuits. Europeans during the nineteenth century were primarily interested in predictable access to the primary exports of the area and its consumer markets. Consular agents, trade representatives, and government officials encouraged regularized trade procedures and the sanctity of contracts. European states aided the central authorities to control dissidence and to do away with arbitrary dealings with both native and foreign merchants. As Europeans acquired land and enterprises they imposed procedures for their protection and transfer. During this period local rulers, trying to revitalize their domains, became indebted to European banks, and eventually turned over control of their finances to foreign managers. At the same time the capitulatory agreements, the protection system, and trade agreements opened up autonomous zones in which European and native interests were able to operate beyond the reach of the sultan. Many Moroccans suddenly discovered that they could make their money, buy their real estate and keep it. Agricultural land and flocks became lucrative investments as there was a relatively steady European demand for such produce. Immune to confiscation, a city-based landowning class began to develop by the 1850s in Morocco using the *khammas* system of tenant farming to work their fields.[3]

The association of land-owning and commercial interests continued throughout the protectorate period. The amount of capital pumped into Morocco in combination with the rewards bestowed by the administration upon loyal would-be moguls served to accelerate the definition of indigenous stratification, although the wealth accumulated was pale in comparison with the fortunes accumulated by the French magnates of Casablanca.

With independence, elements of the commercial elite of the cities and the rural notability moved into the places vacated by the French in the government and private sector. The throne, eager to form a class committed to the regime, allowed the elite to indulge its appetite for spoils, and within a decade a large privileged class developed. Its three major branches are fused through the thorough overlap in personnel and consist of an administrative elite (including the army) linked to private commercial interests, the commercial interests themselves, and a new land-owning class based on modern agriculture. In another decade we should know more precisely if stratification by economic level has superseded vertical family, religious, and tribal ties. It may be indicative of the general trend that despite a falling per capita income in Morocco, total expenditures on luxury goods have shown a steady annual rise.

For the moment it is hazardous to say more than this, and as regards the particular time period of this study, considerations of class are not of primary importance. The Moroccan political elite is not primarily recruited from an economic class, and what lines of class stratification may exist in Morocco today are clouded both by the continued weight of family ties in their dominant groups and by the fact that stability in wealth is as yet so novel a thing that few Moroccans have adapted their cautious behavior to it. The Makhzen is by no means above breaking the fortunes of any of its subjects for arbitrary reasons. Thus, the behavior of the elite can still best be understood as a result of its size, the patterns of interaction of its members, and its social origins; in short, as it has been presented in the preceding pages.

The Moroccan political elite has made no clear break with the social and political past of its country, and while much is new and changing in Morocco, the thread of behavioral continuity that runs through elite activities shapes to a significant degree the style, and ultimately the results, of the political process. The elements that make up the elite generate a good deal of friction, and the ostensible political animosity that results is deceptive. Tension and conflict in Moroccan society have long served as catalysts to group cohesion rather than group disintegration. Segmentation combined with shared interests – the interplay of animosity and dependency among units – is as evident in the political elite as in all other sectors of the society. Economic and family alliances pull together what political and geographic divisions would put asunder.

The behavior of the political elite reflects that of Moroccan society as a whole. Any given actor is constantly building alliance systems through obligations, debts, and patronage in the Moroccan version of contingency planning. The average Moroccan may not be an optimist, nor may he believe that he can control or chart his own destiny, but he is not a fatalist. His name, his wealth, his family, and his reputation are his patrimony which he seeks to defend, and in a cautious way, to augment. The elite member realizes that as a general rule an ostentatious and rapid growth of the patrimony of any one man or group will only arouse the fear and reaction of others.

Power is for defense, and defense is best assured by the group not the individual. A man without a group is a pariah, suspect, and an open invitation to violence. Groups form according to interests that individual members wish to defend, and group patrons justify their existence only so long as they continue to serve the goals of the alliance. Political disputes should not be pushed to the breaking point for that erases an option and closes a door. The rival someday may be in a position to influence the well-being of the group and it is imperative to have contacts with all rivals. Alliances are fluid, and personnel move easily from one to another or enjoy multiple membership. It is difficult to attribute political or programmatic coloration to most groups, and, because there is so little commitment to a political program involved, movements among them are not judged as morally reprehensible. Dogmatic stances are avoided, and the dogmatist is either acting or is a fool.

To maintain their clientele various elite factions must have access to the palace, the ultimate source of spoils and patronage. In turn the palace arbitrates, adjudicates and defines the rules for the competition for the goods that it distributes. The king is not a father figure, although he might like to be. Rather, his self-appointed role is that of arbiter and manipulator of the elite, not its leader. On the one hand he balances elite groups one against another, and, on the other, reminds all members of their basic identity as a group (or family) whose undeniable well-being is dependent upon royal munificence. The smallness and introversion of the elite are crucial to the throne's continued ability to divide it, manipulate it, and use it for its own defense.

Defensive manoeuvres and *attentisme* go hand in hand. Objective circumstances, no matter how compelling, seldom evoke fitting political actions. All members of the elite may in some way find a given situation deplorable but be unable to act singly or in unison to remedy it or exploit its existence. They await instead what might best be called the 'catalytic event'. There is no predictability, no logic to that symbolic happening which triggers some sort of elite response. The assassination of Farhat Hachad in 1952 was such an event, the kidnapping of Mehdi Ben Barka was not. The mid-air arrest of Ben Bella *et. al.* in 1956, and an innocuous circular of the Moroccan Ministry of Education in 1965, came close to triggering a mass response. Strangely, the exile of Muhammed v did so only after a lapse of several months. Elite members, rather than attempting to stimulate some sort of mass reaction, hang back inactive until some stimulus, independent of them and for that reason unforeseeable and uncontrollable, elicits some display of social discontent. Only then will elite members act, capitalizing on the popular ferment ready at hand.

The patterns of elite interaction described in the previous chapters are fragile and temporary. They are fragile because the elite has lost contact with the realities of Moroccan society and is probably incapable of coping with the problems of economic and social development. They are temporary because the composition of the elite and the context in which it operates is likely to change drastically in the near future.* Let us deal first with the fragility of the situation.

Political scientists have often described the difficulty with which the educated elite in various underdeveloped countries communicates with the illiterate hinterland. The general implication is that these men, bursting with ideas to revolutionize their backward societies, are unable to put their worthy and sometimes sound projects into effect for want of making them comprehensible to those whom they are designed to aid. But it may be that in some countries, regardless of the political form of the regime, the problem of communication is posed in a different manner. The elite, after spending a number of years in the rarefied atmosphere of the university at home or abroad, is jammed into the small world of the capital city where most personal contacts are with

* The judgments presented here will be developed in greater detail in chapter 16.

others of their own background. Their major source of information on what is going on in their society is one another, and they seem convinced that the fact of their birth in that society guarantees a profound understanding of it.* Unfortunately they lose touch and occasionally develop misconceptions concerning a population with which they can, indeed, no longer communicate. The elite often falls victim to stereotypes of their own society which, ironically, may have been learned abroad. Plans and projects are drawn up according to these stereotypes and misconceptions and understandably go awry in their application. Sometimes one is almost grateful that the elite has such difficulty in communicating with the masses, for the stolid lack of response on their part has left still-born many plans that should never have seen the light of day.

The homogeneity, smallness, and introversion of the political elite cannot be maintained for much longer, and the elite, as it has been presented, is temporary. Moroccan society has been characterized by balance between component parts, and that balance has been predicated upon a certain stability in the size of diverse groups. Rapid population growth upsets equilibrium at all social levels including that of the elite. The post-1956 emphasis on mass education combined with a veritable demographic explosion has pumped unprecedented numbers of Moroccans into all levels of the educational system. Education has been a key to elite status in the past, and it is unlikely that many of these youths will settle for anything less in the future. Moreover, the new aspirants will not have the common social background of the present elite, the nationalist movement means little to them, and it is improbable that existing alliance and obligation systems will be able to absorb more than a small number of them. Either the elite of today will ignore the future aspirants, and will as a result become obsolete, or it will attempt to absorb them and thus will change utterly its behavior, its size, and its nature. What Berque has said of the *taqbilt* is applicable to the political elite. It is a body that exists in and for itself, beyond whose internal order

* One would assume that leaders of the Mouvement Populaire, a party that claims to represent the peasant masses, would be acutely aware of rural problems. But in calling for a party congress in November 1966, these leaders totally forgot that it was ploughing time. As a result many of the peasants who were obliged to attend the congress did so with ill-concealed discontent. A small example symptomatic of a broader phenomenon of elite isolation.

. . . nothing remains but to recommence on other bases. They [the members] defend themselves to an absurd degree. All the resources of experience and ideas that emigration has gone so far to acquire, are employed to reanimate the old and imperfectable machine. In contact with the world, it cannot evolve. It persists or explodes.[4]

PART THREE

THE ELITE IN ACTION:
TENSION AND STALEMATE

CHAPTER NINE

THE SEGMENTATION OF THE NATIONALIST ELITE

In the following pages the reader will find an interpretive sketch of the politics of the first decade of Moroccan independence. It is not my purpose to treat all the major political events of that period, although most are touched upon. Rather, I have chosen for analysis a number of situations in the breakdown and formation of political groups in order to highlight the dynamics of segmentary behavior. The focal point of this sketch will be the political interaction of elite members with particular emphasis upon elite manipulation on the part of the palace.

Our immediate concern is the split in the Istiqlal Party, con-summated in 1959 but which had been brewing for three years prior to that. In effect, it signaled the coming apart of the nationalist elite into component groups, for the Istiqlal had for years been their rallying point. The party split left in its wake a diverse group of political factions ripe for the manipulative techniques of the palace, and it was the precondition for the king's present control of the elite. But more than that, the party split was the culmina-tion of a long period in which politically active Moroccans were asked to choose between rival leaders and factions, between contradictory policies, between a confrontation with the palace or subservience to its will. The choices were not for petty stakes, nor could many of them be reconciled or compromised. As indicated earlier, it is precisely such situations of either-or choice that Moroccans try to avoid. Thus, the breakdown of the Istiqlal provides us with a good example of Moroccan political behavior, and is, in its own right, an extremely important event.

When Istiqlali leaders prior to 1956 claimed that the party was the organizational reflection of Moroccan society as a whole, perhaps they did not realize to what an extent this was true. Five years of accelerated mass recruitment (1947–52), to which was added the arrest and exile of leaders at all levels of the party hierarchy between 1952 and 1955, served to produce on the eve of independence a party tenuously founded on a collage of disparate patronage groups, mutually ignorant of their relative strengths within the party, and for that reason mutually suspicious of one another. In three years of clandestine activity new leaders had come to the fore, the old had lost touch with the rank and file, while whole sections of the party were allowed to slip away into autonomous activity alongside groups that had been formed with no or very little Istiqlali guidance. The patchwork of political factions that emerged by late 1955 included resistance groups, a Liberation Army, a new labor union, as well as less overt subgroups within the Istiqlal who were for or against the Aix-les-Bains conference,* for or against the use of violence and terror in the nationalist movement, for or against the return of the king. For several months before and after the granting of independence, trials of strength, reprisals, and the settling of accounts were the order of the day within and among Morocco's political organizations, not least among the Istiqlal. The whole shaky, bickering coalition of Istiqlalis had held itself together to defend Moroccan sovereignty and to bring to an end the French protectorate, and it continued to do so in its quest for a homogeneous (i.e. all-Istiqlali) government. On paper the party was impressive, but it is indicative of its internal weakness that the king was able to challenge the party successfully in the formation of his first government. What the king must have feared above all else was that from the wrangling inside the party some leader or faction would gain the upper hand, regroup the remnants of defeated factions, and forge the party into an implement capable of controlling or challenging the throne. It seems apparent that from early on the palace realized that it would be to its advantage to promote the division of the Istiqlal by encouraging disputes among its leaders and by luring away its potential clientele.

On 25 January 1959 a large segment of the Istiqlal did in fact

---

* The Aix-les-Bains conference took place from 22 to 27 August 1955. The French delegation of five ministers was led by Prime Minister Edgar Faure. Most Moroccan political tendencies sent delegates to discuss the future of Morocco.

break away from the parent body, and the following September the split was consumated by the founding of the UNFP. More than any other political event, the split of the Istiqlal has determined the course of politics in independent Morocco. The palace indeed played some role in bringing it about, but in essence its role was marginal. Rather, the scission of the Istiqlal can be attributed to an internally-generated process of spontaneous segmentation. Both because of its historic importance as an event, and because of the insights it provides into the intricacies of Moroccan political behavior, I shall examine the split in detail.[1]

As is most often the case in Morocco, the political disputes involved in the breakdown of the Istiqlal were fought out among faction leaders. Despite public statements to the contrary, these leaders did not act as a result of popular pressures from their followers. Those who claimed that they did were merely trying to consolidate or improve their bargaining position *vis-à-vis* other factions. It is also typical of Moroccan politics that four years were required before these ceaseless manoeuvres for field position resulted in an open declaration of hostilities. Had it not been for a somewhat trivial consideration that will be treated below, this party in-fighting might have continued well beyond four years.

By the winter of 1955–6, Moroccans had begun to consider the Istiqlal not as a unified party but as a coalition of the UMT, the resistance, and the politicians who had organized the party after the Second World War. Although the politicians may have wished to subordinate the UMT and the resistance to the uncontested control of the executive committee, this was not possible in 1955 as a result of three years of discontinuous political leadership in the party hierarchy. Moreover, some politicians, not least 'Allal al-Fassi, wished to emphasize rather than mitigate the party's tripartite order.

It is extremely difficult to generalize about the basic causes of the split of the Istiqlal or to categorize the actions of the various participants. The research that has gone into this chapter has borne out time and again that there are as many motives for and interpretations of the scission as there were major actors. Doctrinal differences and age-group conflicts all figured in the process, but bitter personal rivalries and factors of pure chance render hazardous the grouping of actions according to objective criteria. Of the major contenders, 'Allal al-Fassi and Mehdi Ben Barka have been the most misrepresented. To outside observers they came to symbolize the 'old turbans' and the 'young turks'.[2] But 'Allal al-Fassi was not and is not the obscurantist conservative that some have described, nor was Ben Barka the uncompromising leftist so often depicted by French journalists. It is undeniable that *some* of the younger members felt that their future lay with the UMT and the resistance, but so, for a time, did 'Allal al-Fassi. It is also true that the old guard leaders were ill-prepared for the problems of independence, had no practical program to offer, and were satisfied with the oligarchic party regime, but so were most upper echelon Istiqlalis so long as they felt they had a fair chance to join the oligarchy. What was at stake from 1955 to 1959 was control of the party, and the antagonists were two loose coalitions of party clans, one relying on the UMT and resistance and the other on the patronage groups of the founders of the party. Individuals were constantly shooting off from either of these coalitions, and the boundaries between the two were never fixed. Fundamental programmatic issues at times served to delineate given factions; at other times wholly false issues, such as the internal democratization of the party, were given great play by various contenders, but were no more than devices to force the hesitant to choose sides and to build an acceptable public image for the challenging coalition.

The internal clans of the Istiqlal revealed themselves in the course of several meetings of resistance, union, and party leaders (all nominally Istiqlalis) held in Madrid during the winter of 1955–6 as well as at a party congress held at Rabat on 2, 3 and 4 December 1955. These meetings provided the first opportunity for faction leaders to confront one another and size one another up after the return from exile (17 November 1955) of Muhammed v. Groups of varying composition conducted a long series of *ad hoc* reunions – rump sessions of the party executive committee, certain leaders of the party and the resistance or of the resistance and the union, etc. – aimed at drawing up some sort of party program upon which all factions could agree for presentation at the first party congress. Resolutions adopted at the December 1955 congress and at the later Extraordinary Congress of 19 and 20 August 1956 were, where not actually contradictory, compromise measures arrived at for the sake of party unity.[3]

These meetings went far to create a crisis atmosphere in the Istiqlal, to emphasize the coalition nature of the party, and to set party members thinking not about their place in the party as a whole but their place in any or all of the party factions. Three fairly constant groups became apparent at this time. 'Abdarrahman Yussufi, and Muhammed (Fqih) Basri represented the urban resistance in party circles, while Mahjoub Ben Seddiq, Muhammed 'Abderrezak, Tayyib Bou'azza, and 'Abdullah Ibrahim represented the UMT. These two groups occasionally operated in concert, generally in opposition to the nucleus of the 'old turbans', Ahmad Balafrej, 'Omar 'Abdjellil, Muhammed Lyazidi, Ahmad Mekwar, and Muhammed al-Fassi. The bulk of important Istiqlali leaders, however, were floaters, committing themselves to no faction and somewhat suspect in the eyes of all of them. These leaders were 'Allal al-Fassi, Mehdi Ben Barka, 'Abdarrahim Bou'abid, Boubker Qadiri, and 'Abdulkrim Benjelloun. Two prominent Istiqlalis, Muhammed Laghzaoui and Driss M'hammedi, had, by the summer of 1956, greatly curtailed their party activities and only figured indirectly in the party in-fighting.

'Allal al-Fassi himself was in no small way responsible for much of the stage-setting that went on during 1955 and 1956. His role at that time can be understood only if we consider his peculiarly tenuous position in the party hierarchy. Between 1939 and 1946 al-Fassi had been in exile in Gabon, and in 1944, when the Istiqlal was founded, Ahmad Balafrej was made secretary-general of the new party. Si 'Allal had expected to be named president *in absentia*, but the leaders in Morocco merely conferred upon him the purely honorary title of *za'im* – entailing no functions whatsoever. The *za'im* was deeply offended, and judged, perhaps rightly, that he was being politely jettisoned by his former colleagues. His resentment centered on Ahmad Balafrej, whose urbanity and orientation towards European culture contrasted sharply with the Salafist zeal and Islamic pride of al-Fassi. Thus Si'Allal was a somewhat marginal figure in the party after 1947 and spent most of his time abroad, mainly in Cairo.

After the Egyptian *coup d'état* of 1952, most of al-Fassi's contacts in Cairo were with army officers who made plain their scorn for political parties and gave practical effect to their feelings by abolishing all of Egypt's parties by 1954. The example was not lost upon al-Fassi, but his international renown was founded solely upon his ties to the Istiqlal. Nonetheless al-Fassi quickly adapted to the Nasserist predilection for movements of armed liberation, and soon after the exile of Muhammed V in August 1953, he launched an appeal for terrorist activities against the French authorities in Morocco.[4] This first public declaration was followed by several more over the next two years. Meanwhile in Morocco, obscure leaders with disparate bands of urban resistants were undertaking sporadic activities, and in the Spanish zone plans were laid to form a rural army and to coordinate an uprising with the Algerians on 1 November 1954.* The internal organizers of the Moroccan resistance had no effective support abroad and no tried access to arms and money. Just as Morocco's first nationalists had launched their first campaigns in the name of the sultan, so did the first resistants seek international stature by proclaiming 'Allal al-Fassi honorary president of the Moroccan resistance. And, in fact, he was the sole Istiqlal leader to have condoned Moroccan terrorism.

Suddenly 'Allal was given an implement (or so it seemed to him) to boost his prestige with the Egyptians and to avenge the slights inflicted upon him by the leaders of the Istiqlal. The resistance would be his vehicle to some new form of political organization, one that could dominate an independent Morocco. He let it be known that it was his pronouncements in Cairo that had called the resistance movement into being, and that he was responsible for its operations. His major personal contact with the resistants was his cousin 'Abd al-Kabir al-Fassi, who acted as an arms procurer in Madrid. After the fall from grace of Ziyyad, the nascent resistance organization needed to find a new overall chief and there was talk of either 'Abdullah Ibrahim, who had been released from prison, or 'Abdarrahim Bou'abid taking over this post. But 'Abd al-Kabir al-Fassi was able to stave off either choice and promoted the candidacy of 'Abdulkrim Khatib who had aided him in his missions in Europe. In May 1955, after Khatib had visited the *za'im* in Cairo, 'Allal appointed him as his official representative in Morocco, in effect conferring upon him the status of chief of the resistance. What is particularly significant in all this is that al-Fassi's choice fell not upon party stalwarts, such as Bou'abid or Ibrahim, but upon a man whose attitude towards the Istiqlal was at best lukewarm. But the selection of Khatib is plausible if in fact al-Fassi was trying to move beyond the confines of the party.

* This project went awry when the local chief responsible for this army, Ziyyad, misappropriated most of the funds that had been collected to buy arms.

At the various meetings in Madrid mentioned above (p. 172), al-Fassi stressed the distinction between the Istiqlal, the UMT, and the resistance, assuming for himself the role of spokesman for the latter. At one point, during a rump session of the Istiqlal executive committee in late 1955 (with Bou'abid, 'Abdjellil, and 'Abd al-Kabir al-Fassi present), al-Fassi offered to form a common front with the Istiqlal and the UMT with himself as supreme leader of a three-legged coalition.* As a result it was al-Fassi as much as the 'young Turks' who prepared the psychological ambiance for the breakdown of the Istiqlal, and occasionally he evoked the tripartite image publicly: 'I have just attended a nationalist meeting *with all my comrades of the resistance, of the Army of Liberation and of the Istiqlal, as well as with my comrades of the UMT . . .*' (italics JW).[5] Moreover, al-Fassi did not bother to attend the Istiqlal's first congress in December 1955, and, but for two brief stopovers in Tangier, did not return to Morocco until August 1956.† Like the Tunisian Salah Ben Yussuf, al-Fassi stressed his identification with the *fellagha,* and his absence was designed to show his displeasure with those Istiqlalis willing to negotiate with the French before full independence had been granted. He may also have been hurt that Muhammed V had not appointed him to his first government. In any event he had tried to change horses in midstream, and by 1956 was a man without a sure place in the Istiqlal and rejected by resistance organizations which were, by that time, in the process of being absorbed or dispersed by the state. The uncontested leadership of 'Allal in the Istiqlal is a post-1959 phenomenon (of which more later) and not, as some would believe, a continuous fact from 1946 onwards. Between 1956 and 1959 'Allal al-Fassi was very much in limbo in the party, and, after having set the semantic stage for the split, floated among the contending factions, none of which were prepared to trust him.

Control of the party after independence was in the hands of

---

* At the very time al-Fassi was making these assertions in the name of the resistance, the original organizers were taking their distances from him because they had intended his presidency to be purely honorary, they resented his pretensions, and because his cousin, 'Abd al-Kabir, like Ziyyad before him, had been implicated in the misuse of resistance funds.

† Around March 1956 two Frenchmen on behalf of Resident-General DuBois were sent to Tangier to negotiate al-Fassi's return to the French zone. But al-Fassi, despite all assurances for his personal safety, refused to go.

another floater, Mehdi Ben Barka. He has consistently been identified as the leader of the 'young Turks' but only joined their ranks in the fall of 1958 after the old guard had relieved him of the editorship of the party's French weekly *Al-Istiqlal*. His genius for organization and his ceaseless attention to all aspects of the party's operation was crucial to binding this fragile structure together long enough to achieve an homogeneous Istiqlali government. His single-minded purpose was to make the Istiqlal the sole viable political organization in Morocco, and towards this end the party entered into an often bloody struggle to intimidate the other parties and to subordinate the Liberation Army and the resistance.[6] The assassination in June 1956 of 'Abbas Mass'idi, the field chief of the Army of Liberation in the Rif, the riots at Souk al-Arba' between followers of the Istiqlal and the PDI, the killing of Muhammed Ben Driss Laraqi of the executive committee of the PDI in May 1956, and numerous settlings of accounts in Casablanca, can all probably be attributed to this determined effort to subjugate all sources of potential political opposition to the party. These incidents served to arouse the suspicion of some of the older leaders towards Ben Barka who was, after all, a long-standing member of the executive committee. At the same time, because of his association with the old guard since 1944, the 'young Turks' did not regard him as one of their own. As they often point out, how could they trust a man who personally backed (in August 1956) the appointment of the ex-qaid Lahsan Lyoussi, a semi-educated Berber notable from Sefrou, as Morocco's first minister of the interior?* Or the man who, in his capacity of president of the Moroccan Consultative Assembly, had recommended to Muhammed v in 1957 that his son Hassan be officially designated heir apparent?

Ben Barka was not a dogmatist nor a doctrinaire leftist, although his methods were occasionally radical, his vocabulary characteristically Marxist, and his political concepts authoritarian. But once having defined an objective Ben Barka could be remarkably pragmatic in setting out to attain it. Although no elections were held in independent Morocco before May 1960, there was con-

---

* In an ironic twist, some of Ben Barka's most vehement opposition on this point came from the 'old turbans', particularly Muhammed Lyazidi who was so incensed at the thought of Lyoussi as minister of the interior that he threatened to resign from the executive committee.

stant talk of local elections from 1956 onwards. These elections, it was assumed, would pretty clearly delineate the relative political strengths of the various parties. Ben Barka wanted to be sure that the Istiqlal would triumph in these elections and thus strove to avoid an overt breach in party unity.

Certainly one of the general factors leading to the final split of the party was the question of its reorganization, a question that is inseparable from that of preparing the party for the promised local elections. The problem of reorganization was commonly discussed under the rubric of the internal democratization of the Istiqlal. Thus phrased, the issue was a canard. Ben Barka, confident of his own organizational prowess, was impatient of the haphazard methods of the party elders. He was in fundamental agreement with younger members of the UMT and the resistance that the role of the old guard should be curtailed and that leadership of the party should pass to younger elements. To further this goal, a political committee was set up after August 1956 that included representatives of the union and the resistance. It was suggested that this body would eventually become the supreme executive of the party and was rightly viewed by the elders as a challenge to their hegemony.[7]

Yet this ostensibly democratic move to give greater representation to the rank and file of the party was to some extent negated by Ben Barka. Again, in the summer of 1956, Ben Barka reaffirmed his support of the seventeen regional inspectors of the party and never in ensuing years altered his stance on their utility. But these men, it was claimed by the progressives, had become feudal barons, despoiling the populations of their regional fiefs and thus discrediting the party. It is true, as Ashford has noted,[8] that for many Moroccans the distinction between party cadre and civil servant was at times hazy in the early chaotic months of independence, and local party officials were able to exploit this confusion to their advantage. Party inspectors kept up a steady traffic in membership cards, intervened in court proceedings, put relatives on local payrolls, and sought to control local licensing and contracting. Their impositions were grudgingly accepted by many Moroccans for it seemed wise to be on the good side of an organization likely to dominate local and central government. This state of affairs did nothing to increase the popularity of the Istiqlal. It may well be that, as some of his followers claim, Ben Barka planned eventually to drop the entire system of party inspectors, but the fact that he was so slow in moving in this direction alienated some of the party militants. On the other hand, his vague loyalty towards the inspectors did not put them at ease, and they must have felt somewhat closer to al-Fassi and the elders in general than to Ben Barka.[9] When the scission finally took place, fifteen of seventeen inspectors remained with the old guard.* Ben Barka had tolerated their presence so long as they executed his orders and did not interfere with his personnel transfers, but his trust or misjudgment cost him dearly.

Ben Barka's objectives can be viewed on two levels. On the national level it was to make the Istiqlal the uncontested political force of Morocco, and he hoped to demonstrate its monopoly in the awaited elections. Nevertheless he was not prepared to accept just any Istiqlalis as candidates, and his second objective was to impose his leadership on the party in order to control the selection of candidates. By gradually installing loyal followers throughout the party organization he could bring the regional federations under his control. When discussions commenced in party circles of a party congress to be held in 1958, Ben Barka proposed that delegates be elected by the members of the regional federations. With his own men in charge of these local party elections, Ben Barka could be fairly confident that the delegates to the congress would support him and any proposals he might put forth. Of course the delegates would elect a new executive committee, and, if loyal to Ben Barka, might have wrought considerable changes in the oligarchy in place since 1944. The issue of internal democratization was thus a device by which Ben Barka could extend his administrative responsibility within the party to include the direction of party policy and program. The party in hand, he could see to the nomination of trustworthy candidates in the national elections. It should not be forgotten that national legislative elections were to follow the local elections, and that in 1957–8 the possibility of an elected constituent assembly had not been ruled out. The period was thus one of great expectations with much at stake. Ben Barka wanted the best possible position for the Istiqlal in these elections and for himself in the Istiqlal.

* 'Abdelhai Chami of Casablanca and Muhammed Habib of Marrakesh were the only two inspectors to follow Ben Barka. In addition sixteen local secretaries departed with the 'young Turks'.

The old guard realized that the scheduled party congress could turn out to be the source of a serious challenge to their leadership and therefore opposed Ben Barka's scheme of the election of delegates, suggesting some form of designation instead. Al-Fassi, it appears, was not as intransigent on this point as some of the others for he probably believed that he personally would not be unseated by the delegates. In any case the question of the organization of the 1958 congress became a central issue in the split, and in fact the congress never was held until after the departure of Ben Barka, *et. al.* Ben Barka was willing to force a breach in party unity on the problem of selecting delegates, for he was sure that no matter what the result of the dispute he would come out the winner. Either the principle of the election of the delegates would be accepted and his faction would triumph within the party, or the proposal would be rejected, provoking a split in which the great bulk of the party – UMT, resistance, students, educated cadre, and regional federations with or without the inspectors – would follow him.

None of the factions of the Istiqlal had a detailed program for the party, and one can speak only of differing political orientations and preferences. Despite the fact that the Istiqlal could not form an internal consensus upon the most desirable policies for Morocco to follow, all of its contending members were agreed upon the necessity of asserting its primacy in determining national policy at the expense of the monarchy. Just how this was to be done became a fundamental, if not the fundamental, programmatic issue in the party split. The party elders recommended, in essence, a course of moderation and patience in dealing with the palace. Party wishes should not be imposed upon the king. Moreover, the older members who had worked with Muhammed V since the 1930s believed that, sooner or later, they could bring him around to their way of thinking as they had done in the past. 'After all,' as one remarked, 'four centuries of despotism cannot be overcome in a day.'

The focal point of the differences between the party and the palace was the problem of ministerial responsibility, and the right of unilateral appointment and revocation of government officials possessed by the king. The party wished as a minimum to be consulted on the appointment of all ministers, and, optimally, to place an Istiqlali prime minister empowered to designate his own ministers. Second, the Istiqlal demanded that the ministers be given full responsibility for executing the programs of their departments, and that the prime minister be given effective control over the implementation of governmental policies.

Muhammed v during his lifetime took no steps to comply with the party's demands on this matter. His tactic, now practised by his son, was to express sympathy for party demands but to caution against moving too fast. The party delegations that he would receive were usually dominated by the old guard, and he was adept at putting them off, playing to their sentiments of loyalty, or insinuating that they were allowing younger elements to dictate to them. The 'young Turks' felt constantly frustrated at the executive committee's inability to take a stand against royal prerogative and accused various members of having fallen victim to royal 'feudalism'. The leaders of the UMT and the resistance were the most insistent upon the necessity of imposing restraints on the exercise of monarchical power. This appeared all the more necessary in the early years of independence in that Muhammed v was clearly cutting his ties with the Istiqlal and was encouraging the growth of rival groups to dispute the Istiqlal's pretensions to political dominance. Further, more militant members of the Istiqlal were alarmed at the king's control of the newly-formed army and the Ministry of the Interior responsible for the administration of the country. Even if dominant in any given government, Istiqlalis could not hope to form governmental policy in its entirety if control of that Ministry and the armed forces were to escape them. Without such control they would be helpless to liquidate the 'last vestiges of colonialism'; i.e. the hundreds of French officers remaining as advisors to the Moroccan army and police, the as yet formidable array of private French enterprises and landholdings, and the thousands of French school teachers and technical assistants. The anomaly of this massive French presence was all the more striking when it is recalled that France was doing all in its power to crush the Algerian rebellion with whose objectives the Moroccan government nominally sympathized. The *bête noire* of the 'young Turks' was Prince Moulay Hassan, whom they suspected of having instigated his father's hostility towards the Istiqlal and his temporization towards the French.

In April and May 1958, a governmental crisis occurred which provided the intransigents of the Istiqlal an opportunity to try to impose their views on the party and then upon the palace. They

failed in this attempt, and for all practical purposes entirely withdrew from party activities from then on. This marked the *de facto*
split of the Istiqlal. Before examining this crisis in detail, a brief
look at the actual members of the 'young Turks' is in order. These
men were 'Abdullah Ibrahim, Mahjoub Ben Seddiq, and Fqih
Basri, and while they may have represented a significant body of
opinion within the party, there were no other party leaders of their
stature in their faction. It is true that 'Abdarrahman Yussufi
strongly sympathized with them, but his chronic illness prevented
him from playing a very active role in their cause. Bou'abid and
Ben Barka were viewed as late-comers by this core, and suspicions
bred at this moment did much to poison relations among the
leaders of the UNFP after its formation. During the months
between May 1958 and the formal split of January 1959, both
these men attempted to conciliate the disputants. Ben Barka
wavered between the two principal factions until July 1958 when
he was removed from his post at *Al-Istiqlal*. From then on he
followed – but did not lead – 'Abdullah Ibrahim and the rest.
Bou'abid sought to smoothe over the differences within the party
right up to the time of the final parting of the ways.

The crisis of May 1958 was provoked by the resignation of the
prime minister, M'Barrek Bekkai on 16 April. Bekkai, a political
independent, had announced his sympathy for a motion submitted
to him by two non-Istiqlali ministers and signed by a number of
political personalities outside the government. The motion
protested that, with the approach of local elections, not all
Moroccans were allowed to organize freely in political associations
of their choice, and the signatories demanded a law to guarantee
these rights.* All the Istiqlali ministers† promptly resigned,
accusing Bekkai of having wilfully destroyed governmental unity
in failing to consult with all his ministers before acting.

What ensued was almost a full month of protracted negotiations
between the king and various politicians to form a new government. These weeks of governmental crisis sharpened the internal
divisions of the Istiqlal as it argued out its conditions for participation in future governments. Interminable meetings took place

---

* The motivations of the Bekkai resignation will be discussed fully in
chapter 11.

† The Istiqlal ministers were: Ahmad Balafrej, 'Abdulkrim Benjelloun, Driss
M'Hammedi, 'Abdarrahim Bou'abid, Muhammed al-Fassi, 'Omar 'Abdjellil,
Muhammed Douiri, 'Abdullah Ibrahim, and Ahmad Lyazidi.

at that time on both a formal and informal basis, and the principal actors can no longer recall the details of any particular session. Nonetheless one may trace with some precision the most significant encounters among party leaders.

On 19 April 1958, the Political Commission of the Istiqlal issued a communiqué which stated the party's conditions for the acceptance of further governmental responsibilities. The primary condition was a formal promise from the palace to approve a general policy consisting of these points:[10]

1 the consolidation of independence
2 evacuation of foreign troops
3 strengthening of ties among Maghreb states
4 the establishment of democratic institutions
5 social and economic expansion
6 an homogeneous government
7 permanent guarantees of public liberties
8 a fixed date for local elections
9 institution of a constitutional monarchy

The communiqué had been drawn up on the basis of a memorandum prepared by Bou'abid and Ben Barka. Ben Seddiq, Ibrahim, and Basri showed it to Balafrej, who approved it, and it was then submitted to the Political Commission which also approved it. The memorandum itself was more strongly worded and to the point than the public communiqué. It called for a dahir defining precisely the collective responsibilities of all future governments and the individual responsibilities of each minister. In a sense it was an ultimatum to the palace to limit voluntarily its as yet undefined powers or face the consequences of Istiqlali opposition. This memorandum was presented to the king on 22 April by an Istiqlal delegation consisting of Balafrej, al-Fassi, and Bou'abid.[11] The discussions with the king were stormy, particularly in regard to his right to appoint the ministers of the interior and defense without prior consultation with the Istiqlal. He said that the memorandum was no different from the ultimatums delivered by residents-general Juin and Guillaume.

After this unhappy encounter, more negotiations with the palace took place, and apparently upon his own initiative, the king called in 'Allal al-Fassi, Muhammed al-Fassi, and 'Omar 'Abdjellil to make an appeal to the party elders to talk sense to the 'militants'.

He reasoned thus. First of all, he sympathized with the demand that he give some definition to his own powers, but that for the good of all of Morocco he did not wish to appear to comply with this demand under Istiqlali pressure. Time, and a cooling of passions, would be needed before he could act. Moreover, he was adamant on his right to appoint the ministers of interior and defense. He pointed out that with local elections to be held, it would be far more orthodox and publicly palatable to have as minister of interior a neutral, beholden to no one but his sovereign. Nonetheless he was willing to meet the party halfway, and suggested Mas'ud Chiguer as minister of interior and Ahmad Lyazidi as minister of defense. Both men were reasonably friendly towards the Istiqlal.*

The old guard accepted the king's line of reasoning and announced to the Political Commission that they would be willing to serve in a government according to these new terms. Ben Seddiq and Ibrahim protested vehemently and accused the elders of having betrayed the Political Commission in ignoring the stipulations of the original memorandum. For the 'young Turks' this event demonstrated once again that the old guard was unable to resist the wiles of the palace and could no longer be entrusted with the leadership of the party. They emphasized that the tribal disturbances that had broken out in the Rif may have been encouraged by the king, and that if the party participated in a government in which it did not control the Ministry of Interior it could be seriously discredited by staged revolts. It was imperative therefore that the party put forth its own candidate for that Ministry, and they recommended that this man be Driss M'hammedi, the minister of interior in the previous government.

Bou'abid in this instance aligned himself with the old guard. He did not wish to prolong any longer a crisis that was paralyzing all governmental activity.† In addition, the king's point on the advisability of a neutral minister of the interior seemed sound. For

* Mas'ud Chiguer was one of the signers of the 1944 manifesto and had been a member of the Provisional Executive Committee of the Istiqlal between 1952 and 1955. He also was closely identified with the palace, having served in the first imperial cabinet in 1950 and as director-general of the royal cabinet after 1957. Ahmad Lyazidi, a former officer in the French army, is the brother of Muhammed Lyazidi of the executive committee of the Istiqlal.

† Let us note that it was precisely at this moment that De Gaulle was being brought to power by the French army in Algeria, and that this crisis was hardly an opportune moment for Morocco to traverse without a government.

that matter Bou'abid could not see any reason to provoke a break with the palace over the question of M'Hammedi or Chiguer. The latter at least was a known quantity; a loyal servant of the palace, to be sure, but not one to turn on his party. As for M'Hammedi, despite the warm advocacy of Ben Seddiq and Ibrahim, he was devious and perhaps insincere in his '*progressivisme*' of fresh date.[12] For these reasons Bou'abid was willing to accept a Ministry in the new government in the hopes that the king would make good on his promises. Ben Barka, after initially approving the new government, vacillated between the two fundamental points of view, at times minimizing the importance of Interior, and at others calling for limitations on royal power.

After most of the leaders had voiced their opinions on the crisis, a meeting was held in early May at which a vote was taken to determine who was for or against, as one member put it, 'la volonté royale'. Ibrahim, Ben Seddiq, Basri, and 'Abderrazak all voted against the acceptance of Chiguer as minister of interior. Only Bou'abid abstained, while many of the youngest Istiqlali leaders (see below, p. 189) voted with the old guard to accept Chiguer. Ben Barka was not present for the vote, having left on a visit to Tunisia. Yussufi was also absent, as he felt that all such meetings failed to reflect the base of the party and therefore had no representative quality. The representatives of the UMT and the resistance walked out of the meeting and from that time on cut all ties with the Istiqlal.

Immediately following the rupture, on 12 May* the Balafrej government was formed with Bou'abid as minister of national economy, and by that token the sole minister associated in any way with the 'young Turks'. The press of the UMT became increasingly severe in its criticism of the Balafrej government, and once Ben Barka had returned to Morocco, he cautiously, and after some hesitation, joined in the assault through the pages of *Al-Istiqlal*. In June Ben Barka reprinted a speech that 'Abdullah Ibrahim had delivered to the Jeunesse Ouvrière Marocaine in which he attacked the 'bourgeoisie' of the party.[13] The old guard was stung by this, and *Al-Istiqlal* ceased publication as of 22 June,

* A reliable source reports of having been personally informed by the then Prince Hassan, that on the eve of the formation of the Balafrej government Ben Seddiq and Ibrahim were received by the king. At this meeting, they told him that their stance in the recent crisis should not be regarded as a difference with the palace but as a difference among the leaders of the Istiqlal.

reappearing on 16 August with Muhammed Lyazidi as director. Lacouture suggests that the suspension of publication was carried out voluntarily by Ben Barka, who sympathized with Ben Seddiq and Ibrahim but was reluctant to attack publicly the leaders of his own party.[14] The team that eventually took over the newspaper was directed by Muhammed Boucetta and Muhammed Douiri.* Ben Barka's dismissal apparently ended his hopes of cooperation with the old guard with whom he had worked in the executive committee since 1944, and he threw in his lot, though not publicly, with the UMT and the resistance. Soon after the appointment of the Balafrej government a conciliation committee, consisting of 'Abdulkrim Benjelloun and Boubker Qadiri, was formed, but its efforts were futile.

Following the crisis of May 1958, 'Abdullah Ibrahim withdrew to his private residence in Casablanca, and on 5 June strikes were staged to symbolize worker discontent with the general situation. Summer in Morocco is traditionally the season of political doldrums, and, just as in France, the government grinds to a halt for the August holidays. In contrast, September is typically a month of political ebullience, triggered by the return to school (*rentrée scolaire*), the accepted cue for the renewal of hostilities. The fall of 1958 was no exception. The crisis lay in suspended animation during the late summer, but strikes were held in the early fall in solidarity with Ibrahim who, it was claimed, had been the victim of petty harassment on the part of the Casablanca police. Simultaneously, members of the Balafrej government, including the prime minister himself and Bou'abid, became increasingly aware that they were to be the scapegoats for the spreading tribal disturbances in the Rif. According to this interpretation Balafrej viewed his situation as untenable. On the one hand he was being attacked by a wing of his own party, and on the other was being discredited by internal disorders allegedly taking place to show rural displeasure with the Istiqlali government. Istiqlali offices in the north were closed down, and party officials were coming in for a good deal of local abuse. Yet Balafrej, with Interior beyond his direct control, could take no effective measures

* Muhammed Boucetta is a lawyer from Marrakesh and a former director of Ahmad Balafrej's cabinet in 1957 when the latter was minister of foreign affairs. Muhammed Douiri, from a modest family from Fez, a French trained engineer, is the son-in-law of Balafrej. Both men were members of the Political Commission.

to deal with the situation. During the summer and early fall there were informal contacts between Balafrej, Bou'abid, and Ibrahim. At one point Balafrej told Ibrahim that he would resign, and Bou'abid suggested that a ministerial reshuffle with the introduction of some members of the UMT-resistance faction might save the government. Ibrahim retorted that the horse was already out of the barn, and that the time for forming a government to face the tribal dissidence in the Rif had been in May not in September.

The old guard apparently came to the conclusion that it had been duped, and that the king was not going to live up to his promises of the preceding May.[15] Ibrahim's intransigence was thus vindicated, and discussions of the party congress were recommenced. On 25 September, a four-man committee reflecting the major currents within the party was set up, and the executive committee gave it full authority to work out arrangements for the congress. The members of the preparatory committee were Qasim Zhiri, director of Radio Maroc and a young member of the Political Commission; Muhammed Bennani, strongly identified with the old guard; Muhammed 'Abdarrazak of the UMT; and Muhammed Mansour of the resistance.[16]

The second governmental crisis of 1958 sealed the fate of the Istiqlal, and was brought on by the resignation of Bou'abid[17] from the Balafrej government, made public on 23 November 1958. In prolonged crises in Morocco, it becomes increasingly easy with time to destroy solidarity among individuals and groups as they manoeuvre for ministerial chairs and cabinets. It seems clear that during the weeks between 10 November and 23 December (at which time the Ibrahim government was formed), the palace dropped hints through various intermediaries to all factions that *it* might receive the royal nod in the formation of a new government. In retrospect, all faction leaders have accused the others of having fallen victim to the king's cajolery, and one may thus assume that all were probably approached by the palace. The king could hardly have failed to notice during the preceding six months of factional in-fighting that a divided Istiqlal facilitated the protection of his own prerogatives and that such division should be continued.

Bou'abid resigned because he could no longer tolerate Balafrej' hesitancy in dissociating the government from the revolts (by November the Rif disturbances had taken on the characteristics of tribal dissidence) in the Rif and Zemmour territory.[18] Balafrej in turn resigned in early December, and the king made three separate attempts to designate a new prime minister. In the process, personal animosities were rekindled and the tentative steps toward reconciliation taken in September came to nothing. Al-Fassi was consulted on the formation of a new government, but the 'young Turks' and, one might assume, Balafrej, opposed this solution. M'Hammedi was suggested by the king, but Balafrej likewise found him wanting.[19] Muhammed v then turned to 'Abdullah Ibrahim who agreed to the prime ministership on the condition that his government be empowered to carry out economic disengagement from France, prepare for local elections, and meet the legitimate grievances of the Rif tribes. Most of the old guard congratulated Ibrahim on his appointment, and 'Abdjellil hoped that he would try to bring all party factions into his government. Ibrahim replied that competence would be the sole criterion for his ministers, but that within that limit he would do his best. As a result 'Abdulkrim Benjelloun and Dr Yussuf Bel'Abbes were included in the new cabinet. Muhammed Douiri was offered a post, but his conditions were too stringent, and Ibrahim withdrew his offer. Neither Balafrej, who had played the spoiler throughout the crisis, nor any of his closest associates were in the new government. This was finally installed in office on 24 December 1958, and according to the wishes of both Ibrahim and the king had no party etiquette.

Al-Fassi, who had been ill and was resting in Tangier, came to Rabat to give Ibrahim his support, and he appealed for one last effort to salvage party unity. He suggested that both he and Ibrahim could appear together on 11 January 1959 (the fifteenth anniversary of the founding of the Istiqlal). Ibrahim agreed but felt that there should be a preliminary announcement of a party congress. Al-Fassi would not accept such a declaration, preferring to make first a symbolic display of unity. Neither man would agree to the other's terms, and about a week later al-Fassi allegedly attacked Ibrahim verbally in a closed meeting of party cadre in Rabat. To make matters worse, the preparatory commission for the congress had been inactive since the beginning of the crisis in November, and finally, on 11 January, 'Abderrazak and Mansour publicly declared that preparations were broken off when Zhiri and Bennani insisted upon the designation of one hundred 'notables' to the congress after having accepted the principle of the election of one delegate for each one thousand members. They claimed that this reversal had come at the instigation of Balafrej. On 14 and 15 January, Zhiri and Bennani replied, pointing out that after Bou'abid's resignation *Al-Tali'a* (the UMT weekly) had launched scurrilous attacks on the Balafrej government rendering all further meetings of the preparatory commission futile.[20]

Upon the formation of his government, Ibrahim realized that he was now in the same position as Balafrej a few months earlier, and that he in turn could expect to be attacked publicly by the conservative wing of the party.* With this in mind, Ibrahim and his followers considered for the first time the possibility and desirability of founding a new party. When in fact this occurred, on 25 January 1959, the new body was launched in the name of the Istiqlal: the National Confederation of the Istiqlal Party. Ben Barka, who had cut all ties with the 'old turbans' in November 1958, received most of the public credit or blame for the new organization as neither Ibrahim nor Bou'abid, because of their presence in the government, could openly associate themselves with it. Subsequently Ben Barka explained the move as follows.[21]

It is not a split that has been brought about but a clarification and a reconversion; an indispensable reconversion towards which we have worked for more than three years in order to transform the Istiqlal from the movement or *rassemblement* that it was into a structured, homogeneous, efficient party, capable of playing a role in the execution of the work of reconstruction.

The *de jure* rupture in the Istiqlal will be considered in more detail in the next chapter, but to complete this sketch of the split it is of some interest to note the *ad hoc* manner in which the militants moved from the Confederation to the founding of a totally distinct party, the National Union of Popular Forces (UNFP). According to Ibrahim the necessity of doing so only became clear during the winter of 1959. Al-Fassi returned from Tangier immediately following the founding of the Confederation in order to rally the faithful and to keep control of the regional structure of the party. In a series of communiqués he read out of

---

* In fact an 'independent' journal, *Al-Ayyam*, was started that persistently vilified the Ibrahim government. When Ibrahim was dismissed in May 1960, the last issue of *Al-Ayyam* signed off 'mission accomplished'.

the party those whom he regarded to be the principal offenders, starting with Ben Barka (but not Bou'abid or Ibrahim). In addition, he demanded that the rival faction be denied the right to use the title Istiqlal in any way and initiated legal procedings to this effect. Each time that the Confederation would attempt to open up a local office, the Istiqlalis would drag the issue into the courts. Various localities were devoting all their attention to these local squabbles, and Ibrahim was anxious to re-focus popular thinking on national problems.[22] With the constant repetition of similar events Ibrahim, Ben Barka, and their followers decided that a new party with a new name should be founded. After wading through the summer hiatus, September 1959 witnessed the establishment of the UNFP. Had it not been for the un-anticipated juridical problem however, the two factions might have wrangled on for several months more within the context of the old Istiqlal. Ibrahim and his tiny band had been unable to win the power struggle within the Istiqlal and were forced, perhaps to their own surprise, to abandon the old party and to start from scratch.

When it came time to choose sides, in the winter of 1958–9, a very interesting pattern emerged resembling a checkerboard alliance of generations. It helps explain one of the seeming enigmas of the split; the fact that a good number of Paris-educated Istiqlalis chose to remain with the old guard. Schematically the upper ranks of the Istiqlal looked something like this in 1958–9.

1 The old guard: Balafrej, 'Abdjellil, al-Fassi, and others.
2 The old guard *'jeunesse'*: Ben Barka, Bou'abid, Ibrahim.
3 Paris students of the late 1940s and 1950s in the Istiqlal: Boucetta, Douiri, Muhammed Tahiri, 'Abdulhafidh Qadiri, and others.
4 Paris students 1953–6, plus students who were lukewarm to Istiqlal.

Young Istiqlalis like Muhammed Tahiri and 'Abdulhafidh Qadiri, leaving aside possible enticements from the palace or the old guard, chose to remain with the founders of the party. When in Paris they had been leaders of the Istiqlal student organizations there and were dismayed when those who had preceded them in Paris, such as Bou'abid, passed them over in staffing Ministries and personal cabinets after 1956. Though there was a certain

amount of intellectual indentification between these two consecutive generations of Moroccans in Paris, there had been little
actual contact. One finds the old guard 'jeunesse' giving prominent
positions in the first governments to the likes of Mamoun Tahiri,
Meyer Toledano, Muhammed Lahbabi, and Muhammed Tahiri,*
all of whom played minor or negligible roles in the Istiqlal in Paris.
Ben Barka also made a play for the youngest Istiqlalis, those still
in Paris at the time of independence and after. The net result was
the old guard (no. 1) allying with the Paris nationalists (no. 3), and
the old guard 'jeunesse' (no. 2) allying with the non-Istiqlali Paris
students (no. 4). Many members of no. 3 remained with the old
Istiqlal not out of respect for the elders but out of resentment of
the 'young Turks' with whose programs they were in accord.
Subsequently the old guard publicized the number of young
Istiqlalis who had rejected Ben Barka and Ibrahim, for their
continued presence in the Istiqlal tended to refute the claims of the
UNFP to represent educated youth.[23] It should be noted that
certain members of generation no. 3 were given added incentive to
stick with the old guard by the prospect of moving up in the party
hierarchy once the old guard 'jeunesse' had bolted or had been
driven out. These young men formed a determined core, generally
associated with Balafrej (and to some extent with Prince Hassan)
and perhaps felt the oncoming rupture to be to their advantage.†
In addition, it is important to note the existence of a 'zawiya' of
young agricultural engineers who had begun their careers with the
encouragement of Morocco's first native agricultural engineer,
'Omar 'Abdjellil. Besides 'Abdulhafidh Qadiri and Muhammed
Tahiri, this group included Muhammed Brik, Nureddin al-Ghorfi,
'Abdulhaq Tazi,' Abdelhadi Sbihi, 'Abdullah Bekkali, and others.
Their obligation and loyalty to Abdjellil probably influenced their
decision to remain with the old guard.[24]

Since the breakdown of the Istiqlal in January 1959, periodic
attempts have been made to patch over differences, but what had
started as a power struggle among reduced numbers of elite

---

* I am talking of two men named Muhammed Tahiri. One, a Paris-educated
Marxist, went on to be *chef de cabinet* of Bou'abid and today is in exile. The
other, a Paris-educated agricultural engineer, went on to become director of the
National Office of Irrigation (ONI) in 1960 and stayed with the old guard after
the split. The two are cousins from Fez.

† The best known members of this subclan were: Douiri, Boucetta, Zhiri,
Mehdi 'Abdjellil, and 'Amin Benjelloun. Douiri is the son-in-law of Balafrej.

members took on a life of its own among the rank and file of the Istiqlal and the UNFP who became involved only *after* the split. Elite members learned that, while it may be tactically attractive to conduct their internal in-fighting in the name of the Moroccan masses, once involved the momentum of the latter is hard to reverse. The most notable attempt at rapprochement occurred in 1963 and 1964, at the time of the legislative elections and the parliamentary sessions. In the winter of 1963, a Syndicat National de la Presse Marocaine was the meeting place for journalists from both parties, and in the elections of the following May both agreed not to run their strongest candidates in the same electoral districts. But more cooperation than this was unfeasible as a few months earlier the two parties had been diametrically opposed on the question of the constitutional referendum (12 December 1962). All the violent attacks of the preceding three years could not be quickly forgotten nor could rapprochement be easily explained to the followers of either party. Nonetheless tentative steps were undertaken in this direction, particularly when it became evident that if the representatives of the Istiqlal and UNFP came to a working alliance in the Chamber of Deputies they could control that body. In this vein *Al-Istiqlal* lamented:[25] 'Then they wished to trap us in a dialectic which is completely alien to us: overnight we were baptized by a certain press – you the left, we the right, when in fact nothing of an ideological nature separates us.'

Apart from the king, the greatest beneficiary of the split of the Istiqlal was 'Allal al-Fassi. His precarious position within the Istiqlal has already been discussed, but it was to him that fell the task of holding the party together after Ben Barka and Ibrahim had provoked the split. There is no gainsaying the skill and energy with which he accomplished this task. In the process Balafrej, his old rival and not the activist the situation required, was entirely eclipsed. Most of the old guard wilted in the crisis, and al-Fassi took over uncontested leadership by default. His hour of real glory came at the party congress that was finally held at the birth-place of the Istiqlal, Fez, 8–10 January 1960. His long analysis of the split is an important political document: it is his victory speech in the midst of his party's defeat. After the congress he was no longer simply the *za'im*, he was the President of the Istiqlal.[26]

The UNFP accused the Istiqlal of archaic leadership, lack of ideology, and bourgeois prejudices. Al-Fassi set about to restore his party's image and to counter the charges of the scissionists. On all points the Istiqlal has undergone a significant transformation as a direct result of the split. Morose members of the UNFP, disillusioned over the present state of their own party, complain that their greatest service has been to the Istiqlal which the split saved from atrophy. Considerable changes have been wrought in the executive committee for instance. The old guard is still represented there in force, but their direct participation in party affairs has dwindled. Balafrej by 1962 had ceased all contacts with the party, and the post of secretary-general was incorporated into that of the presidency. In contrast, at the party congresses of 1962 and 1965, young French-educated Istiqlalis were elected to the executive committee. Prominent among them are Douiri, Boucetta, Abdulkrim Fellous, 'Abdulhafidh Qadiri, Muhammed Brik, and 'Abdalhaq Tazi.[27]

A party program based on 'Islamic socialism' has been developed in the past few years. It is vague but iterates all the fashionable causes: land reform, nationalization of key industries, administrative reform, universal education, Arabization, etc. 'Abdulhamid 'Awad, a young economist educated in Cairo, has fleshed out the bones of Istiqlali socialism and has lent it credible economic analysis.[28] Al-Fassi has on occasion promoted Islamic socialism with passion. In a speech to the 1965 party congress, the *za'im* purported to show that Islam contained within it the elements of socialist doctrine and quoted al-Afghani approvingly:[29] 'O miserable peasant, you cleave the heart of the earth to grow that which sustains you and to provide for your family; why then do you not cleave the heart of your oppressor? Why then do you not cleave the heart of those who devour the fruit of your toil?' Statements like the above do little to endear al-Fassi to his age peers who are still unabashed bourgeois, but they have bowed to his judgment thankful that there is still an elder with the energy necessary to run the party. The commercial bourgeoisie of the party may privately deplore al-Fassi's new programs, but they continue to finance it, although on a reduced scale. Such affiliation improves their bargaining position *vis-à-vis* the government, and were the party to return to power, they would be rewarded for their loyalty.

The Istiqlal remains the hybrid it has been since its founding. Active leadership breaks down into the Paris-educated (Douiri,

Qadiri, etc.) and those educated in Arabic. The latter are grouped about the party's Arabic daily, *Al-'Alam*, and include Boubker Qadiri, 'Abdulkrim Ghallab (editor of *Al-'Alam*), Larbi Messari, Mustapha Sebbagh (d. 1966), and Hashimi Filali.[30] Such an arrangement permits reasonably effective communication with the party's two major sources of clientele: members of the governmental administration, private commerce and university students (largely French-speaking), and the rural populations, and the artisans and petty bourgeoisie of several cities (mostly Arabic-speaking). Young or old, progressive or conservative, the party leadership remains urban in origin, often coming from the well-to-do or learned families of Fez, Rabat-Salé, Meknes and Marrakesh. The party's audience has probably not increased since the split, but, despite predictions to the contrary, it has managed to keep intact its following as proved in the 1963 elections.[31]

In concluding this presentation of the split of the Istiqlal I shall make a number of generalizations that seem to corroborate points made in earlier chapters. First, the very nature of the Istiqlal in 1956 was typical of Moroccan social and political organizations in general. It was not a party of individuals joined together according to some sort of concensus on desirable political activity. It was instead an agglomeration of groups which had integrated themselves into the Istiqlal *as groups*, and with purely defensive objectives in mind. The three main groups were the founding politicians, the UMT, and the resistance, but these in turn were divided into subgroups or clans. The latter represented clientele linked to a specific patron such as Balafrej, Ibrahim, or 'Abdjellil.

The breakdown of the Istiqlal brewed for a period of three years (1955–8) before resulting in an open break (May 1958). The open break continued for another eight months before becoming final (January 1959), and the *de jure* break did not reach its logical conclusion, the founding of a new party, until eight months after that (September 1959). Crises in Morocco seem interminable and to speak of crisis at all is misleading. Once again we come up against pervasive tension and friction balanced by a curious immobility. The actors move ponderously, their gestures violent but in slow motion. Most of the actors do not want to be forced to choose sides, and the 'young Turks', initially Ibrahim and Ben Seddiq, could not provoke a movement in their direction – or in any direction – even among their sympathizers. Warm support and promises were of little value, for the neutral participants were distributing them liberally to all the contenders. The faction leaders realized this and were wary of any bold initiatives lest they be left in splendid and impotent isolation. Ibrahim's exit from the party in May 1958 almost resulted in just such a disaster. Moreover, because the Moroccan politician is generally the patron of a clientele group or alliance system, he is more adapted to the kinds of defensive actions inherent in protecting his group's interests and is awkward in taking those dramatic forward steps necessary to see a crisis through to its end.

When confronted with an either-or situation many Moroccans prefer to withdraw. In the months preceding and following the scission of the Istiqlal almost massive withdrawal took place.[32] A victim of this trend was the National Consultative Assembly, designated by the king in 1956 and presided by Ben Barka. All parties, as well as all factions of the Istiqlal, were represented in this seventy-six man body. As the tension mounted among the Istiqlal leaders absenteeism became more and more prevalent within the Assembly. After April 1959 the Assembly never met again.[33] After the split numerous personalities quickly or gradually withdrew from active politics, and by 1962 the following were inactive: Ahmad Balafrej, 'Abdulkrim Benjelloun, Ahmad Tayyibi Benhima, Muhammed Tahiri, Muhammed Laraqi. It was also as a result of the split that many young Jews associated with Ben Barka became political dropouts.

It bears reiteration that the power struggle among the Istiqlal leaders often hinged on personal animosities. Ideological and programmatic disputes tended to be pretexts for, not the causes of, the scission. It is therefore not surprising that those who accepted to choose sides often did so out of loyalty to their patrons rather than out of ideological commitment. Patronage systems and debt alliances came into full play here.[34] For public consumption, of course, all contenders maintained that they were striving to act in the public interest, and that their actions were dictated by popular pressure. But it seems clear that when the factional bickering spilled over into other cities and the blad from Rabat and Casablanca, the local populations involved found the whole crisis distasteful and meaningless and simply 'turned off'. Party cadres to some extent chose sides in the dispute, but the people they ostensibly represented did not budge. Thus the fact that one faction controlled so many inspectors and secretaries and the other so many more was of little import.

The Istiqlal was the most formidable political force facing Muhammed v in 1956. It undeniably included within it the great majority of Moroccan nationalists whatever the mode they had chosen for their actions. Some sort of conflict between the palace and the party was inevitable as the former did not intend to diminish its powers, even in defining them, and the latter, while bearing no malice toward the king, wished to limit the range of his activities. For three years the monarchy was on the defensive, cautiously watching and quietly encouraging the Istiqlal to break up under its own weight, all the while keeping careful control over the army, police, and local and regional administration. The split of the Istiqlal prepared the way for a royal offensive, a gradual subordination of all governmental activity, directly and indirectly, to the palace. Hapless and helpless elite clans have witnessed this process, but, because of old animosities, have been unable to coordinate their resistance. The euphoria and high hopes of the early years of independence have been dissipated, and political actors have come to accept the fact of their own corruptibility. Disillusionment and a cynical quest for spoils now characterize elite behavior, and both traits nicely facilitate the divisive tactics of the palace.

CHAPTER TEN

THE ELUSIVE CLIENTELE OF
THE LEFT

Commentators of Moroccan politics have often singled out the
UNFP as the party of the future. This judgment is based upon
estimates of the UNFP's potential and actual clientele. Because its
program is designed to redress Morocco's economic and social ills,
the UNFP seeks out its followers among those whom it feels are
most aware of the country's problems: laborers, peasants, the
unemployed, and 'enlightened' intellectuals who are the party's
and the nation's 'vanguard'. Taken as a whole this audience may
be conceived as those Moroccans who have broken with old social
patterns and are in the process of adjusting their lives to the
requirements of a modern society. Obviously the inhabitants of
various geographic areas of Morocco experience the problems of
adaptation with varying intensity. Many regions, the most isolated,
or those whose minimal prosperity affords them the luxury of
rejecting 'detraditionalization', remain remarkably unaffected by
the process of modernization. These regions do not for the moment
interest the UNFP for the returns upon any efforts expended upon
them will be meagre. UNFP attention has been fastened upon those
sectors of society that, as identifiable social groups with distinct
characteristics, are the fastest growing and, at the same time, the
most affected by industrialization, urbanization, education, and
bureaucratization. Finally, it is presumed that these sectors are
the most highly politicized and the most responsive to leftist
programs. If indeed Morocco is to become a modern nation, the
UNFP's potential clientele, it is believed, will be preponderant in the
political and economic life of the country. In this chapter the
clientele of the UNFP will be analyzed according to its most salient
social categories: labor, urban migrants (subsumed within this

category will be a discussion of the Moroccan resistance), bureaucrats, and students. My purpose here is to make clear the treacherous terrain upon which the UNFP, or any future party of the left, must operate. This approach is an admitted digression from my immediate concern with elite behavior, but it is requisite to an understanding of the crisis that divided the elite members who founded the UNFP. The following chapter will be devoted to reconstructing the process of fragmentation of UNFP leadership and the party's resultant paralysis. The nature and likely future of UNFP clientele, as well as the party's capacity to organize it, should emerge from this analysis.

1 The Urban Masses

The leaders of the UMT had been in the forefront of the campaign against the old guard of the Istiqlal, and in the newly formed UNFP they and their organization represented the majority of the party's followers. Starting in 1948, Moroccan nationalists had begun to infiltrate the Union Générale des Syndicats Conféderés Marocains (affiliated to the French CGT), and in 1950 displaced the French leadership when Tayyib Bou'azza became secretary-general. After the assassination of Farhat Hachad in December 1952, the union called a general strike that resulted in the imprisonment of Bou'azza and Ben Seddiq. The two were released on 28 September 1954, and on 5 January 1955 founded the Comité d'Organisation pour le Développement du Syndicalisme Libre au Maroc. They followed this move with the creation of the UMT, on 20 March 1955. The protectorate authorities took no measures to curb this activity.[1]

Until 1960 the UMT was Morocco's sole labor and trade union confederation. In that year the Istiqlal organized a rival union, the Union Générale des Travailleurs Marocains (UGTM). Since then all other Moroccan political parties have followed suit but with scant success. The UMT has remained the strongest confederation numerically, and by far the best organized. It is difficult to give membership figures in the UMT with any assurance. At the time of independence, with everyone on the band-wagon, the UMT claimed an impressive 650,000 members, a figure which the union feels has remained constant ever since.[2] Two-thirds of this number is supposedly made up of unionized peasantry and agricultural labor. However, rural labor has proved to be relatively impermeable to UMT efforts, and rural organizations exist more on paper than in reality. Just after independence, when membership was at its peak, farm workers may have been attracted to the UMT for that was a time for all Moroccans to join something. One specific example may be indicative of this initial surge and the subsequent ebb in union membership. Grigori Lazarev, in his studies of the pre-Rif north of Fez, found that in a sample of 563 regularly employed agricultural laborers in 1965, 23 per cent were in fact unionized, 45·2 per cent had been but quit, and 31·8 per cent had never been unionized.[3]

I shall discount rural farm labor and peasantry as of marginal importance to the UMT, and UMT leadership seems tacitly to have done likewise. The real heart of the UMT is made up of twenty-six national federations formed on an occupational or industrial basis, which in turn represent forty-seven local unions. A generous estimate of membership in the federations is 250,000.[4] But a part of this membership is to some extent suspect in the eyes of UMT organizers. The civil servants and the 'intellectuals', organized in ministerial unions or federations such as the Fédération de l'Enseignement National, have proven to be of dubious reliability and predictability. The unionized bureaucrats have, in addition, become a sore point between the divided leaders of the UNFP and UMT, a problem which will be discussed further on. Thus the core of the UMT is the industrial labor force. The economic stagnation of Morocco since 1956 makes hazardous conjectures of the total size of unionized industrial laborers. As of 1964, eleven hundred industries in Morocco provided regular employment for seventy thousand persons, and another sixty thousand are employed seasonally in the food-processing and fibre industries.[5] Without any claims to exactitude and simply to indicate the order of magnitude, I shall put forward a figure of 110,000 permanently unionized UMT members.*

What is particularly worthy of note here is the ratio of employed to unemployed. It is estimated that unemployment in Morocco, strictly speaking a phenomenon of the urban centers, is at a level of 22 per cent of the active city population. In absolute terms, as

---

* This figure is arrived at by adding seasonally and regularly employed – i.e. 130,000 – and subtracting a very rough estimate of those belonging to other unions, perhaps 20,000.

of 1964, this meant that there were 227,000 Moroccans out of work, and 50 per cent of these had been without employment for twelve months or more.[6] Thus for every Moroccan industrially employed there are nearly two seeking jobs. This ratio is most striking in Casablanca, which houses 43 per cent of the entire Moroccan labor force, but where there are upwards of 100,000 unemployed.[7] The implications of this situation are fairly clear. Unionized labor in Morocco represents a distinct elite, and one that is extremely vulnerable. Despite any inclinations to the contrary, union leaders are obliged to be cautious in formulating their demands, for employers, state or private, can easily replace men that have been laid-off or fired for unwarranted union activities. As is often the case in countries with high rates of unemployment, unions tend willy-nilly to center their demands on job stability and job security.[8] When a union is associated with a political party, as the UMT is with the UNFP, conflict between the two inevitably arises over the desirability of involving union members in political strikes. The abortive strike of December 1961, to be discussed below (pp. 221–3), brought this latent conflict to a head among the leaders of the UNFP.

The urban masses, whether recent migrants from the blad or more long-standing city-dwellers, cannot be understood without taking into consideration the fundamental conflict of interest between the employed and unemployed. All Moroccan unions are confronted with this problem, and as long as the economy proves unable to absorb surplus labor, Moroccan unions will be limited in their attempts to make inroads into the steady flood of migrants to the cities. Unions are tempted to try to tap this ample clientele, but being jobless it is virtually impossible to organize it. At the same time it constitutes the greatest threat to the job security of the rank-and-file to whom the unions are ultimately responsible. W. H. Lewis has suggested that unions in North Africa may provide a new framework for reorganizing the lives of migrants to the cities, providing a rock in the storm for those obliged to abandon villages and tribes undergoing a process of social breakdown.[9] But this possible function of unionism will be fulfilled in Morocco in direct proportion to the absorptive capacity of the unions, which at present is constricted by the inability of the economy to generate new jobs for the migrants.

The *bidonvilles* of Morocco are the receptacles for migrants to the cities, and, as the dwelling-place of thousands of displaced, unemployed individuals, have been cited as a breeding ground of likely recruits for radical political movements. Such a view requires considerable modification for implicit in it is the assumption that the denizens of the *bidonvilles* constitute a proletariat in the European sense of the word. As we shall see, this is not the case. Contemporary analysts, while justifiably impressed by the lack of social structure among the urban masses – implied in the term 'uprooted' – do not seem to take into account that this uprootedness has been a common condition in Morocco for a century or more. Miège documents the process of urbanization beginning in the 1830s and devotes particular attention to the massive migration to coastal cities after the famine of 1850. Between 1832 and 1866, the populations of Moroccan seaports grew by the following amounts:[10]

	1834–6	1866–7
Rabat	22,000	26,000
Safi	800	1,100
Larache	2,500	5,000
Tangier	7,500	12,000
Mogador (Essaouira)	10,000	16,000
Mazagan (Al-Jadida)	800	4,000
Casablanca	700	6,000

In 1895, Dr Weisgerber found the Tnaker quarter of Casablanca to be 'composed almost exclusively of *nuwala* [straw huts] swarming with the native proletariat from neighboring tribes or the Suss'.[11] The *nuwala* are simply a rustic forerunner of the *bidonville*, and burgeoning rural centers of today, like Settat or Khemisset, have clinging to them slum areas of *nuwala* in the same manner as Casablanca seventy years ago.

There is then reason to treat with care these symbols of social ferment: rural exodus, unemployment, *bidonvilles*. They are not exclusively the products of the process of modernization although they have been all undeniably accentuated in recent decades.[12] Perhaps there is a tendency to exaggerate social change from both ends, so to speak. On the one hand it could be that traditional social institutions are assumed to be more binding on the individual, more ubiquitous, than they actually were or are. On the other hand, the very real social transformations going on today are too often depicted as totally new departures for which no previous experience provides a precedent. If indeed many Moroccans are uprooted today, they probably always have been to some extent, and if traditional institutions of Moroccan society are gradually decomposing, the process has been at work for longer than one would imagine.

The contours of the rural exodus are most easily discerned in Casablanca, and in 1950 19 per cent of the city's population lived in *bidonvilles*.[13] The migrants come from the east and south of Morocco, with the Chawia and Doukkala plains, because of their proximity to the city, supplying upwards of 40 per cent of all migrants.[14] There are of course many factors that lead to the exodus: crop failures, drought, severe land fragmentation obliging certain members of extended families to emigrate, local disputes of all kinds but often with local authorities, the amenities of the city such as schools and higher wages, and the glamour of the city.[15] In this period 1936–52 (two census years) Morocco's rural population grew by about 1,500,000. Of this 700,000 remained in the blad, 300,000 emigrated to relatively prosperous rural centers, and 500,000 moved to the cities. In that same period Casablanca alone increased its native population by 288,000. Although not all that number can be attributed to rural migration, it is certain that Casablanca did receive the great majority of the migrants.[16] It continues to do so today.

Although some migrants remain permanently in the city, the exodus is generally temporary. Merchants from the south shuttle back and forth between their wives and fields in the Suss and their shops in the north. Inhabitants from the plains may bring their entire family to the city but will often return to the blad for harvests or maintain a lot there to supplement their incomes earned in the cities. Oasis dwellers move north during unfavorable agricultural years and return south when the rains come. Another facet of the exodus is the seasonal migration. The population of Safi, for instance, fluctuates wildly on a seasonal basis (sometimes growing from a base of 80,000 to 120,000 in a given year) when peasants flock in for work in the sardine canning industry, or, during the school year, to place a child in school.[17] Thus contacts with the countryside remain frequent. Relatives visit the emigrant in the city, and he periodically returns to his home for weddings, circumcisions, and the like. More important, he returns at harvest time to make sure that he receives his fair share of the produce of land which his father may have left undivided among his sons. Along these same lines Adam estimates that 65 per cent of the inhabitants of the Casablanca *bidonvilles* return to their homes to find a suitable wife, and that of these the majority marry their cousins.[18]

Though fragile, these links with the traditional world are seldom broken. Despite constant contact with industrial society and modern urban culture the impact on the behavior of the individual migrant, as well as upon his community of origin with which he is in frequent contact, has been remarkably light. He does not break definitively with his upbringing, his childhood period of socialization, nor does he totally reject or defect from his rural culture.[19] The continuity with his social past is not without political significance for the inhabitant of the *bidonville*. He is not the political radical, the alienated proletarian that some would see in him. In fact he may be politically docile, or, if not, he rejects authority in ways common to the rural world. Moreover, it should not be overlooked that not only is he likely to be unemployed it may be that he has *never* been regularly employed. On this score also he fails to live up to the proletarian ideal.* Finally he is, in most phases of his daily life, at the mercy of the state. His shack, according to municipal ordinances, does not legally exist and is by definition temporary. If he is a peddler he depends upon the good will of the police to overlook the fact that he has no license or to keep the one he has. As a veteran or former resistant he depends on a meagre state pension for all or part of his income. If employed he wishes to keep his job at all costs. Certainly he is capable of violence and protest, as the March riots of 1965 amply demonstrate, but his protest is brief, unguided, and formless. He is not a man with nothing to lose. The *bidonville* is more attractive to him than the blad. Graphic evidence of the political timidity of the *bidonvilles* was provided in the constitutional referendum of December 1962. The UNFP had actively campaigned for a boycott of the referendum, but the 'popular masses' of the slums of Casablanca voted more heavily for the proposed constitution than did the

---

* There are 85,000 Moroccans employed in Europe, mostly in France, and the continent is now beginning to cut back the number of foreign workers in Common Market industries. If one day the Moroccans are forced to repatriate, *they* could form a very troublesome proletariat for they will find no work.

city's well-off districts.[20] From all this one may gather that the UNFP probably does benefit from the unexpressed sympathies of the urban dispossessed, but that such sympathies only rarely lead to active support and commitment.

2 Urban and Rural Resistants

Elements of the resistance and the Liberation Army were considered as one of the three major parts of the Istiqlal after independence. While there were significant differences in the personnel of the urban terrorist groups and the rural army, the field leadership of both organizations[21] was in the hands of men of rural origins, often migrants to the cities, often from the south. They point up the fact that the city migrants are not uniformly apathetic and incapable of political action. These men represent the rural *jacquerie* mentioned in chapter 6, and they defy political classification. They favor violent measures but are not by that token revolutionaries. Morocco has traditionally yielded up a strain of such men; agitators without a program, often semi-literate products of Quran schools who feel the need to act and are able to convince others to follow them. The UNFP has tried to build an image of the leaders of the resistance as conscientious revolutionaries striving to end the oppression of the masses, but the resistants themselves failed to live up to their billing, depriving the UNFP thereby of what was to be its activist arm.

The leaders of the resistance, urban and rural, consisted of two groups, one for the procurement of arms, finance, and support abroad, and the other for the training, organization, and execution of terrorist and military operations in Morocco. The first group was dominated by educated members of the urban bourgeoisie, and the second by the above-mentioned rural migrants, although Basri among these served in both capacities. The external team's most important members were 'Abdallatif Benjelloun, 'Abdarrahman Yussufi, 'Abdulkrim Khatib, 'Abd al-Kabir al-Fassi, Ziyyad, Ghali Laraqi, Mehdi Ben 'Abboud, and Hussein Berrada. The members of the internal team were more numerous, but outstanding among them were 'Abbas Mess'idi, Hassan Laarej, Muhammed Meknassi, 'Abdullah Senhadji, Boucha'ib Doukkali, and Muhammed Ben Said. Basri rallied most of these men to the Istiqlal and later led them into the UNFP, but they always remained a distinct group in the party, aloof from the better-educated urbanites. They never fully trusted nor accepted the leadership of the UNFP (Ben Barka, Bou'abid, Ben Seddiq, etc.), and this may be attributed to some extent to their divergent backgrounds. Compounding this suspicion was the assassination of 'Abbas Mess'idi in Fez on 27 June 1956, allegedly executed at the behest of Ben Barka. Relations between Ben Barka and the resistance had never been good for word had been spread that al-Mehdi, a participant in the Aix-les-Bains negotiations of 1955, had favored a solution to the Moroccan problem that would have avoided the return of Muhammed v. Inasmuch as the entire resistance movement had developed as a reaction to the king's exile and was largely aimed at his restoration, Ben Barka's stance could not fail to arouse the hostility of the internal chiefs.[22] Local commanders in the Rif hindered Istiqlali efforts to open party bureaux there, and at one point, in March 1956, Si 'Abbas actually forcefully detained Ben Barka who wished to tour the area. Many resistants in the UNFP today believe that it was this incident that drove Ben Barka to eliminate 'Abbas, utilizing for this purpose a jealous Rifi subordinate of 'Abbas by the name of Hajjaj.* For all the above reasons, the resistants in the UNFP were less than the enthusiastic members continually boasted by the party's founders.

Urban terrorism began soon after the exile of Muhammed v in 1953, but most of the victims were Moroccans considered to be traitors or collaborators. Because of the misappropriation of funds in 1954, the Liberation Army did not undertake any military operations until October 1955 and did most of its fighting after the return of Muhammed v. The heart of the Liberation Army's activities was in the eastern Rif, particularly what became known as the 'triangle of death' described by Aknoul, Boured, and Tizi Ousli. The bulk of the rank and file fighters, who probably never numbered more than six or seven hundred at a time, came from the tribal groupings of Igzinnayan, Bou Yihyi, Mernissa, and Beni Iznassen.[23] These tribes all lay in close proximity to the Spanish zone. Ease of supply and a nearby refuge determined the tribal composition of the Liberation Army, not the innate pugnacity of

---

* Those who wish to clear Ben Barka of blame in this murder claim that he ordered Hajjaj to bring Si 'Abbas from his residence in Fez to Ben Barka's to negotiate a *modus vivendi* with the Istiqlal. Hajjaj did so at gun point, there was a scuffle in the car, the pistol went off and 'Abbas was killed.

the Rifis. The most pugnacious of them all, the Aith Waryaghar, did not participate in the Army of Liberation at all for the tribe lay entirely in the Spanish zone. A contributing factor to the outbreak of fighting in the fall of 1955 was the halt of labor migration from the Rif to Algeria enforced by the French authorities in the summer of that year. This was a severe blow to the incomes of many Rifis and may have touched off attacks in October 1955 led by Si 'Abbas and Hassan ou Hamoush, the *khalifa* of the *qadi* of the Igzinnayan.[24] There were, to be sure, other regional pockets of the Liberation Army, for instance around Taza, in the Middle Atlas back of al-Hajeb, Sefrou and Khenifra, and in the Zemmour country, but the fact remains that the eastern Rif carried the brunt of the fighting.

In January 1956, at a meeting in Madrid, resistance and Liberation Army leaders agreed to a division of responsibilities for future activities. The Liberation Army was divided into three commands: the Rif under Si 'Abbas, the Central and High Atlas under Bel Miloudi and 'Abd al-Qader Bouza'a, and the south under Ben Hamou Misfiwi and the Manouzzi brothers. Dr Khatib was given overall responsibility for these groups, and Basri was entrusted with urban resistance.[25] A brief look at the regional backgrounds of these leaders, and others like them, helps demonstrate a general characteristic of the performance of social and political roles in Morocco. Practically none of the highest ranking field chiefs (except for Bel Miloudi) actually came from the region in which he was active. Not a few had migrated to the cities, and, after the exile of the king, had joined various urban resistance groups. Pursued by the police, many fled to the north to help organize the Liberation Army. This was precisely the case of Si 'Abbas Mess'idi from the Ait Izhak just south of Khenifra, who worked in Casablanca, and was arrested in 1954. After his release he went north to command the Liberation Army. Hassan Laarej, Muhammed Ben Said, Boucha'ib Doukkali and many others were foreign to the Rif. 'Abd al-Qader Bouza'a outdid all others in this respect. Born in Algeria, he had become a French citizen and was serving in Morocco as an interpreter when he defected to the Moroccan resistance. What all this may indicate is that political status in rural Morocco based on ascriptive criteria may not be as prevalent as one would suppose. The tribe or tribal faction, founded on putative or real blood ties, does not always reject leadership from outside in certain situations. It is not in this instance a question of who one is or where one is born, but of the function one assumes or is required to carry out. We have already seen that a murabit's *baraka* was of little avail to him if he failed to live up to the functional requirement of resisting the makhzan. So too a man's birth becomes irrelevant if he is required for a certain task. Dr Khatib from al-Jadida finds most of his political strength in the Rif* in the same way that 'Abbas Kebbaj, from Tangier and of Fassi origins, has his political base among the Sussis in Agadir province. One would like to bring in more evidence to support this contention, but perhaps these few examples will suffice to show the primacy of functionality in the filling of political roles.

Although King Muhammed was back in Morocco, the country's independence had yet to be negotiated in the winter of 1955-6. The French maintained sizeable troop detachments there, and a prime objective of the Liberation Army was to harass these as much as possible in order to provide the king with the best possible bargaining position. All through the winter and spring of 1955-6 the Liberation Army carried out raids on areas of colonization and engaged French troops.

Despite the small numbers of resistants in terrorist groups and the Liberation Army, they constituted in 1956, simply because they were armed, a real danger to public order. Led by men who were little known in Morocco, the resistance was viewed with misgivings by both the Istiqlal and the palace. The former wanted to control it and the latter to disband it. As it turned out, the Istiqlal, and then the UNFP, inherited much of the leadership, but the palace succeeded over a five-year period in dispersing the rank and file.

Initially many urban and rural armed bands were absorbed into the newly created army[26] and police force. Some urban groups had lapsed into banditry, and others, such as the Communists, were regarded as politically unreliable. In both cases, former resistants who had been inducted into the police force were turned loose on groups that had refused to lay down their arms.

* Some will point out that Khatib's wife is from the Boujibar family of the Aith Waryaghar and that she represents his link with the Rif. But she herself was born in Al-Jadida, and, in any event, Khatib's following appears to be not in the Aith Waryaghar but in Beni Iznassen and Igzinnayan where he was active as a leader of the Liberation Army.

In this way a large number of urban resistants were simply liquidated. During the spring of 1956, after the formal granting of independence, and in response to the king's appeals, various contingents of the Liberation Army surrendered their arms.* On 11 February 1956 the French and Moroccans had signed a provisional accord on the internal administration of the country which virtually ended all French offensive military operations against the resistants. Up until that time Moroccan troops in the French army (goums and makhaznis) had been used in operations against their own compatriots. Because the king had never publicly condemned or condoned their role, their status had been ambiguous for a number of months. But the accord of 11 February in effect absolved the Moroccan troops of further responsibility to their French officers, and they melted away into the countryside taking their arms with them. It was at this moment that the Liberation Army swelled its ranks with armed men, augmenting its military potential enormously, but well after its essential task had already been accomplished.[27]

What had been armed bands of a few hundred men became in a matter of weeks an army of thousands. Word was circulated that any resistance chief who could lead a hundred or more of his men to give up their arms would receive an officer's commission in Morocco's new army. This and other enticements attracted about ten thousand so-called members of the Liberation Army into the ranks of the FAR which came into being on 'Id as-Saghir, 14 May 1956. Nonetheless, pockets of the Liberation Army remained at large through the summer of 1956. It was to negotiate their status that Si 'Abbas went to Fez in June. All during July new contingents of the Liberation Army were integrated into FAR.[28] Prince Hassan visited the most troubled areas during July, and it was at this time that diehard elements of the Middle Atlas resistance groups, perhaps at the prince's suggestion, gradually made their way south to the Ait Ba'Amran territory near Ifni. Their departure helped quiet the Middle and High Atlas, but the area around the Spanish enclave of Ifni, and Agadir province in general, fell under the sway of the Liberation Army of the South for a number of

---

* For instance, on 7 April 1956 about 10,000 Rifis went to Rabat, although only a small percentage had been in the Liberation Army, to swear fealty to Muhammed v, *D.M.H.* On 25 and 31 March other delegations had come to Rabat from the Beni Iznassen and Beni Warain.

years. Led by Ben Hamou Misfiwi, and Said and Brahim Manouzzi, the Southern Army utilized members of the Ba'Amran and Rqibat tribes in its operations. But the army is better remembered for its pillaging and banditry in Agadir province than for its efforts to liberate Ifni.*

The National Council of the Moroccan Resistance was created after the king's return to Morocco in November 1955 and met only once, on 18 August 1956. At that time it lamented the fact that the objectives it had struggled to achieve were being abandoned or ignored now that Morocco was free. The delegates stated in their resolutions that:[29]

> Some have begun to wonder at the present time if our revolution has failed after the declaration of independence. The victories that we have attained up to the present are important victories only in so far as their effects result in the liberation of Moroccan sovereignty in the spheres of diplomacy and law. As for internal affairs, the awaited upheaval [inqilab] has not occurred nor has there been any change worthy of note.

The members of the Council at its first and last reunion were:

TABLE 2. *The National Council for Moroccan Resistance*†

Dr 'Abdulkrim Khatib	Said behlaj 'Abdullah
'Abdarrahman Yussufi	Ghali Laraqi
'Allal al-Fassi‡	Hussein Berrada
'Abdallatif Benjelloun	Boucha'ib Doukkali
Hassan Tahar Laarej	Muhammed Ben Said
Said Ben Willat	Said Manouzzi
Belhaj Figuigui Boubou	'Abd al-'Aziz Massi
Millal al-Figuigui	Muhammed Meknassi
Mehdi Madani	'Abdullah Ben Tahar
'Abdullah Senhadji	Muhammed Naciri

* The Southern Army was also responsible for the arrests of two of al-Glaoui's sons in 1957, a move designed to force the king to take measures against the Glaoui family and other collaborators. The resistant, Chafa'i, of Marrakesh directed the arrests, perhaps at the instigation of Ben Barka. He was later killed in the Beni Mellal dissidence of 1960. See below, p. 212.

† This list was given to me by 'Abdallatif Benjelloun, and Dr Khatib corrected and amended parts of it. Both men warn that the list should not be treated as inclusive, but rather as suggestive. Both suggest that others should probably be on the list: 'Abd al-Qader Bouza'a, Col. Bel Miloudi, and 'Abdullah Louggouty. Si 'Abbas was already dead by the time of the Congress.

‡ Al-Fassi was the only member of the Istiqlal executive committee in the Council.

Muhammed Sekouri	Moulay 'Abdesslam
Larbi Zemmouri	Fqih Basri
Hamid Deghmoumi	Al-Failasouf
Ben Hamdoun	Hassan Shadhmi
Sliman Laraichi	'Abderrahman Tannani
Ahmad Lakhsassi	Bouras Figuigui
Mehdi Ben 'Abboud	'Omar Sahli
Belhaj 'Attabi	Muhammed al-Mansour
'Abd al-Qader Yussuf	Moulay Larbi
'Omar Lahrizi	Hassan Laraichi
Muhammed Marwan	Hussein Belqid
Hamid Touzani	Boulihya Tati
Souiri	Abdesslam Jebli
Hussein Doukkali	Mahjoubi Ahardan*
Moulay Tihami	Ben Hamou Misfiwi

The Liberation Army and resistance groups had been fundamental to the return of Muhammed v and the granting of
independence. As Stéphane Bernard has clearly demonstrated,
French military strategists could not risk a major troop build-up
in Morocco, and, when confronted with resistance groups there,
decided to cut their losses and regroup in Algeria.[30] Thus the
extreme importance of their role was undeniable, and the king
found that in rewarding the resistants for their services, he could
also draw their teeth. They were, to borrow a Moroccan elite
expression, 'fonctionnarisés' and 'FARisés'. Local chiefs were made
qaids or khalifas, or *muqaddims* in the early weeks of independence.
The tactic was evident and effective: select the man who is most
dangerous, flatter him with his new status, and put him in charge
of controlling the activities that had won him his post. This sort
of pay-off was common right up to the provincial level where
'Abdullah Senhadji, Muhammed Meknassi, and Ghali Laraqi all
became governors. Hundreds of resistants became army officers,
and others were given high-ranking posts in the police.

In the first few years after 1956 the resistants were further subdued and cajoled through the granting of taxi and transport
licenses, petty commerce franchises, distributions of seized land,[31]
and local contracts of all sorts. Many leaders of the resistance were
from the south where petty trade is a common way of life or means

---

* Ahardan was a controversial member but was accepted on the strength of
reports that he had succeeded in convincing many goums and makhaznis and
Moroccan officers to leave the French army.

to supplement other sources of income, and the commercial possibilities opened to them by the state were particularly attractive.

On 11 March 1959 a dahir was published defining the conditions necessary to qualify as a resistant:[32]

1 Anyone who fought in the ranks of a combat unit of the Liberation Army during the period 15 August 1954 – 7 April 1956.
2 Persons executed, killed, wounded or imprisoned because of armed participation in actions for nationalist purposes in the above-mentioned period.
3 Those who undertook resistance activities revealing a glorious concern for the liberation of the fatherland and the restoration of its sovereignty.

The dahir also brought into being a National Council for the Resistance, a watch-dog body, presided by the prime minister, and composed of the director of the royal cabinet, the ministers of justice and interior, and three members of the resistance designated by the prime minister upon the advice of the minister of the interior. Disputes within and among a myriad of resistance groups that had sprung up since independence prevented the Commission from meeting before 11 July 1960. At that time representatives of six organizations attended a reunion addressed by the king, and the commission finally took shape.[33] The number of resistants serving on the commission has since then risen to seven, but they tend to be unknowns.[34] A National Office of Resistants was set up by dahir in August 1961,[35] and in September 1964 General Bel 'Arbi was made secretary of state for the Resistance, whose task it would be to supervise the dispersal of the remnants of the Liberation Army of the South. Just a few weeks earlier, another dahir had been issued stipulating that 25 per cent of all administrative posts open to competitive examination were to be reserved for resistants, and where there were no specific conditions for employ, resistants would receive absolute priority.[36] At the present time there is an under-secretary of state for the resistance,* who supervises the programs of the National Bureau of the Resistance.

* During 1966–7 the under-secretary was 'Abdesslam Ben 'Aissa, son of a landowner from al-Hajeb, a law student in Paris at the time of the resistance, and a member of the executive committee of the Mouvement Populaire.

Because of the benefits that accrue to resistants in the way of pensions, licenses, contracts, preferential treatment, it has become highly desirable to obtain a resistant's card. Inevitably the distribution of cards has developed into a financially and politically lucrative pastime. At the time of the elections of 1963, a member of the royal cabinet was accused of having influenced voters in Ben M'sik through his control of resistance cards and of having bribed a former resistant not to run against Guedira. In 1966–8 a newspaper appearing irregularly, entitled *Al-Thawra*, lashed out at Ben 'Aissa, accusing him of having sold resistance cards or handed them out wholesale to attract recruits to the Mouvement Populaire.[37] It is reliably reported that at that time there were sixty thousand card-carrying resistants who had, it would seem, met the requirements of the 1959 dahir. But the major point to be made here is that not only was the resistance dispersed or muzzled after independence, the well-being of its members was tied directly to the beneficence of the state.

By 1959, the time of the split of the Istiqlal, very little remained in organizational terms of the Liberation Army and the resistance. Still there was a handful of men, whom the UNFP leaders fondly and perhaps rightly call the 'true resistants', that remained active politically. It is probably not reading too much into the events of 1959–64 to say that the state, with the concurrence of the palace, systematically harassed the tattered remains of the resistance. Lest it sound too one-sided, the state *may* have had good cause. In mid-December 1959, when 'Abdullah Ibrahim was prime minister, the Moroccan police* arrested Yussufi and Basri, both editors of the UNFP's daily *Al-Tahrir*. Muhammed Dehbi, Boucha'ib Doukkali, 'Abdullah Senhadji, and Muhammed Ben Said were arrested on 13 February 1960. These arrests were carried out on suspicions that Basri *et. al.* were plotting to assassinate the crown prince and that they had contacted junior army officers to aid them. The Istiqlali press also accused them of having arranged the assassination of 'Abd al-Aziz' Ben Driss, Istiqlal party organizer in Marrakesh and a close associate of 'Allal al-Fassi, on 24 April 1959. Those arrested had had firearms of untold quantities in their possession. The UNFP claimed that these arms were destined for the Liberation Army of the South.

* The director of the Sureté Nationale at the time and since independence was Muhammed Laghzaoui.

Then on 17 March 1960, the super-qaid of Beni Mellal, Bachir Ben Tihami, and the qaid Ben Hammou killed the police commissioner, Akebli, of that town. Bachir, a Zemmour from Tiflet, a cousin of 'Abdulhamid Zemmouri, and a member of the UNFP, rallied the tribes in the mountains back of Beni Mellal and forced the Ministry of Defense to dispatch troops to quell his dissidence. On 15 April Bachir surrendered and was arrested, but he was not brought to trial until six years later. He intimated that he had acted under orders from 'Abdullah Ibrahim to protest the arrests of the other resistants. His defense lawyer in 1966, however, claimed that his actions were designed to aid the Liberation Army of the South.[38]

Basri, Yussufi, and their companions were released from jail on 3 June 1960, without ever having been brought to trial. The entire episode may be regarded as a sort of warning for what was to happen in July 1963. There is not space nor is there need to go in detail into the plot arrests that took place on 16 July 1963. Once again the charges were intent to overthrow the government and to assassinate the king. The arrested men were accused of storing arms and constituting illegal bands to carry out their plans. Many of those arrested were from the UNFP, but more significantly many were former resistants. One finds that among the 106 accused and brought to trial there were ten members of the defunct National Council of the Moroccan Resistance:*

'Abdarrahman Yussufi	Muhammed Ben Said
Fqih Basri	'Abdesslam Jebli
Said Ben Willat	Ahmad Lakhsassi
'Abdullah Senhadji	Muhammed Meknassi
Boucha'ib Doukkali	Hassan Laarej

Biographical information on the accused also reveals that 33 others had been in the resistance, that at least 24 were from the Suss, that 64 were members of the UNFP, and that 29 were petty tradesmen. There were among the accused only five listed as peasants, and there were no workers. Contacts among the plotters were easily pursued in the course of normal commercial encounters among

---

* Several hundred men had been arrested, but 106 were accused and 85 brought to trial. I have extracted biographical information on the accused from the *procès verbaux* the and *mises en accusation* supplied to me by one of the defense lawyers.

petty tradesmen. The information produced in the course of the trial does not interest us in its bearing on the validity of the charges brought against the accused, but in its biographic portrayal of a large group of resistants. Details on their lives tend to confirm views already expressed to the effect that the resistants were often from the south, frequently tradesmen, and had received their political education in the northern cities (the 'plotters' were concentrated in Casablanca, Rabat, Kenitra, Fez, and Taza). Their commercial networks provided ready-made and efficient means by which to transfer political messages. If it is recalled that the southern merchants often carry on a steady trade with the poorest inhabitants of the cities, i.e. the residents of the *bidonvilles*,[39] then it is not surprising that the political activists among these merchants could act, if not as plotters, at least as party organizers among the dispossessed. Not least among the objectives of state harassment was to discourage the UNFP from using the resistants/tradesmen for this purpose. The brutality involved in the arrests and questioning, despite the subsequent amnesty of those arrested, probably has served and will continue to serve as a major incentive to political docility.

3 The Intelligentsia

We shall now turn to those sectors of the educated population that have become associated with the UNFP. Several members of the liberal professions have been attracted to the UNFP, but to no greater degree than to the other parties. A handful of businessmen, typified by Karim Lamraani and Ahmad Benkirane, have demonstrated a sporadic interest in the party. Government bureaucrats have proven to be a source of recruits for the UNFP, but here again no patterns are clearly discernible, with the possible exception of secondary school teachers. All parties, regardless of their public programs, dip into the pool of the educated elite with about equal success. There is, however, one fairly prevalent characteristic, perhaps even a hallmark, of the educated members of the UNFP: that is their having received an advanced education in France and their immersion in French culture and the politics of the French left. Their intellectual attitudes, not always well-adapted or relevant to the Moroccan milieu, are, for a significant number of them, given daily sustenance by their French, or at least European, wives. As a result, the UNFP, a self-proclaimed party of the masses, has a definite communications problem with these same masses whose culture and mentality they no longer fully understand nor respect. The same communications gap exists within the party itself. In general terms, bureaucrats, lawyers, doctors, etc. – what Manfred Halpern refers to as the new middle class – have not formed a stable clientele for the UNFP, or for any party.

Of far greater dependability have been university students, but their adherence to the UNFP is often confined to their years of advanced education. A member of the UNFP once described the Moroccan Communist Party as a tube, open at both ends, with eighteen-year-old students filing in at one end and, a few years later, filing out the other. The description could be applied to the UNFP.

Moroccan students at home or abroad are highly politicized. Like their counterparts throughout the Near and Middle East the study of law (here taken in the all-encompassing French concept of *droit*) seems best designed to give vent to their political energies. A recent study revealed that of 8,455 Moroccans receiving an advanced education in the country or abroad, 44 per cent studied *droit*, while at the opposite end of the scale agriculture and veterinary studies attracted only 2 per cent of the group.[40] Almost without fail the president of the Union Nationale des Etudiants Marocains (UNEM) is from the Faculté de Droit.

The UNEM is the major Moroccan student union, and, although it insists upon its organizational autonomy, it was always associated with the progressive faction of the Istiqlal and with the UNFP. After the party split, the Istiqlal organized its own student union (UGEM), and in recent years the MP has attempted to do likewise. It was Mehdi Ben Barka who most strenuously wooed the students, and he always felt that they represented the best means to reinvigorate the cadre of the UNFP and to recruit new militants among Moroccan youth.[41] The students have never been restrained in their comments on Moroccan politics and have often given the first public evidence of conflicts and criticisms that had been privately expressed within the confines of factions of the more adult elite. The annual congresses have usually been the scene of programmatic trial balloons. In August 1959, at a time when the Istiqlal was split and Ibrahim prime minister, the UNEM delegates demanded the expulsion of French personnel in the army and police, and reserved their most cutting attacks for Crown Prince Hassan who had been entrusted with the organization of FAR.

The UNEM, as principal spokesman for the students, was, as Ben Barka observed, strategically placed to give political orientation to the increasing flow of university graduates and elite aspirants. As with the resistants, the state has utilized various devices to cow the students into submissiveness. Many have been 'fonctionnairisés', and students themselves suspect the UNEM leaders of having received state subsidies. There is talk of a great *mise en scène*, that the radicalism of the student leaders may be sincere, but that they have agreed with the state to keep it within certain limits. Whether this is true or not is perhaps not as important as the fact that many students believe it to be so. The state has never been faint-hearted in dealing with students, and, in 1963, one of UNEM's officers, Hamid Berrada, was condemned to death *in absentia* for having publicly endorsed Ben Barka's statement on the Algero-Moroccan border conflict. A year later the president of UNEM, Muhammed Halaoui, was arrested for having criticized the sentencing of Berrada. At the same time (5 October 1964) a dahir was published abrogating the dahir of 1961 that recognized the UNEM as an organization of public utility. On 15 October the state prosecutor demanded that UNEM be dissolved, for, it was alleged, its statutes were no longer in conformity with the dispositions of the law of 21 June 1963, forbidding student associations to have any members below the university level. It is true that UNEM did have at one point secondary school students as members, but after its eighth congress in August 1963, the Union adjusted its statutes to conform with the new law. The matter was brought to trial, and on 30 December 1964 the Rabat court threw out the prosecutor's accusation.[42] Since then the UNEM has been continuously kept off balance. In 1966 the king approved a law implementing universal military service, and in July 1966, two weeks before the scheduled UNEM congress, eight members of the executive committee were drafted and sent off for military training at al-Hajeb.[43]

The presentation of the tribulations of UNEM brings to a close my discussion of the actual and potential clientele of the UNFP. It should be clear by now that the view that the UNFP, or any party of a similar nature, has direct access to the most important political audience in Morocco is somewhat superficial. The UNFP has found it extremely difficult to organize Morocco's 'popular masses' as they do not constitute a homogeneous whole. Their political consciousness is shaped as much by the divisions within their own ranks as by the cleavage between them and the economically well-off. To add to the UNFP's dilemma, the state has impeded the party's efforts to contact its followers and has muffled or neutralized strategically-placed middle range cadres – for instance student leaders and resistance activists – who could have implemented UNFP organizational plans. How best to operate under these circumstances became a bone of contention among the leaders of the UNFP and the UMT, and led to the collapse of the UNFP as an effective political party.

CHAPTER ELEVEN

THE TRIBULATIONS OF THE LEFT

At the time of the formal scission of the Istiqlal, Ben Barka declared:[1]

. . . We must bring about a synthesis of the three great forces of Morocco, the syndicalists, the peasantry, and the resistance. It is the resistance that will provide us a bridge to the rural world neglected by previous governments.

This synthesis was never achieved for, as we have seen, the resistance dissolved, and, as we shall see, the leaders of the UMT parted company with the politicians. The split itself revealed a few weak spots in UMT organization. Certain unions of teachers, dockers, and phosphate miners did not follow UMT leadership in the split and joined the Istiqlal sponsored Committee of Autonomous Unions, which on 25 March 1960 became the UGTM.[2] Al-Fassi maintained that the workers had not really abandoned the Istiqlal at all, but rather had been forced to follow Mahjoub Ben Seddiq for fear of losing their jobs. The *za'im* intimated that Ma'ati Bou'abid, minister of labor in the Ibrahim government, would have dismissed any recalcitrant workers in the state sector and would have recalled the *permanents* to full-time employment.[3] On 24 April 1959 the UMT called its first post-1956 congress to reaffirm its organizational solidity, and 'Abderrahim Bou'abid and 'Abdullah Ibrahim, both ministers at the time, attended.

The months during which 'Abdullah Ibrahim was prime minister mark the period of the greatest internal cohesion and general popularity of the UNFP. By making Ibrahim prime minister, the king had given the impression that the left wing of the Istiqlal had become the royal favorite. The appointment indisputably contributed to the final and irrevocable split of the Istiqlal and from that point of view was very much in the interests of the palace. Inveterate bet-hedgers assumed that the new faction in power had best be joined. There was a substantial flow of defectors from other parties, who suddenly professed to see in the Confederation, and subsequently the UNFP, the hope of Morocco.* For a few months the UNFP was indeed at the forefront of Moroccan politics. At its official founding on 6 September 1959, the new party issued a manifesto whose signatories renounced all forms of political affiliation and called upon all 'sincere patriots' to do the same.

The king had formed a government based upon his most outspoken critics. He challenged them, in a way, to act upon their criticisms but deprived of the powers they needed to do so. As it became increasingly evident that the palace was determined to complicate the task of the government and to embarrass its leftist members, dissension among the leaders of the UNFP developed as to how best to cope with the situation. For instance, Ibrahim was forced into the distasteful position of presiding over the legal dissolution of the Communist Party. Then came the arrests of Yussufi and Basri, at the hands of a police force he could not control. The prince seemed to have organized a shadow cabinet whose objective was to harass Ibrahim at every turn, employing the army and the Sureté Nationale under Laghzaoui for this purpose.[4] Some members of the UNFP felt that Ibrahim should have resigned rather than allow the palace to make a fool of him.

The prime minister did not resign, but he did counter-attack in the spring of 1960. At the end of March the UMT staged a successful general strike to protest the sabotage of the Ibrahim government and more specifically the founding of the UGTM. The king until that time had endorsed the principle of the 'unity of the working classes'.† Ibrahim then decided to force a showdown over

---

* The most outstanding renegades were 'Abdulhadi Boutaleb, Ahmad Bensouda, and Tihami Wazzani, all of the PDI, and 'Abdullah Senhadji of the Mouvement Populaire.

† The UMT had hoped that the secretary-general of the government would exercise his authority to oppose the legal formation of any union or association. Instead, on 19 October 1960, a decree was promulgated that officially recognized the UGTM and abrogated the dahir of 17 July 1957 that provided the secretary-general with the above-mentioned discretionary authority.

the question of the attributes of the Ministry of the Interior and Sureté Nationale, and the role of the French police and military personnel in the country. At a cabinet meeting of 13 April an order was drawn up for the repatriation of all French security agents. This was followed on 5 May by discussion of a proposed dahir for the reorganization of the Ministry of Interior, one of whose prime objectives was to subordinate unequivocally Sureté Nationale to the Ministry of Interior. These actions on the part of the prime minister must have decided the king to dismiss him at the earliest possible moment, and his resolve was only strengthened by the surprise victory of the UNFP in the elections to the local Chambers of Commerce and Industry on 8 May. With Morocco's first local elections to be held on 29 May, it appeared that the UNFP might increase its momentum of 8 May and go on to score heavily in Morocco's next electoral test. The most effective way to deflate the UNFP balloon would be to drop unceremoniously its principal representatives in the government. On 20 May the king informed Ibrahim that the mission of his government (i.e. preparation for local elections) had been completed, and on 23 May the king announced that he personally would act as prime minister in the new government to guarantee national unity and stability until the elaboration of a constitution.* The king intended to appoint Prince Hassan as prime minister, but the Istiqlalis with whom he consulted refused to participate in such a government. Thus the king made himself prime minister, and his son vice-prime minister, but for all intents and purposes day-to-day authority was vested in the prince.

Despite this humiliation at the hands of the palace, the UNFP did fairly well in the local elections.[5] In rural areas the electoral campaigns amounted to a series of confrontations between local individuals without much reference to party adherence. But in the cities there was a confrontation of political parties. On a nationwide basis, the Istiqlal won about 40 per cent of all seats in the local councils, the MP 7 per cent and the UNFP 23 per cent; a good showing for a party that was not yet a year old. It won massively in Casablanca and Rabat and did well in Kenitra, Tangier, Safi, Al-Jadida, Tetouan, Settat, and in Marrakesh, Agadir and

---

* The dismissal came on the same day that the Ibrahim government declared *persona non grata* Commander Blair, an American naval officer, whom the prince had attached to his personal cabinet.

Warzazat provinces. The results clearly reveal UNFP strength among workers (through the UMT), bureaucrats, petty tradesmen, and migrants to the coastal cities. In 29 cities and centers of more than 10,000 inhabitants each (representing a total population of 2,860,000) out of 765 seats contested, the Istiqlal won 414, the UNFP 339, and 'independents' 32. The Istiqlal thus won 54·1 per cent of the *seats* in these locales, but each seat did not represent the same number of voters: there were 16,000 electors for a seat on the Casablanca Municipal Council and only 900 for one at Chaouan. Taking into consideration the number of voters rather than the number of seats, we find that the UNFP won 54 per cent of the vote in these 29 agglomerations and the Istiqlal 36 per cent.[6] The UNFP going into the elections still had about it the lustre of power and governmental responsibilities. Its relative triumph marked the peak of its popularity, and it was downhill from then on for the party out of power.

Except for Hassan Zemmouri (minister of agriculture) no members of the UNFP joined the king's government.* They were chagrined not only at their peremptory dismissal, but at the irony of the king's adoption of the central elements of their governmental program as guidelines for his own.[7] UNFP leaders were agreed that they must in some way protest the situation, and adopt a stance of an opposition party, something for which there was no precedent in independent Morocco (with the exception of the PCM). It was in defining its new role and in drawing up an action program for its opposition that the short-lived honeymoon between the party politicians and the UMT came to an end.

The first tangible evidence of the internal tension of the UNFP came in June 1961. The economic situation in the country was not improving, and wages in the public sector had been frozen since independence. As long as Bou'abid was minister of economy the unions had not pushed very strenuously for wage increases, but when the king made Douiri minister of economy† in his government of May 1960, the UNFP/UMT decided to abandon the go-slow policy on wages. Moreover the government had emasculated the

---

* M'hammedi was minister of foreign affairs until October 1960, but he had clearly dissociated himself from the UNFP ever since his stance on the electoral system as minister of interior in the Ibrahim government.

† It will be recalled that Douiri was a prominent member of the Balafrej clan in the split of the Istiqlal, and when both he and Boucetta became ministers some saw in this a royal reward for their instrumental role in the split.

five year plan prepared by the Ibrahim government. In early June 1961 the Fédération Nationale des Fonctionnaires, containing within it unions of employees of the Ministries of Education, Public Works, Interior, Health, Posts, Telephone and Telegraph (PTT), Finance, Agriculture, Customs, Foreign Affairs, and Radio (RTM), adopted a unanimous motion to call a general strike. Their communiqué stated that in the period 1956–61 retail prices increased by 38 per cent while wages were held stationary.[8] Douiri warned that a law of 5 February 1958 forbade civil servants to strike and that if they did, severe sanctions would be applied. On 17 June the government received a UMT delegation of Hachemi Bennani, Muhammed 'Abderrazak, and Driss Medkouri, after which it was announced in a communiqué signed by 'Abderrazak and Guedira that the Superior Council of the Civil Service would meet on 13 July to discuss the union claims. The UMT claimed a great victory, and no general strike occurred. Many unionists and UNFP members regarded the 'victory' as a total sell-out. The scheduled meeting of the Superior Council of Civil Service never did take place.

Several members of the UNFP believed that the legitimate grievances of the public sector employees should be used as a springboard to a more general form of political protest, that the UMT should enlarge the scope of its objectives to include political as well as economic demands. Critics of the UMT point out that the union leaders began to play a double role. In their capacity as members of the executive committee of a political party they agreed wholeheartedly to the suggestions of their party colleagues outside the UMT. However, in their capacity as leaders of the UMT, they would ignore or criticize the very policies they had approved as politicians.

Plans were reformulated for a general strike in December 1961. At a meeting of the Administrative Commission of the Federation of PTT, it was decided that PTT workers would go on strike if their wage demands were not met by 20 December. This decision was made public in *L'Avant-Garde* of 2 December, and it was stated that Civil Service unions stood ready to join PTT in the strike. As the big day approached there was a considerable amount of shuffling behind the scenes as the government sought to convince the UMT to call off the strike. On 20 December, PTT workers, led by their secretary-general, Wasfi Boucha'ib, struck but were joined only by employees of RTM and Foreign Affairs. Members of the PTT Federation assert that what in effect had happened was that Ahmad Guedira, the minister of interior, had privately threatened Ben Seddiq with strong reprisals against the strikers. It is alleged that Ben Seddiq told Guedira not to worry, that PTT would be left out on a limb, but that the government should concede a few of its demands so that the UMT as a whole would not lose face.* The upshot was that the minister of PTT, 'Abdesslam al-Fahsi al-Halfaoui, received a union delegation and made a few token concessions. Guedira promptly announced that in view of these concessions and the settlement with PTT, any further strikes would be subject to sanctions. Some doubted that Guedira could in fact apply sanctions. In the Ministry of Foreign Affairs, high-ranking employees representing the elite of the educated bureaucracy, and, at that time, devoted to the UNFP, decided to call Guedira's bluff. Some two hundred of them went on strike, and one hundred and sixty-eight of them were immediately fired, not to be reinstated until 8 December 1962. Despite the debacle, the headlines of *L'Avant-Garde* of 23 December 1961 trumpeted 'Triumph of the UMT'.

It seems certain that the UMT ceded to governmental pressure for the following reasons. First, UMT leaders were told that if they backed the general strike, they would be obliged to share their headquarters with other unions on an equal basis. In 1961 such sharing could only have meant with the UGTM. All UMT office space, from the giant central headquarters in Casablanca to all their smallest locals, is supplied rent free by the state which also pays the water and electricity bills. In the same vein the question of the *permanents* was raised once again. It would be absurd to suppose that Ben Seddiq could not live without his salary from the Railroad, nor were the other *permanents* in the National Bureau of the UMT vulnerable on this count. But scores of lower echelon UMT officials who were at the same time *permanents* probably did rely to a great extent on their state salaries. The government threatened to end their privilege of full-time union duty and recall them to active government service. In that event, they could either accept reintegration or quit their public jobs. In the first case the

* Telephone workers claim that they tapped Ben Seddiq's phone and recorded his conversation with Guedira. Contacts between the two were frequent, and 'Abderrazak may have acted as liaison between the UMT and the royal cabinet.

UMT would lose much of its cadre and in the second would have to provide for their welfare. Neither solution seemed happy, and the UMT knuckled under to the government's warning. In addition, the abortive strike of December 1961 led to a more lasting *modus vivendi* between the royal cabinet and the UMT. In effect the government told the UMT that it would tolerate all UMT activities of a strictly syndical nature, but were the union to push its members beyond demands concerning workers' welfare and into organized forms of political protest, then the UMT could expect a strong reaction from the government. The consequences of agreeing to this arrangement are clear: the UMT would have to drop all *practical* affiliation with the UNFP.

The political leadership of the UNFP in the few years since the party's creation had lost control, even access,* to its one source of organized followers, the UMT. Personal animosities among the top leaders did not help matters, but it is perhaps worthy of note that Ben Barka was not physically present in Morocco at this time, having left the country in early 1960 upon the arrests of the resistants.† One can assume nevertheless that he had his say in the direction of the party even from abroad, and it is certain that his assumption of the role of spokesman for the Moroccan left in the *tiers monde* was viewed with a jaundiced eye by some. When he returned to Morocco in the spring of 1962, a major attempt was made to shore up the party. The second UNFP congress, held the first few days in June, was called in order to work out a satisfactory relationship between the party and the union. The original impulse for the congress may have come from some of the younger members who could no longer tolerate the petty jealousies of the party's leaders.[9] The commission that prepared and managed the congress was a careful balance of the contending forces. Ben Barka did not wish to adumbrate the central issue, even if it meant offending the feelings of his UMT colleagues. In his address he belabored the theme of party primacy in its relation to the union:[10]

> The working class is a major force, but it must establish clearly the relation between its syndicalist role and its political goals. . . .

* Apparently UMT leaders would not allow UNFP organizers and recruiters to contact union members directly.

† It might also be noted that soon after the UNFP had fallen from power, some of its most ardent supporters – Boutaleb, Bensouda, and Tihami Wazzani – abandoned the party as of November 1960. Thus they do not figure into the UNFP-UMT divorce.

The efforts of the party are a blend of syndicalist and political objectives. But we must not allow certain factors to prevent this blend: such as weak ideological formation, unemployment, and pressure and corruption on the part of the central authorities. . . .

The UNFP, in its role as a revolutionary implement, is alone capable of assuming the position of leadership in the struggle of all other revolutionary groupings [itals. J.W.]. . . . This means that the party alone has the right to undertake the coordination of the political struggle and to study and define the programs of all revolutionary movements in the country.

The role of our cadres and militants within mass organizations that have particular goals and missions must be the integration of these limited struggles within the broad horizons laid down by the party as the pre-eminent political implement.

The relationship described by Ben Barka was viewed by the UMTists as 'feudalistic'. No effective compromise was reached at the congress on this issue despite a show of unity in the unanimous adoption of rather belligerent resolutions.[11]

After the 1962 congress, for all practical purposes, active cooperation and regular consultation between the UMT and the UNFP ceased. At the time of the constitutional referendum in December 1962, the UNFP called for a boycott, but the UMT recommended to its members the less risky course of abstention. It is clear from the results that many members of the UMT ignored even this tepid proposal and voted for the constitution anyway. At its third congress, in January 1963, the UMT announced that it was independent of all political organizations and had as its sole objective the welfare of the laboring masses. In the legislative elections the following May, the UMT refused to endorse UNFP candidates specifically, nor did it run any of its own. Instead it suggested to its members that they vote for the 'progressive' candidates. The only candidates identifiable according to this criterion were those of the UNFP, but the ambiguity of the UMT statement was both unmistakable and intentional.

Perhaps more than all these incidents members of the UNFP resent the comportment of the UMT during the arrests that took place in the summer of 1963 in connection with the plot to assassinate King Hassan. In July, UNFP leaders began to debate the advisability of running candidates in the forthcoming local elections. They believed that the legislative elections had been rigged, and that the local authorities were doing all in their power to hinder UNFP candidates from registering in the local elections. Perhaps the best course would be to boycott these elections entirely. For its part, the UMT had presented its own candidates in opposition to the UNFP in several places.[12] The Administrative Commission of the UNFP had become inoperative because its members from the UMT no longer participated in it, but on 16 July at Casablanca there was a meeting of all UNFP party representatives in parliament, and provincial secretaries. The purpose of the meeting was to decide party policy in the local elections. The police interrupted the meeting and arrested all present on suspicion of plotting. Naturally there was no one from the UMT there. The UMT did withdraw from the local elections after the arrests, as did the Istiqlal. But it seemed to UNFP members that the UMT was only shedding crocodile tears over the plight of those arrested. They were further embittered when, in March 1964, Yussufi was denounced in court after months in prison for having failed to inform the authorities of approaches made to him by the plotters, while Ibrahim and Ben Seddiq, both of whom had received the same overtures and had said nothing, were never arrested nor even called for testimony.

One cannot treat relations between the UMT and the UNFP adequately without giving some attention to 'Omar Benjelloun. In December 1961 Benjelloun was the UMT official responsible for the local PTT union of Casablanca. As a result of the strikes of June and December, he became thoroughly disenchanted with the national leadership of the UMT. He perhaps epitomizes in his views on politics and unionism that sector of the well-educated Civil Service that has given its support to the UNFP. Benjelloun is an avowed Marxist and received his university education in political science in Paris. The strategy he recommends for Moroccan unions is one of total political commitment and ceaseless agitation, whatever the cost. Like Ben Barka, he feels that the educated cadre of Morocco, in view of their crucial role in the development of the country, should be the motor-force of unions and parties. In a Sorelian vein, Benjelloun is certain that six months of all-out opposition – i.e. a general strike – on the part of the civil servants would paralyze the regime and force the monarchy to accede to the demands of the opposition. But, he asserts, the National Bureau of the UMT had lost its nerve and courage as a result of coddling over a number of years by both the parties and the government.

National federation heads had become used to an easy life and no longer knew the feelings of the workers. On the other hand, UMT organizers retort that Benjelloun's ideas are unrealistic, that he has forgotten that the guts of the UMT are the workers, not the 'spoiled' bureaucrats. The latter can afford to take dramatic political actions, but it is always the workers who pay. Every action, political or economic, must be carefully weighed and prepared before mobilizing the masses. Benjelloun has been unimpressed by such arguments, and, stealing a leaf from Ibrahim's and Ben Seddiq's book, has decided to challenge the leadership and try to reform the UMT from within.

The Federation of PTT was to spearhead this action. It had been a thorn in Ben Seddiq's flesh from the fall of 1961 on. After the strike of 19 June 1961 had been annulled, the PTT Federation decided to force the UMT's hand by publicly declaring their intention to strike again. All during 1962, the UMT prepared for its third congress, and, just as had been the case in the Istiqlal in 1958, a prime question was the selection of delegates. The PTT leaders accused Ben Seddiq of having insisted upon designating the delegates for fear that elected delegates would be hostile to the National Bureau.[13] On 3 January 1963, just before the third congress was to convene, Benjelloun was briefly kidnapped and badly beaten by several members of other UMT federations.[14] He was among a group of PTT employees who claimed to be duly elected and authentic representatives of PTT, but this delegation was barred from the congress. A week after the congress, 'Abderrazak informed the minister of PTT that the Federation of PTT had been dissolved, and that its officers had been suspended. Until the federation was reconstituted, the UMT would recognize only the members of a Provisional Committee of Management and Organization as the legitimate representatives of the PTT employees.[15] Intermittent efforts were carried out by the ostracized leaders and their obvious following to gain acceptance within the UMT – the unity of the working class is taken lightly by no Moroccan leader. But no compromise could be reached, and at a congress on 23 and 24 May 1964, the PTT Federation reaffirmed its existence, suggested that its autonomy was not voluntary, and announced its determination to work for the democratization of the UMT from within.[16]

'Omar Benjelloun has been a member of the Administrative

Commission of the UNFP since 1962, and has been a central figure in party organization. He has occupied himself with all phases of party activity, but above all his pet project has been to bring all the Civil Service federations around to his way of thinking, to challenge, and if need be to renew, the national leadership of the UMT and restore an active political role to the UMT in close conjunction with the UNFP. This is a tall order, and his task has not been aided by his arrest in 1963 as one of the accused in the plot trial and his subsequent sentencing to death (he was pardoned in 1965). He was arrested once again in March 1966 on charges of having incited school children to go on strike. These events lend credence to his own assertions that because of the collusion between the government and the UMT, he will inevitably be immobilized. His removal from active politics* has been followed by declarations of triumph from the UMT which claims that PTT employees, after four years of tyranny, have driven from their midst Wasfi and other provocators. There is still, however, an autonomous union of PTT, loyal to Wasfi and Benjelloun.[17] In addition, employees of the Ministry of Education, mostly secondary school teachers, founded an autonomous union of school teachers in August 1966, denounced Driss Medkouri of the National Bureau of the UMT for negligence of his duties, and protested Benjelloun's imprisonment.

The kidnapping of Mehdi Ben Barka added fuel to the fires of UMT-UNFP enmity. It should be clear by now that Ben Barka personified the UNFP's belief in the necessity of political unionism, and his assertiveness on this point had caused a good deal of friction between the politicians and the labor leaders. His disappearance provided the UMT with the opportunity to demonstrate the organizational feebleness of the UNFP and, at the same time, to take a thinly veiled slap at the missing leader. UNFP leaders had been unable to organize any sort of impressive demonstrations to attest to Ben Barka's and the UNFP's popularity in the days immediately following the kidnapping.† The UMT initially limited its protests to the printed word. Then on 12 and 13 November the union called a general strike whose objective

---

* Benjelloun was sentenced in June 1966 to a year in prison, and after his release he was banned from Rabat and Casablanca.

† There were student strikes in Rabat and elsewhere, but, to my knowledge, there was no public demonstration resulting from the passing of Ben Barka.

was to make clear the workers' serious dissatisfaction with the state of emergency (proclaimed the previous June) and to express their demands for the institution of an 'authentically democratic regime'. In its communiqué the UMT pointedly declared that the general strike[18] 'answers the feelings of profound indignation elicited by the degradation of the situation of our country, *a situation of which the disappearance of Ben Barka constitutes but a single aspect* (itals. J.W.) . . . By calling the strike, the UMT seemed to serve notice to the UNFP, as it had done periodically in the past, that the party without the union was powerless, and that it could not evoke any popular response without the UMT as intermediary.

The UMT in 1963 had declared itself independent of all political parties and stressed the primacy of its syndical activities. Yet in severing effective relations with the leadership of the UNFP,* it lost its political arm and political facade.

In late 1965 and the first half of 1966, the UMT, in a desultory fashion, groped its way towards some sort of working arrangement with the Istiqlal. After five years of mutual vituperation the two organizations proclaimed one another, over the prostrate body of the UNFP, the only two legitimate nationalist organizations in the country. A common program for remedying the nation's ills was published simultaneously,[19] and Boucetta entered into frequent contacts with UMT counterparts.[20] Ben Seddiq tried to prepare the way for reconciliation with the Istiqlal among UMT cadres in February 1966, and both organizations tossed one another roses at the time of the May Day celebrations of 1966.[21]

The party split of 1959 had almost come full circle, but neither group was prepared to go beyond verbal accolades. For all intents and purposes, by the summer of 1966 the matter had been shelved, and 'Abdullah Ibrahim was busying himself with the organization of a Permanent Secretariat for Action and Coordination (SPAC),[22] to move beyond, as he put it, the obsolete political carcasses of the past. Ibrahim's own judgment of his success in this endeavor and of the obstacles in his path are of a more general validity: 'All

---

* UMT leaders that are at the same time members of the UNFP General Secretariate (Ben Seddiq, 'Abderrazak), and others closely identified with the UMT (Ibrahim, Ma'ati Bou'abid, Tihami 'Ammar) insist that there is no division between the UMT and UNFP, but rather a division among the leaders of the UNFP. They maintain this fiction in spite of the fact that the executive committee of the UNFP has not met regularly with all members present since 1962 as a direct result of their continued absence from it.

political groupings are extremely jealous of their autonomy; no leader feels that he can make the first step and wants all the others to come to him.'[23]

The divorce between the UMT and the UNFP has vitiated the left in Moroccan politics. Mehdi Ben Barka wanted his party to join in the revolution of the *tiers monde* and to sweep out the 'feudal remnants' of Morocco. Today the UNFP no longer challenges the Moroccan regime, no longer has as its *immediate* objective the thorough remodeling of the government and the economy. The objective conditions for a party of radical protest may not yet be present in Morocco, and the UNFP has seen its clientele, or its access to various sectors of it, stripped away little by little. The urban unemployed are more docile than had been imagined, but, in any case, there is no practical way to organize them. They will continue to alternate between long periods of quiescence and short bursts of rioting and sabotage, their only form of protest. Organized laborers on the other hand are above all job conscious and are a privileged minority in the sea of unemployed. The UMT's greatest attraction and the essence of its cohesion is its ability to provide and maintain jobs for its members. This reputation it will not risk for the sake of ritualistic political agitation. The resistants, the men who were to be the shock troops of the UNFP, were sponged up into the administration, army, and police. The few leaders who remained in the UNFP lost most of their following and may have lost most of their nerve after the plot arrests of 1963. Now, the best the UNFP can hope for is survival, and its sweeping programs for political reform have been replaced by marginal demands designed to gain fringe advantages in the manner of the other parties in Morocco.[24]

The breakdown of the left completes the process of the dispersion of the nationalist movement. The absorption of the resistance, the scission of the Istiqlal, the UMT-UNFP divorce, and the withdrawal and quiescence of formerly active Moroccan politicians, are the principal benchmarks of this disintegration. Thus, by 1960–1 Morocco's segmented political system had emerged, and it is upon this system of manipulatable groups that the present strength of the throne is predicated. Moreover, it is the continuation of this system that has increasingly become the overriding objective of the domestic policies of the king.

Ineluctably there will be a revival of the left in Morocco. The tasks of economic development, the pressures exerted by a political climate among the developing countries favorable to the left, the existence, for all its slipperiness, of an increasingly vast clientele, all favor a regrouping of the Moroccan left wing. How this will take shape is impossible to predict with any precision.

However, one may be reasonably certain that a re-merger of the UNFP and the UMT, with the same leaders in command, will be no more successful than the half-hearted attempt to bring together once again the UMT and the Istiqlal. In fact, following the June War of 1967, there was a formal reconstitution of the UNFP. This came about as a result of Mahjoub's Ben Seddiq's arrest in July. He was sentenced to a year and a half of prison for what were judged to be insulting remarks regarding the government's alleged collusion with Zionist interests. The king seized this opportunity to prove that the UMT was just as vulnerable as the UNFP, and that, as had been the case with Ben Barka, the abrupt removal of the UMT's leader would provoke little more than perfunctory protests.[25] Other than a strike that the police easily broke, such was the case.

The manifest weakness of the UMT in its confrontation with the throne propelled it along the path to reunion with the UNFP, a path that it had leisurely followed after the reconciliation with the Istiqlal had petered out. UNFP leaders, along with almost all politicians, voiced their shock over the arrest, and appeared willing to swallow their pride and try to build anew on the shambles of their two organizations. In early August a new political bureau for the UNFP was established, made up of Ibrahim, Ben Seddiq (in absentia), and Abderrahim Bou'abid. It was to undertake the reorganization of the UNFP, and in a communiqué it stressed that within the new organization the UMT would retain full responsibility for all decisions concerning union affairs.[26]

Numerous meetings during the fall of 1967 moved this project no nearer to reality. Many former UNFP members refused to take part in the effort, preferring, as one of them remarked, to let the younger generation try their hand free from the feuds of their elders. For their part, UMT cadres were reluctant to renew an experience that had been so distasteful in the past.

Thus, despite the various attempts of the Istiqlal, UMT, UNFP, and even Dr Khatib to form some sort of alliance during the state of emergency, the same pieces remain on the chess board, somewhat weaker, somewhat wearier, and somewhat easier to move.

What I have sought to demonstrate in the last two chapters is both the fragility of the left's clientele in Morocco and the style of leftist politicians coping with the problems of maintaining a viable movement. The left has fallen victim, at least for the time being, to the context within which it operates, as well as to the behavior of its principal leaders. Many of those who joined the UNFP band-wagon in 1959–60, did so because it was the party in power, and they dutifully mimicked the party's socialist slogans to show their good faith. But for most of these fair-weather friends, the UNFP was but a convenient path to the sources of patronage, and the ideology or outlook that it represented was of negligible importance (leaving aside students) in attracting adherents. The handful of leaders that sincerely believed in the party's program suffered, like most Moroccan politicians, from a certain incapacity to impose their doctrine and program for action on their followers. They could not bring themselves nor oblige others to make distasteful choices and to take risks that would commit members to an un-alterable line of conduct. The failure of the party to determine its policy *vis-à-vis* the regime was covered up by rhetoric announcing the imminence of the final confrontation with 'le pouvoir absolu'. Neither moving forward nor backward, the UNFP simply dispersed, individuals and clientele grouplets gradually moving away. This process continues today with the palace conscientiously gathering in the UNFP remnants.

In examining the dispersion of the left, we find once again examples of the behavior of Moroccan political factions in periods of prolonged crisis. Moreover, crises are drawn out because of the unwillingness of political actors to damage their lines of com-munication with opposed groups. Consequently, the initial fervor that some political leaders tried to diffuse among their clientele is dissipated, and, equally important, the issue that lay at the heart of the choice remains unresolved. Prolonged crisis, as it wears down the emotional and ideological content of the problems at hand, simultaneously leads to a reassertion of value neutrality, and, concretely, to greater flexibility in alliance-building. Allies are then chosen for the strength they can add to the new aggregate, with relatively few normative considerations influencing the choice. In this light it was really not incongruous that the UMT, the Istiqlal, the Khatib forces, and factions of the UNFP all considered one another perfectly plausible allies. But because the issues that had originally led to dissension – the role of labor unions within political parties and the correct tactics to be used in dealing with the palace – remained unresolved, it has proven difficult to consummate any possible alliances as a result of the complexity involved in the coordination of policy positions.

Again, it seems unlikely that the present leftist factions will be able to effect any practical form of joint action, but younger elements may indeed be moving in that direction. They hope that reconciliation can be achieved with the consent of the principal leaders involved; if not, it will be achieved despite them.

CHAPTER TWELVE

AGENTS OF SEGMENTATION:
THE MOUVEMENT POPULAIRE

The palace had played an active role in the division of the nation-alist elite, but such division was not in itself sufficient to establish the control and room for manoeuvre that the palace sought. The king needed to impose some degree of cohesion upon his clientele so as to present a credible counterforce to the nationalists. This process had begun well before the actual scission in the Istiqlal and led to the formation of new parties and coalitions and to the bolstering up of loyal political groupings already in existence. How these new pieces in the segmentary system were brought to life has received little detailed analysis. In this and the following chapter I shall try to fill in some of the gaps with special attention to the formation of the Mouvement Populaire and the FDIC. I have adduced a considerable amount of factual detail for the record so to speak, but this should not obscure the central focus upon political behavior. The king's clientele in this respect proved just as vulnerable to internal segmentation and the dilemmas of choice as had the nationalist elite.

One hesitates to suggest that the king and his closest advisors had devised a master-plan for establishing and maintaining the political pre-eminence of the throne in the months following the sovereign's return to Morocco. Occasionally, however, events have worked themselves out to the advantage of the palace to such an extent that pure chance and political agility are inadequate explanations. The king's break with the Istiqlal in the winter of 1955–6 was abrupt and clear-cut. To assert his mastery of in-dependent Morocco he had to take on his largest source of potential trouble. The king gambled and won. The Istiqlal could not impose its will upon him, but in so trying led to its own fragmentation. Occasional nudges in one direction or another, well-timed raps on the knuckles of one faction, pats on the back of another, were all that was required of the palace to keep the Istiqlal moving on its internally generated course towards breakdown. But this was essentially an exercise in negativism, and the king clearly was in need of a group or groups whose loyalty to the throne was unquestionable. In this respect somewhat more direct monarchical participation was required in the political process than had been the case in the division of the Istiqlal. Disparate clientele groups had to be propelled toward one another, with the discreet, and sometimes not so discreet, encouragement of the palace serving as the catalyst to the process. Ready at hand was a rallying point: the post-1956 arrogance of the Istiqlal, its pretensions to a monopoly of nationalist sentiment and nationalists, its constant reminders to all who had never served in its ranks that they were unfit to share in the fruits of victory. The fruits of course were ministerial posts, patronage, and graft, the life-blood of patron-clientele alliances. The control of the flow of patronage, no matter how well founded the Istiqlali claims to it, remained securely with the palace.

The first order of business was to keep alive any groups rival to the Istiqlal. These amounted to the PDI of Hassan Wazzani and the Liberal Independents of Rachid Mouline and Reda Guedira. Both parties were amply rewarded in the first government of Si M'barrek Bekkai.

This worked to the advantage of the PDI in particular, which picked up strength in diverse tribal areas immediately following independence. It is illuminating to examine the reasons why. There had been, to be sure, a number of rural notables who participated in the nationalist movement, and, in so doing, accepted Istiqlali (urban) leadership. Yet, in a general way, and leaving aside the very small group of resistance and Army of Liberation types, the rural world was on the outer edges of the nationalist struggle. One can hardly speak in global terms here. How tribesmen collectively and individually regarded the nationalist movement cannot be accurately assessed. As has been noted before, the local notable can generally control the orientation of the group to which he belongs without the positive assent of the bulk of its members. If he has constructed his systems of alliance and patronage with sufficient skill, few will defy his lead which is binding in a moral ('ar) sense.

The discussion in the next few lines will be concerned with the motivations of the leaders and not the led. The former were left very much out in the cold at the time of independence. They had not kept their doors open to the Istiqlal, and despite the presence of Lahsan Lyoussi as minister of interior in the first government, Istiqlali personnel, hostile and scornful towards the rural notables, were rapidly infiltrating the blad as interior, police, justice, education, and public works employees, as well as party organizers. The intruders impinged upon the alliances carefully constructed under the protectorate, upset local patronage systems, and, in a more general way, often revealed a lack of understanding of rural politics. These factors all led to charges of 'Fassi colonization' on the part of rural notables. They had to find a channel to the top, an alternative to the Istiqlali steamroller. There was the PDI ready at hand with six ministers and the king's ear. The fact that it was no less Fassi than the Istiqlal (possibly more so) hardly seemed to matter. It served the purpose at hand, and, as pointed out in the previous chapter, this is the prime consideration in the choice of leaders and alliances.

It is curious indeed to find Hassan Wazzani a Berber leader, but such was his fortune during much of 1956 and 1957. There were pockets of PDI strength scattered through the Middle Atlas, in Tafilalt province (thanks to the encouragement of Governor Addi ou Bihi), and in the Rif. For all its functionality, this was a somewhat unnatural arrangement, particularly when there were available Berber notables who fancied themselves political leaders on a national scale. The king was aware that the old bilad as-siba would be resistant to Istiqlali penetration, and that it offered a clientele loyal to the person of the king as well as a counterweight to the Istiqlal. There was much talk of, but few steps taken toward, the establishment of a rural party. Tribal bigwigs, Amharoq among the Zayan, ou Bihi in the Ait Izdeg, Moha ou Said of the Ait Wirra, and Lyoussi of the Ait Youssi, may have all entertained thoughts of a party to oppose the Istiqlal. Probably the king would have preferred to see Bekkai or Lyoussi undertake steps in this direction, but no one was willing to take the initiative.

The first attempt to give concrete form to anti-Istiqlal sentiment was singularly inept. This was Governor Addi ou Bihi's 1957 revolt at the instigation of Lyoussi, in which everyone – the Berber notables, the king, and the French – except the Istiqlal came off looking badly. In 1956, the customary tribunals in Berber-speaking areas had been done away with, and were replaced by courts of first instance (*as-saddad*). The new judges assumed the legal powers granted the qaids and pashas under the protectorate pertaining mostly to criminal infractions. Much of the new judicial personnel that moved into the blad was identified as Istiqlali.* Addi ou Bihi regarded his province as his fief, and the whittling away of the legal and administrative powers at the disposal of himself and his retainers was seriously undermining his power base. He became extremely apprehensive when Lyoussi was replaced as minister of interior by Driss M'hammedi in May 1956.[1] Between then and January 1957, ou Bihi and Lyoussi evidently conjured up a plan to turn the Istiqlali tide.

As is almost always the case, the moment chosen to act was simultaneous with the king's departure, this time on a Mediterranean cruise. Having received arms through French officers in Morocco, ou Bihi, on 17 January 1957, closed down Istiqlali headquarters in Midelt, threw all offending personnages in jail, including the police chief and judge, and sealed off Midelt and Rich, the heart of his domain. The governor claimed his sole objective was to safeguard the throne from the machinations of the government. In the absence of the king, Prince Hassan dispatched two battalions of FAR to restore order and to bring back ou Bihi. Shortly thereafter, the governor surrendered on the strength of the *aman* (amnesty) offered him by General Kittani.

Something of what had gone on preceding and during his brief revolt came out in testimony in his trial in January 1959. The timing of the trial itself is important, coming as it did when the Rif was in revolt, and when the newly founded Mouvement Populaire had not yet had its party statutes accepted by the government. In the course of the trial, it became clear that the PDI in 1957 was ou Bihi's counterforce to the Istiqlali incursions into his territory.[2] Tihami Wazzani, an important PDI leader, was the governor's defense lawyer. One of the qaids armed by ou Bihi, Boutoulout of Talsint, testified in favor of his patron and in so doing the simplistic nature of rural politics was underlined. He professed his

* 'Abdulkrim Benjelloun of the executive committee of the Istiqlal was minister of justice from 7 December 1955 to 23 December 1958.

hatred of the Istiqlal and bemoaned the presence of Istiqlali judges in the province. Nevertheless, he himself had been a member of the Istiqlal from 1947 to 1955.[3] The question of 'Fassi colonization' or the intrusion of city boys into the blad was not really at stake here. The qaid of Midelt at the time was an Istiqlali but was also from the douar of Tashawit two kilometers away. Many of the judges who testified to mistreatment at the hands of ou Bihi's retainers were Berbers and almost certainly graduates of Azrou. What was at stake was ou Bihi's patronage system, and the issues of Berber vs. Arab and the PDI vs. the Istiqlal were bent to fit the inexorable need to defend the governor's nest egg.

The Istiqlal (both wings) wanted to make the most of this trial to discredit its rural opponents and to break down the barriers they had erected to impede the Istiqlal's development in their realms. A great number of prominent rural figures were accused of complicity in the governor's revolt. Lyoussi, who fled Morocco during the trial, was an obvious target. Others implicated by the prosecutor were Lahidi Ahardan, brother of the founder of the Mouvement Populaire, the brother of Commandant Oufqir,* and the Temsemani brothers of the eastern Rif. The death sentences[4] that were meted out to Lyoussi and ou Bihi were an implicit warning to the palace not to meddle in political affairs. The king had housed ou Bihi in the palace at Rabat for six months after his arrest in 1957,[5] and kept Lyoussi on as one of three members of the Crown Council until his flight in January 1959.

The revolt of Addi ou Bihi focused attention on the resentment of many regions of Morocco toward the Istiqlal. But it was also made plain that the older notables had little idea how to exploit this resentment in a practical way. Mahjoubi Ahardan, governor of Rabat province, became impatient with his clumsy elders. He did not have their wealth nor their reputation, and he was not taken very seriously by the palace.† Nonetheless he decided to precipitate matters. In the months following Addi ou Bihi's arrest, there were constant rumors of a new party.[6] Certainly

* The Oufqir family is from Bou Denib in the Tafilalt province where Oufqir père had been qaid. Commandant Oufqir's brother was secretary-general of the province during ou Bihi's governorship.

† Ahardan is from Oulmès (Ait 'Ammar) between the large Zemmour and Zayan tribal confederations. He had been a captain in the French army and was qaid at Oulmès at the time of the king's exile in 1953. He refused to sign the Glaoui petition of deposition and recognition of Ben 'Arafa.

Bekkai, Lyoussi, Wazzani and the king were aware of the talk, but the animators at this point were Ahardan and Dr Khatib. In October 1957 tracts appeared announcing the new party signed by one Haddou 'Rifi'. This was actually Haddou Abarkash of al-Hoceima, a graduate of Qarawiyin, and today president of the Mouvement Populaire. About a month later Ahardan gave a press conference in which he identified himself with the new party and declared that 'we did not fight for independence [*Istiqlal*] to lose our liberty'. Driss M'hammedi, a friend of Ahardan and the man who had originally introduced him to Khatib, was forced to dismiss him as governor for engaging in partisan activity.*

But the new party had no finances, no program, and was not even legal. Its founders were such neophytes that they constantly botched the drawing-up of party statutes and did not know the proper procedure for registering. Istiqlal officials were consequently able to hold up recognition of the party for months on a series of legal technicalities. The party did have the good will of several people, including the king and the prince, but most were skeptical as to whether Ahardan could bring off his venture. Typically the palace practised private assistance without running the risk of public association. Ahardan's press conference had precipitated matters in a relative sense only, and the project simmered until April 1958. At that time, it will be recalled, Prime Minister Bekkai approved a declaration drawn up by several politicians, including Wazzani, Khatib, and Ahardan, to the effect that, with local elections coming up, not all Moroccans enjoyed their full rights to political association. At issue was legal recognition of the Mouvement Populaire, and Bekkai† submitted his resignation as a symbol of his solidarity with the new party.

To dramatize the restlessness of rural Morocco and its desire to have a greater voice in the direction of the country's affairs, minor incidents, along the lines of closing down Istiqlali bureaus and manhandling local officials, occurred in various areas of Morocco, but particularly in the Rif. Similar incidents, whose

* In an interview with Ahardan, in Rabat (18 April 1966), he told me that had he not acted then, nothing would ever have come of the new party for no one appeared willing to budge.

† Bekkai had served as an officer in the French Army and was pasha of Sefrou when Muhammed v was exiled. He refused to sign the Glaoui petition and probably convinced Lahsan Lyoussi, the qaid there, to do likewise. Bekkai is a notable from the Beni Iznassen and his family property is at Berkane.

spontaneity is questionable, plagued the Balafrej government throughout the summer of 1958.

The alleged rural discontent, the ostensible *raison d'être* of the Mouvement Populaire, was to be symbolized by the transfer of the body of Si 'Abbas Mess'idi, who had been buried in Fez, to Ajdir,* a former center of Liberation Army activities in the Igzinnayan tribal area. Si 'Abbas in the popular mind had become a martyr of the Istiqlal's implacable ambition to bend all Moroccans to its will. Although permission to transfer the body had been requested by Khatib and Ahardan, it had been denied. They decided to move his remains anyway, and this was carried out on 2 October 1958, the third anniversary of the first military action of the Liberation Army.[7] Around five thousand tribesmen turned out for the reburial. Mehdi Essqalli, inspector-general of the Ministry of Interior and a well-known Istiqlali, arrived on the scene to try to disperse the crowd. He only managed to aggravate the situation and was obliged to call in elements of the *Forces Auxilliaires*. In breaking up the demonstration there was some bloodshed. The king met with Essqali and Laraqi, the governor of Fez, in Fez the following day, and it was decided that Khatib, Ahardan, and 'Abdullah Louggoutty† would have to be arrested for the illegal transfer of the body.

As a result of the arrests three distinct movements of tribal dissidence developed‡ and occupied the attention of national leaders for more than three months. The Rif, primarily Igzinnaya and Aith Waryaghar, was the major trouble spot, but there were also armed bands around Oulmès (Ahardan's hometown) led by Bel Miloudi and around Tahala south of Taza in the Beni Warain led by ex-qaid Moha ou Haddou. The events in the first two regions are directly attributable to the arrests of the leaders of the MP, while the last has but a tenuous connection. All the confusion, it should be added, was taking place simultaneously with the scission of the Istiqlal and the long governmental crisis of November–December

* Not to be confused with Ajdir near al-Hoceima which had been a center of operations for 'Abdulkrim al-Khattabi in the Rif War.

† 'Abdullah Louggoutty is of the Beni Iznassen, a resistant, and a former super-qaid in Oujda province who resigned in protest of the actions of the governor of Oujda, Muhammed Ould 'Amar Amidou, himself a former resistant and an Istiqlali. The governor, it is claimed, harassed anyone who dared speak ill of his party.

‡ A fourth insurrection occurred in the Midelt region but was touched off by the sentencing to death of Addi ou Bihi.

THE COMMANDER OF THE FAITHFUL

1958. It was, of course, the armed revolt in the north that had prompted Bou'abid to resign from the Balafrej government in the first place.

For two months, Khatib, Ahardan and Louggoutty held court in prison, while increasingly befuddled politicians came to negotiate with them. Some Istiqlalis had hoped that their arrests would nip the MP in the bud, but the reverse was proving true. On 23 October three battalions were sent against Bel Miloudi and his Zemmour backers in the Karrouba massif south of Oulmès, and the fire was eventually put out there. But the Rif was still boiling. Tracts had been distributed threatening a tribal onslaught on Fez if Khatib and Ahardan were not released.* On 11 November a group of tribesmen from the Aith Waryaghar presented a list of grievances and a petition to the king, after Lyazidi, the minister of defense, had visited the region. Troops had taken up positions in the north, but there were no engagements.[8] A royal commission, headed by 'Abderrahman Aneggai of the royal cabinet, was dispatched to the troubled area to assess popular feelings. On 3 December, during the inquest and at a time when the country had no government, Khatib, Ahardan and Louggoutty were released from prison. After a press conference at the Tour Hassan Hotel on 4 December, Khatib and Ahardan mysteriously departed for Madrid. A week later the royal commission presented its initial findings to the king. Local grievances were summarized under the following headings:

1 A feeling of abandonment and frustration. Independence had not brought the north what it had brought other regions.
2 Unemployment: difficulty of going to Algeria for work. Also many former soldiers who served in the Spanish Army were without work.
3 Fiscal injustice.
4 Lack of hospitals, roads, schools, agricultural credit.
5 Administrative snarls.

Aneggai in a public statement declared that everywhere he went in the provinces of Nador, al-Hoceima, and Taza, the people told

* The tracts were drawn up by Hussein Hassoun, an Ahardan stalwart from Oulmès, with the help of Driss Cherradi. Cherradi was in touch both with Ahardan and the prince. His father had been pasha at Khouribga and was considered to be a collaborator with the French but, somewhat late in the day, he made his peace with the nationalists.

him that they wanted administrators of integrity, no matter where they came from. These must be apolitical, and certain elements that have 'trespassed' into the administration must be eliminated.[9] All concerned viewed these complaints as more or less legitimate,[10] and a Rifi, Captain Medboh,* was made minister of PTT on 25 December. On this note the first phase of the Rif uprising came to a close.

The newly formed Ibrahim government pledged itself to remedy some of the ills that had arisen in integrating the ex-Spanish zone into the preponderant French zone economy. The grievances of the region were many. The Spanish had done little to develop their zone, and the general economic situation reflected that of the home country. The exploitation of the mineral and agricultural resources of the northern zone was in no way comparable to the French endeavors in the south. School and road construction and port development were minimal. The economies of the two regions functioned at very different rhythms, and their integration could only be brought about at considerable cost to the less advanced. Prices in the northern zone rose sharply with the introduction of the southern zone currency which was pegged to the French franc. The *tertib* tax was introduced, the use of the forests for grazing and fuel was put under strict control, and *kif* (a form of hashish) cultivation and trade was impeded. Tangier was deprived of its international status, and foreign businesses there began to close down, thus shutting off the most important source of labor demand in the north. The problem of unemployment was aggravated by the inaccessibility of Algeria during its revolution. The Rifis in particular had a long history of labor migration to Algeria. Finally, in the eyes of the northerners, independence seemed only to bring an influx of condescending southerners to administer the north, without any noticeable influx of capital to alleviate the region's economic depression.

Everyone hoped that Ibrahim's pledges would calm the aroused Rifis, and the departure of Khatib and Ahardan for Spain perhaps reflected their own belief that what they had started was now finished. But another round of tribal dissidence occurred in

---

* Captain Medboh is from the Igzinnayan (Dar Caid Medboh) where his father had been qaid. Captain Medboh had four times previously been a provincial governor. How much popularity the family enjoys in the Rif is problematic: Medboh *père* aided the French against the great Rifi hero, 'Abdulkrim.

December and January requiring substantial military intervention. The characteristics of the second phase differ markedly from those of the first, and brief mention of them may help resolve, to some degree, contradictory interpretations of the events of winter 1958-9.

Ernest Gellner was intrigued by at least two aspects of the uprisings which had little historical precedent; first that the uprisings collapse fairly easily and second that captured leaders are treated with leniency.[11] He explains this anomalous behavior as a facet of the new national game of politics, in which political leaders construct patronage systems whose ramifications run out from the capital city and intertwine with the administrative apparatus. These systems must be tested, must be shown to exist, so that the patron's potential power is made sufficiently evident. These tests are brief and are brought to a close by the patron himself once they have produced the desired effect. He sees to it that those locally responsible are treated lightly.[12] At the same time Gellner reprimands some analysts for having read into the uprisings 'attempts by tribesmen to recover their erstwhile tribal independence'.[13]

The Rif uprising lends itself to both interpretations, that sustained by Gellner and that which he seeks to refute. The question turns on which phase of the events one is considering. The first phase, spring 1958 through to the following November, can be interpreted according to Gellner's hypothesis of the 'political nervous system', but the second phase, particularly January 1959, fits better a reanimation of the tribal quest for autonomy. The tribe of Aith Waryaghar, or at least a large part of it,* ceded to the temptations of siba. Muhammed Hajj Sillam, referred to in the press as 'Amezzian', the *muqaddim* of the Waryaghar fraction of Beni Bou'Ayyash, was the ring leader of phase two.[14] He was joined by Mess'ud Aqjuj, leader of a fraction of the Igzinnayan. 'Abdullah Senhadji supported their actions and was active at Nador. He may have been in contact with Spain, and it seems certain that the Spanish tried to supply arms to the dissidents.[15] Sillam apparently promised the Aith Waryaghar great quantities of arms, and they were ready to follow him on the strength of this promise. He was never able to deliver on his

---

* Hart contends that in this uprising the Aith Waryaghar acted as a corporate group, probably for the first time since the Rif War.

pledge. This was no mere response to a patron's signal, as had been the case in phase one. Sillam, along with his partisans, had simply taken the bit in his teeth. There was no question of leniency in suppressing this uprising.

The king had issued an ultimatum that the tribesmen of the Rif must lay down their arms by noon, 7 January. Both Sillam and Aqjuj ignored the ultimatum, although Aqjuj did surrender a few days later. FAR detachments liberated the airstrip at Imzuren near al-Hoceima. Artillery barrages and aerial bombardments were used on dissident areas, and on 9 January Prince Hassan arrived at Tetouan to direct military operations. Infantry columns pushed into Waryagharland from Tetouan, Oujda, and Nador,[16] and on 16 January both Prince Hassan and Prime Minister Ibrahim entered al-Hoceima. By the end of January peace had been restored, and Sillam had fled to Spain. Casualty figures are hard to come by for this operation, but now, several years after the event, some of those who were involved are ready to admit that the suppression of the revolt was a good deal more brutal than had been stated at the time.

Despite the impromptu performances of the Rifis, the stage had been set for the launching of a rural based party. The Mouvement Populaire was legally recognized in February 1959, but it did not hold its constituent congress until November 1959. In the meantime, a Provisional Committee of Direction was established to draw up a program (it had done so by 1 June 1959), and to find some sort of financial support. The palace may have come to its aid at this juncture, but the MP has always seemed to hover on the brink of insolvency. Moreover, the new party did not wish to impose dues payments upon prospective recruits, for such impositions had become linked with the Istiqlal. Bekkai, in his capacity of President of the Association of Veterans and War Victims (perhaps 100,000 members), was able to encourage individual donations to the party from veterans' pensions.* There were also a few individual donors such as Driss Cherradi's father and Dr Khatib himself. Recourse to the Lyoussi family, and probably the Amharoqs, was avoided at this time by the party's founders, for they neither wanted the party to be dominated by the bloc of Middle Atlas tribes nor identified with what the

* Since Bakkai's death in 1961, Mahjoubi Ahardan has been president of this Association.

Istiqlalis called 'feudalist' elements. In addition Lyoussi was against the transfer of the body of Si 'Abbas and had told his Ait Youssi followers not to attend the ceremony at Ajdir.*

Two full years after Ahardan's press conference the Mouvement Populaire held its constituent congress at Rabat, 9–11 November 1959. This, it will be noted, came close on the heels of the UNFP's first congress in September, and Ben Barka had hoped to attract several members of the new rural party to his own. He was not very successful in this endeavor, but 'Abdullah Senhadji did (briefly) join the UNFP. Ahardan repeated several times that as far as he and his supporters were concerned the difference between the Istiqlal and the UNFP was negligible: both parties were equally bad.

The program that was presented to the delegates of the Rabat congress was based on a doctrine of 'Islamic socialism'.[17] The reader may judge for himself the solidity of the new ideology, but it is further evidence that pretensions to socialism in Morocco had not only become acceptable, they had become politically necessary. That Islamic socialism became the stock-in-trade of the MP was re-emphasized at its second congress in October 1962 and in the years between. But the title was misleading, for the real pitch was defense of the blad and unabashed 'Berberism'. For instance the 1959 program stated:[18]

The *jama'a*, living cell of the local community, and the existence of collective lands, should be the basis of our efforts toward the institution of socialism.

or again in 1962:[19]

A socialism within the context of Islamic doctrine and in accordance with the traditional vocation of the Moroccan people of which the collective lands and the *twiza* are vestiges full of meaning.

Moreover, the MP has consistently called for the distribution of state and *habous* land to local collectivities and tribes.

Direct appeals to Berber sentiments have been common themes. A constant demand of the MP has been the setting up of school programs to teach Berber dialects 'in order to safeguard the unity of the homeland'.[20] Addi ou Bihi's death in 1961 stirred the depths

* Much of my information on the MP has been extracted from one or more interviews with the following: Mahjoubi Ahardan, Dr Khatib, Hussein Hassoun, Muhammed Boukharta, Mustapha 'Alawi, 'Omar Chbouki, Driss Cherradi, Hassan Wazzani, Patrice Blacque-Bélair.

of Ahardan's Berber pride. In a speech at Sefrou[21] he defended his ancestors who had gone into siba, never against the monarchy but against corrupt intermediaries. He extolled the virtues of Addi ou Bihi, who, if he had really been a traitor, would have started a civil war. To be sure, he had received arms from the French, but there were no others with which to defend the king. In the same speech, Ahardan referred to the separation of judicial powers in 1956 and declared: 'In fact, when we were guided by *izref* (customary) law our situation was much to be preferred to that in which we find ourselves today. For Islamic justice has been rendered unrecognizable by the deviationists.'

Above all, however, the central tenet of the MP program has been unconditional support for the throne. In 1959 Khatib dwelt on the monarchical fervor that had inspired the Liberation Army, whose loyalty and Islamic beliefs 'the Europeanized intellectuals' ignored completely. The courage and devotion of the people triumphed despite these 'pseudo-intellectuals' and the 'excommunications launched by our ambassadors in exile'. This clearly was aimed at the Istiqlal and UNFP and the ambivalent attitude of their leaders towards the use of force in 1955. Still, it was a little embarrassing that a fair number of resistants had joined the UNFP, and the 1959 congress called for the suppression of armed groups that still infested the country (probably referring too the Southern Liberation Army) and demanded that the leaders of these bands be brought to justice.

After the 1959 congress the leaders of the new party undertook a major organizational effort.* Regional meetings were held in winter and spring 1960 throughout Morocco, and local bureaux were opened in all areas. Of course the immediate objective was to make a showing in the local elections of 29 May. This was not an auspicious moment to make a political debut, and, in the end the MP won only 7 per cent of the local seats contested. Unsurprising was the party's evident strength in the north – Oujda, Taza, and Nador – and also in Beni Mellal province.[22] To thwart the Istiqlal to the greatest extent possible, the Mouvement Populaire may have swallowed its pride and backed certain UNFP candidates. But much of the Rif had been under military administration since the

---

* The inspectors of the party were Louggoutty and Abarkash, and their principal assistants were Hussein Hassoun, Moulay 'Ali Zerhouni, Boukharta, Cherradi, Najjem Guerrouj, and Tayyib Bel'arbi.

fall of 1958, and in al-Hoceima province all political parties had been banned. In that province 57 per cent of the registered voters failed to turn up at the polls.

In late October 1962 the party held its second congress at Marrakesh where it had been making some headway. There the party called for a constitutional monarchy (it got its wish six weeks later) and proclaimed its unreserved support of the king. Dr Khatib was ratified in his post of president of the National Council and Ahardan as secretary-general of the party. The two thousand delegates elected a National Council of one hundred and eighty members and a Central Committee of twenty-one who, in the ensuing years, constituted the backbone of the party.

Altogether in keeping with the earnest but haphazard atmosphere that generally characterizes MP gatherings was the 'great goat debate'. After expounding the finer points of Islamic socialism for several hours, MP leaders found that many of the delegates were considerably more aroused by the vicissitudes of goat raising, specifically the fact that forest rangers would not let the goats graze near their precious trees. It seems Ahardan intervened energetically and suggested the importation for breeding purposes of special Spanish goats that do not eat leaves and bark. As a result of this debate, Ahardan earned himself the nickname of 'goat man' (*rajl al-ma'az*).

The resolutions of the 1962 congress also reiterated with feeling the rural world's lack of representation in the government, and, more particularly, its desire for a giant Ministry of Rural Affairs. It is true that when King Hassan constituted his first government (1 June 1961) after his father's death, Khatib and Ahardan were both in it, the first as minister of state for African affairs and the second as minister of defense. But this left the party still nibbling on the outer edges of patronage sources to which other parties had what seemed to be unjustified access. During the summer of 1962, Khatib and Ahardan privately threatened to resign if their party was not more favorably treated. Their resignations were not accepted, nor were their demands immediately met. Still, before the constitutional referendum of December 1962, on 18 October to be precise, Khatib was made minister of health (replacing the Istiqlali Yussuf Bel'Abbas). Finally, on 20 August 1964, Ahardan became minister of agriculture and agrarian reform, and his appointment was construed as the fulfillment of the party's previous demands. He was succeeded in this post in February 1966 by another member of the MP, Haddou Chiguer.*

It has already been posited that the monarchy does not wish to see any political party become too strong, nor, conversely, does it wish to see any party wither away entirely. In this respect there is no very meaningful distinction made between parties of opposition and parties of support. Few Moroccans, the king included, take very seriously the political labels fixed upon various groupings, and it is the better part of wisdom to tolerate, even encourage, division in groups whose loyalty to the throne is as yet unquestioned. If the Moroccan left lies shattered, the Moroccan right is hardly in better shape.

The unavoidable personality clashes that had lain dormant in the MP came to light in 1963 with the formation of the Front pour la Défense des Institutions Constitutionelles (FDIC). Here for the first time was a coalition of pro-monarchical forces more or less explicitly united on the basis of loyalty to the throne. The creation of FDIC was announced on 20 March 1963 by Reda Guedira, its prime mover, at the time of the departure of the king on an official visit to the United States. The Front was composed of the PDC,† the Liberal Independents, the MP, and several independent political figures It is said that the leaders of the MP agreed to enter the coalition only after having been urged to do so by the king. Mahjoubi Ahardan in particular was cool to the whole idea, and he had always manifested misgivings at joining forces with any other groups. A political novice, he generally felt ill at ease with the smoother, more articulate city politicians (of whom no better example can be found than Guedira), and his somewhat shaky Arabic did not bolster his self-confidence. As a result he became very jealous of the organizational autonomy of the MP which he regarded as his brain-child and his responsibility. His apprehensions of being lost in a bigger pond were repeatedly explained to his followers as his refusal to entrust their fate to perfidious politicians. Dr Khatib, while personally close to Ahardan, was not always in complete accord with the latter's often impulsive political deeds. Moreover, he was more than a little ill at ease in an atmosphere increasingly permeated by pure 'Berberism'. Despite his

* Chiguer was replaced by Muhammed Zeghari in March 1967.

† When Boutaleb, Bensouda, and Tihami Wazzani joined the UNFP in 1959, the PDI changed its title to Parti Démocratique Constitutionnel (PDC).

Rifi support, Khatib has few personal claims to being a Berber. His upbringing in al-Jadida, his medical studies in France, made him at home with the urban elite. But he too had misgivings about FDIC.

Thus it was with great reluctance that the MP entered Guedira's alliance. 'Abdullah Louggoutty was dead set against participation, and there was talk of ejecting him from the party. Ahardan, minister of defense, accompanied the king on his trip to Washington, and when he returned, he found, so he claims, that Khatib had made a deal with Guedira and was integrating the MP into FDIC. It is true that Guedira wished to make of FDIC a unified political party, and Ahardan suspected that Khatib had arranged with Guedira to subordinate the MP to FDIC and to dump the secretary-general in the process.[23]

The choice of candidates for the legislative elections and the elections themselves accentuated difficulties within the party. It was only after exhausting negotiations that Ahardan agreed to the list of candidates that would run on the FDIC ticket. Even then, in many rural areas, there were renegade candidates, including Louggoutty at Ahfir, who refused to abandon the MP label. To make matters still worse, in the legislative elections themselves Khatib won easily at Aknoul while Ahardan was crushed at Khenifra.

The commencement of parliamentary life in Morocco served to crystallize differences within the MP. On 13 November 1963 the king formed a government which included several ministers who had been defeated in the elections, among them Mahjoubi Ahardan. This seemed grossly unfair to those who had won seats in the name of FDIC. Their champion became Dr Khatib who had been dropped from the government (his brother 'Abderrahman, however, became minister of interior), and they elected him president of the Chamber of Deputies.* Khatib's election as president was the result of a tactical accord with Guedira, who sought someone capable of controlling the MP. The MP, with its forty-odd deputies, was the majority of the majority, and many of their deputies were not willing to rubber stamp everything passed

---

* FDIC, with 69 representatives, had a relative majority of the 144 seats in parliament. There were 41 Istiqlalis, 28 UNFP, and 6 independents. Of FDIC's representatives there were about 42 members of the Mouvement Populaire.

their way by ministers, who, having been rejected by the electorate, did not hesitate to show their scorn for the Parliament.

Still, the parliamentary delegation hoped that it would receive its just rewards through the good offices of Ahardan. He had never stinted in his criticism of the manner in which Guedira and his clan had monopolized the patronage of the majority to the exclusion of the MP.* Citing the preponderance of MP deputies in the FDIC delegation, he recalled to Guedira and his cohorts, 'we brought the grain, and you brought the chaff'. Coordination among the component parts of FDIC became increasingly difficult, and, in January 1964, in the middle of the first parliamentary session, Ahardan urged upon his followers a complete break with FDIC. Guedira countered on 14 April by founding a new party, still nominally within the FDIC coalition, called the Parti Socialiste Democrate (PSD) and grouping all the representatives and ministers of FDIC who did not belong to the MP. The fact that 'Abderrahman Khatib was a founding member of the PSD reenforced Ahardan's view that Dr Khatib was in league with Guedira. Ahardan as usual had an aphorism ready for the occasion, and alluding to the Rabat clan in the PSD, intoned 'We did not conquer the *Tala'a* [a sector of Fez associated with the Fassi bourgeoisie] to fall victim to *Bouqroun* [a quarter associated with the Rabat elite.]' All this came to a head in the second session of Parliament when the UNFP presented a motion of censure of the government's economic policy (see below, p. 263). It came as no surprise that the Istiqlal decided to vote for the UNFP motion, but part of the majority threatened to bolt FDIC on this issue. Hussein Hassoun announced that many MP deputies sympathized with the motion, and that the government should not take its majority for granted. The palace would have to appease the disgruntled majority of the majority. In July, Khatib and Ahardan agreed that a ministerial reshuffle should see Louggoutty, Cherradi, and Boukharta included in the new government, but, with Khatib absent abroad in August, Ahardan submitted to the king the names of Haddou Chiguer and 'Abdesslam Ben'Aissa. Accordingly, in the

* Ministers not belonging to the MP but associated with FDIC in the 13 Nov. 1963 government were: Ahmad Bahnini, Fall Ould Omeir, Guedira, 'Abdelhadi Boutaleb, 'Abdelqader Benjelloun, Yussuf Bel'Abbas, Driss Slaoui, Tihami Wazzani, Moulay Ahmad 'Alawi, and Muhammed Benhima. Against this array the MP could boast only Ahardan, 'Abdarrahman Khatib, and two undersecretaries of state, Haddou Chiguer and 'Abderrahman al-Kohen.

government formed on 20 August 1964, Chiguer became minister of PTT, Ben'Aissa under-secretary of state for the resistance, and Ahardan became minister of agriculture. Khatib, not to mention Louggoutty, Cherradi, and Boukharta, felt betrayed.

A new nucleus of MP deputies formed around Louggoutty who, as second vice-president of the Chamber of Deputies, often presided over the parliamentary sessions. This group, more or less encouraged by Khatib, made war on the government. Driss Cherradi had been dismissed in the winter of 1964–5 as director of Royal Air Maroc (RAM) by Muhammed Benhima, the minister of public works, under whose jurisdiction RAM falls. When, on 25 January, the annual budget of Public Works was submitted to the deputies for approval, fifteen members of the majority voted against it. Istiqlal and UNFP delegates had made a habit of voting against any government proposal, but the fifteen added votes brought this particular budget down to defeat. Almost simultaneously the insurgent faction began to accuse Ahardan of a multitude of sins: dictatorship within the party, racism, exaggerated Berberism.[24] Khatib bemusedly formed an arbitration committee, but about a week later those loyal to Ahardan founded a new weekly, *Al-Haraka*, because the official organ of the party, *Al-Maghreb al-'Arabi*, was controlled by Khatib.

After the Casablanca riots of March 1965 there was, needless to say, much talk of a censure motion, but this time Khatib was in the forefront of the move. By this time the king had given up hope in his parliamentary majority and was entertaining thoughts of a government of 'national union'.* At one point he sounded out Khatib on his willingness to be prime minister, but Khatib placed too many conditions on his appointment. On 19 May the Istiqlal proposed a modification to the Press Code which, if it were to be approved, would forbid non-Moroccans to publish in Morocco. This motion came to a vote on 7 June (with Louggoutty presiding) and was approved 55–22 despite the fact that FDIC had submitted a countermotion of its own. The rebels within FDIC had struck again, this time through abstentions. The king hesitated no longer, dissolved Parliament, and proclaimed the state of emergency the same day.[25] Khatib publicly voiced his disaccord with the king's move and stated his confidence that the majority was still viable

---

* It was at this time that he pardoned those arrested in 1963 for the plot and started negotiations with Ben Barka in Europe.

and that parliamentary institutions had not been endangered.*

After conferring with the king at Ifrane, Ahardan agreed to participate in a government presided over by the king himself. Khatib had been invited to consult with the king also, but he pleaded illness and did not go. On 12 June Ahardan announced to the Central Committee of the MP that he and Chiguer had been asked to join the new government. Khatib, Boukharta, the Louggoutty brothers, and Muhammed Bekkai objected strongly to such participation, but the majority of the Central Committee

The Split of the Mouvement Populaire†

* It had been on the basis of Art. 35 of the constitution that the king had acted. Art. 35 gives him the right to declare a state of emergency 'should any event interrupt the course of action of the constitutional institutions. . . .'

† From *Al-Kawalis*, 3 Dec. 1965.

Mahjoubi Ahardan, to the right, declares: 'Anyone who wants to, can get out.' Khatib, to the left, replies 'So long.' Khatib, the wealthy city dweller, is heading off in the direction of his birthplace, al-Jadida, while Ahardan seeks his support back in his blad in the area of Khemisset. Khatib is portrayed as well dressed, leading a plump goat, the pejorative symbol of the party. The crescent on his voted approval. Khatib and his followers stalked out of the meeting. Subsequently Ahardan read out of the party the two Louggouttys and Boukharta. He did not touch Khatib for the sake of party unity nor Bekkai because of his illustrious name. Khatib answered back in the pages of *Al-Maghreb al-'Arabi*, denouncing Ahardan for 'tribalism' and high-handedness, and demanded a national congress of the party to pass judgment on the expulsions.[26] About a week later *Al-Maghreb al-'Arabi* was closed down by order of General Oufqir, minister of interior, who has generally aided Ahardan in his struggle with Khatib. During the summer there were rumors of Khatib's intentions to found a new party, perhaps with UMT support.[27] Nothing came of these rumors, and most of 1965 and 1966 went by with one faction demanding a national congress and the other denying there was any need for it. The Khatibists called the others opportunists who would do anything to hold on to their government sinecures.* The Ahardanists retorted that the Khatibists were only upset because they had lost their parliamentary salaries.† There was a scramble for party members as each faction jockeyed for position. As usual few Moroccans were willing to choose until a winner had emerged.

Following form, Ahardan made his winning move when Khatib was on an official voyage to Saudi Arabia. Abruptly Ahardan convoked the Fifth National Congress (where the third and the fourth were is difficult to ascertain) of the MP, at Kenitra, on 4 November 1966. This stratagem followed a meeting of Khatib's partisans in Rabat on 17 October. They had noted that there had not been a congress in four years, and that, according to the party statutes, the secretary-general must be elected every two years. The group judged that Ahardan had ceased to be secretary-general two years ago and proceeded to elect Khatib provisional secretary-general. Two days later, Ahardan formally excluded Khatib from the MP and consummated the deed at the impromptu congress.

At the congress Ahardan easily had his way with the delegates, a new Ahardanist Central Committee was elected, and Haddou

---

breast indicates his supposed sympathies for the Arab cause and language. Ahardan is presented as the underfed country boy, with sandals and a scrawny goat, but the crown on his breast symbolizes his primary loyalty to the throne.

* There seems some justification in this charge: many of those who went along with Ahardan had some sort of state function: Cherradi, Hassoun, Al-Kohen, Zerhouni, Rahmani, Bel'arbi, Rahali.

† The Khatibists willingly admit this charge.

Abarkash became the new president of the Mouvement Populaire. The congress stole Khatib's thunder and called for an end to the state of emergency.[28] In February 1967, Khatib acknowledged the *fait accompli* and announced the birth of a new party, the Mouvement Démocratique Populaire, under his leadership. The new party has so far remained inactive, but it represents yet another potential pawn in the king's chess game.

In the intricate and complicated machinations that led to the formation and the eventual split of the Mouvement Populaire certain elements stand out. Once again we find the reluctance of Moroccans to take initiative even when those concerned are agreed that it is essential to do so: thus, the months that elapsed between the first attempts to found a Berber party and the actual founding of the Mouvement Populaire. Like all other political groupings, the MP was a coalition of patronage groups, brought together with great difficulty, and prepared to coexist but not to cooperate. The latent crisis between the two major factions – those of Khatib and Ahardan – over the division of spoils and patronage re-enforced the internal paralysis of the party. In turn, the nascent split in the party festered from March 1963 (the founding of FDIC) to June 1965 (the proclamation of the state of emergency), before it was openly acknowledged. It was not until November 1966 that Ahardan decided to break with Khatib. Because of the usual phenomenon of dropouts both factions lost strength as a result of the split, and the king was able to pick up his favorite kind of clientele; unattached individuals.

CHAPTER THIRTEEN

AGENTS OF SEGMENTATION: FDIC

A situation of political imbalance in Morocco spontaneously elicits corrective processes. The preponderance of the Istiqlal in 1956 stirred into action disparate personalities and factions whose primary, if not sole objective was to cut the Istiqlal back down to size. The monarchy was a direct participant in this process; its focal point and its animator. There were enough willing and eager hands to undertake the task without the throne openly involving itself in the muzzling of the Istiqlal. One of the most avid opponents of the Istiqlal, of 'single-party dictatorship', has been Reda Guedira whom we left, along with the Liberal Independents, in suspended animation at the beginning of the preceding chapter.

Guedira's following among educated Rabatis was to play the same role among the urban elite as the Mouvement Populaire among the rural elite: it was to serve as a rallying point for those who had no place in or had been alienated by the Istiqlal. Like Ahardan and Khatib, Guedira had great difficulty in attracting clientele and in forming effective alliances, particularly in bringing about an urban-rural coalition. But FDIC was essentially that, a fragile alliance between the rural Mouvement Populaire and the urban supporters and sympathizers of Guedira. Various figures had, at one time or another, worked towards this coalition, but it was the possibility of a major Istiqlali victory in the 1963 legislative elections that finally, though temporarily, brought them together. It was the problem of selecting candidates for these elections, and then the difficulties of directing the coalition in the new Parliament that led to FDIC's disintegration. Because the elections and the brief parliamentary experience had such a great influence upon the evolution of FDIC, a brief analysis of both is presented in this chapter.

In 1955 the 'Friends of Rachid Mouline', until that time an informal grouping of Rabati politicos, became a political party, the Liberal Independents. As such, they were awarded one Ministry – Guedira as minister of information – in the first government. Mouline joined Guedira in the second government as minister of state for the Civil Service. But it was Guedira who was closely linked with the palace through his intimate association with Prince Hassan. Even when the Liberals were driven from the government from May 1958 until June 1961, Guedira remained in close contact with the prince and his cabinet whose behind-the-scenes manoeuvres so irritated the Ibrahim government.* When Hassan became king, Guedira became, without much exaggeration, his grand vizir. From 1961 to November 1963 he occupied the post of director-general of the royal cabinet with delegated powers equivalent to those of a prime minister.[1] At about the same time he was appointed minister of the interior and of agriculture, posts which he occupied through the elections of May 1963.

The political mentor of the Liberals was Rachid Mouline, a member of an important Rabat family and whose father had once been minister of habous under the protectorate. However his 'friends' were considerably younger than he, and their ambitions and energy eventually led them to break with him. The Liberals, whether the followers of Guedira or Mouline, have all been from Rabat (with the exception of Badr ad-Din Senoussi who is from Casablanca but did not join until 1958), and were secondary school students (several at the College Moulay Youssef) during the early years of the nationalist movement. The two most important Rabatis in the Istiqlal, Balafrej and Lyazidi, were their seniors and had no hold over them. When the National Party split in 1937 over what they felt to be a senseless issue, they followed Mouline into a neutral position.

Like the leaders of the UNFP, most of the Liberals received their higher education in France, but unlike the former they became impregnated with the liberal philosophy associated with the

---

* Not all of Guedira's actions at that time were hidden. In 1959, the journal *Les Phares* was started under the direction of Muhammed Ziani, one of Guedira's closest associates, and its self-assigned task was to make life difficult for Ibrahim.

Radical Party in France. They judged the leadership of their own association to be old-fashioned, and that they would have to move beyond their *za'im*, Mouline. Guedira became the effective leader of the group, and one of his colleagues remarked that Guedira was to the Liberals what Ben Barka was to the Istiqlal. Guedira's principal lieutenants were and are M'faddel Cherkaoui and Muhammed Ziani, and his most constant supporters: the two Bargache brothers, 'Omar Ben Brahim, 'Omar Ben Mess'ud, Dr Ben Boucha'ib, Muhammed Regregui, Fatmi Britel, and Muhammed Belgnaoui.

Guedira has always believed that Morocco can maintain its cohesion only if there are a number of political groups competing for governmental power. If any one party were to become dominant, it would destroy the nation's political stability in two ways. First, it would obviate the necessity of an arbiter in politics and thus would render the monarchy obsolete. But the monarchy, because of its long political history and its religious attributes, is the symbol of Moroccan social cohesion and the focal point for national consensus. Second, any party is likely to represent only one or a few of the many elements that constitute Morocco's highly complex society. Its triumph would be artificial, could be sustained only through coercion, and would inevitably lead to a new form of siba. In keeping with his own analysis, Guedira has ceaselessly worked to prevent single-party dominance, and in his own view the major threat in this respect has come from the Istiqlal. A series of initiatives undertaken by him and other like-minded Moroccans, beginning in 1958, finally culminated in the creation of FDIC, a loose coalition whose aim was to counterbalance the Istiqlal.

FDIC was five years in the making and had several false starts. It was always the presumed imminence of elections that galvanized anti-Istiqlali factions into action. From 1958 to 1960 the local elections were perpetually just around the corner, and after the 1962 constitutional referendum there was the prospect of a whole series of national, local, and occupational elections. FDIC and its forerunners have been passed off by some as mere electoral alliances, temporary and negative in intent. This may be so, but almost all Moroccan political groupings are coalitions, more or less temporary, and more or less defensive in their aims. Moreover, the fact that oncoming elections served as a catalyst to coalition where all else failed is indicative of the great importance attached to election results in determining the political demography of the country. In 1960 and 1963 all politicians tacitly, though some not publicly, accepted the elections as a legitimate test of their strength and as a challenge to live up to their advance press. Thus, to slough off the FDIC as a simple electoral coalition is to underestimate the crucial nature of its task, temporary though it may have been.

To return once again to April 1958, one finds in embryo the allies who were to form FDIC five years later. On 15 April, Hassan Wazzani, 'Abdelhadi Boutaleb, Dr Khatib, Mekki Naciri,* Ahardan, Rachid Mouline, and Reda Guedira (the latter two were the only ministers) presented a motion to Prime Minister Bekkai. The motion stressed that 'with the approach of local elections not all Moroccans are fully endowed with their democratic rights. Associations and political parties cannot constitute themselves freely. All signatories [of the motion] agree to work together to guarantee and promote the interests of all Moroccan citizens and demand a law guaranteeing these rights.'[2] Bekkai presented the motion to the king, approved its intent, and submitted his resignation.

It was, as we know, the status of the MP that was at issue in this manoeuvre. Somewhat less than a year later it became a legally constituted party. At the same time the ardor for the coalition cooled as the likelihood of local elections became more remote under the governments of Balafrej and Ibrahim. But almost on the eve of the local elections of 1960 the anti-Istiqlalis came to life again. On 15 May 1960, Ahardan, Wazzani, and Bekkai signed a *Protocol of Entente and Unity of Action between the Mouvement Populaire and the PDC*.[3] The protocol called for, among other things, the resignation of the Ibrahim government and the formation of one of national union (the demand was met within a few days). The PDC and MP pledged that neither one would enter such a government without the other.† A committee of liaison‡ was set up with a secretariat at Casablanca run by

* Naciri, before independence, had been the leader of the Islah (Reform) Party at Tetouan. He is a member of the venerable Naciri family of Salé.

† The signatories were adequately rewarded for their timely demand. Bekkai, Khatib, and Muhammed Cherkaoui all became ministers on 26 May.

‡ The committee was composed of Khatib, Ahardan, Cherradi (MP), and Wazzani, Cherkaoui, Maaninou (PDC), and Bekkai as an independent.

Driss Cherradi (MP) and Muhammed Cherkaoui (PDC). It had been hoped that the electoral alliance could be prolonged and developed into a merger of the two parties and probably including the Liberals, but Ahardan refused to scale down the autonomy of the MP.[4]

The alliance between the PDC and the MP bore fruit only once. The king, in late August 1960, chose a seventy-eight man constitutional council from the nation's political,* economic, regional, and cultural groupings, to write a draft constitution. The constitutional council held elections for its presiding officer in January 1961. The two candidates were Muhammed Zeghari and 'Allal al-Fassi, and the latter won easily, 44–27. After his victory, two other members of the council, Ahardan and Maaninou, announced in the name of their respective parties their withdrawal from the body.

The withdrawal of these two parties, taken in conjunction with the absence of the UMT and the UNFP, deprived the council of any credible claims to representivity and effectively paralyzed it. The death of Muhammed V in February 1961 sealed its fate, and it was never convened after Hassan's accession to the throne.

The constitution itself,[5] particularly in its clauses regarding a national bicameral legislature, served to rekindle the fires of anti-Istiqlalism. In lieu of the constitutional council the final text of the constitution was drawn up literally behind closed doors. Guedira and his closest associates are not at all shy about claiming substantial responsibility for the draft. The constitutional prohibition of a single-party system mentioned above is Guedira's brain-child and, according to M'faddel Cherkaoui, is the consummation of seven years of indefatigable labor.[6]

Once the constitution was approved, Guedira was faced with protecting his invention. He was particularly concerned by the series of elections that were to commence six months after the referendum. As he put it, 'We had built a house that would be inhabited by our adversaries; we had to make room for our friends.'[7] It is a bit difficult to pin down the justification for his fears. The UNFP was the only (legal) party to oppose the constitution, and received the tepid approval of the UMT in this respect. The UNFP objected to the document on several scores: the secrecy involved in its preparation, the 'excessive' powers retained

* Protesting the fact that it was an appointed and not an elected body, the UMT and UNFP refused to participate in it.

by the throne, the ambiguities inherent in a government responsible, according to the constitution, to both king and Parliament. To supplement these secular criticisms the UNFP resorted to the religious pronouncements of Moulay Larbi al-'Alawi who condemned the principle of primogeniture as the new rule of dynastic succession. The UNFP stance against the constitution evidently drew little popular response at the time of the referendum as the constitution was overwhelmingly approved. Having been thoroughly drubbed in the first round, the UNFP, revealing great flexibility to say the least, decided to present candidates for Parliament in an attempt to recoup its losses. Still, it did not announce its intentions to do so until May 1963, well after the foundation of FDIC.

The Istiqlal, for its part, had not stinted in its efforts to encourage approval of the constitution.[8] Despite its support, Guedira and many others suspected the party's motives. It was believed that the Istiqlal would claim that its appeals had guaranteed popular acceptance of the constitution, and that it would then strive to obtain a majority in the new Parliament. If this were to be the case, the Istiqlal could then proceed to amend the constitution to fit more exactly its own preferences. Moreover, in the weeks following the referendum, Guedira could not be sure that the UNFP and the Istiqlal would not form an alliance for the legislative elections. To deflate the Istiqlal's ego after its self-proclaimed triumph in the referendum, the three Istiqlali ministers (al-Fassi, Boucetta, Douiri) were given a good excuse to resign, which they did. This marked the first time since independence that no Istiqlalis were represented in the government.

Rumors of a governmental party began to circulate immediately following the referendum. Because of the Gaullist style of the constitution, it was thought that the new party would probably call itself the Union pour la Nouvelle Monarchie. In fact it had been planned to name the party Front pour la Monarchie Constitutionnelle. The king was very much involved in preparations for the Front, and he was fully aware that the throne was 'dans le jeu', but ultimately it was decided to expunge the word 'monarchy' so as not to compromise the king.[9] 'Omar Ben Brahim, a Liberal, became director of the royal cabinet in January 1963 (Guedira remained as director-general), and he was rumored to be the secretary-general of the Front. Guedira does not pretend that FDIC was any more than a device to forestall an Istiqlali victory in the elections. He would have liked to have built something durable but realized that his allies of the hour boded ill for the life of FDIC. But at least the MP and PDC shared his concern for the monarchy and the constitution. The allies came together only after the urging of the king, and to get the party off the ground several ministers announced their adhesion to it.* But no sooner formed, the alliance began to come unstuck. The ill-will among the component parts of FDIC, generated in the process of selecting a slate of candidates for the elections, was stifled just long enough for FDIC to win its parliamentary majority. After that, there was no controlling personal grudges.

Most observers had expected the electoral series to begin with local elections, followed by professional, provincial, Chamber of Counsellors, and finally Chamber of Deputies elections. However in mid-April the king reversed the order. He loftily justified the reversal in this manner:[10] 'I wished them [the elections] thus in the hope that the political climate of our public life will be rapidly cleansed, avoiding a useless extension of sterile, destructive polemics.' He then went on to endorse in all but name the candidates of FDIC. If, he said, the country wishes governmental stability then it must elect a clear-cut majority in the Chamber of Deputies. He recommended that all Moroccans vote for those who are 'determined, like you and me, to remain faithful to its [the constitution's] orientations and principles'.[11]

On 2 May, two weeks before the elections, the UNFP decided to enter a slate of candidates. It termed this action 'opening a front in the very ranks of the forces of reaction. . . . It is not a question of ameliorating the regime, of modifying or adapting it. For the UNFP, it is a question of its abolition.'[12] Once having decided to join in the game, the situation seemed to dictate an alliance with the Istiqlal, but the barriers to such an arrangement proved insurmountable. The Istiqlal and UNFP had traded epithets at the time of the referendum, not to mention the entire period since the party split, and these remarks could not easily be forgotten. Also it was certain that the Istiqlal, after its success and the UNFP's failure in the referendum, would claim that its members were

* Besides Ahardan, Khatib, and Guedira, Moulay Ahmad 'Alawi, 'Abdelhadi Boutaleb, Driss Slaoui, Ahmad Bahnini all joined FDIC. Prince Moulay 'Ali, Muhammed Benhima, and Yussuf Bel'Abbas were active sympathizers.

responsible for the election of any winning UNFP candidates.[13] The parties were able to agree not to run rival candidates in districts in which one or the other party was known to be strong.

The results of the elections satisfied no one.[14] FDIC won only a relative majority, and seven ministers went down to defeat.* The Istiqlal and UNFP accused Guedira of having grossly rigged the elections as minister of interior, while defeated FDIC candidates charged that he had not done enough. From the point of view of my analysis, what is most striking in the results is the practical effect of the lack of coordination between the UNFP and the Istiqlal. FDIC, with sixty-nine seats, won only 24 per cent of total votes cast. The Istiqlal (41 seats and 21 per cent) and the UNFP (28 seats and 16 per cent) won a relative majority (37 per cent) of total votes cast. Looked at another way, the median vote cast per elected candidate was: FDIC – 16,810; Istiqlal – 24,541; and UNFP – 26,823.[15] If one adds up the votes cast for party candidates, there still remains 39 per cent of the voters unaccounted for. These represent the non-partisan voters of Morocco, and, as such, with only six deputies, were the most underrepresented sector of the electorate.

The Istiqlal and UNFP contested the representivity of the legislative elections, aiming their most telling blows at Guedira.† On 4 June he gave up his post as minister of interior to clear the atmosphere and was replaced by Ahmad Hamiani, a neutral. Hamiani then became responsible for the ensuing local, professional, and Chamber of Counsellors elections. But alleged harassment of UNFP and Istiqlal candidates seeking to register led both these parties to consider boycotting the elections. The UNFP's fairly strong showing in the legislative election had surprised FDIC, which had concentrated on stopping the Istiqlal. The local elections, which had been scheduled for 28 June, were postponed a full month, probably so that the FDIC could regroup to stave off the UNFP. It seems more than likely then that the UNFP protests were well-founded. The plot arrests of 16 July came after the decision of the UNFP to boycott the elections, but the arrests, including those of duly-elected members of Parliament, helped

* Ahardan, Bel'Abbas, Benhima, Boutaleb, Bahnini, and Alawi were all beaten by Istiqlalis, while Driss Slaoui lost to a UNFP candidate.

† The Istiqlal press reported that on 24 June a faithful party member from the Chawia was arrested for having named his dog 'Guedira'.

decide the Istiqlal and UMT to boycott also.[16] As a result FDIC candidates ran virtually unopposed and, indeed, in all subsequent elections. Of the 120 members of the indirectly-elected Chamber of Counsellors, 78 had party labels, and of those 74 were FDIC.* Although many ministers and other important figures, defeated in the elections to the Chamber of Deputies, were able to regain a modicum of their prestige through the election to the Counsellors, the body was, as a whole, not quite 'the quintessence of the elite' described by an official journal.[17] The body included thirteen illiterates and the educational level of the bulk of its members was abysmally low.

The Parliament, like FDIC, was probably doomed to failure before it ever convened. In particular, King Hassan had been greatly deceived by the slender victory of FDIC, and what he had hoped would be a cooperative body to legitimize the acts of his government had not come to pass. On the other hand, the Istiqlal and the UNFP, convinced in advance that FDIC would crush them at the polls, had minimized the importance of the Parliament. After their relative victory in the elections they were the prisoners of their own pre-election rhetoric.[18] The individuals that made up the majority very definitely took their new status seriously, but the rivalries within FDIC prevented them from ever acting as a coherent group. Only if FDIC had established some sort of internal unity would it have been possible to have realized one of Guedira's prime objectives: governmental responsibility to the majority. As it was the government could safely ignore the majority, and was inclined to do so in any case, as so many of the ministers had been defeated in the elections. For all these reasons then, there was practically no one committed to the successful operation of the Parliament.

From the outset of parliamentary life it appeared that the king wished to make a mockery of the experiment, and it is only fair to note that all concerned aided him admirably in his task. The opposition parties resorted to debilitating tactics designed in general to embarrass the government. The latter reciprocated with systematic hostility.[19]

For instance, the second parliamentary session convened three

* Eighty were elected by provincial assemblies all dominated by FIDC. The other forty were elected by the Chambers of Agriculture (16), the Chambers of Commerce and Industry (14), Chambers of Artisans (5), and the Chambers of Wage Earners (5). The elections took place 13 Oct. 1963.

weeks late, on 18 May 1964. Two days later the price of sugar was raised without any advance warning to the Deputies, and on 21 May the Istiqlal and UNFP delegates left the Parliament in protest over procedural irregularities. Then on 15 June came the UNFP's censure motion of government economic policy.[20] The debates were televised, and government representatives did their best to convert them into a public trial of the UNFP. Bahnini, 'Alawi, 'Abderrahman Khatib, and Guedira sought to draw the UNFP deputies into a political debate. At one point 'Alawi challenged the president of the UNFP parliamentary group, 'Abdellatif Benjelloun, to come before the assembly and the cameras and publicly dissociate himself and his party from Mehdi Ben Barka, who had been condemned to death *in absentia* some months earlier. Throughout the debates never once did Driss Slaoui, the minister of economy, or Mamoun Tahiri, the under-secretary of state for finance, appear before the Parliament to defend the government's economic policy.

When the king dissolved Parliament, he could emphasize the futility of the body by pointing to the fact that it had passed only two laws in its two years of existence. The majority, as we have already seen, had become untenable. The creation of the PSD (see p. 249) in April 1964 merely gave substance to a division that had been awkwardly patched over since the preceding summer. The new party offered up basically the same program as that of FDIC, but its founders did not include any members of the MP or PDC. On the other hand, many of the founders were ministers who had been defeated in the elections and who had ridden rough-shod over their own parliamentary majority. In addition, a few previously uncommitted personalities, such as Laghzaoui, Yussuf Bel'Abbas, and Zeghari, became formal members of the new organization. The creation of the PSD only managed to rankle the MP delegates even more, and probably explains to some extent Hussein Hassoun's threat to vote with the UNFP and Istiqlal in favor of the censure motion. According to the journal of the PSD, *Al-Watan*, the 'aereopagus' of the party was:[21]

President: Ahmad Bahnini	Muhammed Laghzaoui
Sec.-Gen.: Reda Guedira	M'Faddel Cherkaoui
Yussuf Bel'Abbas	Tihami Wazzani
'Abderrahman Khatib	(cited as 'the father of the
Moulay Ahmad 'Alawi	party's ideology')

One can imagine that Guedira was severely disillusioned by the dreary spectacle of the Parliament and its bickering majority, and he was certainly aware that his disappointment was matched by that of the king. The founding of the PSD, in this light, can be regarded as a last-ditch attempt to give a minimum of guidance to the majority. Nonetheless the king had begun a slow process of whittling away Guedira's powers. First, in June 1963, he was relieved of Interior, and in November 1963 he became minister of foreign affairs but was obliged to give up Agriculture. As minister of foreign affairs, he found himself in an unenviable position *vis-à-vis* the 'hawks' of the Moroccan general staff as he strove to find a diplomatic as opposed to a military solution to Morocco's border dispute with Algeria. In the summer of 1964 the government agreed to initiate special courts to try all cases involving corruption in public employ. Guedira privately opposed the project, for there were already in existence adequate means to handle administrative corruption, and, in any case, the victims would surely be petty offenders. The creation of these courts led to Guedira's resignation from all public functions, on 15 August 1964, and the decision taken against his counsel represented the final act in the breakdown of the long-standing *entente* between the king and himself. He had already been replaced as director-general of the royal cabinet by Driss M'hammedi in November 1963.

The PSD limped along into 1965, but after the March riots it was every man for himself. On 23 May Bel 'Abbas resigned and was soon followed by Laghzaoui. By early June practically all the founding members, including Bahnini, had formally quit the party. However, the demise of FDIC and the PSD did not entail the death of their component parts. These are still ready at hand to be called forth when needed. If there is ever to be another referendum or new legislative elections, one can be sure that something resembling the old coalition will have to be resurrected.

The fate of FDIC and the PSD may be taken as symptomatic of the king's relation to the elite. Many had joined both organizations upon the urging of the king, and they left it because the king had made evident his displeasure with the two groups and their leader, Guedira. The latter had once attracted clientele because of his obvious access to the king. When this situation no longer obtained, association with Guedira became a political liability. These men belong to the core of the king's clientele, and their success is measured in their degree of access to the king. As autonomous and semi-autonomous groups have been whittled down in their prestige and strength, the king has proportionately added to his own clientele. This process tends to be cumulative, for as the balance has shifted more and more in favor of the palace, more and more elite members have felt it expedient to commit themselves to the king lest they be excluded from patronage. It would now be extremely difficult for any autonomous or opposition organizations to reverse this process, as long as they operate with the same personnel. Indeed, the Istiqlal and the UMT have made clear their willingness to cooperate with the palace. They have become in a way the king's loyal opposition, not out of respect for the throne, but because the king manifestly has the upper hand in terms of power and goods. This, in effect, was what the first decade of independence was all about, the unequivocal assertion of monarchical control. The king achieved this by breaking up some groups and pulling together others, all the while subordinating their interests to his. Morocco's segmentary system was thus restructured and reoriented, but it remains to be seen what tools the king developed to sustain his control.

The National Ballet of the Devotees of Politics *

السياسة في دولة الهواة

Torres   Yussuf Bel'Abbes   Allal al-Fassi   Moulay Ahmad 'Alawi   Mohammed   Majhoubi Ahardan
Ahmad Bahnini   Mohammed Cherkaoui   'Abdulhadi Boutaleb   Benhima   Ahmad Reda Guedira
  Hassan Wazazni

* From *Al-Kawalis* (The Corridors), 19 Nov. 1965.

266

CHAPTER FOURTEEN

THE MONARCHY AS ORCHESTRATOR
OF THE SEGMENTED SYSTEM

The extent to which the king dominates and determines the course of politics in Morocco is not easy to determine. The two poles of thought on this matter present him on the one hand as all powerful, ruthlessly crushing any opponents and enslaving his friends, and, on the other, as an absolutely neutral referee who conscientiously keeps clear of the political squabbles of his subjects. It may be neither satisfactory nor precise to say that his role lies somewhere between the two poles, but it is to this judgment that one is reduced. Whether by chance or design, the fact remains that the factions that in combination have made up Morocco's major political organizations have been for some time divided within and among themselves. These same factions are not to be regarded merely as fragments or pieces of some larger structure, but as segments. In so speaking, I emphasize their dynamic interrelation hinging on their mutual opposition at several possible levels. Opposition may spring from social divisions (city/city or urban/rural), from personality clashes (Balafrej/al-Fassi), from organizational contiguity and dependency (UMT-UNFP), or from combinations of the above. The competition for scraps of power and patronage does not seem to cause opposition so much as to maintain it.

Muhammed v, relying on his personal prestige, announced himself as the retainer of the nation's sovereignty and no group was able to contest the assertion. His claim, in a sense, was a self-fulfilling prophecy, as he simply exercised secular powers commensurate with his pretension in the absence of any coordinated challenge of his right to do so. It is perfectly conceivable that the Istiqlal might have laid claim to the nation's sovereignty after

267

1956, that it might have monopolized the distribution of rewards and punishments, and of course during the first two years of independence there was an obvious rivalry between the king and his erstwhile colleagues in this sphere. But the Istiqlal could not make good on its claims. The monarchy was then able to convert its undeniable moral authority into political power in the sense that it acquired the tools of coercion and enticement with which it could impose its will. Today most elite members recognize the palace as the only source of patronage and legitimization, and as the policeman of the political process. Every move on the part of a political actor is calculated with respect to the likely reaction of the palace.

Within this set of circumstances the king does not have to act very often or, when he does, very obviously. His coercive powers are seldom used but often enough so that it is plain to all that they exist. However, the powers of enticement are constantly employed and are extremely effective within the context of the relatively few individuals who make up the elite. As mentioned in Part Two, the king – and here we have in mind Hassan II – is in all respects a member of the elite with firm links to both its rural and urban sectors. He is personally acquainted with almost all elite members and knows their individual idiosyncrasies and rivalries. This knowledge, taken in conjunction with the means at his disposal, has enabled him to maintain a high degree of segmentation among elite factions and to control their competition for patronage. Naturally he cannot afford to have any one faction acquire inordinate strength, but conversely he does not wish any of the factions to disappear for that would not only leave him with fewer elements to manipulate but would also deprive him of convenient foils for his own actions. For their part, elite factions have come to accept the game pretty much as defined by the king. Their demands and challenges are, for the most part, 'positive' designed to elicit marginal advantages from a regime no one of them rejects entirely. A faction that steps out of line and is chastised will stir little more than verbal protests and crocodile tears among equally vulnerable counterparts. The king is almost always able to deal with elite segments one at a time. The price to be paid for this balance is stagnation, as no faction alone can take a bold initiative, nor taken together are they capable of positive action. The king's chosen role is not to lead but to orchestrate what a political cartoonist captioned 'the national ballet of the devotees of politics' (see p. 266). In this chapter I shall consider the specific tactics and techniques resorted to by the monarchy in performing this role. The next chapter will examine the king's instruments of orchestration, and chapter 15 will present the elements of his long-term strategy.

Tactics and Techniques

The carrot as opposed to the stick has been the king's preferred tool for elite manipulation. Here his major asset is a wide range of public offices that he controls through his personal powers of appointment. The king enjoys the right to appoint the following sorts of public officials by royal dahir :[1]

1 The government, and, if necessary, the ministers individually, as well as the secretaries and under-secretaries of state and the high commissioners.
2 The secretary-general of the government.
3 The governors of the provinces.
4 The qaids and super-qaids.
5 The magistrates of secular justice (Supreme Court, regional tribunals, *Saddad*) and religious justice (*qadis*).
6 Officers of FAR and Gendarmerie Royale.
7 Diplomatic representatives.
8 In a general manner, all high ranking employees.

Beyond such appointments, there is a sprawling system of contractual arrangements, channelled through Muhammed Bahnini, the secretary-general of the government, by which large numbers of middle-range and even petty bureaucrats are able to adjust their pay and promotion scales outside the normal Civil Service procedure. Such contracts can serve as a form of monarchical control over even the lowest ranks of the bureaucracy.

The king's control over these appointments is taken for granted by elite members. There is occasional talk, harking back to the dispute over the Ministry of the Interior in 1958, of enabling the prime minister to form his own government, but the king may act with full confidence that no one will seriously contest his prerogatives in the formation of governments and the definition of their tasks. It may have been as early as 1958, when the 'young Turks' of the Istiqlal felt they could control the government once party ministers were given defined responsibilities, that the throne had gained such mastery of the administration that few bureaucrats, even those who considered themselves Istiqlalis, would have risked their careers in a party-palace confrontation. Almost without knowing it they had been added to the king's clientele.

The lure of public employ is too strong for most Moroccans to ignore, and there are always plenty of eager individuals willing to assume public responsibilities regardless of the strictures placed upon their freedom of action. The king has stated that 'sometimes I say to my ministers: if tomorrow none of you would accept to govern, I would say to my chauffeur: be minister.'[2] Hassan II has never been confronted with such a situation, for his ministers only too gladly accept to 'govern'. At play here may be a factor of unabashed power hunger. To so state is not to judge the moral comportment of Moroccans, for, as Fred Riggs has argued, transitional societies provide few outlets for the ambitious other than through the exercise of political power. This power, although influenced by non-governmental groups, is lodged primarily in the government.[3] Further, within the Moroccan context, access to government positions is the only sure way to maintain patronage-clientele alliances.

The appointment consequently has become the be-all and end-all of elite manoeuvres. Scarcely a week goes by without rumors of a government shake-up. The rumors themselves are often planted by the palace or by ministerial hopefuls (the Moroccans refer to the latter as *ministrables*). Moroccan politicians may not take the gossip too seriously, but neither can they afford to ignore it. As a result the king is able to keep the elite constantly off balance with incumbents apprehensive that they may lose their jobs and the *ministrables* jockeying for position. Palace-watching and second-guessing becomes an elite obsession, and every little hint or stray remark is seized upon as a possible indication of things to come. During the state of emergency, by definition a temporary situation, the tactic of elite-baiting has reached the level of an art. The meeting of the king with a UMT delegation, or the dispatch of Guedira to Paris on a special mission, or the appointment of Dr Khatib as his personal representative to a conference, or a fond smile in the direction of General Oufqir, all are taken as important clues to the waxing and waning of various political stars. In this manner the state of emergency has now covered a longer time span than that of the Moroccan Parliament. King Hassan has not benefited from the immense moral authority that his father had accreted during his years in exile. For this reason Hassan II has had to be careful in his choice of ministers and advisers, and where his father relied on ties of loyalty, Hassan must rely on expediency. His choice has fallen upon men who have little or no following and only remote chances of building one. These men are without groups and have nowhere to go. They are presented with the 'unique alternative' – service to the king or oblivion. Typical of this tactic was the reappointment of the ministers defeated in the 1963 elections. Once reminded of the fragility of their power base, they were reconfirmed in their former functions.

A variation on this theme, applied to friend and foe alike, is to demonstrate a man's vulnerability publicly through some sort of punishment, and then, with the lesson learned, make an about-face and reward him with a post.* For instance in May 1966, Ahmad Benkirane, director of a French language daily, *Maroc-Informations*, had his publication closed down by order of the minister of interior. The paper had had a reputation for being mildly critical of the regime, but it had ties with no political parties. Its suspension instigated a few verbal laments from the party press but nothing more. Benkirane got the message and decided to cease publication entirely. A few months later he was appointed director of the Caisse de Dépot et de Gestion.

To deal with organized clientele groups, to deflect their challenges, and to disarm them, the king may resort to a tactic of 'pre-emptive appointment'. All political groupings in Morocco lack organizers and leadership at all levels. Not infrequently an organization may depend on the devotion of a few individuals or may have set its sights upon an up-and-coming student leader, or apprentice lawyer, etc. These key individuals are generally well known within the confines of the elite, and the palace will often make a special effort to attract them itself. In the same vein, and of equal importance, are strategic appointments. The object is twofold: first to propagate an image of political broadmindedness

* One of the most striking North African examples of this technique is Tunisian, i.e. Bourguiba's dressing down of Ahmad Ben Salah followed by his appointment to a key Ministry. Hassan II may have hoped to win Ben Barka in the same manner.

through the presence of opposition elements in high places, and second, to deaden the criticisms of the opposition group from which the appointee came. This tactic has worked with remarkable consistency and has frequently had the additional effect of eventually leading the parent group to disown the appointee. Often the palace has been able to draw these men from the pool of dropouts or incipient dropouts who have taken their distances from a divided party or group. Any given strategic appointee may enter into the contract with the purest of motives, perhaps believing that having an opportunity to put his ideas to work is better than sterile criticisms from the sidelines. His group may find it advantageous, at least on a short-term basis, to have a protector well placed to defend group interests.

The palace can and does easily maintain contacts with all sectors of the elite. Sometimes this is done publicly between the king and the leader of a given faction or privately through one of several possible intermediaries. The palace, Moroccans point out, has had its flanks covered by Laghzaoui (right), M'hammedi (left), and its center by Guedira. These are only three of several such politicians. Through these men there are constant negotiations, in the broadest sense of the word, between the palace and elite factions. The objective of the king is generally announced to be a government of national union, and any government that has representatives from the major political groups, no matter how fragile their links with these groups, will be so proclaimed (such as the governments from May 1960 to January 1963). Failing this the government will be announced as one of neutral technicians 'alone capable of dealing with the nation's problems calmly and with perseverence' (1963 to the present). Still, it is certain that if he can have it on his own terms, the king would prefer a government of national union.

In all negotiations the king has proceeded with great deliberation. What is important for him is not so much the results of the contacts but the contacts themselves. As long as they are maintained then elite members are still abiding by the rules. Ever since the plot arrests of July 1963 there has been a sporadic dialogue between the palace and the UNFP with regard to a government of national union. 'Abdellatif Benjelloun, in the peroration of his speech condemning the government's economic policy in June 1964, called for a government of national union under the guidance of the king. Vague discussions were held between Bou'abid and M'hammedi in late 1964 followed by direct contacts with the king after the March riots of 1965. At that time the king acknowledged the seriousness of the economic situation and spoke favorably of a UNFP entry into the government. But he felt that no steps in this direction could be taken before the Casablanca Conference of Arab heads of state in September 1965. During all this he dropped hints of his estime for the UNFP, such as the appointment of 'Abdulhamid Zemmouri to the royal cabinet during the trial of the plotters, and the pardon in April 1965 of many of those who had been condemned. However, the talks came to an abrupt halt after the kidnapping of Ben Barka in late October 1965.*

With the UNFP negotiations out of the question, the king turned promptly to the UMT, which had been more or less ignored since the preceding spring. The king wanted to show that the opposition was still willing to work within the family, and for this purpose the UMT had as much symbolic value as the UNFP. On 25 November 1965 the king received a UMT delegation, led by Ben Seddiq, which deplored the economic situation of the country and warned that only a government enjoying the confidence of the laborers and all the 'forces vives' of the country could treat these economic ills.[4] Simultaneously tentative conversations between the UMT and the Istiqlal were started, and it was widely assumed that the Istiqlal would never have taken this step without the knowledge and probable approval of the palace. Of course the UMT and Istiqlal could not temper their criticisms of the regime even in the process of negotiating an entry into the government. The more virulent the attacks the better from the king's point of view, for once having brought his critics into the government he could then claim to have unified the divided political ranks of the country. But the Istiqlal, the UMT, and the king have been very wary of one another, the first two feeling that they might fall victim to the old palace manoeuvre of handing over to its critics responsibility for implementing policies they have recommended and then hampering them in their efforts to do so. The king, for his part, has been not at all averse to prolonging contacts indefinitely, or until the UMT and the Istiqlal join in the government under his conditions. Thus,

---

* On 12 Nov. 1965 the royal cabinet issued a statement denying that in its contacts with Bou'abid the possibility of a UNFP entry into the government had ever been discussed.

months elapsed after the first breathless rumors of an Istiqlal-UMT government, and the king seemed able to continue the process for some time thereafter.[5] Meanwhile, appetites were whetted and incumbent ministers unnerved by small government reshuffles.*

---

* The reshuffles occurred in June and July 1965, February 1966, and March 1967. Essentially they represent personnel juggling and no far reaching changes of ministers or policy orientation takes place. Locally such a reshuffle is known as a *replâtrage* (replastering).

CHAPTER FIFTEEN

THE INSTRUMENTS OF ORCHESTRATION

1 The Bureaucracy

The king's monopoly of the patronage system not only facilitates his manipulation of elite factions but also gives him effective control of the administration. The palace has gradually placed trusted personnel in practically all Ministries. The success of the palace in this respect can be divided into a period of defense (1955–60) and a period of offense (1960–present). In the first period it was faced with a challenge from the Istiqlal and clung stubbornly to the police and army. With respect to the Ministries, it would often have to negotiate a list acceptable to the Istiqlal and also allow a party minister to designate high ranking appointees within his jurisdiction. Under the Ibrahim government, the king was obliged to draw up a list of governors, qaids, and other officials, that was satisfactory both to himself and M'hammedi. But after May 1960, when the king for the first time became prime minister, all governmental posts of any importance were filled unilaterally by royal dahir. These posts included not only ministries, but also the directors of state and semi-public banks, credit agencies, and national offices. The king's increasingly firm grip on the governmental apparatus was symbolized in March 1961 by Hassan's simultaneous assumption of the prime ministership, the Ministry of Defense, the Ministry of Agriculture, and the Ministry of Interior.* His incumbency in these offices, brief though it was, stirred almost no political comment.

* Hassan became king and prime minister upon his father's death in Feb. 1961. He was already minister of defense. Hassan Zemmouri resigned as minister of agriculture in January 1961, and the Ministry of Interior fell vacant at the same time when M'barrek Bekkai died.

A special note regarding the national offices and semi-autonomous state banks is in order here. During Bou'abid's tenure as minister of national economy (1956–60), a number of bodies were instituted to deal with specific economic problems. Of particular importance were the National Bank for Economic Development (BNDE), the State Bank for Industrial Participation (BEPI), and the National Office for Irrigation (ONI). These institutions had served as poles of attraction for numerous technicians who, it may be judged, were activist and eager to undertake vast projects. However, the social and economic dislocations inherent in their plans were apparently felt to be too high a price to pay for results that would not necessarily favor the regime. For a while the king may have toyed with the idea of controlling these organizations through the Ministries under whose jurisdiction they fell. But recently it is clear that this method has been found to be overly cumbersome, and the probable objective now is to do away with the autonomy of these offices entirely. There may well be exceptions to this surmise, such as the Sherifian Office of Phosphates (OCP), but the outlook that it represents has in effect become public policy:[1]

... these offices exist in a completely artificial situation characterized by high salaries and numerous privileges ... these offices exist on the outer limits of the state, thanks to the autonomy they have been given, in such a way that their management escapes the control of the state.

Our venerated king has decided ... to confront these organizations in the very interior of their redoubts. .... Our independent regime in fact demands total harmony among the institutions and sectors that are an integral part of the general apparatus of the state.

In brief, the king's control of the administration, including access to it and the activities of the office holders once appointed, is his major instrument of rule. There are of course several strata within the administration, each of which exhibits somewhat different behavioral norms. I shall be most concerned with the uppermost level, those who are appointed officials and not career civil servants, but mention will be made of the others as well. For the appointee the award of high office is considered an open invitation to aggrandizement. This may in part reflect a traditional Moroccan attitude to public office which, under the makhzan, was seldom salaried. A government official had to live off fees (*sukhrāt*) for his services, and the going rate was subject to bargaining. When a sultan appointed a qaid or an *amil* or the like, they knew that they would have to feather their own nests quickly for the sultanic favor could be withdrawn at any moment. This precariousness of appointment is still very much a factor influencing ministerial behavior.* The royal nod is interpreted as 'enrichissez-vous'. The patronage may go towards personal acquisitions (real estate, import licenses, commercial licenses, non-competitive contract bidding), or may trickle down the arteries of patron-clientele alliances. Ministries change hands fast, and one must act quickly lest the tap be turned off. The rate of changeover in the last ten years has been such that most elite factions have had access to the benefits of governmental office and are, so to speak, all in on the game. This has been referred to elsewhere as 'keeping the elite happy' and few elite members have resisted temptation in this respect.[2]

Many ministers or high ranking officials tend to circulate through the administration in the company of a few selected associates who generally staff their personal cabinets. They are a given minister's team and may form the nucleus of a political clan with lines running outside the governmental apparatus, or occasionally running into other sectors of the government itself. These are patronage groups in the most precise sense, for the patron protects his wards and shares his good fortune with them. They are consequently obliged to follow his ups and downs, and he can usually rely on them in the event of a political crisis of one kind or another. These rather tight associations reflect in microcosm the relations between the king and various chosen sectors of the elite. That the behavior of ministerial cabinets may have been getting out of hand was indicated in the Royal Memorandum submitted to all political parties following the March riots of 1965. That document declared.[3] 'It is necessary that there abound in the members of the ministerial cabinets ability and honor; in order to uphold the dignity of the cabinets as regards the administration and the people.' It was further recommended that the secretary-general of each Ministry, in principle a non-partisan technician, be given responsibility for the day-to-day operation of the Ministry.[4] Thus the secretary-general becomes in effect a counterbalance to the minister and, if need be, a watch-dog.

* Another aspect of the contemporary administration reminiscent of the old makhzan is the flexibility of ministerial jurisdictions. Ministers range far and wide beyond the confines of their competence.

Immediately below the ministers and their staffs (as well as below the directors of Offices, autonomous bureaux, and public agencies) is an intermediate group of high-ranking Civil Service career employees. This group is a sort of reservoir for the highest posts, and individuals of particular brilliance may be the objects of a certain amount of competitive attention between palace and parties. The pre-emptive appointment often comes into play here. In regard to this intermediate stratum it is worth quoting the comments of a knowledgeable analyst of Moroccan bureaucracy:[5]

The majority of high-ranking Moroccan employees are young men, having an average age of thirty-five. They exercise their responsibilities generally with dash, often with competence, but rarely with determination or with a sense of public service. . . .

[It is] a young group, of bourgeois origins, with modern training. A concern for efficiency would on the whole render them as favorable to a program of the left as to a dynamic program supported by the monarchy. Having acceded at an early age to their responsibilities, they will block for a long time the upper posts of the administrative hierarchy.

This leaves us with the great bulk of civil servants, the clerks, the middle range section heads, the school teachers, and the like. They are promoted according to seniority, and very few will be snatched from the ranks by an appreciative superior. Their salaries have, with some exceptions, been frozen since independence, and the uppermost ranks of their departments are, as noted above, probably closed to them for some time to come. Needless to say, as literate members of an illiterate society, with superiors whose competence is often questionable, they are not very happy with their lot. Added to these is a growing number of Moroccans having advanced technical educations who often are shuttled off by an apprehensive and less qualified superior to some obscure bureau where they quietly waste their time and talents. Discontent in the lower and middle echelons of the bureaucracy may take the form of a cynical negligence of individual duties and not infrequently petty corruption.* At times, as with secondary school teachers,

* The creation of the corruption courts which have systematically tried only petty offenders, just as Guedira safely predicted, has only served to deepen administrative cynicism, perhaps anomie, for the sins of the patrons are well known.

this discontent seems to take on the aura of widespread political opposition.

The evolution of administrative recruitment has in itself constituted a built-in process that I shall call 'administrative drain'. Political parties have been manipulated in their competition for public office, but they have also had the potential for expanding their clientele seriously undermined by the monopoly of valued cadres by the administration. The growth of the Moroccan administration, both central and local and including the police, has been accentuated since 1956. Figures regarding this expansion vary greatly and are not always easy to come by. I shall be concerned mainly with the order of magnitude and the implied rate of absorption or 'drain'. One source estimates that between 1955 and 1964 administrative personnel, excluding the military, grew from 60,000 to 145,000.[6] Another, which includes the military, gives figures for the same years of 68,000 and 255,000.[7] These figures are indicative of the obvious needs of the government for massive staffing at all administrative levels following independence.

Prior to 1956 political parties in general, and the Istiqlal in particular, were well-endowed with young, educated Moroccans whose energies went into party work. They often undertook nationalist activities precisely because they had been excluded from, or relegated to, minor posts within the protectorate administration. Opportunities after independence have been far better, and the Civil Service has drained off most of the last decade's secondary and university level students. Parties no longer have the middle-range organizers with ample time for their duties that they once had. It is, of course, possible today to be both partisan and a civil servant, but there is an increasing premium placed on the apolitical employee. Those who have maintained party ties and party duties have found themselves to be ordinary mortals, with jobs and families to worry about, and little energy left over after a day's work for party affairs. All political parties and organizations have been afflicted by administrative drain. In 1965 al-Fassi acknowledged the penury of cadres before the party congress:[8] 'The Istiqlal, after having nourished the nation with its trained personnel since independence, finds itself today in need of new personnel to undertake the organization of the nation [*sic*] and to continue to give it a sound orientation. . . .' Or again, in standard

UNFP jargon, '. . . without battle-tested cadre, there is no revolutionary option'.[9] In sum, the autonomous process of administrative drain, taken in conjunction with the manipulative techniques of the palace, have served to keep political groups malleable and organizationally feeble.

2 The Ministry of the Interior

I have so far treated the administration globally, merely singling out for attention a few salient characteristics of its relation to the palace. Within the administration, however, one Ministry stands out from all others as an instrument of monarchical control – the Ministry of the Interior. It has been the recipient of extensive powers delegated to it over the years in a continual process of affirming its direct relation to the throne.

It will be recalled that some elements of the Istiqlal were bent on gaining the Ministry of Interior for a party member in order to control the internal administration of the country as well as the police. Subsequently these same men have come to place little importance on the post of minister of interior *per se*. The reason is that the peculiar nature of the appointment system would permit the king to bypass his minister entirely and deal directly with his governors, qaids, etc. All officials of Interior (just as was the case under the makhzan) are appointed by royal dahir, and the symbolic link is with the king, not the minister who may only advise in these matters. As laid down in the dahir of 20 March 1956:[10] 'The appointments, promotions, dismissals of personnel, demotions, revocations, with or without loss of pension rights, transfers, placement in reserve status, separation of qaids or governors are pronounced by dahir.' Conflict between the king and his minister of interior has seldom arisen, and he has generally sought the minister's advice in the selection and movement of personnel. The minister maintains direct and daily contact with all regional and local officials through the Direction of Political Affairs. The title of this Direction is a holdover from the protectorate and was changed towards the beginning of 1966 to the Direction of General Affairs. Under General Oufqir, the Direction has been supervised by the under-secretary of state for interior, Muhammed Ben'Allem. It is attached almost directly to the minister's cabinet and is basically an executory device for the current policy of the minister.

The local agents of Interior have at their disposal contingents of *Forces Auxilliaires*, a sort of national guard, that they may use to quell local disturbances and to maintain order. More ambiguous is the agents' relation to the local police of Sureté Nationale. In principle the latter are responsible to the qaid or pasha, but in practice they have enjoyed considerable autonomy in their actions. Thus, the two chains of command of the police and Interior tend to rival one another. For added assurance both are under the surveillance of the Gendarmerie Royale. Besides affording the king three sources of intelligence, the rivalry existing between these organizations tends to check the ambitions of any one of them.

Despite the assiduously maintained traditional relationship between the monarch and his local administrators, there have been profound changes in the nature of the corps and in the duties of individual members. There are today in Morocco twenty provincial governors, two governors of prefectures (Rabat and Casablanca), the *préfet maritime* of Casablanca port, created in September 1967, twenty-four pashas, and 350 qaids. This corps is now increasingly composed of career officials, salaried,[11] and to a growing degree not native to the locality in which they serve. Governors and super-qaids, because of the size of the territories within their jurisdiction, may come from their province or district. At the other end of the scale, *khalifas* of city quarters, the *muqaddims* of rural douars, and the shaykhs of tribal fractions, should be members of the group they administer. However, the intermediate officials, the qaids, because their reduced territory may have within it several tribal fractions or lineages, are chosen, in the interests of impartiality, from other regions.[12]

Ernest Gellner has nicely summed up the change in role of the qaid since 1956. Gellner points out that the qaids under the protectorate:[13]

had great formal powers and even greater informal powers, and legally authority was elusively located between them and the French officers [*officiers des affaires indigènes* and *contrôleurs civils*], in such a way that power was often uncontrollable and unchecked: either of its two components could always put the blame on the other. The officer could blame an exaction on the will of the tribe, expressed by its leader, and the leader [the qaid] on the unintelligible exigencies of the higher European administration. After independence, these local caids were abolished: the name survived,* and was applied to the district officer who was now a Moroccan rather than a Frenchman.

Immediately following independence the administrative agents of Interior were changed drastically and in an improvised manner. The protectorate corps was largely discredited because of its collaboration with the French during the nationalist movement. New replacements had to be found quickly in early 1956 with the blad in ferment as a result of the activities of various bands of the Liberation Army. The gap was filled with a massive influx of ill-prepared resistants and Istiqlalis – anyone whose local prestige might be sufficient to maintain order. Ill at ease in their new functions, the new administrators sought comfort in the party and set about building local clientele groups through administrative and party favors. Local populations began to resent their activities and ceased to resort to the qaid in solving local problems. In addition, the qaid through the separation of powers lost his judicial weight in the community. A serious lack of contact between the administrator and his wards developed.[14]

When M'barrek Bekkai became minister of interior in May 1960 he determined to rid Interior of party hacks and replace them with competent, apolitical administrators. He also changed several provincial governors. The new governors were requested to comment on all personnel under their jurisdiction and were authorized to weed out any they found undesirable. They followed their instructions to the letter, and, in filling the gaps thus created, the governors constructed clientele groups, often including their relatives, that then followed them from post to post.[15]

The qaid corps today is ostensibly apolitical and competent. Without being able to cite precise figures, one finds a high percentage of qaids who had started their administrative careers as interpreters for protectorate officials in the court system and Interior.† Of these the majority are graduates of the *Collège* of Azrou.

Specialized training for qaids has been stressed in recent years. In 1957, the old Cours des Affaires Indigènes that had been used

---

* Even the name has now been changed: a qaid is a *chef de circonscription rurale*, a super-qaid, *chef de cercle*, and a pasha, *chef de circonscription urbaine*.

† Many entered the administration during the Second World War when experienced French officers were recalled to France and were replaced by younger officers without training in local dialects.

to train French administrators was converted into the Centre d'Orientation Marocaine. It started its functions with a one-month crash course for the amateurs who had taken over the administration after 1956. In March 1963 it was decided to initiate a four-month course. The new school, now known as the Centre de Formation des Agents d'Autorité, was transferred to Kenitra in 1964, and its curriculum expanded to cover two full years of preparation. Entrants now must have a degree from the School of High Administrative Studies or any university level degree (*licence*). In addition to military training, and the study of French and Arabic, courses are given in economic development, sociology, public accounting, rural equipment, topography, rural engineering, and agriculture.[16] One class of approximately fifty qaids has graduated and been posted to regions chronically understaffed. One wonders, in view of their university educations and increasing urban representation, what changes in the nature of the qaid corps these new recruits will bring about as they infiltrate the hierarchy.

Locally, the qaid or super-qaid is an extremely important figure. All other administrative employees (except perhaps police) – those in Public Works, Health, Education, PTT, and so forth – must report to him periodically and must clear all local projects with him. Like the French *officiers* before him, he has been in need of a foil and has been provided one in the form of the local councils, elected first in 1960 and again in 1963. These were first instituted by Muhammed v to give Moroccans some experience in democratic procedure under strict controls without running the risks of national legislative elections. In both 1960 and 1963 the elections, run according to a system of individual candidatures and election by relative majority, were designed to inject new life into the old, dispersed, and discredited rural elites. This objective was achieved, and qaids now have elected councils who share responsibility with them for unpleasant tasks, while the council members themselves have been able to regain some of their former lustre.[17]

The competence of the local councils was not defined until a month after the elections – on 23 June 1960.[18] The broad powers implied in the following, 'the council regulates through its deliberations the affairs of the *commune*, and in particular it prepares and votes the local budget' (Art. 19), were emptied of all substance by the right of surveillance and veto vested in the qaid. In effect, the local council can make no moves independently: it must submit the agenda of all its meetings to the qaid for preliminary approval; he may veto any point in it or the agenda in its entirety; and in the actual meeting he may insist that discussions be confined strictly to the agenda. Bourely has observed that the council 'may voice its wishes (*voeux*) concerning all local affairs, notably in the sphere of administration, economy, finance, sociocultural activity, and religion. These wishes are transmitted to the competent agencies. It is forbidden at all times to formulate wishes of a political nature or wishes foreign to goals of local interest.'[19] Much the same can be said of the powers of the provincial assemblies (elected 6 October 1963) *vis-à-vis* the governors.[20] Finally, in the event that a given council exceeds its powers or discredits itself in any way, the minister of interior is empowered to dissolve it and call for new elections.*

New functions have steadily devolved upon the Ministry of Interior, and there is probably no facet of domestic policy in which it does not have at least an advisory voice. Relative to all other Ministries the king has chosen Interior as his favored instrument and has left its attributes loosely defined. Recently the Ministry of Interior was given *de facto* control, although not responsibility for day-to-day operations, of the bulk of the programs of the Ministry of Agriculture.

On 9 November 1966 a series of decrees were published pertaining to the decentralization of the Ministry of Agriculture.[21] The decrees announced the creation of seven regional offices† to execute regional policies of agricultural development. In the process, the existing structure of the Ministry of Agriculture was completely done away with, including the national offices. ONI, responsible for irrigated acreage, had been supplemented by the creation in 1962 of the National Office of Rural Modernization (ONMR), responsible for dry-farming (*bour*) acreage. The two offices were merged in May 1965 to form the Office de Mise-en-Valeur Agricole (OMVA). Falling vaguely within the jurisdiction of this amalgamated office were the Centres de Gestion et d'Exploita-

---

* In November 1965 the Ministry of Interior dissolved the Municipal Council of Salé as a result of its illicit financial activities.

† The regions are Doukkala, Tadla, Gharb, Moulouya, Haouz, Warzazat, and Tafilalt, corresponding to the major irrigated areas of Morocco; see map, p. 285.

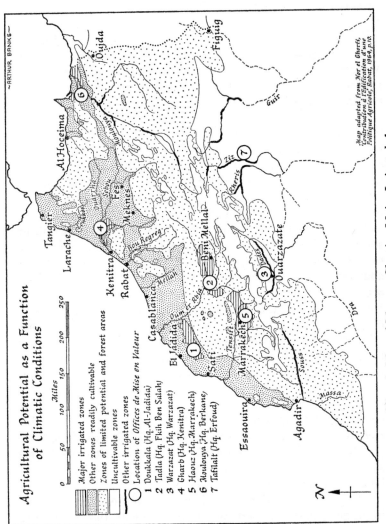

~ARTHUR BANKS~

Agricultural Potential as a Function
of Climatic Conditions

Miles
0   50   100   150   200   250

Major irrigated zones
Other zones readily cultivable
Zones of limited potential and forest areas
Uncultivable zones
Other irrigated zones
Location of Offices de Mise en Valeur
1 Doukkala (Hq. Al-Jadida)
2 Tadla (Hq. Fkih Ben Salah)
3 Warzazat (Hq. Warzazat)
4 Gharb (Hq. Kenitra)
5 Haouz (Hq. Marrakech)
6 Moulouya (Hq. Berkane)
7 Tafilalt (Hq. Erfoud)

N

Climatic Map of Morocco Showing Major Irrigated Areas

Map adapted from Nor el Gharb,
"Contributions à l'Edification d'une
Politique Agricole, Rabat, 1964, p.10.

285

tion Agricole (CGEA). These had been instituted as a sort of 'parking-lot' for acreage taken over by the state in September 1963 from land of official colonization. The centres were responsible for about 220,000 hectares.[22] They proved to be inefficient, and production on acreage under their management fell substantially.[23] A non-official study maintains that of the 356 blocs of land under CGEA management, 180 were confided to 'bureaucrats' of the Ministry of Agriculture, 26 had no official management, and 150 were turned over to 'private managers' ranging from wealthy peasants to merchants and chauffeurs.[24]

OMVA and the CGEA no longer exist as such. In their place are the above mentioned regional offices. The offices will be managed by a council of administration presided over directly by the sovereign or the minister of agriculture. The council of administration will include the existent Interministerial Economic Council, which will present an annual program to the government. But immediate responsibility for the regional offices will fall to local technical councils presided over by the governors. They will be assisted by the directors of the local offices and representatives of the provincial, municipal, and local elected councils. It seems abundantly clear, despite the fact that the modalities of the reorganization have not yet been worked out, that the Ministry of Interior will have the final word on the operations of the local offices. Governors will be able to keep under close surveillance office directors who have had a tendency to move too quickly at times. The association of elected representatives in this endeavor will once again provide a foil for the governor, but will at the same time boost their prestige by giving them tasks of apparent importance. The Ministry of Agriculture has very little left with which to occupy itself, and will as a result have little appeal for elite factions looking for patronage. Conversely, Interior will have greatly augmented its control of patronage, and it is likely that some of this will see its way, as in the past, into the hands of the king's loyal administrators.

The scope of Interior's jurisdiction was further enlarged when, in August 1967, the services of urban affairs (*urbanisme*) and housing (*habitat*) were detached from the Ministry of Public Works which had been responsible for them since their creation after the second world war. Broadly speaking, the field of action of these services are the *bidonvilles*, and the transfer of the services to Interior signifies that Ministry's direct concern in controlling rural migration to the cities.

3 The Army

The Moroccan Army has coordinated its operations with those of the Ministry of the Interior, and, as a recent official publication stated: 'Its activity is not limited uniquely to defense and safe-keeping of the national territory but equally to contribute effectively and efficiently to social endeavors.'[25] The king himself has often explicitly stated the non-military vocation of FAR:[26]

We have confided to certain of Our officers the duty of participating in the administration of the country, as ministers, governors, or *agents d'autorité*. Our army has participated in the training of these agents of the Ministry of Interior, determined as We are to associate the moral qualities and physical aptitudes of the officer to the diverse attributions and competences of the administration.

Military personnel has shuttled back and forth between civilian and military duties. There has been a close feeling of identity between FAR and Interior, for so many Interior officials are Berber, have had military experience, are graduates of Azrou, or have close relatives with such career experiences. The very atmosphere of Interior is markedly military: the officials locally wear military uniforms, the centralized command system is unparalleled in the Civil Service, and the tenure of Berber military personalities, Bekkai and Oufqir, as minister of interior has re-enforced the *esprit militaire* of the Ministry. Thus transition from military to civilian duties and back again involves no very drastic changes in life-style for Moroccan officers. Because of their training and discipline, officers and recruits of FAR have been called into all sorts of projects, from building schools to caring for flood victims. In 1963, two years after the launching of the rural development program known as Promotion Nationale, twenty-five specially trained officers were attached to provincial governorates to act as special assistants in administering local programs and as liaison with the Délégation-Générale of the Promotion Nationale in Rabat.[27]

The simple presence of FAR as a coercive arm is never forgotten by any political participants. On the one hand it implements programs of a social and economic nature and thereby steals the thunder of the opposition, and on the other lies ready to nip in the bud any extra-legal political manœuvres. The Moroccan Army, particularly as regards the upper echelons of its officer corps, has been unlike that of many of Morocco's eastern neighbors. The general staff of FAR has been dominated by a group of officers from the French, and to a lesser extent, Spanish armies. Many maintained their ranks in these armies right up until 1956. Not only did they miss the nationalist bandwagon, but some even participated in repression of the nationalists. This fact has promoted a conservative outlook among the older officers, and they have systematically weeded out junior officers smacking of leftist or strongly nationalist opinions.[28] The counterpart of their aversion for politics is loyalty to the throne. Their past and their lack of following in Morocco leave them little choice – another example of the unique alternative.

But these officers represent only a small percentage of the entire officer corps, numbering 1,500 today.[29] Although recruitment of troops was held down from 1956 to 1958, the training of junior officers was massive and selective. In July 1956 it was decided that any candidate for the Military Academy (Dar al-Beida) at Meknes would have to have at least reached the second round of the baccalauréat examinations. This move alone served to redress the Berber-Arab balance in the officer corps. The sons of rural notables were disadvantaged vis à vis their urban rivals who could afford the requisite education. 'Thus in the area of recruitment of officers, the major difference between the army formed by the protectorate and that of the new state consists of the erection of a new line of social demarcation no longer traced by the privileges of birth but by money.'[30]

A serious gap separates junior from senior officer. All promotions were blocked from 1956 to 1959 by General Kittani. He acted out of prudence and concern for the smooth integration of French, Spanish, and Liberation Army officers into FAR. In a period of high politicization (one will recall the declamations of UNEM towards FAR and the prince as well as the Istiqlal's aim to control the Ministry of Defense), Kittani, the prince, and Muhammed V sought to avoid stimulating factional jealousies through the promotions of junior officers that would ineluctably have given rise to ill-feeling and possibly to disloyalty. The rank-freeze served to re-enforce the prominence of the ex-French Army officers who were mostly senior grade, and gave them an opportunity to shape FAR in their own image.

FAR, even more than Interior, has been symbolically tied to the palace. Prince Hassan was made responsible for its organization, and the king has final authority in all promotions. Each promotion has been carefully weighed, and King Hassan has made sure that the material needs of the army as a whole are satisfied. Again, as is the case with Interior, it is doubtful that the officer corps will maintain its present characteristics. The emphasis on advanced education, technical training, and the inevitable increase in urban, politically aware recruits and junior officers moving up the promotion ladder, may undermine the army's loyalty to the throne.

4 The Royal Cabinet

Under Hassan II the royal cabinet has taken on some of the aspects of a shadow government that closely follows all ministerial activities. It has become the body within which most major policy decisions are made. It was not always thus. At its inception in 1950, as the imperial cabinet, the body grouped a few confidants of King Muhammed v. It was directed by Muhammed Bahnini (now secretary-general of the government) who had been the professor at the Imperial Collège of Princes Hassan and 'Abdullah. Bahnini's adjoint was Mas'ud Chiguer. On 12 February 1956, however, a more elaborate cabinet was organized, with Chiguer as director, Muhammad 'Awad (also a former palace tutor) as chef de cabinet, and Moulay Ahmad 'Alawi as press officer. In addition there were six attachés.* Yet its role was reduced and informal. A former member described its function following independence as being one of informed advice from a handful of discreet collaborators to a king who felt unsure of himself in his new capacity as head of state. In the early years, perhaps by coincidence or because of acquaintances arising from proximity, the royal cabinet favored non-Fassi elements, particularly those of Salé (Hajji, Zniber, Sbihi, 'Awad) and Tetouan (Annegai, Bennouna). The successive directors under Muhammed v were Chiguer, very briefly Rachid Mouline, 'Abderrahman Annegai

* These were Ahmad 'Osman, 'Abdullah Chorfi, Ahmad Tahiri, 'Abdesslam Hajji, Muhammed Zniber, and Ahmad Melchimi.

(killed in an auto accident in January 1959), Ahmad Hamiani, and Muhammed 'Awad. The latter was the first to bear the title of director-general, a position hitherto tacitly attributed to Prince Hassan.

The importance of the royal cabinet has been considerably augmented under the reign of Hassan II. His two directors-general, Ahmad Guedira and Driss M'hammedi,* have assumed powers enjoyed by no other ministers.[31] Broadly speaking, its functions are as follows. First and foremost, its highest ranking members are generally the king's most trusted political advisers. Besides Guedira and M'hammedi one may cite in this connection Driss Slaoui, 'Abdulhafidh Boutaleb, Yahya Benslimane, Tayyibi Benhima, and Moulay Ahmad 'Alawi. Trust is a relative word, and with Hassan II has been easily placed and easily withdrawn. The royal cabinet also provides the king expert technical advice on all problems, as well as evaluations of various ministerial proposals. In 1966, for instance, there were three engineers in the cabinet: Tayyib Zaamoun, Muhammed Dadi, and Muhammed Ben 'Abderrazik.† The royal cabinet services the king with speech writers (for instance 'Abdellatif Khatib of Tetouan is fluent in Spanish, French and Arabic), legal advice (Muhammed Rachidi), and public relations (Tayyib Bel'arbi). Commonly referred to in Rabat as the 'garage' or the 'ministerial seedbed', the royal cabinet is a way station for elite members in transit to or from government employment. One may also find within this function an occasional strategic appointee for whom there is no other post readily available. The bulk of the attachés generally are men who have been parked temporarily in the cabinet. A final, rather minor, function is appointment to the royal cabinet, for purely honorific purposes, of some loyal servant of the throne. But it bears reiteration that the royal cabinet, as it stands today, is the framework for all major policy decisions and is the king's instrument to supervise the implementation of the policies thus chosen.

---

* Driss M'hammedi died suddenly in March 1969 and was replaced as director-general of the royal cabinet by Driss Slaoui.

† In the summer of 1967, the king in effect established a new branch of the royal cabinet. The new creation is called the Private Economic Council and consists of the king's favored economic advisers: M'hammed Zeghari, Prince Moulay al'Hassan ben al-Mehdi, 'Omar 'Abdjelil, 'Abdelmajid Benjelloun, Karim Lamraani, Muhammed Benkirane, Ahmad Benkirane, 'Abd al-'Aziz 'Alami, Mohammed ben Larbi. For their positions see p. 107.

5 The Judiciary

The administration of justice in Morocco can be effectively influenced and guided by the palace. It constitutes a convenient instrument with vast possibilities for role legitimization among elite factions. In this respect the king literally incarnates the function of dispenser of justice. He may intervene in the judicial process through the simple fact that he exists, by use of his spoken and written word, and by direct manipulation of the judicial apparatus. We shall examine a few examples of royal intervention in this sphere, and, in the process, the possibilities open to the king should become clear.

The Moroccan magistracy is no less aware of the king's appointive powers than any other group of state employees. The 1962 constitution grandly reaffirmed the separation of the executive and judicial powers, but maintained the king's right to appoint all magistrates. He is to consider the proposals of the Superior Council of the Magistracy in these appointments, but he presides over this council himself, and the majority of its members are appointed by him.

The king's word may be law. Article 19 of the constitution merely inscribes what have long been the traditional attributes of Morocco's sovereigns: he is commander of the faithful, and defender of the faith and the constitution. The official faith of Morocco is Islam (Art. 6). Louis Fougére has speculated in the light of these constitutional attributes.[32]

> The king is thus constituted as the guarantor and guardian of the very substance of the Moroccan community. Is it going too far to admit that he even could and should refuse to promulgate a law that might in some way threaten it, and that he retains in this light, an implicit general competence that is not exhausted by the enumeration of his powers made by the constitution?

No, it is not going too far, and there have been numerous precedents even before the writing of the constitution that have indicated this 'general competence'. At issue is the legal value of a royal pronouncement, and one court, in 1960, stated the case thus:[33]

> An order or declaration of the king representing the nation has the force and value of law, since it is the king himself who proclaims the law. Such a declaration or order of the king has the force and value of

law even without being published in the Official Bulletin or dis-
seminated by press or radio.

The issue has never been settled conclusively. In two cases judged
by the Supreme Court, that of the dissolution of the PCM and the
sentencing of the Bahais in Nador, the king's word was treated as
law in one and overlooked in the other. Never, however, has the
Supreme Court ruled against the legal value of the king's word.

In September 1959, Prime Minister Ibrahim was obliged to sign
an order dissolving the Moroccan Communist Party (PCM). It had
been judged, by the minister of justice, that the party's statutes
violated an article of the 1958 dahir regulating the rights of
association: to wit, the PCM had objectives designed to undermine
the government and the monarchy. The PCM was able to bring the
matter to court in Casablanca where its case was upheld on the
basis that the state had failed to produce adequate evidence of the
party's intentions. The state appealed against the verdict and a
new trial was set for the Court of Appeals in Rabat. Just prior to
the second trial, Muhammed v gave a speech (18 November 1959)
in which he roundly condemned 'materialist doctrines'.[34] At the
Court of Appeals the state prosecutor based his case squarely on
the king's words which, he claimed, had the force of law. The Rabat
court upheld the prosecutor's case, and the PCM appealed against
the verdict to the Supreme Court. In May 1964 the Supreme
Court finally rendered its judgment and rejected the party's
appeal. The court argued that when neither party presents adequate evidence, the judges are fully justified in relying upon the
legal pronouncements of the king.[35]

The second instance to be considered is that of the trial of the
Bahais in the Criminal Court of Nador in December 1962.
Bahaism has always raised the hackles of Muslims because of the
civil strife it caused in Iran in the last century, and because it
openly seeks to supersede Islam as well as Judaism and Christianity.
In 1962 there had been reports of Bahai activity in northern
Morocco, and 'Allal al-Fassi, who was at the time minister of state
for Islamic affairs, managed to have the matter pursued in the
courts. Fourteen Bahais were brought to trial on charges of
corrupting youth, forming an illegal association, and seeking to
destroy Islam and the Moroccan state. After the trial had begun,
King Hassan, in a press conference, described Bahaism as 'a true

heresy' and therefore unacceptable in Morocco.[36] A day later the court at Nador sentenced three Bahais to death and five to life imprisonment. The trial caused a national and international reaction, there was talk of a Moroccan 'inquisition', and some likened al-Fassi to Torquemada. The verdict was appealed to the Supreme Court which, in December 1963, dismissed the judgment of the Nador Court, pointing out that the Bahais had undertaken no criminal activities covered by the Moroccan penal code.[37] The Supreme Court chose to ignore the king's words, and it may be that Hassan II rigged the incident to embarrass al-Fassi and to help force the Istiqlalis from his government. What is clear, however, is that the king can have it any way he wants: either his words can be binding legally or, if he so decides, of no legal importance. The Moroccan court system will accept his recommendation in either case.

The plot arrests of 1963–4 furnish an example of the direct manipulation of the judicial system with at least the acquiescence of the king. No judgment will be passed here as to the validity of the charges, but even if there were not a shadow of a doubt as to the existence of a plot against the king's life, the police and court handling of the accused violated most norms of judicial procedure

The government always denied that the fact that so many of those arrested were members of the UNFP could be construed necessarily to mean that the UNFP had organized the plot. At the same time, the government did nothing to dispel such an assumption. The arrests were carried out on 16 July 1963, at a UNFP party meeting at Casablanca. Some believe that the government had become so preoccupied with defeating the Istiqlal in the legislative elections of May that it neglected the UNFP. The surprisingly strong showing of the UNFP necessitated some action to halt its momentum before the local elections of June. These were postponed one month, and the arrests were carried out in the interim.

Those arrested and subsequently brought to trial (eighty-five in all) were held *incommunicado* from 16 July to 15 August when the plot was officially announced. During this month, their testimonies or 'confessions' were registered by the police through individual questioning. All the accusations were based on this testimony. Very little evidence gathered before the arrests was ever introduced into court. The defense claims that the prisoners were systematically tortured until they had incriminated one another. Some of the victims charge that it was a trial of their thoughts and dreams, that under torture they were forced to confess that they had thought of, or discussed with others, the demise of the king. 'But,' as one remarked, 'what Moroccan hasn't?'[38] Circumstantial evidence of two networks of plotters led by Shaykh al-'Arab and Moumin Diouri, as well as arms caches at Skhirat and near Agadir, will not concern us here as the focus of this analysis is the procedural rather than the substantive aspects of the affair.[39]

Defense lawyers were pleased when the trial was scheduled for 25 November in the Criminal Court of Rabat. In view of the border conflict with Algeria, and the condemnation of Ben Barka *in absentia* for treasonous remarks regarding the conflict, the defense had feared the trial would take place before some sort of military tribunal. The defense was dismayed, however, when a prosecutor from Oujda and another from Beni Mellal were brought in as presiding magistrates, apparently to ensure the outcome. The defense protested that they had no right to sit on the Rabat Court, but their objection was overruled. The court refused to accept evidence of police tortures, despite Diouri's testimony to this effect, and ordered supplemental medical examinations by a military physician only months after the alleged tortures took place. None the less the fact that there were fifty-three defense lawyers, that the trial was open to the public and the press, that the accused were free to talk of their tortures, all lent an aura of suspense to the proceedings. It was a political trial in that while the verdict may have been a foregone conclusion, the process itself was gripping and charged.* Otto Kirchheimer described the function of the political trial thus:[40] '. . . the desired third-party effect of a trial rests less on the message of the verdict than on the tension generated by the public sense of participation in an unfolding drama, the outcome of which remains doubtful until the very last moment. Planned justice can scarcely communicate this experience.' Manipulated justice can and did convey this experience. The UNFP was in fact on trial, and the public was invited to witness the revelation of its guilt. The condemnations were

---

* For the prisoner who dramatically tore off his shirt to reveal the scars caused by lye poured on his stomach, the Prosecution produced with fanfare the tape of Fqih Basri's confession of trying to organize a plot.

accessory to the staging.* Having equated the UNFP with disloyalty in the public mind, the king could then retouch his own image of the magnanimous father of the country by pardoning his errant subjects – which he did a year later.

6 Propaganda and the Press

The palace has diverse means to reach its public and to disseminate propaganda. Foremost among these is the Radio-Television Marocaine (RTM) which is entirely state-controlled. But it is peculiar that the principal instruments of press support for the king are a privately owned newspaper chain and a privately-owned wire service. There has always been an official newspaper in Arabic, but its daily circulation has seldom exceeded three to five thousand. Essentially the same publication has appeared since 1956 under the titles of *Al-Ahd al-Jadid*, *Al-Fajr*, *Akhir Sa'a*, and *Al-Anba*. They have all been of negligible importance.

The Mas Press, owned by Yves Mas, a former bastion of the protectorate regime,[41] publishes two dailies, *Le Petit Marocain* (average daily circulation is 45,000) and *La Vigie* (30,000). Mas has for some time controlled most newspaper advertising in Morocco, and his enterprise, unlike most other Moroccan newspapers, is profitable.† But the anti-nationalist reputation of the Mas Press won it few friends after 1956. To protect his investment Mas has diligently sung the praises of each successive government, while reserving his most lavish accolades for the palace. Hardly a day passes without the *Petit Marocain* headlining the fantastic progress of the country in some domain or other under the inspired leadership of His Majesty. This is carried to such extremes that one suspects that the writers are hammering out their eulogies maliciously, announcing the success of projects that have only just been discussed in the council of ministers, or turning a natural disaster into an occasion to trumpet that only King Hassan will lead the country out of its plight.‡

* On 14 March 1964, the verdicts were made public: 12 were condemned to death (3 in Morocco and 9 *in absentia*), 67 were condemned to various prison terms, and the rest were released.

† *España*, published in Spain but with a daily Moroccan circulation of perhaps 30,000, is probably an exception, but the bulk of its readers are in Spain.

‡ According to the *Petit Marocain*, 15 March 1966, the king is still well equipped with *baraka*. After a long drought the rains came to Berrechid just an hour after the king's passage through the town.

Despite the hostility of the Istiqlal, the Mas Press has managed to thrive, its continued existence founded upon the ambiguity of the Press Code of November 1958. The Code contains two contradictory articles. Article 12 flatly states:

. . . All proprietors, associates, stockholders, partners, financiers, or other participants in the financial life of publications edited in Morocco, must be of Moroccan nationality.

But Article 27 expressly authorizes foreign publications to be published in conformity with the other clauses of the Code. The directors of foreign publications were given six months to conform with the Code's dispositions. On 23 May 1959, five days before the expiration of the six months' grace, Prime Minister Ibrahim informed the directors that their requests for authorization were still under study, and that, pending a decision, they were 'authorized, beginning 28 May, to continue to publish provisionally'. No subsequent decree of authorization has ever been issued to end this provisional status.[42]

Since 1963, however, the Mas Press has been under steady attack from both the Istiqlal* and the UNFP. They have demanded that the foreign press in Morocco be closed down in conformity with Article 12 of the Press Code.[43] The case has been in the courts for some time and was also the object of a law proposal of the Istiqlali parliamentary group. The Supreme Court was finally presented with the question, and, without touching upon the problem of the contradictory articles of the Press Code, decided that it was not competent to judge the legality of Ibrahim's temporary authorization as it was an 'administrative act'.[44] The question has been returned to the courts, and it appears that the debate can be drawn out interminably.

The palace and the royal cabinet have always had access to a certain number of 'independent' publications in which rumors and trial balloons are planted. Gossip sheets have proved to be a convenient outlet in this respect.† A minister can thus be anony-

---

* It should be noted that the Istiqlal now has a French language daily of its own: *La Nation Africaine*, 1963–1965, and *L'Opinion* to the present.

† At its peak (1964–5) Morocco's now defunct *Akhbar ad-Dunya* had a circulation of 30–35,000 as a weekly. Its editor, Mustapha 'Alawi, now publishes the daily *Al-Misa*, closely tied to the MP. It occasionally indulges in gossip which is a standard way for elite members to communicate with one another and the palace in anonymity.

mously discredited, reaction to a new policy or appointment tested, or a certain political climate encouraged. For instance *Al-Misa* of 9 February 1967 ran an editorial that described the Istiqlal as being divided into three rival groups. It is reliably reported that all Interior officials were ordered to report on local reactions to the article. This came at a time of renewed talk of a constitutional referendum and legislative elections, and the seemingly unmovable bulk of the Istiqlal is still the major obstacle to controlling such projects. The article may represent a small part of a larger policy of stimulating latent divisions within the party, and to encourage among others an image of a divided Istiqlal.

The existence of several independent publications in Morocco is often cited as evidence of the country's freedom of expression. Party publications do indeed enjoy a right of criticism uncommon for most other nations of the Middle East and North Africa. This freedom, however, is hedged about by a number of regulatory devices that encourage self-censorship and editorial timidity. The Press Code in Articles 71 and 72 permits the minister of the interior to initiate proceedings against any publication he judges to have offended or caused injury to the king or any members of the royal family. He may also order the administrative seizure of any publication that he feels is of a nature to trouble the public order. This latter clause has frequently been invoked.[45] Judicial action can be undertaken with regard to any newspaper or periodical up to one year from date of publication (Article 78), and if a publication is condemned to pay a fine and does not do so within fifteen days of the sentence, it may be suspended (Article 76). The upshot is that several publications (most often *Kifah al-Watani* of the PCM, *At-Tahrir/al-Muharrir* of the UNFP, and to a lesser extent *Al-'Alam* of the Istiqlal) are periodically hauled into court and fined. No newspaper, other than the Mas dailies, makes any money in Morocco.

One of the more under-exploited media of royal image making is the Friday prayer (*khutba*) in the mosque. This prayer throughout the Muslim world is pronounced in the name of the sovereign and has often been the occasion for panegyrics. In Morocco today there does not seem to be any uniform policy of using the mosque for propaganda. The *khatib* who pronounces the prayer, and of whom there may be twelve thousand in Morocco, is frequently allowed to write his own text. However, on feast days, royal birthdays, and any occasions of national importance, the Ministry of Awqaf (Habous) and Islamic Affairs distributes an obligatory *khutba* text. At other times it may distribute an indicative text.* A sample from an obligatory text on the occasion of the birthday of Muhammed v reads :[46]

Verily our Imam, our Lord Muhammed v is the greatest guarantor of the interests of this nation. His stances and sayings testify to this as do his behavior and deeds. Verily the 'Alawite house is glorious, and at its head is this great hero worthy of the confidence, obedience, fidelity, and loyalty of all Moroccans. All of the Islamic world is witness to this heroism and devotion.

The administration in a global sense, but particularly the Ministries of Interior and Justice, the army and police, the royal cabinet and the press are the essential instruments of royal control. They constitute the means or channels by which the king can intervene directly in the political process. Through the administration the king is able to maintain the inner conflicts of the elite and to reaffirm the primacy of the throne in the allocation of goods and power. Through the Ministry of Interior and the army he is able to supervise the competition among factions, change the rules of the game, eliminate certain players, and, if need be, simply defend himself. But these manœuvres, while carried out with aplomb and sophistication, represent no more than an intelligent holding operation designed to sustain the regime in the face of inevitable challenges from new elites, and to tide it over the present period of economic stagnation.

---

* This information was supplied to me by 'Abderrahman Doukkali (the son of Boucha'ib Doukkali) the sec.-gen. of Islamic Affairs, in an interview, 1 Dec. 1965, Rabat. He estimates that there are 10,000 mosques in Morocco and that their staffing totals about 32,000. No attendance figures are kept for mosques.

CHAPTER SIXTEEN

THE ABSORPTIVE CAPACITY OF
THE ELITE

Few European powers in administering foreign territories ever ventured very far down the path of universal education. As a result most recently independent countries share a common characteristic of a governmental and political monopoly vested initially in the hands of an educated elite. Such elites have attracted a growing amount of attention from western social scientists, whose concern is often to determine to what extent any given elite is capable of coping with the process of social and political change going on within the society from which it is issued. The task confronting these elites is variously defined, but all definitions revolve about the Janus-faced problem of simultaneously integrating primordial attachments into a comprehensive, national, political culture, and promoting economic development. The survival of any regime and the elite that it represents is contingent, at least to some extent, upon its capacity to undertake this two-part task. However, it is conceivable that a regime that succeeded in raising the standard of living and in expanding GNP could survive whether or not it was able to pursue to a positive conclusion its integrative revolution. Conversely, no matter how successful a regime may be in this latter respect, its triumph will go for nought if not accompanied by at least a modicum of economic expansion.

One may take this observation a step further and postulate that crucial to the process of integration and development is the ability of any regime to absorb the educated and semi-educated cadres of its country and to satisfy their aspirations for prestige as well as their material needs. Economic stagnation or retrogression does not in itself constitute an automatic threat to a regime. It does constitute a threat if there is a large and disgruntled would-be elite willing to seize upon the economic situation as a lever to gain access to or overthrow the incumbent elite. Elite aspirants may also exploit primordial sentiments toward the same end. In the long run, however, prolonged economic stagnation will place severe strictures upon the absorptive capacity of an elite faced with growing numbers of educated aspirants. Only economic expansion can effectively generate career jobs, both in the public and, where it exists, private sectors. Failing this, the regime is reduced to contrived bureaucratic expansion and make-work projects to sponge up excess cadres.[1] It may be argued, then, that the most immediate danger to many regimes in developing countries is not so much economic feebleness or cultural heterogeneity, as the existence and growth of groups with national aspirations capable of exploiting these weaknesses.

The problem of elite absorption is only just beginning to be felt in Morocco, and it may not become acute for some years to come. There has been no serious challenge to the present elite educated under the protectorate, and it has become so set in its ways that it seems oblivious, except in the most abstract fashion, to its growing isolation *vis-à-vis* the still inchoate mass of young, educated Moroccans. Two factors have served to blunt the thrust of those produced by the 'education explosion' that has taken place in Morocco since 1956. First, as already noted, the expansion of the administration following independence, combined with the replacement of foreign personnel by Moroccans, provided ample opportunities for the educated to exercise their talents profitably. Second, while neither GNP nor per capita income have grown as fast as the population, the government's administrative role in the economy has expanded. In addition to this, there has been a steady Moroccanization of the private sector proportionate to the gradual departure of European economic interests. Recently it has become apparent that neither the government nor the private sector of the economy will be able to absorb, as effectively as before, the educated elite aspirants who have already begun to form a dangerous 'intellectual proletariat'. Government officials now speak of administrative saturation and diminishing returns upon each individual employee added to the Civil Service roster. As regards the economy, it has failed to generate much new employment. Morocco, like many countries at a similar level of development, is simultaneously plagued by a severe shortage of technically trained

TABLE 3 *Moroccan Students*
Attending Institutions of Higher Learning
*in Morocco and Abroad**

Disciplines		No. of Students	%
Law (Droit)		3,581	
Administration		130	
Economy and Commerce		138	
Commercial Technique		71	
	Total	3,920	46·36
Literature		1,059	
Pre-university Lit.		404	
Sociology		167	
Orientation		29	
Ecole Normale Sup., Teaching		670	
	Total	2,329	27·54
Pre-university Science		248	
Sciences		209	
Preparation for Prof. Schools		144	
Industrial Technique		598	
	Total	1,199	14·18
Medicine		501	
Pharmacy		172	
Dental Surgery		43	
	Total	716	8·47
Agricultural Technique		136	
Veterinary Medicine		31	
	Total	167	1·98
Other		124	1·47
	Total	8,455	100·00

* From Nor el-Ghorfi, *op. cit.*, p. 507, based on figures for 1962. These figures may be far from accurate as many students register in more than one faculty, but the trends indicated are probably valid. An unpublished study of projections of enrolment for the period 1967–72 indicates that in 1966–7 there was a total of 6,853 university-level students, 2,681 of which were abroad, and 2,961 of which worked for degrees in 'droit'.

personnel and an over-abundance of high school and university graduates educated in the humanities and liberal professions (see table 3, p. 301). These students have merely retraced the educational experience of their elders and feel, for the most part, fully qualified to take up the reins of power.

Universal education early on became a nationalist battle-cry against the French elitist educational policy. The nationalist promises to redress the wrongs committed during the protectorate years had to be honored, albeit with misgivings, after 1956. A considerable part of budgetary resources have annually been allocated to expanding the educational system at all levels, diverting funds from pressing and more immediately productive investments in industry and agriculture. Budgetary allocations for education have generally represented about 17 per cent of the total state budget.[2] Political parties and unions, taking advantage of the widespread popular yearning of most Moroccans for social and economic betterment through the education of their children, have, in conjunction with the employees of the Ministry of Education themselves, persistently pressed for even greater investment in the educational system.[3] Caught between the millstones of economic rationality and political expediency, successive Moroccan governments have financed nothing less than an educational explosion (see table 4, p. 303) characterized by steadily deteriorating standards at all levels. The products or victims of the post-1956 educational system that make up what Ashford calls the third generation elite[4] may have received instruction greatly inferior to that of their elders (Ashford's second generation and the men that constitute the present elite), but, for all that, aspire to positions commensurate with their own exaggerated estimate of their competence.

The political problem posed by a growing in-school population is not confined solely to the absorption of secondary school and university graduates. Primary school graduates and secondary school dropouts constitute, in relative terms, skilled personnel by the simple fact that they are literate. Table 2 indicates the dimensions of the absorption problem that has developed in the last decade.

Moroccan planners have projected the size of the in-school population at these three levels for the next twenty years, assum-

TABLE 4

The Growth of the In-School Population of Morocco
1953–65*

Level	1953	1956	1961	1965
Primary	157,000	292,000	856,525	1,100,000
Secondary	4,648	28,000	60,291	174,000
Advanced	2,800†	—	4,639	9,297
Total	164,448	320,000	921,455	1,283,297

* Reconstructed from figures taken from A.Ayache, *op. cit.*, p. 321; C.F. Gallagher, 'Morocco Goes Back to School', *A.U.F.S. Report* (Sept. 15, 1958), p. 4; *B.E.S.M.*, Vol. 16, No. 58 (1952), p. 543 and Vol. 28, No. 100 (Jan.–March 1966), p. 155. Figures do not include private and religious enrolment.

† This figure includes 2,429 students in the Center of Legal Studies, The Center for Advanced Scientific Studies, and the Institute of Advanced Moroccan Studies (IHEM). The rest (*c.* 400 students) were university students.

ing that universal primary education will be a fact by that time and that the population will continue to grow at a rate of 3·3 per cent per year. On that basis primary school students will number 7,220,000 in 1985, and secondary and above 1,661,000. This would mean that the student population would grow seven times over in those twenty years and would necessitate the training by the end of the period of some 178,000 teachers, a number roughly equivalent to the entire Civil Service of 1965.[5]

Clearly if present growth rates in the school-going population were maintained in future years, education would come to dominate all Morocco's development plans. Despite political pressure to the contrary, the government has begun to stabilize its educational programs and to redraft its projections for the years to come. Indeed, with somewhat less than half of those eligible to begin primary school actually enrolled, there are numerous indications that the spontaneous demand for education at this level has been satisfied. One may conjecture that education has not turned out to be the panacea described by the nationalists, that schooling has not brought the children what their parents expected, that having put at least the eldest child in school many Moroccans may no longer feel any need to educate the others.

Nonetheless, if one keeps in mind that between 1912 and 1954 only two thousand Moroccans ever reached the *baccalauréat* examination, the more modest prognostications for the future simply reduce the intensity of the explosion without in any way avoiding it. Taking into account only the secondary school cycle (seven years) we find that the revised projections estimate a rise from the present (1965–6) 175,000 students to a figure of 336,000 in 1975–6. By that time the number of students passing the Moroccan equivalent of the *baccalauréat* examination, and thereby eligible to move on to university training, will grow to 14,000 annually as compared with 2,355 in 1965–6.[6] This post-nationalist generation of educated Moroccans is of particular political importance. The nationalist generation, whatever the nature and level of its training, was small enough numerically to find a meaningful and rewarding niche in the post-1956 political process. The 'fourth generation', that of the 1980s and 1990s, may, despite great numerical size, have received technical training adequate to find a career role in the administration of the economy.

The third generation, however, is too big to be pacified piece-meal in the manner of their elders, and, as regards the administration and economy, they are simply obsolete. Their inevitable frustration may lead to the formation of formidable counter-elites whose demands on the present regime may be far more radical and far more threatening than any that have been made heretofore. Before taking up some of the characteristics of the third generation elite we would do well to outline in somewhat greater detail the limitations upon the absorption of educated cadres inherent in Morocco's stationary economy.

It has already been posited that the monarchy is unwilling to sponsor dynamic programs of economic development that would have as one of their results a certain amount of social and economic upheaval. The short term necessity of political control has consistently superseded the long term necessity of vigorous economic growth. The fact that Morocco, relative to many other countries in the Near and Middle East, has considerable economic potential, may have lulled the monarchy and the elite into a false sense of security. A low level of investment, a steady capital flight, and a high birth rate have stifled the modest economic growth rate since independence.

Over 65 per cent of active Moroccans are dependent upon agriculture for a living, and about 45 per cent of Morocco's foreign earnings come through the export of agricultural produce and food products.[7] These exports consist largely of citrus fruits and vegetables, but up until 1959 Morocco had exportable surpluses of food grains. However, the production of cereals, while sometimes varying spectacularly from one year to another due to lack of rainfall, has not progressed significantly beyond the maximal levels of the 1930s.* Since 1936 the population has grown from c. 7,040,000 to 13,500,000 in 1966. Per capita production of cereals has fallen from 364 kilograms in 1936 to 218 in 1965 and 115 in 1966.[8] It is small wonder then that about 100,000 Moroccans annually feel compelled to abandon the blad for the cities. Moroccan agriculture is underexploited, and although yields are high on acreage farmed by modern methods, little attempt has been made to improve yields on traditionally-farmed acreage.

The agricultural depression has been singled out in this context because it weighs so heavily on the rest of the economy. Added to increasing rural underemployment, diminishing caloric intake and falling per capita production, are annual food deficits met by imports from abroad. The payments in hard currency for these food imports, as well as those for sugar, tea and tobacco, pre-empt funds from investments in social and economic infrastructure and industry. This comes at a moment in the economic development of Morocco when public and private investment in industry and manufacturing must be massive in order to take up the slack paid out by departing European interests and to sustain the production levels they established.

In 1953, at the height of the postwar boom, gross investment in fixed assets rose to 18 per cent of GNP, exclusive of foreign military investments. Between 1951 and 1955 Gross Domestic Product grew annually by 4·1 per cent. Taking 1952 as our base year (1952=100) the level of investment plummeted to 47 in 1957, rose to 55 in 1958 and to 60 in 1962. Investments since that time have not exceeded an annual level of 11 to 13 per cent of GNP.[9] Moreover, public outlays provided for by Moroccan planners since independence have not been fully utilized.[10] Nonetheless, mining and industrial output increased by 4·2 per cent annually between 1961 and 1964, thanks largely to the steady growth in phosphate production which is Morocco's greatest export item. The textile and food processing industries also have manifested significant expansion since 1958.

* Abundant rainfall in 1968 and 1969 led to record cereal harvests estimated and over 40 million quintals for both years.

THE COMMANDER OF THE FAITHFUL

As in so many other developing countries, population growth smothers the modest rate of economic expansion. In Morocco, in recent years, the two rates have been in equilibrium with population and economic growth averaging 3 to 3·5 per cent annually.[11] Over the five year period, 1960–4, it is estimated that agricultural production increased by 11 per cent, industry and mines by 21 per cent, and GNP by 13·7 per cent. During the same period the population grew by about 14 per cent.

It is to be hoped that the preceding few paragraphs have given some indication of the stagnation and immobility of the Moroccan economy. The country's relative wealth in economic resources

TABLE 5

General Economic Indices*

	1960	1961	1962	1963	1964
Population in millions of inhabitants	11,850	11,940	12,242	12,680	12,950
Harvests in millions of quintals	25·1	11·9	27·8	30·5	27·0
GDP index constant prices. 1960=100	100	97	108	113	114
Ind. Prod. index constant prices. 1960=100	100·0	104·5	109·0	110·0	121·0
Agric. Prod. index constant prices. 1960=100	100·0	84·6	105·6	126·0	111·0
Per Capita GNP, 1960 prices 1960=100	100·0	94·5	97·0	101·0	103·7
Gross Investments constant prices. 1960=100	100·0	109·1	114·0	132·0	131·0
Investments as % of GNP	9·9	11·7	11·0	12·1	11·4
Balance of payments in current prices: billions of Francs	—	−28·8	−15·8	−27·0	−31·2

* From the 1966 report of the Association Marocaine des Sociétés, reproduced in *Maroc-Informations* (27 Feb. 1966), p. 4.

306

has kept the situation from reaching crisis proportions, but the point is that it does not appear likely that there will be any significant economic expansion for some years to come. In fact Moroccan planners have tacitly concurred that Morocco would do well simply to maintain present growth rates and levels of per capita income (about $188·00 annually) for the next twenty years.[12] Thus it may be concluded that career openings dependent upon the growth of the Moroccan economy will be extremely limited for members of the third generation elite.

The dilemma of the third generation is compounded by the poor quality of the education it has received. Bearers of the Primary School Certificate (CEP) in the first few years after independence were rapidly inducted into the administration to exercise modest functions such as clerks and office boys. The shortened primary school cycle, combined with massive enrolment and rapid Arabization have subsequently rendered holders of the CEP unfit for the administration. As much as 65–70 per cent of Moroccan pupils terminate their schooling after five years of primary education, and they now swell the ranks of the literate unemployed. But even the students who pass on to secondary school, and obtain the Secondary School Certificate (CES) after four years of high school, have become liabilities. Both the administration and private enterprises are now wary of hiring bearers of the CES, which since 1960 has continually declined in prestige. In 1966, 7,205 Moroccans (of which 1,040 were monolingual in Arabic) were awarded the CES. Of course the plight of those who drop out of the secondary cycle before obtaining a certificate is more pronounced, and on this score students trained exclusively in Arabic are particularly disadvantaged. For any kind of promotion within the administration a good knowledge of French is a prerequisite, and those without this knowledge are badly handicapped in gaining access to and advancement within the bureaucratic hierarchy. These students are rightly embittered by this state of affairs, for Arabic is after all the national tongue. In March 1964, secondary school students in the Islamic institute of the Kasba of the Cherrada in Fez went on strike to demand the abrogation of the requirement of a knowledge of a foreign language for the *baccalauréat*. They further demanded that certificates granted by traditional and modern institutions be considered as equivalent. Students in Meknes, Oujda, Tetouan, and al-Hoceima joined in the strike which continued until mid-April.[13]

Too poorly educated to undertake employment in the adminis-tration or private enterprise, all these students are too highly educated, within the Moroccan context, to undertake menial work at low salaries. Many have opted for jobs as manual laborers in Europe, which at least is relatively remunerative. The Ministry of Education and the royal cabinet are fully justified in speaking, as they did in the Royal Memorandum on Education of August 1966, of the 'educated unemployed'.[14]

One area where there is a pressing demand for Moroccans having the CES or having the *baccalauréat*, is that of secondary school teachers, and there also the supply does not meet the demand because of the poor quality of the graduates. By 1975 15,000 new teachers will be needed to staff the secondary cycle; 12,000 for the first four years (first cycle) and 3,000 for the last three (second cycle). At the present time (1965) there are some 9,500 secondary school teachers, of which 5,100 are foreigners, and of the Moroc-cans 3,000 handle only materials in Arabic.[15] There would seem to be great opportunities for the third generation in this sphere, but the fact is that so few secondary students are able to meet the reduced standards of the *baccalauréat* examinations (only 1,712 in 1966) that the supply of candidates falls far short of required levels.[16] Again, even those that have passed these examinations are not educated to meet the country's needs for teachers versed in the sciences. Only 35 per cent of those who passed the *baccalauréat* in 1966 majored in the sciences, and of Morocco's estimated 7,000 university students in the same year only 25 per cent were majoring in the sciences. This is one of the most salient aspects of the obsolescence of the third generation elite. There does not seem to be any immediate and financially feasible remedy to the situation.[17] For the next decade or more a high proportion of secondary school teachers will continue to be French, the government will mark time on Arabization of secondary school curricula, and there will be no massive effort to retrain the poorly equipped products of the post-1956 school system. The Royal Memorandum which was circulated to all the political parties stated the crux of the matter: 'Whatever reforms and options we may adopt, it is incum-bent upon us not to overstep the limited financial range allotted to education.'[18] Put more baldly, there will be no attempt to salvage the third generation elite. Such a non-policy may be financially advisable[19] but will almost certainly entail grave political risks.

Even were these new elite aspirants to be happily ensconced somewhere in the administrative apparatus or in the private sector, the implications for the incumbent elite would be no less profound. The sheer numbers and social diversity of the third generation elite are such that the whole context of national politics, as described in the preceding chapters, will be radically changed as its members reach maturity. With secondary school and university students now numbering in the tens of thousands, the possibility of pervasive intimacy and mutual acquaintance among elite members will rapidly disappear. Further, these young Moroccans come from diverse social, economic, and geographic milieux. Most are unfamiliar with and little interested in the spider web of familial, commercial and political alliances that bind together members of the nationalist elite and that are part and parcel of elite behavior. Nor do the aspirants share with their seniors the common experience of participation in the nationalist movement (many were not even born in 1944), and their esteem for nationalist leaders, or for any elite members for that matter, is minimal. Today there are secondary schools and *lycées* in almost every urban center where before there was but a handful for the entire country. This fact has entailed not only a democratization of the educational system, but has also led to a diminution of the prestige of the original *collèges* and *lycées* and the old-school tie spirit associated with them during the nationalist years. In this respect it is significant to note the dramatic decline of the *Collège* of Azrou which is now merely another regional secondary school. Berbers now attend secondary schools in closest proximity to their homes, and this may mean schools in Fez or Rabat or Marrakesh. The number of students taking the *baccalauréat* examination has fallen off sharply since 1956 at Azrou. The *Collège* has lost its symbolic status as the Eton of the Berber elite, and its name holds no magic for the third generation.

It is no easy task to summarize the political attitudes of the third generation elite. Toward the present elite, young educated Moroccans display feelings of hostility, contempt and indifference, but almost never admiration. They are exponents of a sort of glib radicalism, more remarkable for its cynicism than its idealism. All the clichés of the French left come easily to them and have even filtered into everyday Arabic. One of the most common of these catch-phrases is *option révolutionnaire*, which became the title of a selection of Mehdi Ben Barka's writings: *Al-Ikhtiyar al-Thawri fil-Maghrib* (The Revolutionary Choice in Morocco). Yet they have very little more confidence in the leaders of the left than in any others. All politicians, it is generally assumed, line their pockets when in public office, make money off the backs of the people, and share a general culpability that cuts across all political tendencies. But, at the same time, the young allow that they might be bought too. As mentioned earlier, many suspect their own student leaders of being palace puppets, whose revolutionary ardor has been cooled by substantial rewards. They are not outraged, just bitter, and some only demand their chance to dip into the public till. It is precisely this opportunity that will largely be denied them. Members of the second generation elite who are still relatively young have choked off access to the more lucrative positions, and in view of their age are unlikely to budge for some years to come. This fact exacerbates the resentment of the aspirants and arouses the suspicion and defensiveness of the incumbents. It does no good to tell these youngsters that their ambitions have outstripped their technical capacities. Doubt in their ability to handle tasks of great complexity or in the wisdom of their views is not typical of the would-be elite. Secondary school students are notable for their intolerance, impatience, lofty ambitions, and a proclivity for absolutist views.[20]

The resentment and hostility of elite aspirants is diffuse and unorganized, expressed only by individuals or small groups. The UNEM, the UNFP, and the various federations of employees may in some measure be the spokesmen for the frustrations of the would-be elite, but such bodies have, as yet, been unable to rely upon the young for concerted action. The facility and conviction with which they manipulate the contemporary jargon of third world socialism masks a fundamental confusion regarding their individual wants and the image they should establish among their peers. Apter has argued that the young in modernizing societies 'are not merely driven by ordinary motives of political gain', and that because their identity problems are so exaggerated, they have a predilection for all-embracing ideologies or 'political religions'.[21] Morocco's third generation elite would to some extent conform to this judgment, but it is important that we do not lose sight of 'ordinary motives of political gain'. A recent survey of a sample of *lycée* students in Fez and Casablanca revealed that in answer to the question 'What are the things that you would most like to have, but have not?', over 40 per cent of all male respondents checked 'personal pleasures', while only 2–3 per cent listed 'religious, political, or altruistic hopes or wishes'.[22] Satisfaction of personal pleasures has been the leitmotif of the monarchy's policy of keeping the elite happy. Confronted with the swollen ranks of the third generation elite, a continuation of the policy, while desirable, is probably no longer feasible.

Members of the incumbent elite often talk of Youth and the rising generation, but their grasp of the problem seems bemused and abstract. Some indeed are aware of the potential trouble that could be caused by the educated unemployed, but few realize to what an extent current elite modes of behavior will become anomalous in the next decade. Politicians tend to regard students as clientele but not, except for a few chosen individuals, as future partners. They assume that present-day youth will repeat the patterns of political evolution of the nationalist elite, that student radicalism will give way to political pragmatism and flexibility. There has been a failure of communications between the second and third generation elites, reflected within each organization in which both age groups are represented.

I have stated that Morocco's economic depression has not yet reached crisis proportions, nor has third generation discontent taken on organizational form. But it seems only a matter of time before both the crisis and the development of articulate counter-elites occur.[23] Graphic evidence of the interdependence of the educated unemployed and the retrogression of the economy was provided by the March riots of 1965. At that time the monarchy was openly denounced, but in a more general way the entire elite was challenged. Political parties and labor unions had nothing to do with provoking the riots, nor could they control them once the violence spread. All elements of the elite were taken by surprise by the events. Perhaps for the first time since independence elite factions were presented with the practical effects of a set of circumstances whose implications they had until that time, considered only in the abstract.

In the winter of 1965, the minister of education, Yussuf Bel 'Abbas, issued a ministerial circular which crystalized a policy that previously had only been hinted at. The secondary school cycle of Morocco is divided into two periods. The first period of four years culminates in the examinations for the CES. A certain number of students continue on into the final three-year period, finishing up with the *baccalauréat* examination, and, if successful, a chance to go on to the university. Bel'Abbas' circular stated that any student eighteen years old or older in his fourth year of secondary school would be prohibited from continuing on to the final three-year period. They would be reoriented toward vocational and technical schools, as would any students that repeated one year in the first four-year period. This stirred the anger of many secondary school students who had, through no fault of their own, exceeded the age limit or repeated, and were to be deprived of a chance to have a university education. The number of students who might suffer from the circular was probably not too great, but the issue supplied a pretext for other groups, which had been nursing their grievances over a long period of time, to voice their protests.

Moroccan secondary school teachers had become increasingly dissatisfied with low wages that had hardly increased since independence. European teachers were earning about twice as much (in part paid for by the French Ministry of Education) for the same work. Their demands for a rectification of the situation were discussed in November 1964 when the three-year plan was being drawn up, but the upshot was an increase in their work load without an increase in the salaries. By January 1965 there was widespread talk of a strike of the secondary school teachers. Thus when protest strikes broke out in Casablanca on 22 March regarding the ministerial circular, the teachers more or less joined in. A day later strikes and demonstrations took place in Fez, Marrakesh, Meknes, and Rabat.

At about this point, the students and teachers were joined by masses of unemployed Moroccans and street gangs looking for trouble. The demonstrations became violent, and rioters ran loose through the Nouvelle Medina of Casablanca. On 24 March the UMT called a general strike for noon to 6 p.m., ostensibly to demonstrate its solidarity with the rioters, but perhaps also to give some direction and orderliness to the mobs. As casualties mounted, the Ministry of Interior intervened brutally. Mobile Security Units (Groupes Légers de Securité) were moved into Casablanca and were given a free hand to disperse the rabble.[24] Official sources reported that seven were killed in the repression, but witnesses with access to the hospitals suggested figures of 300–400 dead. There were several hundred arrests made.[25]

Initially the riots were attributed to outside interference – apparently a handful of Ba'athi Syrians and Iraqis who taught in the secondary school system. With a few days reflexion, however, and with the immensity of what had happened slowly sinking into government circles, the king chose to call a spade a spade. In his speech of 30 March, the king deplored the anarchy and violence of the demonstrators. He accused the teachers of cowardice in pushing their pupils to acts of violence, and flatly stated, 'there is no danger for the state as grave as that of the so-called intellectual. It would be better if you were all illiterate.' He then went on to admit that the economic situation was scarcely promising, and that much of the violence came from the unemployed. Sugar prices had been increased, imports restricted, and goods had become scarce. The economic crisis of 1964–5 led to the dismissal of over ten thousand workers. The king stated his belief that these factors, and not outside agitators, had led to the riots. The rioters had denounced the throne, but Hassan II sought to place the blame elsewhere:[26]

My people, since the arrival of the deputies to parliament, the legislative service has been paralyzed, as well as the Official Printing House, and the Official Bulletin has published only three laws although we are already in our third year of constitutional experience. Who then is responsible? He who elaborated the constitution? Those who adopted it? No, and again no. Rather it is those who apply it.

The implication was that Parliament and the political parties had failed to reflect popular aspirations and that the riots came as a natural, if deplorable, consequence. But the riots reveal more than that. They represent the first open and generalized manifestation of the alienation of the third generation elite and of its challenge to the incumbent elite, which includes the king.

In recent years the elite has bemusedly begun to concern itself with youth, and the March riots may have highlighted the urgency of the problem. But the state of emergency, proclaimed a few months after the riots, has become a state of normalcy and with it has come political torpor. Elite members, now that the memory of the riots has grown somewhat dim, have ceased to worry about their successors and have returned to the womb of their own internal intrigues. The king has admonished the students for their failure to recognize their debt and duty toward the state and for their lack of civic spirit. Perhaps acting on his stated preference for illiterates, he has done nothing to stem the flow of expatriate 'so-called intellectuals'. To vitiate the third generation elite, he may encourage the emigration of surplus brains, pick off promising leaders through pre-emptive appointments, draft troublemakers, and harass the rest.

The king's growing preoccupation with students has led him to institute a more elaborate system of control. Perhaps alarmed at the student upheavals in France and Senegal of the spring of 1968, the king appointed three ministers responsible respectively for primary, secondary, and higher education. In addition there is a minister of youth and sports, a minister of state responsible for traditional education, and another responsible for technical training (*formation des cadres*). Moreover, the king has ordered the establishment throughout the kingdom of 'Houses of Thought' to encourage right thinking and to counter the nefarious influences of foreign ideas. Each province is to keep up-to-date lists of all those youths with a primary or secondary school diploma but without work. They are to be inducted into a sort of youth corps to carry out public projects.[27] Thought control and the plans to absorb the literate proletariat and the urban unemployed may well be beyond the technical and financial means of the state, but it is yet another, somewhat ominous, step in the direction of regimentation.

When the Moroccan political elite will break apart under outside pressure or submerge its existing traits in an onslaught of new recruits cannot be pinpointed in time. In the immediate future, the incumbent elite will continue to monopolize national politics. The major concern of the monarchy will remain short-term survival, manifested in the minutiae of day-to-day elite manipulation. The king may rely increasingly upon the military-civilian cleavage which he has so far skillfully managed to straddle. For any civilian factions that lose patience in the game as defined by the king, and that proceed to recommend or undertake radical measures to remedy the situation, there is the sword of Damocles of military intervention as a constant reminder and restraint.

But the king has no desire to become beholden to the Moroccan general staff, and to forestall any thoughts that the army is the sole support of the throne he will not allow important civilian groups to lose their organizational credibility. For the moment, the civilian counterweight to FAR is the UMT, a solid, nationwide organization that would prefer the continuation of the *status quo* to the repressive measures that would surely follow a military takeover. The arrest of Mahjoub Ben Seddiq in the summer of 1967 may seem a clear deviation from this policy. On the other hand, Ben Seddiq's leadership has been under increasing fire from within the UMT, and a period in prison could refurbish his image and dispel accusations that he is a stooge of the palace.

In modern Morocco there has been a territorial inversion of the blad as-siba and the blad al-makhzan. The mountains are now the source of the surest support for the monarchy while the urban centers of the Atlantic plains have become the most likely environments for dissidence. The king strives to remain the sole Moroccan with a following, influence, and authority in both camps. As was the case in pre-protectorate Morocco, the educated urban bourgeoisie, the politicians, bureaucrats, and merchants are unable to exercise any positive role in the evolution of the regime. They are once again victims of fundamental political and social divisions that are kept in precarious equilibrium, and while they would like to mitigate these divisions and bring about a re-ordering of Moroccan society within an explicitly nationalist framework, they shy away from positive actions for fear of the upheaval their endeavors would entail. The monarchy is a marvelous excuse for the Moroccan elite to benefit from a system that it refuses to espouse and for whose shortcomings it shirks all responsibility. The king realizes that the perfunctory grumblings of his clientele will most probably never take the form of an overt challenge to his regime upon whose rewards the elite has come to depend. Inescapably, new elites, with little or no stake in the present but great hopes in the future, will take up the responsibilities their elders have refused to assume.

CONCLUSION

Throughout this study I have viewed Moroccan politics from two perspectives: that of patterns of political behavior evident at all levels of society, and that of the national political elite. In the first and more general approach, I have sought to explain discernible patterns of political behavior in terms of the traditional structure of Moroccan society. In the second, I have tried to determine the extent to which these same patterns have influenced and are manifest in elite behavior. It has been contended throughout these pages that the political style and attitudes of Moroccan elite members are still largely shaped by attitudes that arose in an historical situation that no longer applies. Such a contention is by no means original and has been made often before about other elites and other societies.

It is a commonplace that politics in underdeveloped societies are generally founded upon a blend of 'traditional' (ascriptive, affective) and 'modern' (rationalistic, achievement-oriented) norms. Morocco is not unique in its particular blend of factors: on the contrary, I would suggest that Morocco resembles, in varying aspects, other countries in the Middle East. However, I have not been content to accept the Moroccan situation as so commonplace as to require no further analysis, nor to note simply that tradition influences contemporary politics, that primordial sentiments still have great weight in Morocco, and leave it at that. Such an attitude, unfortunately, has been evident in much of the literature of the Middle East, and each new student to the area is obliged to work out for himself the exact weight of various factors on the spectrum between tradition and modernity. It will be possible for us to discern changes in the weight of these factors only if we have a clear idea of their configuration at some given point in time. Without such a 'snapshot', future changes will be interpreted in an informational vacuum.

The Moroccan political elite has provided me with such a snapshot. Its contours should be generally familiar to those who have studied the formation of other elites in the colonial context. An advanced education, while not a requisite to elite membership, is almost a guarantee of access to elite status. As elsewhere, the protectorate authority nurtured a small elite, scions of the well-to-do who were judged to have a material interest in the *status quo*. It was further hoped that this new, secularly educated elite would be fully assimilated into the exogenous culture, and that its members would eventually become the apostles of the new civilization within their own society. What assimilation did take place was generally shallow, and the cultural values learned by the westernized elite were turned against its mentors. At the same time, the protectorate never generated enough of an impact to wrench Moroccans entirely from their habitual modes of behavior. Fanon has argued that this can only be done through the catharsis of communal blood-letting in a revolt against both the traditional indigenous culture and that imposed from the outside. But had he lived, he would have seen even Algeria relapse, after seven years of armed revolution, into some of the behavioral patterns of the past.

If even the products of the westernized educational system, who composed the bulk of the elite, could not be turned fully into new ways of thought and behavior, so much less was the impact of the protectorate upon the remainder of the elite. Army officers were encouraged to maintain their links to the traditional rural notability, religious leaders were steered away from the modernizing tendencies of Islamic reform, and Muslim commercial interests were given little incentive to update their practices. Thus, even the most advanced elements of the Moroccan elite bore heavy traces of the country's traditional political culture at the time Morocco became independent, while the rest of the elite was only beginning to divest itself of and to transform its primordial sentiments. The phenomenon of cultural lag on both a society-wide basis and within given elites is common to most developing countries. Yet with regard to Morocco it can be argued that the contrast of new and old attitudes within a 'mixed' political culture is particularly striking in that the full impact of the exogenous culture

was crammed into a single generation. Some Moroccans underwent childhood socialization under the makhzan, formal education
under the French, and found career opportunities in the government of independent Morocco.

The social origins, recruitment, education, and political development of the Moroccan political elite are not unlike that of other
colonial elites of the Arab world. Further, it has operated since
independence as part of a monarchical regime that, at one time or
another in the recent past, has had counterparts in the majority
of the countries of the area. The leading member of the Moroccan
political elite is also head of a three hundred year old dynasty, and
is a monarch who intervenes directly and continuously in the
political process. The monarchy has achieved for the moment
remarkable control of elite politics, and the two aspects of its
domination have been, on the one hand, a policy of elite division
through the manipulation of punishments and rewards, and, on the
other, the direct subordination of the armed forces and police to the
throne. The essential dilemma of such a monarch is to promote
economic development without upsetting the delicate political
stalemate that he has helped maintain. The recent development of
Iran would indicate that, under highly favorable economic circumstances, a monarch can encourage, at least on a short-term basis,
economic development while maintaining the political status quo.

Unlike Iran, however, Morocco receives no massive revenues
from the sale of its natural resources, and King Hassan has no
financial cushion with which to meet the country's economic
crisis.[1] Moreover, elite paralysis may lead Morocco even further
from coping with its fundamental economic problems, and the
elite may be deposed if conditions continue to worsen. The possible paths that Morocco might follow in future years are myriad
and there is little point in making predictions. Morocco could fall
victim to the military – either in the form of a coup to sustain the
monarchy, or one to do away with it. The elite might find new
strength by rejuvenating its leadership, regrouping and imposing
some sort of political cohesion among its squabbling factions. The
king may some day feel compelled to abandon his cautious economic policies and lead a crusade for economic development, regardless of the risks to his dynasty. Or, as seems to be happening now,
faced with a deteriorating economic situation, he may clamp down
on anyone capable of exploiting these ills. Were he to continue to

do this, he would eventually snuff out what few intermediaries remain between the throne and the masses. These are but a few of the possible developments that might take place in the next phase of Moroccan politics. All that can safely be predicted is that the type of elite stalemate analyzed in these pages cannot continue for too much longer.

The trends of education in the past decade, I have argued,* in combination with a stagnant economy, pose a set of problems whose solution will require radical changes in the size and behavior of the elite. Here, one must insist upon the problem of elite absorption. Until recent years this has been no problem at all, and demand for educated personnel generally exceeded the supply. But that happy situation has come to an end. The development of significant would-be elites is a serious threat to the incumbent elite. Without them, there would be few spokesmen for those victimized by economic stagnation. Without them, grievances could pile up indefinitely for want of those who could exploit them, articulate them, and use their weight as a lever or a hammer to attack the incumbent elite. But in Morocco there is no doubt that such would-be elites are taking form particularly among the youths who have completed their educations since 1956. One can only speculate as to how they may organize, what programs they may adopt, and how the present elite may react. However, they cannot simply be ignored. Were the incumbents to try to integrate their challengers into the present family, they would destroy the intimacy and introversion upon which the style and content of elite politics is predicated. Were they stubbornly to resist all efforts to adapt to the new situation, they would inevitably be thrust aside. The latter reaction on the part of the incumbent elite has been the more common in other countries of the Arab world.

Segmented elite politics in Morocco is then of a relatively temporary nature. But what can be said of the underlying patterns of political behavior that are to be found throughout Moroccan society? Will they survive the demise of the elite? The likelihood is great that these patterns will endure for quite some time, although it is equally likely that their grip on Moroccans will gradually diminish. Their tenacity has been evident elsewhere in the Middle East, and even under the revolutionary regimes the ostensible dynamism of the 'modernizing elites' often seems to

* In chapter 16.

319

mask poorly some of the old defense-oriented, negative patterns discussed in this study.

In general, the politics of independence has given rise to a new political vocabulary employed primarily within and among elites. A variety of political regimes now function in the area, and there is a rapid turnover in governments if not in personnel. But despite the diversity of political form, the style and content of politics have not evolved so rapidly. Communal, segmented politics are still prevalent in North Africa and the Middle East. This is so because similar forms of social organization and social relations have been common to the entire area. The organization of the family, tribe, and city quarter; the traditional economic, social and political roles of the commercial bourgeoisie, 'ulema, governmental officials, and religious and ethnic minorities; the interaction of city and country, urbanite and tribesman, folk religion and orthodoxy, and government and dissidence have all been fundamentally similar throughout the Arab world. Finally, all this area fell under the direct or indirect suzerainty of Europe for extended periods of time and underwent, to varying degrees, a far-reaching process of cultural challenge and shock.

The existence of general patterns of political behavior can be seen to flow logically from this shared social, cultural and historic background. Yet seldom has the relation between contemporary politics and the social organization and political culture of the Middle East been explicitly and extensively analyzed. This I have tried to do for one country during a somewhat brief moment in its political history. As such, this study suggests a more general approach to the politics of the entire area, one oriented to the social factors influencing the formation of attitudes toward and the actual use of power and authority. The frequently-observed tension and the accompanying immobility of Middle Eastern politics are rooted in the defense-oriented attitudes characteristic of segmented societies. To understand any given problem within the area would require intensive interdisciplinary analysis with a view to situating strictly political acts in the context of all social activity within the society, country, region or group under study. My generalizations about the behavior of the Moroccan political elite may have a general validity within the Middle East, and could help others determine the relation between the mixed political culture and the contemporary politics of the area.

Not only are the defense-oriented politics of stalemate and tension specifically appropriate to the cultural heritage of the Middle East, but they are also part and parcel of political competition in general. Moreover, others have noted that in developing societies there is a tendency towards intense factionalism, or the formation of cliques, in political organization.[2] These become the vehicles for the expression of interests and personal ambitions that are often a blend of the primordial and the objective. Such factions tend to persist well into, and despite, the process of the decay of traditional institutions. They adapt to the politics of mass urbanization and the single party as easily as they do to nominally plural, liberal systems. To date no one can say with any assurance at what point in a society's development these cliques lose their pivotal place in political competition.

One need not be a seer to predict that the processes of urbanization, industrialization, bureaucratization, and mass education will substantially transform Moroccan society in the next decades, and, as a result, will transform the elite and its style. A challenge from the growing intellectual proletariat seems inevitable, and the incumbent elite, as it is presently constituted, is not prepared to meet this challenge. Further, the challengers will have a growing clientele at their disposal in the bureaucracy, in the schools, among detribalized agricultural laborers, growing urban masses, industrial labor, and perhaps even in the army. But one should not conclude from this that factional politics will become obsolete, any more so than they are today, nor that there will be an abrupt rupture in behavioral continuity. In the Middle East, Egypt, Syria, and Algeria, whose politics are ostensibly very different from those of Morocco, have revealed a continued propensity for factional tension and stalemate. It may well be that in Morocco political behavior will fail to evolve at the same pace as, and in relation to, the social transformations that Moroccan society is undergoing. Whether or not the incumbent elite adjusts to the changed situation, or is displaced for its failure to do so, may not be as important as the political behavior and style adopted by future elites. This study will have served a useful purpose if, in addition to clarifying certain aspects of contemporary political development in Morocco, it helps others to understand what is to come.

A SELECT BIBLIOGRAPHY ON MOROCCO

The following lines represent a summary of those books, articles, and publications that I found most useful in my research. I have made no attempt to be complete, and many worthy publications are not mentioned here. The selections are my own and constitute my tribute to some of those who made Morocco more understandable to me.

History

The standard works on Moroccan history are H. Terrasse, *Histoire du Maroc* (2 vols), Casablanca, 1950; C.-A. Julien, *L'Histoire de l'Afrique du Nord* (2 vols), Paris, 1964; and Ahmed Khalid al-Nasiri al-Slaoui, *Kitab al-Istiqca: Chronique de la Dynastie Alaouie du Maroc*, Archives Marocaines, vols, 9 & 10, Paris, 1906. Jean-Louis Miège, *Le Maroc et l'Europe* (4 vols), Paris, 1962, has presented a thorough internal and diplomatic history of Morocco in the nineteenth century. Supplementing him are Eugène Aubin, *Le Maroc d'Aujourd'hui*, Paris, 1905; Dr L. Arnaud, *Au Temps des Mehallas*, Casablanca, 1952; J. Erckmann, *Le Maroc Moderne*, Paris, 1885; and F. Weisgerber, *Au Seuil du Maroc Moderne*, Rabat, 1947. Fresh attempts to reinterpret Moroccan history are to be found in Jean Brignon *et al.*, *Histoire du Maroc*, Paris-Casablanca, 1967, and Muhammed Lahbabi, *Le Gouvernement Marocain à l'Aube de XXe Siècle*, Rabat, 1958.

Society

In anthropology, Jacques Berque's *Structures Sociales du Haut-Atlas*, Paris, 1955, and Robert Montagne's *Les Berbères et le*

Makhzen dans le Sud du Maroc, Paris, 1930, are now classics. More recently Ernest Gellner has published several articles treating tribal organization, particularly with regard to the Central High Atlas, and D. M. Hart has written extensively on the Rif and Ait Atta of the Sahara. Of a somewhat different nature are two other classics: E. Westermarck, *Ritual and Belief in Morocco* (2 vols), London, 1926, and R. Le Tourneau, *Fès avant le Protectorat,* Casablanca, 1949. The most solid study of Moroccan Jewry, though limited in scope, is P. Flamand, *Les Communautés Israelites du Sud-Marocain,* Casablanca, 1950. Two good but dated studies on urban development are André Adam's 'Le "bidonville" de Ben M'Sik à Casablanca,' *Annales de l'Institut d'Etudes Orientales,* vol. 8 (1949–50), pp. 61–198, and Robert Montagne (ed.), *Naissance du Proletariat Marocain,* Paris, 1950. In addition, various Moroccan periodicals and scholarly journals have printed the sociological studies of Abdel-kabir al-Khatibi, Grigori Lazarev, Paul Pascon, and Abdulwahad Radi.

Economy

The most recent survey of the Moroccan economy is that of the IBRD Mission, *The Economic Development of Morocco,* Johns Hopkins Press, 1966. Other worthy studies are those of Samir Amin, *L'Economie du Maghreb* (2 vols), Paris, 1966; Albert Ayache, *Le Maroc: Bilan d'une Colonisation,* Paris, 1956; Charles F. Stewart, *The Economy of Morocco 1912–1962,* Harvard, 1962; and André Tiano, *La Politique Economique et Financière du Maroc Indépendant,* Paris, 1963.

The Protectorate and the Nationalist Movement

On the organization of the protectorate, a useful book is André de Laubadére, *Les Réformes des Pouvoirs Publics au Maroc,* Paris, 1949. The period is ably analyzed by Jacques Berque, *Le Maghreb entre Deux Guerres,* Paris, 1962; Stéphane Bernard, *Le Conflit Franco-Marocain: 1943–1956,* Brussels, 1963; and Ladislav Cerych, *Européens et Marocains 1930–1956: Sociologie d'une Décolonisation,* Bruges, 1964. The nationalist movement is best treated by J. P. Halstead, *Rebirth of a Nation: The Origins and Rise of Moroccan Nationalism, 1912–1944,* Harvard, 1967; C.-A.

Julien, *L'Afrique du Nord en Marche*, Paris, 1952; R. Rézette, *Les Partis Politiques Marocains*, Paris, 1955; and Allal al-Fassi, *The Independence Movements in Arab North Africa*, Washington, D.C., 1954.

Politics

The most thorough treatment of the early years of independence is D. E. Ashford's *Political Change in Morocco*, Princeton, 1961. On the same period see also J. & S. Lacouture, *Le Maroc à l'Epreuve*, Paris, 1957. More recent and more specific studies are those of Jacques Robert, *La Monarchie Marocaine*, Paris, 1963; and I. W. Zartman, *Destiny of a Dynasty: The Search for New Institutions in Morocco's Developing Society*, University of South Carolina Press, 1964, and *Morocco: Problems of New Power*, Atherton Press, 1964. Two articles of a general nature are of particular merit: Jules and Jim Aubin, 'Le Maroc en Suspens', *Annuaire de l'Afrique du Nord*, vol. 3 (1964), pp. 73–88, and Octave Marais, 'La classe dirigeante au Maroc', *Revue Française de Science Politique*, vol. 14, no. 4 (1964), pp. 709–37. Also the electoral and parliamentary studies of Paul Chambergeat in the *Annuaire de l'Afrique du Nord* are of high quality. Charles Gallagher in his *American Universities Field Staff Reports* has given extensive attention to Morocco since independence. Finally, one could well consult three books that range beyond Morocco in their subject matter: L. C. Brown (ed.), *State and Society in Independent North Africa*, Middle East Institute, Washington, D.C., 1966; C. F. Gallagher, *The United States and North Africa*, Harvard, 1963; and Abdullah Laroui, *L'Idéologie Arabe Contemporaine*, Paris, 1967.

Newspapers, Periodicals, Brochures

For general coverage of current events in Morocco, *Le Monde* is unexcelled. *Jeune Afrique*, a Paris weekly, often reports on Morocco. *Maghreb*, published on a bimonthly basis, is an excellent press digest and economic and political review directed by Louis Fougère. In Morocco the most reliable newspaper, in the sense that it is never seized by the police, is *Le Petit Marocain*, while the best quality daily is *Maghreb-Informations*. In Arabic, *Al-Alam* is the best of the dailies, while *Kifah al-Watani* is the best weekly. *Lamalif* (in French) is a sometimes excellent monthly cultural, economic, and cautiously political review. Moroccan scholarly journals and periodicals of high quality are the *Bullétin Economique et Sociale du Maroc*, the *Revue de Géographie de Maroc*, *Hespéris*, and the *Annales Marocaines de Sociologie*.

Without equal in scope and quality is the *Annuaire de l'Afrique du Nord*, published since 1962 at the University of Aix-en-Provence. It presents complete annual bibliographies, resumés of all political, economic and social developments for each year, as well as important scholarly articles and book reviews.

NOTES

INTRODUCTION

[1] Clifford Geertz, 'Politics Past, Politics Present', *European Journal of Sociology*, vol. 8, 1967, p. 11.

[2] See L.Binder, 'Prolegomena to the Comparative Study of Middle East Governments', *A.P.S.R.*, vol.LI, no. 3, 1957, p. 653.

[3] S.Verba, 'Comparative Political Culture', in L.W.Pye and S.Verba (eds), *Political Culture and Political Development*, Princeton, 1965, p. 513.

[4] Most of the above paragraph is adapted from Clifford Geertz, 'The Integrative Revolution', in C.Geertz (ed.), *Old Societies and New States: The Quest for Modernity in Asia and Africa*. New York, 1965, pp. 109-20.

[5] Col. Justinard, *Le Caid Goundafi*, Editions Atlantides, Casablanca, 1951, p. 159.

[6] See R.K.Merton, 'Puritanism, Pietism, and Science', in his *Social Theory and Social Structure* (revised edn.), New York, 1964, pp. 574-606 (quotation from p. 606).

[7] D.E.Ashford, *Political Change in Morocco*, Princeton, 1961, p. 405.

CHAPTER ONE

[1] H.Terrasse, *Histoire du Maroc: des Origines à l'Etablissement du Protectorat Francais*, vol. 1, Casablanca, 1949, p. 343.

[2] See Ernest Gellner, 'Tribalism and Social Change in North Africa', mimeo. (July 1964), p. 5. This article has subsequently appeared in W.H.Lewis (ed.), *French-Speaking Africa: The Search for Identity*, New York, 1965, pp. 107-18. All citations are from the unpublished mimeo.

[3] See Robert Montagne, *Les Berbères et le Makhzen dans le Sud du Maroc*, Paris, 1930, p. 372.

[4] Quoted by E.Michaux-Bellaire, 'L'organisation des finances au Maroc', *Archives Marocaines*, vol. 11, 1907, p. 250 (note).

[5] A vivid example of dynastic instability is that of the period 1358-1465, in which seventeen Merinid sultans reigned. Seven were assassinated, five more were deposed, and only five died in office. Three of the seventeen sovereigns were children of the ages of ten, five and four. See Henri Terrasse, 'Sur quelques traditions historiques du Maroc', *Maroc: Bulletin d'Information*, no. 34, Sept. 1953, p. 25.

[6] Gellner, *op. cit.*, p. 6.

[7] Montagne, *op. cit.*, p. 385.

[8] Eugène Aubin, *Le Maroc d'Aujòurd'hui* (2nd edn.), Paris, 1905, p. 135. See also E.Michaux-Bellaire and H. Gaillard, *L'Administration au Maroc: Le Makhzen, étendue et limites de son pouvoir*, Tangier, 1909, p. 14; and Ahmed Khalid an-Naciri as-Slaoui, *Kitab al-Istiqca: Chronique de la Dynastie Alaouie du Maroc*, Archives Marocaines, vols. 9 and 10, Paris, 1906, vol. 10, pp. 167–8 and p. 278.

[9] *Ibid.*, p. 46. Cf., I.W.Zartman, 'The King in Moroccan Constitutional Law', *The Muslim World*, part 2, July 1962, p. 187.

[10] See C-A.Julien, *Histoire de l'Afrique du Nord* (2nd edn.), vol. 2, Paris, 1962, p. 243. Under Muhammed Ben 'Abdullah (1757–90) the land of siba expanded after the forceful reign of Moulay Isma'il (1672–1727). From this period on until 1912 the makhzan could no longer use the road linking Fez to Marrakesh by way of Tadla, not to mention the Fez–Tafilalt route.

[11] See Jules Erckmann, *Le Maroc Moderne*, Paris, 1885, pp. 195–211; and Es-Slaoui, *op. cit.*, vol. 10, pp. 324–39.

[12] See Terrasse, *op. cit.*, p. 261, and S.Schaar, 'Conflict and Change in 19th Century Morocco', unpublished Ph.D. thesis, Department of Oriental Studies and History, Princeton, November 1965, pp. 61–100.

[13] See Es-Slaoui, *op. cit.*, vol. 9, pp. 56–68, Aubin, *op. cit.*, pp. 174–94. On the formation of guish tribes see J. Le Coz, 'Les tribus guiches au Maroc', *Revue de Géographie du Maroc*, no. 7, 1965, esp. pp. 1–10.

[14] Montagne, *op. cit.*, p. 377.

[15] Moulay Isma'il, once he had constituted the corps, presented it with the *Sahih* of al-Bukhari, and told them that all, sultan and soldier alike, are slaves in the presence of Allah and His law. Whence the name '*abid* (slaves) of Bukhari. See Es-Slaoui, *op. cit.*, vol. 9, p. 77.

[16] Mohammed Lahbabi, *Le Gouvernment Marocaine à l'Aube de XXᵉ Siècle*, Rabat, 1958, p. 167. Under Moulay Isma'il the Wadayya tribe was particularly favored, as both the sultan's mother and wife came from that tribe. Consequently it was used to garrison the turbulent areas of the Sais plain and the mountain of Zerhoun near Meknes in addition to Fez al-Jadid; Aubin, *op. cit.*, p. 190, and Julien, *op. cit.*, p. 231.

[17] See Augustin Bernard, *Le Maroc* (6th edn.), Paris, 1922, p. 252, and Erckmann, *op. cit.*, p. 254. The basis of recruitment in guish tribes was one combatant per household. The southern tribes of 'Abda, Ahmar, Rahamna, and Manahba, supplied troops but were not exempt from taxes. See Henry Terrasse, *Histoire du Maroc*, Casablanca, 1949, vol. 1, p. 350.

[18] Erckmann, *op. cit.*, pp. 266–77.

[19] Aubin, *op. cit.*, pp. 193–4.

[20] Bernard, *op. cit.*, pp. 235–44; also Lahbabi, *op. cit.*, pp. 137–8. The most recent chamberlain, Hassan Ben Ya'ish, died in September 1966, having served the makhzan under Moulay 'Abd al-'Aziz and Moulay Hafidh. He was made *qaid al-meshwar* under Moulay Yussuf and *hajib* by Muhammed v. King Hassan appointed the son of the deceased, 'Ali, to fill the vacancy.

[21] *Kharaj* was replaced by the *naiba*, levied on conquered territories (whence the *nuwaib* tribes). See E. Michaux-Bellaire, L'organisation des finances...', p. 221.

[22] In the eighteenth century, the Sultan Muhammed Ben 'Abdullah levied *maks* on the sale of clarified butter and oils. Fassi merchants cried heresy, but the sultan's right to levy such taxes was upheld by a *fatwa* (legal pronouncement) of the *'ulema*. They argued that, in his capacity as defender of the faith, the sultan had the right to resort to non-Islamic taxes if that were the only way he could maintain his army. See Aubin, *op. cit.*, pp. 246–7, and Es-Slaoui, *op. cit.*, vol. 9, p. 275.

[23] See Aubin, *op. cit.*, p. 204, and Lahbabi, *op. cit.*, pp. 161–4.

[24] Erckmann, *op. cit.*, pp. 222–7, and Terrasse, *op. cit.*, p. 346.

[25] Erckmann, *op. cit.*, pp. 120–9, 219; and Lahbabi, *op. cit.*, pp. 137–8.

[26] See Bernard, *op. cit.*, p. 255, and Montagne, *op. cit.*, *passim*.

[27] Lahbabi, *op. cit.*, pp. 35–9 and 77–8; for the powers of the pasha see Erckmann, *op. cit.*, p. 138.

[28] Bernard, *op. cit.*, p. 202. For a thorough treatment of the *zawiyas* and murabitin, see Georges Drague, *Esquisse de l'histoire Réligieuse du Maroc, Confréries et Zawiyas*, Paris, 1951; regarding Al-Jazouli see pp. 49–64; also G.H.Bousquet, *L'Islam Maghrébin* (4th edn.), Algiers, 1954, pp. 64–158.

[29] This idea is developed in Montagne, *op. cit.*, pp. 409–12, and in Elaine C. Hagopian, 'The Status and Role of the Marabout in Pre-Protectorate Morocco', *Ethnology*, vol. 3, no. 1, Jan. 1964, pp. 42–52.

[30] Bernard, *op. cit.*, p. 204.

[31] There were exceptions to' Alawite enmity toward the brotherhoods. It was rumored at the time, that Sultan 'Abd al-'Aziz, deposed in 1907, was a member of the zawiya of the redoutable Ma al-'Aynin. Members of the makhzan, despite official policy, often belonged to zawiyas. See Aubin, *Le Maroc d'Aujourd'hui*, p. 231, and Jamil Abu Nasr, who notes that Moulay Hafidh was a member of the Tijaniyya; *The Tijaniyya: A Sufi Order in the Modern World*, Oxford, 1965, p. 175.

[32] Drague, *op. cit.*, p. 106, 118–20. For a good account of recent developments, see F.S.Vidal, 'Religious Brotherhoods in Moroccan Politics', *M.E.J.*, Oct. 1950, pp. 427–47.

[33] See Mission Scientifique du Maroc, 'Ouezzan', *Villes et Tribus du Maroc: Rabat et sa Région*, vol. 4, Paris, 1918, p. 229.

[34] See Michaux-Bellaire and Gaillard, *op. cit.*, p. 4.

[35] Montagne, *op. cit.*, p. 367. A latter day practitioner of this distinction was Addi ou Bihi, who revolted against the government to save the king in 1957. See chapter 11.

[36] Schaar, *op. cit.*, p. 110.

[37] See Terrasse, *op. cit.*, pp. 243–4.

[38] *Ibid.*, p. 361.

CHAPTER TWO

[1] See J.L.Miège, *Le Maroc et l'Europe* (4 vols), Paris, 1962, esp. vol. 3, pp. 1–18.

[2] Clement H.Moore, 'The National Party: A Tentative Model', *Public Policy*, vol. 10, 1960, p. 265.

[3] This interpretation is developed by F.Weisgerber, *Au Seuil du Maroc Moderne*, Rabat, 1947, pp. 330–66. Cf. Justinard, *op. cit.*, pp. 111–24. See also Terrasse, *op. cit.*, p. 319, for the origins of this system under Moulay 'Abderrahman in 1854.

[4] A.De Laubadère, *Les Réformes des Pouvoirs Publics au Maroc*, Paris, 1949, p. 49; see also Jean Célérier, *Le Maroc*, Paris, 1953, p. 107.

[5] See Gen.A.Guillaume, *Les Berbères Marocains et la Pacification de l'Atlas Central (1912–1933)*, Paris, 1946, *passim*, and Capt.G.Spillmann, *Les Ait Atta du Sahara et la Pacification du Haut Dra*, IHEM, Rabat, 1936.

[6] Guillaume, *op. cit.*, p. 73.

[7] Figures from Vincent Monteil, *Maroc*, Paris, 1962, p. 154. The bulk of these losses consisted of Moroccan 'partisans', Algerian *spahis*, and Senegalese. The French supplied the officers and the Foreign Legion. Guillaume may have been

inflating these figures to prove the extent of France's sacrifices in Morocco and hence its obligation to hold fast to its hard-won possession. Many of the deaths probably resulted from disease and exposure rather than combat.

[8] See for instance Robert Rézette, *Les Partis Politiques Marocains*, Paris, 1955, pp. 60–1.

[9] Quoted by Pessah Shinar, 'Abd al-Qader and Abd al-Krim: Religious Influences on their Thought and Action', *Asian and African Studies*, vol. 1, 1965, p. 175; see also D.M.Hart, 'Clan, Lineage, Local Community, and the Feud in a Rifian Tribe', typed MS, April 1958, to be published.

[10] For the text of the Treaty of Fez, see H.J.Liebesney, *The Government of French North Africa*, Pennsylvania (U.P.), 1943, pp. 128–30.

[11] De Laubadère, *op. cit.*, pp. 23–4.

[12] *Ibid.*, pp. 12–13.

[13] See Albert Ayache, *Le Maroc: Bilan d'une Colonisation*, Paris, 1956, p. 83.

[14] Liebesney, *op. cit.*, pp. 28–35.

[15] De Laubadère, *op. cit.*, p. 25.

[16] *Ibid.*, p. 22.

[17] In the period 1912 to 1956 some 600 billion old francs in public funds were invested in Morocco. Monteil, *op. cit.*, p. 105.

[18] *Loc. cit.* More will be said of Yves Mas in reference to the press after 1956 (chapter 14). For a thorough presentation of French economic interests in Morocco see René Gallissot, *Le Patronat Européen au Maroc (1931–1942)*, Rabat, 1964, esp. pp. 41–54.

[19] Stéphane Bernard, *Le Conflit Franco-Marocain: 1943–1956* (3 vols), Brussels, 1963, vol. 3, pp. 43–5; also Ayache, *op. cit.*, pp. 92–3.

[20] De Laubadère, *op. cit.*, p. 59.

[21] For more information on regional and local administration, including the Berber dahir, see Bernard, *op. cit.*, vol. 3, pp. 47–56; C.-A.Julien, *L'Afrique du Nord en Marche*, Paris, 1952, p. 146; Liebesney, *op. cit.*, pp. 35–50; De Laubadère, *op. cit.*, pp. 51–61. French policy toward the Berber notability and the Berbers in general, educational policy in Berber areas, and the role of the *Collège* of Azrou will be examined in detail in chapter 5.

[22] Figures taken from F.Taillard, *Le Nationalisme Marocain*, Paris, 1947, pp. 81–4. More attention will be devoted to educational policy past and present in chapter 16.

[23] See Bernard, *op. cit.*, vol. 3, p. 88, and below, chapters 5 and 6.

[24] For more on the Council of Government see Bernard, *op. cit.*, vol. 3, pp. 31–5, and Rézette, *op. cit.*, pp. 44–55.

[25] De Laubadère, *op. cit.*, p. 15.

[26] This view is developed by M.M.Knight, *Morocco as a French Economic Venture*, New York, 1937; and Charles Stewart, *The Economy of Morocco: 1912–1962*, Harvard, 1964; Ayache, *op. cit., passim.*

[27] For a full treatment of the notion of nationalism being essentially a manifestation of the reaction of social elites to the problems of social and economic change, see M.Halpern, *The Politics of Social Change in the Middle East and North Africa*, Princeton, 1963, pp. 196–214.

[28] L.C.Brown, 'Islamic Reformism in North Africa', *The Journal of Modern African Studies*, vol. 2, no. 1, 1964, p. 55.

[29] Much of the information on the Salafists has been taken from the following sources: Jamil Abu Nasr, 'The Salafiyya Movement in Morocco: The Religious Bases of the Moroccan National Movement', *St. Antony's Papers*, no. 16 (Middle Eastern Affairs, no. 3), London, 1963, pp. 90–105; Allal al-Fassi, *The Independence Movements in North Africa*, Washington D.C., 1954, pp. 11–15 and *Hadith*

al-Maghrib fil Mashriq, Cairo, 1956, pp. 3–29; Marston Speight, 'Islamic Reform in Morocco', *The Muslim World*, vol. 53, no. 1, January 1963, pp. 41–9.

[30] Jacques Berque, *Le Maghreb entre deux Guerres*, Paris, 1962, p. 74; see also R.Le Tourneau, 'North Africa: Rigorism and Bewilderment', in G.Von Grunebaum (ed.), *Unity and Variety in Muslim Civilization*, Chicago, 1955, p. 243. One moment of crisis between the residency and the palace came in 1946 when Muhammed v forbade the founding of any zawiyas without his permission. See Al-Fassi, *Hadith* . . ., p. 21.

[31] For a biography see 'Abd al-Qader Sahrawi, *Shaykh al-Islam, Muhammed Bin al-'Arabi al-'Alawi* (in Arabic), Casablanca, 1965.

[32] See J.Berque, 'Ca et là dans les débuts du réformisme réligieux au Maghreb', *Etudes d'Orientalisme dédiées à la Mémoire de Lévi-Provençal*, Paris, vol. 2, pp. 483–86.

[33] Berque, *Le Maghreb* . . ., p. 397.

[34] Montagne, *op. cit.*, p. 419. See also Jean and Simone Lacouture, *Le Maroc à l'Epreuve*, Paris, 1957, pp. 83–7.

[35] See J.P.Halstead, 'The Origins of Moroccan Nationalism: 1919–1934', Ph.D. thesis, Department of History, Harvard Univ., April 1960, pp. 204–5. This thesis has subsequently been published in expanded form: *Rebirth of a Nation: the Origins and Rise of Moroccan Nationalism, 1912–1944*, Harvard, 1967. All citations are from the original thesis.

[36] De Laubadère, *op. cit.*, p. 89.

[37] See M.E.Girardière, 'L'Ecole coranique et la politique nationaliste au Maroc', *La France Méditerranéenne et Africaine*, fasc. 1, 1938, pp. 99–109; also Halstead, *op. cit.*, pp. 179–81, and his article, 'The Changing Character of Moroccan Reformism 1921–1934', *Journal of African History*, vol. 3, 1964, pp. 439–40.

[38] Dr Weisberger claims that at the time of the signing of the Treaty of Fez, all Fassis, from the 'ulema to the simple grocers, were disgusted by the 'sell-out' of the imam who had come to power five years earlier as the sultan of *jihad*. p. 272. *op. cit.*,

[39] See R.Montagne, *Révolution au Maroc*, Paris, 1953, p. 178. Steeg was advised by Urbain Blanc and Michaux-Bellaire. Ben Ghabrit and Moqri, both wazirs, as well as Muhammed Ben Yussuf's tutor, Mammeri, all concurred in the choice. See J.Lacouture, *Cinq Hommes et la France*, Paris, 1961, p. 183.

[40] See Halstead, *op. cit.*, pp. 212–9; and 'Allal al-Fassi, *'Aqida wa Jihad* (Faith and Striving) (in Arabic), Rabat, 1960, pp. 9–10, where he gives the names of the members of the first zawiat.

[41] Girardière, *op. cit.*, p. 103; see also Ashford, *Political Change* . . ., p. 44; Rézette, *op. cit.*, pp. 282–3.

[42] *Istiqlal Party Documents 1944–1946*, Paris, Sept. 1946, pp. 2–3. J. S. Lacouture, *op. cit.*, p. 134, give a different interpretation of the text of the declaration, stating that it was the work of the younger members of the party. I cannot conclusively refute this contention, but it is clear that Lacouture is wrong in stating that the text called for constitutional monarchy. See also Al-Fassi, *Hadith* . . ., pp. 100–1.

Many of my observations concerning palace-nationalist relations between 1930 and 1944 have been taken from interviews with some of the founders of the Istiqlal.

[43] *Loc. cit.*

[44] See Taillard, *op. cit.*, p. 127, and Rom Landau, *Mohammed V, King of Morocco*, Rabat, 1957, p. 45.

[45] R. Le Tourneau, *Evolution Politique de l'Afrique du Nord Musulmane*, Paris 1962, pp. 219-21.

[46] For an account of this session of the Council of Government and related speeches by those present, see Marcel Rouffie, *Le Protectorat, a-t-il fait faillite?*, Casablanca, 1951, pp. 50-3. Of the seventy-five members of the council only ten were elected, and it was precisely this group that left the session with the addition of 'Abbès Kebbaj of Agadir.

[47] Quoted in J.Lacouture, *Cinq hommes . . .*, p. 211.

[48] See Walter B.Cline, 'Nationalism in Morocco', *M.E.J.*, Jan. 1947, p. 23, and J. & S. Lacouture, *Le Maroc à l'Epreuve*, p. 134.

[49] For more information on this crucial aspect of Moroccan urban development, see R.Montagne (ed.), *Naissance du Prolétariat Marocain*, Paris, 1950; André Adam, 'Le *bidonville* de Ben M'sik à Casablanca', *Annales de l'Institut d'Etudes Orientales*, vol. 8, 1949-50, pp. 61-198, and chapter 9.

[50] For a brief presentation of the reform see Republic of France, French Embassy, Press Service, *The Reforms of September 1953 in Morocco*, New York, Oct. 1953.

[51] See Montagne, *Révolution au Maroc*, p. 221, and Bernard, *op. cit.*, vol. 1, pp. 148-215.

[52] See *ibid.*, p. 232, where this view is developed further. For a fuller treatment of the obscure period after 1952 see Ashford, *op. cit.*, pp. 75-92; Bernard, *op. cit.*, vol. 3, pp. 259-301; I.Lepp, *Midi Sonne au Maroc*, Paris, 1954; and Muhammad al-Khattabi, *Al-Maghreb fi Tariq al-Istiqlal* (Morocco on the Path to Independence), Casablanca, 1955.

[53] For all the resolutions and two differing interpretations, see Al-Fassi, *Hadith . . .*, pp. 107-8, and Rézette, *op. cit.*, pp. 190-3. The PDI was founded in 1946 by Bel Hassan Wazzani. The two Spanish zone parties were the National Reform (*Islah*) Party of 'Abd al-Khaliq Torres and the Moroccan Unity (Ittihad) Party of Mekki an-Naciri.

[54] See Al-Khattabi, *op. cit.*, pp. 36-43.

[55] The other members of the Committee were Muhammed Douiri, Mas'ud Chiguer, Muhammed Boucetta, 'Abdulkrim Ghallab; see Ashford, *op. cit.*, pp. 76-8; and J. & S. Lacouture, *Le Maroc . . .*, p. 137.

[56] For details on the urban terrorist groups see Bernard, *op. cit.*, vol. 3, pp. 259-75.

[57] Much of my information on the Liberation Army has been taken from *ibid.*, vol. 1, pp. 376-82 and vol. 3, pp. 287-97; and from interviews with 'Abdallatif Benjelloun and 'Abdulkrim al-Khatib. See also chapter 9.

[58] See Al-Khattabi, *op. cit.*, pp. 151-2.

[59] For the king's speech see Republic of France, French Embassy, Press Service, *Documentary Background on Recent Political Events in Morocco*, New York, Jan. 1956.

CHAPTER THREE

[1] Jacques Berque, *Structures Sociales du Haut-Atlas*, Paris, 1955, p. 449.

[2] E.E.Evans-Pritchard, *The Nuer*, Oxford, 1940, and *The Sanusi of Cyranaica*, Oxford, 1949.

[3] Evans-Pritchard, *The Nuer*, p. 150. See also Evans-Pritchard, *The Sanusi . . .*, p. 59, and Paul Bohanon, *Social Anthropology*, London, 1963, pp. 137-40.

[4] R.F.Murphy and L.Kasdan, 'The Structure of Parallel Cousin Marriage', *American Anthropologist*, vol. 61, Feb. 1959, p. 17.

[5] M.D.Sahlins, 'The Segmentary Lineage: An Organization of Predatory

Expansion', in Ronald Cohen and John Middleton (eds), *Comparative Political Systems*, New York, 1967, pp. 89–119.

[6] See D.M.Hart, 'Segmentary Systems and the Role of "Five Fifths" in Tribal Morocco', *Revue de l'Occident Musulman et de la Méditerranée*, vol. no. 3, 1967, pp. 65–95; W.H.Lewis, 'Feuding and Social Change in Morocco', *The Journal of Conflict Resolution*, vol. 5, no. 1, 1961, pp. 43–54; Jeanne Favret, 'Relations de Dépendance et Manipulation de la Violence en Kabylie', unpublished manuscript, presented at Colloque de Groupe de Recherches en Anthropologie et Sociologie Politique, Paris, 30 March, 1968.

[7] See Murphy and Kasdan, *op. cit., passim*; and Fredrik Barth, 'Segmentary Opposition and the Theory of Games: A Study of Pathan Organization', *Journal of the Royal Anthropological Institute*, vol. 89, 1959, pp. 5–21.

[8] Lewis Coser, *The Functions of Social Conflict*, New York, 1964, pp. 50–5.

[9] Barth, *op. cit., passim*, suggests that the Pathans have devised an alliance system of political factions grouping opposed agnates that handles specifically objective conflict.

[10] See Sahlins, *op. cit.*, p. 93. Sahlins sets forth the economic rationale of the segmentary system, but insists, I believe erroneously, on the tendency of such systems to direct conflict and hostility outwards.

[11] David Hart has worked out the possibilities of conflicting alliances among the Aith Waryaghar. See his 'Emilio Blanco Izaga and the Berbers of the Central Rif', *Tamuda*, vol. 6, no. 2, 1958, pp. 203–7. Cf. Barth, *op. cit., passim*.

[12] Cited by Coser, *op. cit.*, p. 77. For Coser's general discussion of conflict situations, see pp. 76–80. See also Max Gluckman, *Custom and Conflict in Africa*, Oxford, 1959, p. 2.

[13] Barth, *op. cit.*, in a fascinating application of games theory to Pathan coalitions, presents a convincing explanation of this tendency towards rough parity of power.

[14] That such behavioral norms in segmentary systems have wide applicability is clear from R.A.Levine's analysis of the Gusii of Kenya. 'Socialization, Social Structure, and Intersocietal Images', in Hebert Kelman (ed.), *International Behavior: A Social-Psychological Analysis*, New York, 1965, pp. 43–69. See also Murphy and Kasdan, *op. cit.*, p. 20.

[15] Again this principle has wide applicability. See R.F.Murphy, 'Intergroup Hostility and Social Cohesion', *American Anthropologist*, vol. 59, no. 6, 1957, p. 1018, on the Mundurucu of Brazil; and Coser, *op. cit.*, p. 107.

[16] See R.Patai, *Golden River to Golden Road: Society, Culture and Change in the Middle East*, Pennsylvania, 1962, pp. 177–250.

[17] See Montagne *Les Berbères et le Makhzen*, pp. 201–5.

[18] See Sahlins, *op. cit.*, p. 90, and David Easton, 'Political Anthropology', in B.J.Siegal (ed.), *Biennal Review of Anthropology 1959*, Stanford, 1959, pp. 210–62.

[19] M.G.Smith, 'Segmentary Lineage Systems', *The Journal of the Royal Anthropological Institute*, vol. 86, part II, 1956, p. 48.

[20] *Ibid.*, p. 50.

[21] *Loc. cit.*; cf. Aidan Southall, 'A Critique of the Typology of States and Political Systems', in *Political Systems and the Distribution of Power*, A.S.A. Monographs 2, London (Tavistock Pub.), New York (Praeger), 1965, pp. 127–9.

[22] For an example from the Fulani see Smith, *op. cit.*, pp. 63 and 75.

[23] See R.W.Nicholas, 'Factions: A Comparative Analysis', in *Political Systems and the Distribution of Power*, p. 28; cf. R.W.Nicholas, 'Segmentary Factional Political Systems', in M.J.Swartz *et al.* (eds), *Political Anthropology*, Chicago, 1966, p. 53.

NOTES PAGES 68–84

²⁴ Eric Wolf has analyzed the conversion of the lineages of Quraish into commercial clientele groups. See his 'The Social Organization of Mecca and the Origins of Islam', *Southwestern Journal of Anthropology*, vol. 7, 1951, pp. 329–56
²⁵ See Patai, *op. cit.*
²⁶ See Nicholas, 'Segmentary Factional Political Systems', p. 55, and Geertz 'The Integrative Revolution', *passim.*
²⁷ See Ernest Gellner, 'Patterns of Rural Rebellion in Morocco: Tribes as Minorities', *European Journal of Sociology*, vol. 3, no. 2, 1962, pp. 297–311; and Jeanne Favret, 'Le traditionalisme par excès de modernité', *European Journal of Sociology*, vol. 8, no. 1, 1967, pp. 71–93.
²⁸ See Berque, *Structures sociales . . ., op. cit.*, p. 298; and on the anti-Arab siba of the Middle Atlas, see Terrasse, *Histoire du Maroc . . ., op. cit.*, p. 310.
²⁹ See Le Tourneau, *Fès avant le Protectorat*, Casablanca 1949.
³⁰ P.Bourdieu, *Sociologie d'Algérie*, Paris, 1958, p. 55.
³¹ For some examples see Patai, *op. cit.*, p. 244.
³² Le Tourneau, *L'Afrique du Nord Musulmane . . .*, p. 196.
³³ From an interview with 'Abdulhadi Tazi (Mukha').
³⁴ See Arnaud, *op. cit.*, pp. 136–52. For comments on similar phenomena in sub-Saharan Africa, see P.C.Lloyd, 'The Political Structure of African Kingdoms: an Exploratory Model', in *Political Systems and the Distribution of Power*, p. 93; on Mecca at the time of the prophet, Wolf, *op. cit.*, p. 336. I shall give more attention to clientele groupings in chapter 4.
³⁵ Paul Pascon suggests that the head of the patriarchal family must devote a considerable amount of time to consolidating his position *within* the family. See his 'La main d'oeuvre et l'emploi dans le secteur traditionnel', *B.E.S.M.*, nos. 101–2, 1966, p. 134.
³⁶ I owe much of my interpretation of defensive alliances and bet-hedging to Larry Rosen, who has provided me with some insights garnered in the course of his research in Sefrou. The Moroccan metaphor may be the expression 'sensing a change in the wind', an image used repeatedly by Hadj Salim al-'Abdi in his interviews with Arnaud, *op. cit.*
³⁷ Bourdieu, *op. cit.*, p. 86.
³⁸ For some examples see Berque, *Structures sociales . . .*, p. 436.
³⁹ David Hart notes that in the Rif financial debt (*amarwas*) is like a spider web, everyone owing to everyone else. It may even be that the liquid cash earned by Rifi workers in Europe and Morocco is partially devoted to maintaining debt relations (private communication, 5 Nov. 1966). See also, E.R.Leach, *Social and Economic Organization of the Rowanduz Kurds*, Monographs in Social Anthropology, London, 1939, pp. 42–3.
⁴⁰ See Coser, *op. cit.*, pp. 76–80.
⁴¹ For comments on variations in pluralism, see Pierre Van Den Berghe, 'Pluralisme social et culturel', *Cahiers Internationaux de Sociologie*, vol. XLIII, 1967, pp. 67–78, esp. pp. 70–4.

CHAPTER FOUR

¹ Driss Chraibi, *Le Passé Simple*, Paris, 1954, p. 243.
² Raymond Aron, 'Catégories dirigeantes ou classe dirigeante?', *R.F.S.P.*, vol. 15, no. 1, Feb. 1965, p. 17; cf. T.B.Bottomore, *Elites and Society*, London, 1964, p. 14.
³ F.W.Frey, *The Turkish Political Elite*, M.I.T., 1965, p. 16, uses formal positions of power to set the contours of the Turkish elite.
⁴ For an excellent analysis of the Moroccan elite, with which the author is in

334

basic agreement, see Octave Marais, 'La classe dirigeante au Maroc', *R.F.S.P.*, vol. 14, no. 4, Aug. 1964, pp. 709-37.

[5] Ayache, *op. cit.*, p. 320, gives a figure of twenty thousand for total enrolment in the *écoles-libres* in 1954. The great bulk of these were primary school students.

[6] Marais, *op. cit.*, p. 718.

[7] See Verba, *op. cit.*, pp. 544–6.

[8] See Arnold Hottinger, 'Zu 'ama' and Parties in the Lebanese Crisis of 1958', *M.E.J.* (Spring 1961), pp. 127–40.

[9] See Ernest Gellner, 'Political and Religious Organization of the Berbers of the Central High Atlas' mimeo. (Aug. 1964), 10 pp.

[10] Mehdi Ben Barka, *Problèmes d'édification du Maroc et du Maghreb: Quatre entretiens avec el-Mehdi Ben Barka* (with Raymond Jean), Paris, 1959, p. 32.

[11] See Berque, *Structures sociales . . ., op. cit.*, p. 432.

[12] Cited by Edward Westermarck, *Wit and Wisdom in Morocco: A Study in Native Proverbs*, London, 1930, p. 176.

CHAPTER FIVE

[1] From R. Le Tourneau, *La vie quotidienne à Fès en 1900*, Paris, 1965, p. 32.

[2] The city-dwellers' fear of the tribes is summed up in Dr Linarès' term 'amazigophobia': i.e. hatred of Berbers who, in the Middle Atlas, refer to themselves as *amazigh* (pl. *imazighan*): freemen. See le Tourneau, *La vie quotidienne . . .*, p. 39. Among the cities themselves there were important differences in attributed characteristics, local solidarity, and, to a lesser degree, political style: thus Rabat, Salé, Tetouan, Meknes, and Marrakesh.

[3] In this subcategory are to be found the al-Fassis, Bensoudas, and Boutalebs. Thus the grandfather of 'Allal al-Fassi (himself a graduate of the Qarawiyin and an 'alim) was an *imam* at the imperial mosque of Fez and his father was a member of the Council of 'Ulema. On all these categories see le Tourneau, *Fès avant . . .*, pp. 482–91.

[4] At Tangier the Ben Daoud, at Marrakesh the Knichash, and at Meknes the Ben Ya'ish are three examples of such families. See Aubin, *op. cit.*, pp. 214–38, and for genealogical information on makhzan and local notables, see Marthe and Edmond Gouvion, *Kitab Aâyane al-Maghrib 'l-Akça*, Paris, 1939, *passim*. I am indebted to Yahya Ben Sliman who shared with me many of his own highly instructive views on makhzan families.

[5] See Mission Scientifique du Maroc, 'Ouezzan', *op. cit.*, and Edward Westermarck, *Ritual and Belief in Morocco* (2 vols), London, 1926, vol. 1, pp. 35–261.

[6] See le Tourneau, *Fès avant . . .*, pp. 257 and 488–9.

[7] For more details see, Idriss al-Kittani, 'The Traditional Moroccan Family; its Formation, Customs, Traditions, and Social Structure' (in Arabic), *Cahiers de Sociologie*, no. 1, Sept.–Oct. 1965, p. 30.

[8] See G.Pallez, 'Les marchands Fassis', *B.E.S.M.*, nos. 49 and 51, 1951, no. 51, p. 57.

[9] See Ch. René-Leclerc, 'Le commerce et l'industrie à Fès', *Renseignements Coloniaux*, no. 7, July 1905, p. 219.

[10] Pallez, *op. cit.* (no. 49), p. 194. For the principal families engaged in cloth trade with England and their agents in Manchester, see Leclerc, *op. cit.*, p. 231.

[11] *Ibid.*, p. 252.

[12] Chraibi, *op. cit.*, p. 253. This novel is an important source on the political and economic behavior and attitudes of the Fassi bourgeoisie, the relation between father and son of two generations in conflict, and the uses of power of a Moroccan patriarch.

[13] These names have been taken from the biographic data presented by Halstead, *The Origins of Moroccan Nationalism* . . ., appendix I. We may add to this list, for indicative purposes, other names of important graduates taken at random: Moulay Ahmad 'Alawi, the Bahnini brothers, Ahmad Hamiani, Muhammed Lahbabi, Muhammed Tahiri, Muhammed Zeghari, Driss Slaoui, Majid Benjelloun, Muhammed Douiri, Col. Ahmad Dlimi, Ahmad Reda Guedira, and Mehdi Ben Barka.

[14] For an interesting discussion of the role of French in North Africa in general, see C.F.Gallagher, 'Language and Identity in North Africa', in L.C.Brown (ed.), *State and Society in Independent North Africa*, M.E.I., Washington, D.C., 1966, pp. 73–96.

[15] For the proverb and the purposes of endogamy in Fez, see al-Kittani, *op. cit.*, p. 22.

[16] Le Tourneau, *Fès avant* . . ., p. 504.

[17] Kittani, *op. cit.*, p. 30.

[18] See Berque, *Le maghreb entre deux guerres*, p. 185.

[19] 'Allal al-Fassi, *'Aqida wa Jihad* (Faith and Striving) (in Arabic), Rabat, 1960, pp. 11–12.

[20] For more information on the UMCIA see Ashford, *Political Change* . . ., pp. 376–81.

[21] Le Tourneau, *Fès avant* . . ., p. 447.

[22] Berque, *Le maghreb entre deux guerres*, p. 229.

[23] For an interesting discussion of the 'marginality' of Moroccan tribes, see Gellner, 'Tribalism and Social Change in North Africa', pp. 5–6.

[24] See Guillaume, *op. cit.*, p. 98.

[25] See Ayache, *op. cit.*, pp. 305–6; a few of the 'feudalists' Ayache may have had in mind are Moha ou Hammou, his son Amharoq, Muhammed Cherradi, of Oulad Bhar, the qaid Ayyachi of the Ait Ayyachi, Ghali al-Mernissi, Nejjai of the Gharb, etc. See M. & E. Gouvion, *op. cit., passim.*

[26] See Bernard, *op. cit.*, vol. 3, pp. 51–2. He remarks (p. 82) that almost all the 3,500 pashas, qaids, and shaykhs after 1912 came from the medium landowning class.

[27] See André Ammoun, 'les F.A.R. et le trône chérifien', *Etudes Méditer-ranéennes*, Nov. 1960, p. 59.

[28] J. & S. Lacouture, *Le Maroc à l'épreuve*, p. 85.

[29] For a list of the 118 amnestied in 1963, see *B.O.*, no. 2664, 8 Nov. 1963, Dahir no. 1-63-279, p. 1762.

[30] Aubin, *op. cit.*, p. 148.

[31] The gift took place on the king's trip to the Middle Atlas. He stopped at the Tizi n Tretten to receive the allegiance of the tribes in the same spot where five years before Maréchal Juin (at that time no longer resident-general), had come to give a fillip to the movement against Muhammed v. See Lacouture, *Cinq hommes* . . ., p. 221. Sultan Moulay Hafidh himself had married Amharoq's sister as well as a daughter of Madani al-Glaoui. See Arnaud, *op. cit.*, p. 245.

[32] For an interesting discussion of this, see Jean Ougrour, 'Le fait berbère', *Confluent*, Sept.–Oct. 1962, pp. 617–34.

[33] As told to Dr Arnaud, *op. cit.*, p. 173. These remarks, which are vague and impressionistic, will take on some clarity in chapter 11, where the MP is examined more closely.

[34] Ayache, *op. cit.*, p. 321, gives a figure of 121 Muslim girls enrolled in secondary school in 1952 and two girls at the university level.

[35] Consult on these communities, Willner and Kohls, 'Jews in the High Atlas

Mountains of Morocco: a Partial Reconstruction', *The Jewish Journal of Sociology*, vol. 4, no. 2, Dec. 1962, pp. 207–41; H.Z. (J.W.) Hirschberg, 'The Problem of the Judaized Berbers', *Journal of African History*, vol. 4, no. 3, 1963, pp. 313–39; Pierre Flamand, *Les Communautés Israélités du Sud-Marocain*, Impriméries Réunies, Casablanca, N.D. (1950?).

[36] For the commercial position of the Moroccan Jews in the nineteenth century and their contact with the makhzan, see Miège, vol. 2, pp. 86–98, and vol. 3, pp. 24–30.

[37] See le Tourneau, *Fès avant* ..., p. 451.

[38] Miège, *op. cit.*, vol. 2, pp. 90–3. Two well-known teams of the era were BenChimon-Ghassal in Tangier and Bendahan-Britel in Rabat.

[39] Ayache, *op. cit.*, p. 313.

[40] For a general treatment of North African Jews, see André Chouraqui, *Les Juifs d'Afrique du Nord*, Paris, 1957.

[41] See *Le Monde*, 18 Jan. 1961, p. 4.

[42] David Amar, through his journal *La Voix des Communautés*, in 1963, did little to give the impression that Jews were at all interested in political integration.

CHAPTER SIX

[1] Westermarck, *Wit and Wisdom* ..., p. 350.

[2] From 'Back-ground d'une situation impossible', *L'Avant-Garde* (UMT), 25 June 1966.

[3] For an excellent study of the growth of nineteenth century Casablanca, see J.-L.Miège, 'Origines du développement de Casablanca au XIXe siècle', *Hésperis* (1st and 2nd Trimestre, 1953), pp. 199–226.

[4] This tariff was enacted on all imported goods varying upwards from 20 per cent of the value of the goods. See J.P.Meynaud, 'L'Expérience économique marocaine', *Economie et Politique*, Feb. 1962, p. 66.

[5] For a Marxist interpretation of the Moroccan situation see Hadi Messouak, 'Structures de classe et tâches de la révolution marocaine', *Confluent*, Sept.–Oct. 1962, pp. 576–91. A balanced critique of 'liberalism' as the guiding principle of Moroccan economic development is to be found in 'Chronique économique', *Maghreb-Informations*, 8–9 Jan. 1967, pp. 1 and 4.

[6] See F.W.Riggs, *Administration in Developing Countries: the Theory of Prismatic Society*, Boston, 1964, pp. 141–2, 212–6.

[7] Abbès Lahlou, 'La bourgeoisie, symbole et reflet direct de l'occidentalisation de la société marocaine', *Civilisations*, vol. 14, nos 1–2, 1964, p. 73.

[8] Marais, *op. cit.*, p. 734.

[9] Again, the characteristics of elite enterprises and governmental protection seem to correspond closely to F.W.Rigg's 'canteen model', *op. cit.*, pp. 106–9.

[10] I hope to publish a study of the politics of trade in Casablanca in which I will set forth in detail the evolution of the Sussi petty tradesmen. A useful article on the ideal Sussi type is that of E.A.Alport, 'The Ammeln', *Journal of the Royal Anthropological Institute*, vol. 94, part II, pp. 160–71.

[11] See André Adam, 'La population marocaine dans l'ancienne médina de Casablanca', *B.E.S.M.*, no. 48, 1950, p. 22.

[12] *Loc. cit.* Also Montagne *Naissance du prolétariat*, p. 108.

[13] Adam, 'ancienne médina', p. 17. The exogamous marriage of a Sussi with a Fassiya may often be complemented by an endogamous wife back in the Suss.

[14] Figures cited in Kingdom of Morocco, Haut Commissariat à la Jeunesse et aux Sports, *Regards sur l'Emploi et le Chômage au Maroc*, Cahier d'Education Populaire, no. 2, March 1962, Rabat, p. 28. In 1960, in retail trade in food,

drinks, and tobacco, there were 95,075 Moroccans. See Kingdom of Morocco, Délégation Générale à la Promotion Nationale et au Plan, Service Central des Statistiques, *Résultats du Recensement de 1960*, vol. II (Population Active), Rabat, 1965, p. 326.

[15] *Loc. cit.* Figure may be too low as a result of the non-declaration of profits.

[16] For more details see Grigori Lazarev, 'Le salariat agricole des fermes de colonisation', *B.E.S.M.*, nos. 101–2, April–Sept. 1966, pp. 51–2.

[17] For the Istiqlal's candidates and the party's position, see *Al'Alam*, 17 Aug. 1966.

[18] See *Le Petit Marocain*, 25 Aug. 1966, p. 3.

[19] Miège, *Le Maroc et l'Europe*, vol. 3, pp. 1–36.

[20] For the king's lengthy speech, see *Al-Anba*, 11 Oct. 1966. The king noted that this speculation affected the poor more than the rich. In some of the poorer sections of Casablanca land sells for *c.* $32·00 per square meter while in the heart of town it sells for $12·00 per square meter. This attests to the fact that with the slowdown in industrial and commercial activity since 1956, resulting from the steady exodus of European concerns, office and business space 'downtown' can no longer fetch high prices. On the other hand the population of the city has continued to grow, and the state has encouraged slum clearance and building projects. Speculators realize that most housing projects will have to be built on the outskirts of the city, and real estate values there have correspondingly sky-rocketed.

[21] Pallez, *op. cit.*, no. 49, p. 195.

[22] See G. Lazarev, 'Structures agraires et grandes propriétés en pays Hayaina (pré-Rif)', *Revue de Géographie du Maroc*, no. 9, 1966, esp. pp. 41–52.

[23] Figures cited by Monteil, *op. cit.*, p. 142.

[24] See Nor el-Ghorfi, *Contribution à l'Edification d'une Politique Agricole*, INRA, Rabat, 1964, p. 23. On page 10 Ghorfi gives a figure of 4,742,499 hectares as being under cultivation in Morocco.

[25] See Kingdom of Morocco, Ministry of National Economy, *Tableaux Economiques*, Service Centrale des Statistiques, Rabat 1960?, p. 47; also Ayache, *op. cit.*, p. 154.

[26] Samir Amin gives a figure of 500,000 hectares in *L'Economie du Maghreb* (2 vols.), Paris, 1966, vol. 1, p. 338. A Moroccan review claims that figures supplied by Conservation Foncière (the land deeds office) reveal that 300,000 hectares were bought in this manner in the period 1956–9 alone. See 'Les lots de colonisation', *Lamalif*, no. 6, Oct. 1966, p. 13.

[27] I have seen no precise figures on the acreage owned by these companies, but some of the major interests involved were: Compagnie Marocaine, Domaine de Béni 'Ammar, Société Marocaine de Culture et d'Entreprises, Grands Domaines de Meknès, Société Agricole des Oulad Daho. See Ayache, *op. cit.*, p. 160.

[28] For instance, Lazarev, 'Structures agraires . . .', p. 53, mentions that the city bourgeoisie have lost interest in the Haya'ina region, productively poor, and are selling their property there to cover purchases of *colon* land in the rich Sais plain.

CHAPTER SEVEN

[1] J. & J. Aubin, 'Le Maroc en Suspens', *Annuaire de l'Afrique du Nord*, vol. 3 (1964), p. 85.

[2] Dankwart Rustow has claimed that throughout the Middle East 'oriental despotism' was more a frame of mind of the rulers than an actual political fact.

The despots were always hedged in on all sides by rivals, 'ulema, guilds, janissaries, tribes and distant governors. The same general observation seems applicable to Morocco. See his 'Politics and Westernization in the Near East', in Richard Nolte (ed.), *The Modern Middle East*, New York, 1963, p. 73.

³ Kingdom of Morocco, Embassy of Morocco, *The Constitution of the Kingdom of Morocco*, Washington, D.C., 12 Dec. 1962, p. 9.

⁴ Ahmad Reda Guedira, *interview*, Rabat, 28 Feb. 1966.

⁵ For the text, see Kingdom of Morocco, Ministry of Information, *Le Maroc en Marche: Discours de Sa Majesté le Roi Hassan II depuis Son Intronisation*, Rabat, 1965, p. 206.

⁶ J. & J. Aubin, *op. cit.*, p. 75.

⁷ I.W.Zartman, *Destiny of a Dynasty*, Carolina (U.P.), 1964, p. 41; see also his *Morocco: Problems of New Power*, New York, 1964, pp. 149, 240.

⁸ See *Maghreb Digest*, May 1965, p. 24.

⁹ The very ambiguous remarks of the king have inevitably been subject to great controversy in view of Ben Barka's disappearance, and judging from the official text there is room for several possible interpretations of what he actually meant: 'I have pardoned those who plotted against the Throne of this country and who have been deprived of their civil and political rights.

'I have likewise pardoned those who committed the crime of jeopardizing the internal security of the state in regard to whom sanctions have been pronounced and who have been interned by the Justice.

'I *would have wished* [author's italics] that my pardon encompass all those against whom judgments have been pronounced for jeopardizing the external security of the state [i.e. Ben Barka, Berrada, etc.] that they committed, had they not fled the justice of their country and sought refuge abroad and continued in the path of error. All those whom my pardon and clemency have touched have committed grave and odious crimes; those who have sought refuge abroad in order to avoid confronting the justice of their country have also committed crimes that are no less ignoble.'

On the strength or weakness of this statement Ben Barka decided it was wiser to continue his exile abroad. Text of Hassan's speech in *Le Maroc en Marche*, pp. 496–8.

¹⁰ *Ibid.*, pp. 497–8.

¹¹ See Miège, *Le Maroc et L'Europe*, vol. 2, p. 237 and vol. 3, pp. 18–19.

¹² Zartman, *Destiny of a Dynasty*, p. 28 (note).

¹³ See *Le Petit Marocain*, 27 Dec. 1966, p. 3.

¹⁴ See *Le Maroc en marche*, pp. 358, 517–8.

¹⁵ See *Le Petit Marocain*, 13 March 1968, p. 3. The body is called the Conseil Supérieur de la Promotion Nationale et du Plan and was provided for in the 1962 constitution.

¹⁶ From Kingdom of Morocco, Royal Cabinet, *Tawjihat* (Orientations) (in Arabic), April 1965, p. 40.

CHAPTER EIGHT

¹ Quoted from the Quran by 'Allal al-Fassi, *AL-Naqd adh-Dhati* (Auto-Critique), Tétouan (n.d.), p. 89.

² Cf. Barrington Moore's study of Mogul India in his *Social Origins of Dictatorship and Democracy*, London 1967, esp. 322–8. See also Schaar, *op. cit.*, pp. 93–5.

³ *Ibid.*, pp. 160–1.

⁴ Berque, *Structures sociales . . .*, p. 441.

CHAPTER NINE

[1] The split has already been ably treated by Ashford, *Political Change . . .*, esp. pp. 219–69. However, Ashford's research does not go beyond summer 1959, and his approach is considerably different from that of the present writer. The author also believes that information gathered through extensive interviews with many of the major participants warrants a second look at this event. Those interviewed one or more times in relation to the split are: 'Abdarrahim Bou'abid, 'Allal al-Fassi, 'Abdullah Ibrahim, 'Omar 'Abdjellil, Muhammed Boucetta, Muhammed Douiri, Muhammed Tahiri, Boubker Qadiri, 'Abdulhafidh Qadiri, 'Abdulkrim Benjelloun, Muhammed 'Abderrazak, Hassan Zemmouri, Muhammed Lahbabi, and 'Abdarrahman Yussufi.

[2] See the brilliant reappraisal of Al-Fassi in Abdullah Laroui, *L'Idéologie arabe contemporaine*, Paris, 1967, pp. 44–7.

[3] For more details on these meetings in Madrid, see al-Fassi, *'Aqida wa Jihad*, pp. 25–9; and on the two party congresses, C.F.Gallagher, 'Morocco's Crisis comes to a Head', *AUFS Report*, 30 Aug. 1956; and Benjamin Rivlin, 'Towards Political Maturity in Morocco', *Current History*, July 1959, p. 27.

[4] See Rézette, *op. cit.*, p. 221, for excerpts from the first appeal in October 1953.

[5] Quoted in *Le Petit Marocain*, 17 June 1956, p. 4.

[6] Ben Barka's links to the resistance were even more tenuous than those of al-Fassi. See his brother's remarks in Abdelkader Ben Barka, *El Mehdi Ben Barka Mon Frère*, Paris, 1966, pp. 92–3.

[7] See Ashford, *Political Change . . .*, pp. 224–6.

[8] *Ibid.*, p. 196.

[9] Taking into consideration their education, lingual abilities, and social background, the inspectors were pronouncedly more oriented toward al-Fassi than Ben Barka; *ibid.*, p. 234.

[10] See *Le Petit Marocain*, 20 April 1958, p. 3.

[11] *Le Petit Marocain*, 23 April 1958. The same day Muhammed v consulted with Fqih Basri, Bouch'aib Doukkali, and Hassan as-Safi of the resistance, and Ben Seddiq, Bou'azza, and 'Abderrazak of the UMT.

[12] When in fact M'Hammedi was replaced at Interior by Chiguer, he joined vigorously in the attacks against the old guard launched by Ibrahim. J.Lacouture marvels at this new-found radicalism of M'Hammedi. See *Le Monde*, 2 July 1958, p. 4.

[13] See Ashford, *op. cit.*, p. 227.

[14] J.Lacouture, *Le Monde*, 2 July 1958, p. 4.

[15] See Ashford, *op. cit.*, p. 228.

[16] *Loc. cit.*

[17] Bou'abid had actually resigned on 10 November, but this was kept secret for two weeks. On the second governmental crisis of 1958, see *ibid.*, pp. 105–11.

[18] See Bou'abid's letter of resignation, finally published in *La Vigie*, 23 Nov. 1958; cited in *ibid.*, p. 107 (note). Balafrej had made one abortive effort to stand up to the king. He approved a party motion to veto the appointment of King Muhammed's brother-in-law, Prince Moulay Hassan al-'Alawi, the former pasha of Meknes, as governor of Meknes Province. But the king convinced Balafrej to withdraw the party veto, saying that he had to reward the prince for services rendered. In Morocco there is no answer to such an argument.

[19] *Ibid.*, p. 108, and al-Fassi, *'Aqida wa Jihad*, p. 57.

[20] See *Le Petit Marocain*, 11, 14 and 15 Jan. 1959.

[21] From Ben Barka, *op. cit.*, pp. 26–7. See also J.Lacouture, 'Tension politique

à Rabat', *Le Monde*, 27 Jan. 1959), p. 7, and 'Mehdi Ben Barka; le rebelle', *Le Monde*, 30 Jan. 1959, p. 6.

[22] For instance there was bloodshed at Bou'Arfa (a scene of party fighting in September 1958) in early April 1959. The insurgent Istiqlalis attempted to open headquarters, the stalwarts protested and were arrested by the local qaid, a melée ensued in which two people were killed. Boucetta went to the scene of the incident and accused the Ministry of Interior (under M'hammedi) of favoring the scissionists. See *Al-Istiqlal*, 11 April 1959, p. 4.

[23] For instance Tahiri, Qadiri, Boucetta, Douiri, and Zhiri were the stars of an important meeting of the National Council of Cadres in November 1959. See their speeches in Istiqlal Party, *National Council for Cadres: The Fez Meeting Nov. 29, 1959* (in Arabic), n.p., n.d. Many of these younger members had already indicated their sentiments in May 1958 when they voted with the old guard to accept Chiguer as minister of the interior.

[24] In May 1960, this group founded the Association Nationale de Téchniciens de l'Agriculture. Al-Ghorfi became president and Brik vice-president. 'Omar 'Abdjellil was named honorary president by acclamation of the Association's members. See *Al-Istiqlal*, 18 June 1960, p. 6.

[25] See 'Lettre d'un militant de l'Istiqlal à un militant de l'UNFP', *Al-Istiqlal*, 16 June 1963, p. 4. The article places the blame for the split upon Ben Seddiq and suggests that he would be happy to wreck the UNFP also. As we shall see, the UNFP was indeed beset by internal problems in 1963.

[26] See al-Fassi, '*Aqida wa Jihad, passim.* Like Ashford, I am obliged to relegate one element of al-Fassi's analysis to a footnote. He claims that a fundamental cause of the split was the Demnati Bank project, allegedly launched by Basri, a certain Demnati, and 'Abdulkrim Khatib, involving French capital. Al-Fassi maintains that the party elders vetoed the 'imperialist' scheme and so poisoned the atmosphere that future efforts at conciliation were of no avail. *Ibid.*, pp. 49–50.

[27] Elected to the executive committee in 1962 but not re-elected in 1965 were 'Abd al-Kabir al-Fassi and Qasim Zhiri. They are still members of the National Council of the party and in good standing.

[28] See 'Abdulhamid 'Awad, *Al-Istiqlaliya: Economic Principles and Contemporary Socialism* (in Arabic), Rabat, n.d. (1965?).

[29] 'Allal al-Fassi, *M'araka al-yum wal-ghad* (The Battle of Today and Tomorrow) (speech given to the 7th Istiqlal party congress, 12–14 Feb. 1965), Rabat, 1965, p. 30.

[30] It is probably with this group, somewhat in the Salafist tradition, that al-Fassi is most at ease. For instance in his speech '*Aqida wa Jihad*, p. 70, he singles out as heroes in saving party unity: Hashimi Filali, Bouchta Jema'i, Ahmad Mekwar, Muhammed and Ahmed Medkouri, 'Abd al-'Aziz Ben Driss – all known for their education in Arabic and Islamic training.

[31] In those elections the Istiqlal averaged 20 per cent of votes cast in rural areas and 35 per cent in urban areas, for a total of 998,478 votes, or 21 per cent of all votes cast. Figures from Octave Marais, 'L'Election de la Chambre des Représentants du Maroc', *A.A.N.*, 1963, pp. 98–102.

[32] For details of a specific example of this withdrawal, that of the Istiqlal and UMT scouts and youth organizations, see Abdelwahad Radi, 'Naissance et Evolution des Mouvements de Jeunesse au Maroc', Diplôme d'Etudes Supérieures de Philosophie (unpub.), Sorbonne, 1963–4, esp. pp. 52–3 and 107–10.

[33] For a history of this Assembly, see Pierre Ebrard, 'L'Assemblée nationale consultative marocaine', *A.A.N.*, 1962, esp. pp. 65–70. See also his more

detailed (unpublished) study of the same title at CHEAM (Comité des Hautes-Etudes de l' Afrique et l'Asie Moderne), Paris, 1959, vol. 146, no. 3100.

[34] One informant succinctly put what many had told the author in a less direct manner: 'I couldn't abandon the boss (patron) in this question. After all he found me a job in 1957 after I came back from France.'

CHAPTER TEN

[1] For more information on the founding of the UMT see H. Bérenquier, 'Le syndicalisme Marocain', *L'Afrique et l'Asie*, 1èr Trim., 1961, pp. 28–9; and for a less balanced view, G.P. Jouannet, 'Le syndicalisme au Maroc',*Revue Politique et Parlementaire*, Jan. 1955, pp. 43–52.

[2] Willard Beling, *Pan-Arabism and Labor*, Harvard, 1961, p. 73, cites a figure of 880,000 members of the UMT. The figure was drawn from the U.S. Department of Labor, Office of International Labor Affairs, *Directory of Labor Organizations: Africa*, Washington, 1958. This figure represents a serious overestimation on somebody's part.

[3] G.Lazarev, 'Le salariat agricole des fermes de colonisation', *B.E.S.M.*, April–Sept. 1966, p. 63.

[4] This figure reflects the contemporary situation. For an earlier view, see D.E.Ashford, 'Labor Politics in a New Nation', *Western Political Quarterly*, June 1960, pp. 317–18. Ashford cites a figure of 576,000 for the twenty-six federations, of which perhaps 300,000 actually pay dues.

[5] Figures taken from *The Economic Development of Morocco* (IBRD Mission), mimeo., Rabat, Dec. 1965, published by the Johns Hopkins Press, 1966; citations are from mimeo, pp. 172–3. There are 31 enterprises in Morocco employing more than 500 manual laborers, and they alone account for 43,000 of the regularly employed work force.

[6] See Kingdom of Morocco, *Regards sur l'emploi . . .*, pp. 35 and 45. In rural areas there are few adults who are actually unemployed. There, underemployment is the major problem and involves about 50 per cent of the active population.

[7] *Ibid.*, p. 24.

[8] For a general discussion, see Bruce Millen, *The Political Role of Labor in Developing Countries*, The Brookings Inst., May 1963.

[9] W.H.Lewis, 'The New Nomadism in North Africa', *M.E.J.*, Summer 1957, p. 277.

[10] Miège, *Le Maroc et l'Europe*, vol. 3, pp. 17–19; figures p. 14.

[11] Weisgerber, *op. cit.*, pp. 15–16.

[12] For one of the most perceptive analyses of these problems, see Pierre Bourdieu and A.Sayad, *Le Déracinement: La Crise d'Agriculture Traditionnelle en Algérie*, Paris, 1964, esp. pp. 117–77.

[13] See Adam, 'Le bidonville de Ben M'sik', p. 69.

[14] *Ibid.*, pp. 100–1. See also Montagne, *Naissance du prolétariat*, pp. 91–105.

[15] *Ibid.*, p. 125, and Pierre Suisse, 'L'Exode rurale', *B.E.S.M.*, Trim, 1955, pp. 460–2.

[16] Figures from André Adam, 'L'Exode rurale', *Session d'Etudes Administratives, Diplomatiques, Economiques*, Faculté de Droit du Maroc, Rabat, 1959, pp. 70–2.

[17] From an interview with Tayyib Amara, Pasha of Safi, 15 March 1966.

[18] Adam, 'L'exode rural', pp. 80–1.

[19] Anthropologists seem to be more attuned to the resilience of traditional social institutions in transitional societies than political scientists. See, for instance, Robert Redfield, *The Little Community: Peasant Society and Culture*,

Chicago, 1963, p. 29. For a vivid account of the life of one nominally uprooted Moroccan, see Driss Ben Hamad Charhadi, *Une Vie Pleine de Trous* (with Paul Bowles), Gallimard, 1965; in English, *A Life Full of Holes*, London, 1964. For a sociological view, Ladislav Cerych, *Européens et Marocains 1930–1956: Sociologie d'une Décolonisation*, Bruges, 1964, pp. 263–78.

[20] See Paul Chambergeat, 'Le référendum constitutionnel du 7 décembre 1962 au Maroc', *A.A.N.*, 1963, pp. 192–3, 201.

[21] The urban resistance consisted of a number of separate organizations. There was in 1953 the Black Hand of 'Abdesslam Bennani, and in 1954 the *Munatham as-Sirri* (Secret Organization) of Fqih Basri. The PCM organized the Black Crescent. Casablanca and Kenitra were the locales for much terrorist activity. For a complete analysis see D.E.Ashford, 'Politics and Violence in Morocco', *M.E.J.*, Winter 1959, pp. 11–25; J. & S. Lacouture, *op. cit.*, p. 137; and Bernard, *op. cit.*, vol. 3, pp. 259–85.

[22] See 'Mehdi Ben Barka', *Maghreb*, no. 13, Jan.–Feb. 1966, pp. 21–4.

[23] For a general treatment of the Liberation Army, see particularly Bernard, *op. cit.*, vol. 1, 317–82, and vol. 3, pp. 287–91.

[24] I am obliged to D.M.Hart for having allowed me to read over field notes he gathered in regard to the Liberation Army and also the uprising of the Aith Waryaghar in 1958–9. In the future in citing these notes I shall simply use *D.M.H.*

[25] From an interview with Dr 'Abdulkrim Khatib, 16 Jan. 1967, Rabat.

[26] For a complete treatment of the creation of FAR see Zartman, *Problems of New Power*, pp. 62–117.

[27] See Bernard, *op. cit.*, vol. 3, p. 379.

[28] Zartman, *Problems of New Power*, pp. 72–4.

[29] From a brochure, *The Conference of August* 1956 (in Arabic), National Council for Moroccan Resistance, n.d. (1956), p. 8.

[30] Bernard, *op. cit.*, vol. 3, pp. 259–300.

[31] For a specific example of land distribution, see Paul Pascon, 'Recherche d'une forme d'exploitation nouvelle', *Les Hommes, La Terre, et L'Eau* (ONI), no. 7, March 1964, pp. 294–313. Pascon remarks cryptically, 'The distribution had been understood as a gratification, as a profit in privileges for services rendered to the national cause, or more prosaically, perhaps as the price of appeasement. Throughout history in Morocco the supporters of triumphant causes and the faithful servants have retained land free from taxes: a plot of guich land!' (p. 309).

[32] From Kingdom of Morocco, Ministry of Information and Tourism, *The First Resistant: His Majesty Muhammed V*, (in Arabic), Rabat, n.d. (1960?), pp. 23–4.

[33] *Ibid.*, p. 21.

[34] For those designated in 1966, see *Le Petit Marocain*, 1 Oct. 1966.

[35] See *B.O.*, no. 2548, 25 Aug. 1961, 'Création de l'Office National des Résistants', p. 1197.

[36] *B.O.*, no. 2711, 19 Aug. 1964, 'Le régime d'accès aux emplois des administrations publiques réservés aux résistants', p. 1222.

[37] For one such attack see *Al-Thawra*, 10 Sept. 1966, pp. 1–2. Ben 'Aissa is accused of having processed 20,000 resistants in one year in this manner.

[38] The trial started on 9 November 1966, and on 30 December 1966 Ben Hammou was condemned to death and Bachir to life imprisonment. See *Le Monde*, 31 Dec. 1966, and *Maghreb-Informations* from 10 November to 30 December, 1966. The murder may have resulted from a dispute involving a local flirt.

[39] See Adam, 'Le bidonville de Ben M'sik', p. 130.

[40] See Nor al-Ghorfi, *op. cit.*, p. 507 (table).

[41] For a statement of his belief in the crucial nature of youth support for the UNFP, see Mehdi Ben Barka, *The Revolutionary Choice in Morocco* (in Arabic), Beirut, April 1966, p. 14.

[42] On this action against the UNEM, see A.Adam, 'Chronique sociale et culturelle', *A.A.N.*, vol. 3, 1964, pp. 206–8; and UNEM, *Complot contre les Etudiants Marocains* (Document No. 1 sur l'UNEM), Casablanca, 1964.

[43] The congress was held anyway, and a new executive committee was elected. Then on 14 Feb. 1967 the new president of UNEM, Fathallah Walalou, and another member of the executive committee along with twenty-five students, were arrested for attempting to hold a 'cultural' meeting at the Law Faculty that the university had refused to authorize. Those arrested were secretly flown to Tarfaya. The king was absent in the U.S., but after his return the students were released. See *Le Petit Marocain*, 1 March 1967, p. 1.

CHAPTER ELEVEN

[1] Quoted in *L'Express*, 12 Feb. 1959, p. 23.

[2] See Ashford, 'Labor Politics...', pp. 329–31.

[3] See al-Fassi, *'Aqida wa Jihad*, pp. 62–3. A *permanent* is a union official who is granted the right by the state to devote all his time to union duties and still draw his state salary.

[4] For the UNFP apprehensions at that date, see the pamphlet *Pour comprendre la situation au Maroc au seuil de 1960* (Comité de Liaison Franco-Maghrébin), Paris?, 1960. It was pointed out that the harassment of the UNFP became particularly acute during King Muhammed's voyage to the Middle East, 7 Jan.–7 Feb. 1960.

[5] There are a number of good accounts of the elections, as well as of preparations for them: see P.Chambergeat, 'Les élections communales Marocaines du Mai 29, 1960', *R.F.S.P.*, no. 1, vol. 11, March 1961, pp. 89–117; Zartman, *Problems of New Power*, pp. 196–243; Ashford, 'Elections in Morocco', pp. 1–15; and XXX, 'La physionomie politique du Maroc à la lumière des élections de 1960', *Lamalif*, March 1967, pp. 21–30.

[6] For an interpretation of the results see *ibid.*, p. 27, and Chambergeat, 'Les élections communales', pp. 112–3. Official detailed results have never been published.

[7] On 22 May the king declared that the task of his government was to establish a constitutional regime, bring about economic liberation, industrialization, struggle against unemployment, implement an agrarian reform, maintain a foreign policy of nonalignment, achieve the evacuation of all foreign troops, recuperate the usurped territories of Morocco, and work towards Arab and African solidarity. See UNFP comments in *Al-Rai al'Am*, 23 May 1960.

[8] See *L'Avant-Garde*, 10 June 1961, p. 1.

[9] *Akhbar ad-Dunya*, 25 May 1962, claims that in Feb. 1962, a month after the December strike, Mehdi 'Alawi, Hachemi Bennani, Muhammed al-Habib, Brahim Ba'amrani, Muhammed Bahi, Ahmad Chakir, and Tihami 'Ammar, all young party and union men of secondary importance, demanded that a congress be called in the interests of party unity. In the event, the congress was held simultaneously with that of the FLN in Algeria and the Arab Socialist Union in Egypt. Ben Barka emphasized this fact and talked of Morocco's role in the 'great revolution from Cuba to China'.

[10] Ben Barka, *The Revolutionary Choice*, pp. 40, 76–8.

[11] For the resolutions, see *A.A.N.*, vol. 1, 1962, pp. 763–8. One resolution stated 'that it is objectively impossible to pursue a policy of national liberation and transformation of economic structures within the framework of an archaic power, deprived of all popular underpinning, and within that of an irresponsible, rotten, and inert administration' (p. 767).

[12] See P. Chambergeat, 'Les Elections Communales au Maroc', *A.A.N.*, vol. 2, 1963, p. 123 (note). The places in question were Casablanca, Rabat, Tangier, Meknes, Safi, Kenitra, Yussufiya, Marrakesh.

[13] On this point, as well as for a general resumé of the internal vicissitudes of the UMT, see, 'Pour imposer la démocratie ouvrière intérieure au sein de notre centrale l'UMT', *La Voix du Postier* (Bulletin intérieur de la Fédération Nationale du Personnel des PTT), Special issue, Sept. 1965, p. 12 and throughout.

[14] *Ibid.*, p. 13.

[15] 'Abderrazak's letter to the minister, in *ibid.*, pp. 20–1.

[16] *Ibid.*, p. 32.

[17] For UMT claims, see *L'Avant-Garde*, 20 Aug. 1966. The autonomous federation held its second national congress in March 1967; see *Al-Muharrir*, 24 March 1967.

[18] Text in *Maroc-Informations*, 16 Nov. 1965, p. 1.

[19] See *Maroc-Informations*, 15 Nov. 1965, p. 1.

[20] Muhammed Boucetta, interview, 21 Oct. 1966, Rabat.

[21] See *L'Avant-Garde*, 4 May 1966, and *Al-'Alam*, 3 May 1966.

[22] See *L'Avant-Garde*, 7 May 1966. Just what Ibrahim had in mind is hard to say. He did begin to organize discussion groups with employees of the Ministry of Education (see *Al-Misa*, 17 June 1966, p. 1), but the summer hiatus and Ibrahim's absence abroad put a damper on these activities.

[23] Abdullah Ibrahim, interview, 24 Jan. 1967, Casablanca.

[24] I have developed this notion of the marginality of UNFP programs elsewhere. See my 'Marginal Politics and Elite Manipulation in Morocco', *European Journal of Sociology*, vol. 8, no. 1, 1967, pp. 94–111.

[25] See 'La situation politique au Maroc', *Maghreb*, no. 23, Sept.–Oct. 1967, pp. 7–10.

[26] See Louis Gravier, *Le Monde*, 13–14 Aug. 1967, p. 4.

CHAPTER TWELVE

[1] For a good account of the Ou Bihi revolt, see Zartman, *Problems of New Power*, pp. 80–2.

[2] Hassan Wazzani explains that the French dismissed ou Bihi from his post of qaid in 1947 or 1948 and banished him to Berrechid. At one point he found that his property near Rich was being vandalized while the French turned a blind eye. He managed to contact Hassan Wazzani in Casablanca who was organizing the PDI there, and 'Abd al-Qader Benjelloun, a lawyer and leading member of the PDI, undertook to defend ou Bihi's rights. This was the start of Wazzani's association with the governor, and the former proudly claims a role in the latter's revolt against a 'single-party dictatorship'; interview, 29 June 1966, Fez.

[3] For his testimony see *Le Petit Marocain*, 5 Jan 1959, p. 3.

[4] See *Le Petit Marocain*, 28 Jan. 1959. The court refused to recognize the validity of the *aman* granted by General Kittani, and ou Bihi and Lyoussi (*in absentia*) were condemned to death. Ou Bihi died in prison on 30 Jan. 1961. In Feb. 1962 Lyoussi was allowed to return to Morocco from Spain.

[5] See *Le Petit Marocain*, 31 Jan. 1959, p. 3.

[6] See Ashford, *Political Change*, p. 320.

[7] For more on this event, see Zartman, *Problems of New Power*, pp. 87–91, and Ashford, *Political Change*, pp. 211–8, 319–26. Also Jean Lefèvre, *Le Monde*, 4 Oct. 1958, p. 4.

[8] *D.M.H.*; and Jean Lefèvre, *Le Monde*, 2–3 Nov. 1958, p. 1.

[9] For the commission's report and Aneggai's statement see *Le Petit Marocain*, 9, 10 Dec. 1958.

[10] The well-founded charge of under-administration has been substantiated by Ashford, 'National Organizations and Political Development in Morocco', *Il Politico*, vol. 28, no. 2, 1963, pp. 372–3. In the Rif, 48 per cent of all Interior posts were vacant, with corresponding percentages of 45, 45, and 40 for Larache, Nador, and Chaouan. No other region of Morocco had more than 31 per cent vacancies.

[11] Ernest Gellner, 'Patterns of Rural Rebellion in Morocco: Tribes as Minorities', *European Journal of Sociology*, vol. 3, no. 2, 1962, p. 297.

[12] *Ibid.*, pp. 310–1.

[13] *Ibid.*, p. 296.

[14] For a portrait of Sillam, see *Al-Mashahid* (in Arabic), Rabat, vol. 4, no. 26, 1959, p. 10.

[15] Lefèvre, *Le Monde*, 9 Jan. 1959, p. 3 and 18 Jan. 1959.

[16] Zartman, *Problems of New Power*, p. 90.

[17] From a brochure, Mouvement Populaire, *Congrès Constitutif du Mouvement Populaire*, Rabat, 1959. Bekkai attended the congress as a sympathetic observer.

[18] *Loc. cit.*

[19] See *Le Petit Marocain*, 26 Oct. 1962. The *twiza* is, ideally, a form of voluntary communal labor for projects of collective utility (repair of roads, irrigation ditches, storehouses, etc.). Some qaids distorted this into obligatory or even forced labor.

[20] From the resolutions of the 1959 congress.

[21] Text, in *Traductions et Analyses de la Presse Arabe*, 23 Feb. 1961.

[22] See Chambergeat, 'Les Elections communales', *R.F.S.P.*, p. 113. Muhammed v had assured MP leaders that the elections would not be for some time. But the UNFP victory in the CCI elections forced the king to hold the local elections before the left gathered more steam. The MP as a result was badly prepared for the campaign.

[23] Ahardan recounted his difficulties with Khatib from 1963–5 in an interview, 18 April 1966, Rabat. He later repeated much of this in his speech to the Fifth National Congress of the MP, 4 Nov. 1966. See *Al-Haraka*, 11 Nov. 1966.

[24] See the interview with 'Abdullah Louggoutty, 'Ne tombons pas dans le régionalisme', *Jeune Afrique*, 24 Jan. 1965, p. 15.

[25] For a concise account of the life of the Parliament see P.Chambergeat, 'Bilan de l'expérience parlementaire marocaine', *A.A.N.*, vol. 4, 1965, pp. 101–116.

[26] See *Al-Maghreb al-'Arabi*, 3 July 1965. Khatib was not on a very firm footing in his call for a congress, for neither he nor Ahardan had thought one necessary regarding the party's adhesion to FDIC.

[27] In a clandestine issue of *Al-Maghreb al-'Arabi*. 20 Aug. 1965, Khatib praised the UMT and called for unity of the working class. His article was partly designed to vex Ahardan and his Union des Syndicats des Travailleurs Libres (USTL) originally organized by Hussein Hassoun.

[28] For the new party program, see *Al-Misa*, 4 Nov. 1966.

CHAPTER THIRTEEN

[1] *B.O.*, no. 2531, 28 April 1961, 'Délégation de pouvoir et de signature à M. Ahmed Réda Guédira, Directeur-Général du Cabinet Royal', p. 629.

[2] I have paraphrased the original motion published in *Le Petit Marocain*, 17 April 1958.

[3] The text of the protocol was supplied to me by Hussein Hassoun. In an interview, 9 April 1966, at Fez, Hassan Wazzani informed me that although Guedira did not sign the protocol (because of his position in the prince's cabinet?) he was active in promoting the *entente*.

[4] From Wazzani, interview, 9 April 1966.

[5] There has been a good deal written concerning the constitution and the referendum. The most thorough treatments are: Zartman, *Destiny of a Dynasty*, pp. 16–87; Jacques Robert, *La Monarchie Marocaine*, Paris, 1963, pp. 241–310; L.Fougére, *op. cit.*, pp. 155–67; W.A.Beling, 'Some Implications of the New Constitutional Monarchy in Morocco', *M.E.J.*, Spring 1964, pp. 64–79; C.F.Gallagher, 'Toward Constitutional Government in Morocco', *A.U.F.S. Report*, vol. 9, no. 1, 15 Jan 1963, and 'The Moroccan Constitution: Text and Comment', *A.U.F.S. Report*, vol. 9, no. 2, 20 Jan. 1963; Chambergeat, 'Le référendum constitutionel', pp. 167–207; Maurice Duverger, 'La nouvelle constitution marocaine', *Le Monde*, 30 Nov. 1962, p. 10; the special issue 'La constitution marocaine', *Confluent*, no. 7, Jan. 1963; and Michel Bourely, *Droit Public Marocain*, vol. 1 (Institutions Politiques), Rabat, 1965, pp. 235–300.

[6] M'faddel Cherkaoui, interview, 25 Feb. 1966, Rabat.

[7] Guedira, interview, 28 Feb. 1966, Rabat.

[8] For the Istiqlal's favorable interpretation of the constitution, see 'Abdulkrim Ghallab, *This is the Constitution* (in Arabic), n.d., Rabat.

[9] From an interview with M'faddel Cherkaoui, 25 Feb. 1966, Rabat. For more on the king's involvement in the creation of FDIC see Marais, 'L'élection de la chambre . . .', p. 86.

[10] For his speech, 18 April 1963, see *A.A.N.*, vol. 2, 1963, p. 883; see also Jacques Robert, 'Les élections législatives du 17 Mai et l'évolution politique interne au Maroc', *Revue Juridique et Politique d'Outre-Mer*, April–June 1963, p. 266.

[11] *A.A.N.*, 1963, p. 884.

[12] UNFP communiqué, 2 May 1963, included in a private dossier on the 1963 elections prepared by Bachir Awad.

[13] The apprehensions of the UNFP were recounted to me by 'Abderrahman Yussufi, interview, 26 Oct. 1965, Casablanca.

[14] For a detailed presentation of the returns, see Marais, 'L'élection de la chambre . . .', *passim*; also C.F.Gallagher, 'The Meanings of the Moroccan Elections', *A.U.F.S. Report*, vol. 9, no. 5, June 1963; and Stuart Schaar, 'King Hassan's Alternatives', *Africa Report*, Aug. 1963, pp. 7–12.

[15] Figures from Gallagher, 'The Moroccan Elections', p. 6. Bachir Awad estimates that had there been an effective alliance between the UNFP and the Istiqlal, FDIC would have won only 14 seats.

[16] See P.Chambergeat, 'Les élections communales au Maroc', *A.A.N.*, vol. 2, 1963, p. 123.

[17] See *Akhir Sa'a*, 1 Oct. 1963, in *Traductions et Analyses de la Presse Arabe*, 2 Oct. 1963. M'faddel Cherkaoui was elected president of the Chamber of Counsellors.

[18] This interpretation is borrowed from Chambergeat, 'Bilan de l'expérience parlementaire . . .', pp. 101–2.

[19] *Ibid.*, p. 103.

[20] Bahnini had presented his government's program to parliament on 12 January 1964, and he did not allude to any grave financial difficulties. Then, on 20 May, the price of sugar was raised drastically in order to curtail consumption and to reduce the outflow of hard currency used to pay for sugar imports. The outflow had reached disastrous proportions, and the UNFP decided to use this issue for a general critique of the government's economic policy. See UNFP, *Motion de Censure Contre la Politique Economique et Financière du Gouvernement*, Casablanca, June 1964. The brochure in Arabic bearing the same title is far more detailed reproducing the texts of speeches of UNFP deputies and the debates with the ministers.

[21] See *Al-Watan*, 26 Sept. 1964, cited in *Traductions et Analyses de la Presse Arabe*, 27 Sept. 1964. See also 'Le Maroc a un parti de plus', *Jeune Afrique*, 20 April 1964, p. 7; and 'Création du Parti Socialiste Démocrate', *A.A.N.*, vol. 3, 1964, pp. 609–32.

CHAPTER FOURTEEN

[1] This enumeration of appointive powers is taken from Bourely, *op. cit.*, pp. 183–4.

[2] From an interview in *Réalités*, no. 250, Nov. 1966. The complete text of the interview was published in *Maghreb-Informations*, no. 160, 15 Nov. 1966.

[3] See Riggs, *op. cit.*, pp. 74, 131–2.

[4] See *L'Avant-Garde*, 27 Nov. 1965, p. 4.

[5] Each week sees its speculations on a ministerial shake-up, and every now and again the pundits of the Balima Hotel say this time it's for sure. Such occasions have occurred with a statement by Al-Fassi (*L'Opinion*, 10 June 1966), at the beginning of the Ben Barka trial (J. Ben Brahem, 'L'Hypothèse d'un remaniement ministériel est sérieusement envisagée à Rabat', *Le Monde*, 17 Sept. 1966), and prior to King Hassan's trip to the U.S. ('Le serpent de mer et la constitution', *Jeune Afrique*, no. 316, 29 Jan. 1967, p. 19.

CHAPTER FIFTEEN

[1] From a broadcast commentary of RTM, 5 Jan. 1967, published in *Presse Marocaine de Langue Arabe: Traductions*, French Embassy, Rabat, 6 Jan. 1967.

[2] For a far more systematic analysis treating administrative behavior in transitional societies in general, see Riggs, *op. cit.*, esp. on 'strategic spending', pp. 141–2, and on 'transfer index', pp. 212–4.

[3] Kingdom of Morocco, Royal Cabinet, *Tawjihát* (Orientations), in Arabic, 20 April 1965, p. 7.

[4] *Ibid.*, p. 8. A few ministers have tried to transfer the directors of their personal cabinets to the post of sec.-gen. The ideal sec.-gen. is described in Bourely, *op. cit.*, p. 311.

[5] Marais, 'Classe dirigeante', pp. 728, 730.

[6] Jules et Jim Aubin, *op. cit.*, p. 76. Figure includes diplomatic corps.

[7] Samir Amin, *op. cit.*, vol. 1, pp. 338–9. M. Amin estimates that of the 68,000 employees in 1955, 41,000 were non-Moroccan. Of the 255,000 in 1964 only 15,000 were non-Moroccan. He further indicates the growth of the administration in terms of Morocco's operating budget which increased from 77 million dirhams in 1955 to 220 million dirhams in 1964 (p. 339). For still more figures, see Ashford, *Political Change*, pp. 118–24. Ashford quotes an estimate of a possible 110,000 civil servants by the end of 1958 (p. 119). Other pertinent

articles are; Paul Buttin, 'La relève au Maroc des cadres français par les cadres marocains', *Civilisations*, vol. 11, no. 1, 1961, pp. 52-61; and Muhammed al-Fassi, 'Le problème des cadres au Maroc', *Problèmes des Cadres dans les Pays Tropicaux et Subtropicaux*, INCIDI, Brussels, 1961, pp. 41-51.

[8] Al-Fassi, *The Battle of Today and Tomorrow*, pp. 126-7.

[9] From the proceedings of the 2nd UNFP Congress, May 1962, at which time the party's lack of personnel was discussed. For the effect of administrative drain on youth movements, see Radi, *op. cit.*, p. 110.

[10] *B.O.*, no. 2267, Dahir no. 1-56-046, 6 April 1956, 'fixant le statut des Gouverneurs', p. 341; and Dahir no. 1-56-047, 'fixant le statut des caids', p. 342.

[11] Under the makhzan and under the protectorate, qaids had no fixed salaries and, in the latter period, lived on rake-offs from *tertib* collections (agricultural taxes). See Bernard, *op. cit.*, vol. 3, pp. 51-2.

[12] Octave Marais states that in 1960 qaids that were locally recruited still represented a high proportion of the corps, varying according to the province from 20 to 50 per cent. See his excellent study, 'L'administration locale et les élus au Maroc', paper presented to the General Assembly of the Mediterranean Social Science Research Council, 12-16 Sept. 1966, Beirut, p. 18.

[13] See Ernest Gellner, 'From Ibn Khaldun to Karl Marx', *The Political Quarterly*, vol. 32, no. 4, Oct.-Dec. 1961, p. 385; also, J.R., 'Un aspect du Maroc actuel: le bled sans caid,' *L'Afrique et L'Asie*, no. 40, 4e Trim, 1957, pp. 52-4.

[14] Marais, 'L'Administration rurale . . .', p. 3. I am obliged to Boris de Parfontief for his insights on these early problems of organizing Interior, and especially the training of administrators. One could also usefully consult in this connection Ernest Gellner, 'Independence in the Central High Atlas', *M.E.J.*, Summer 1957, pp. 237-52.

[15] Marais, 'L'Administration rurale . . .', p. 8.

[16] See 'Centre de formation des agents d'autorité relevant du Ministère de l'Intérieur', *Provinces et Communes*, no. 2, April-May 1964.

[17] See Marais, 'L'Administration rurale . . .', pp. 5-6.

[18] Dahir no. 1-59-315, 23 June 1960, 'relatif à l'organisation communale'.

[19] Bourely, *op. cit.*, p. 365, and for his discussion of the councils in general, pp. 347-68. See also Marais, 'L'Administration rurale . . .', p. 13. I have also consulted an unpublished study by Muhammed Bouzidi, 'Les obstacles à la coopération entre les autorités locales et la population rurale', 1966, 27 pp.

[20] See H. Nicholas-Mourer, 'Les collectivités locales dans l'administration territoriale du Royaume du Maroc', *A.A.N.*, vol. 2, 1963, pp. 129-60.

[21] *B.O.*, no. 2819, 9 Nov. 1966, pp. 1266-82. The dahirs are summarized in *Maghreb-Informations*, 12 Nov. 1966, pp. 1 and 4.

[22] Of these only 16,000 had been redistributed to Moroccan peasants by the state. For a chronological and regional breakdown of this redistribution, see *La Vie Economique*, 3 June 1966, pp. 1 and 3.

[23] Their failure had become so obvious that the minister of agriculture and the king felt obliged to make public statements regarding their performance. For Chiguer's remarks, see *Maroc-Informations*, 12 March 1966, and for the king's see *Le Petit Marocain*, 1 and 7 July, 1966.

[24] See 'Les Lots de colonisation', *Lamalif*, no. 6, Oct. 1966, pp. 14-15. The period referred to, 1964-5, corresponds to the pork-barrel incumbency of Mahjoubi Ahardan as minister of agriculture.

[25] *Maroc 66*, as quoted in *Le Petit Marocain*, 3 March 1966.

[26] From the speech of Hassan II on the tenth anniversary of the founding of FAR; text in *Le Petit Marocain*, 15 March 1966.

[27] See Patrice Blacque-Bélaire, 'La Promotion Nationale Marocaine: bilan

en 1963', *A.A.N.*, 1963, p. 164. André Tiano gives more and somewhat varying details: 10,000 recruits, 313 corporals, 956 chief corporals, 458 junior officers, and 85 officers, all of whose active duty had been terminated, have been put at the disposition of Promotion Nationale by FAR. See his *La Politique Economique et Financière du Maroc Indépendant*, Tiers Monde, Paris, 1963, p. 57.

[28] See the excellent study of FAR of M.B., 'Le Maroc' in *Le Rôle Extra-Militaire de l'Armée dans le Tiers Monde*, Paris, 1966, pp. 31–55; his remarks on apolitical officers, pp. 46–7.

[29] 'Maroc 66', *op. cit.*, gives this figure. Army recruits are numbered at 40,000. Jean Lacouture estimates that in 1956 about 300 Moroccan officers serving in the French army joined FAR. See his 'L'Armée est-elle au Maroc un élément de la stabilité monarchique?', *Le Monde*, 17–18 August 1958, p. 6.

[30] M.B., *op. cit.*, p. 36. Since 1961, Oufqir and Ahardan have tried to check this trend and have favored loyal Berber candidates.

[31] The rank of director-general is equivalent to that of minister. See *B.O.*, no. 2667, 12 Dec. 1963, Dahir no. 1–63–349, 12 Nov. 1963, 'Fixant la composition du Cabinet Royal et du Secrétariat particulier de Sa Majesté le Roi', p. 1907. The dahir provides for 1 director-general, 1 director, 1 chef, 1 judicial advisor, 4 attachés, and 8 *chargés de mission*.

[32] Fougére, *op. cit.*, p. 164.

[33] The judgment was handed down in a trial of cooking oil salesmen and was published in *Le Monde*, 23 April 1960. The quote is in Zartman, *Destiny of a Dynasty*, pp. 34–5 (note).

[34] For the text of the speech and other relevant documents, see *Un Procès d'Inquisition*, Paris–Provence–Impression, 1960, 189 pp.

[35] The official text of the judgment was provided to me by the Supreme Court: 'The Moroccan Communist Party vs. the State Prosecutor', Rabat, 28 May 1964, handtyped, 4 pp.

[36] For the king's remarks, see *Le Maroc en marche . . .*, p. 209; and for a resumé of the case, see 'L'Affaire des Bahaistes', *Confluent*, Dec. 1963, pp. 968–86.

[37] Kingdom of Morocco, Supreme Court, 'Abd al-Aziz al-Waryashi vs. the State Prosecutor', Judgment no. 300-S-7 (in Arabic), Rabat, 11 Dec. 1963, 2 pp.

[38] A good account of the arrests and trial are to be found in 'Le complot contre le Roi', *Confluent*, no. 41, May 1964, pp. 470–510. A foreign observer's views in, Erik Poulsson, 'The Treason Trial in Morocco', *Bulletin of the International Commission of Jurists*, no. 18, March 1964; for the UNFP arguments, see *La Vérité sur le Complot* (supplément en langue française du journal *AT-Tahrir*), Nov. 1963; and *Bulletin du Comité d'Information et d'Etude sur la Situation au Maroc: Numero Spécial*, Paris, January 1964. I have also consulted the *procès verbaux* and the *mises-en-accusation* put at my disposal by one of the defense lawyers.

[39] The evidence is well presented in the issue of *Confluent*, May 1964. The accused claim that Shaykh al-'Arab was like a 'diseased rat' working on police orders, and biting as many members of the UNFP as possible with his talk of assassinating the king. Once he had completed his task, the police were obliged to get rid of him. He was in fact shot down in a gun battle with the police in Casablanca, 7 Aug. 1964. He had been sentenced to death *in absentia*, but had returned secretly to Morocco from Algeria.

[40] Otto Kirchheimer, *Political Justice*, Princeton, 1961, p. 426.

[41] For an account of the press under the protectorate see Bernard, *op. cit.*, vol. 3, pp. 125–32.

[42] For a detailed discussion of this problem and the press in general, see

Pierre-José Mollard, *Le Régime Juridique de la Presse au Maroc*, Collection de la Faculté des Sciences Juridiques, Economiques et Sociales, Rabat, 1963, pp. 45–9.

[43] Their case is carried by the Syndicat National de la Presse Marocaine, *Pourquoi Nous Combattons la Presse Mas*, Rabat, n.d. (1963).

[44] See *Maroc-Informations*, 10 Dec. 1965, p. 1.

[45] See Mollard, *op. cit.*, pp. 78–9, 80–2. For an extensive party critique of the Press Code see, *Al-'Alam*, 18 May 1966.

[46] From a selection of mimeographed *khutba* texts printed by the Ministry of Awqaf and made available to me by Muhammed at-Tanji of that Ministry. Kingdom of Morocco, Minister of Awqaf, *Sermons of Orientation and Guidance* (in Arabic), Rabat, 1964.

CHAPTER SIXTEEN

[1] In other Middle Eastern countries this has been a political fact of life for some time. As regards Egypt, see Leonard Binder, 'Egypt: the Integrative Revolution', in *Political Culture and Political Development*, pp. 412–3; and Malcolm Kerr, 'Egypt', in J.S.Coleman (ed.), *Education and Political Development*, Princeton, 1965, pp. 169–94.

[2] See the speech of King Hassan in *Le Petit Marocain*, 4 March 1967, p. 3.

[3] Aziz Belal, in an address to the National Federation of Teachers, recommended an increase in educational outlays to 25–30 per cent of the annual state budget. See *L'Avant-Garde*, 15 April 1967, p. 3.

[4] See D.E.Ashford, *Second and Third Generation Elites in the Mahgreb*, Policy Research Study, U.S. Department of State, Washington, 1964. This study is pertinent to the discussion throughout this chapter.

[5] Figures from Kingdom of Morocco, Division du Plan et des Statistiques, 'Projections de Population-Répercussions sur Certains Aspects de l'Economie du Pays et Solutions Proposées', July 1965, mimeo. p. 11.

[6] Figures from Kingdom of Morocco, Royal Cabinet, Royal Memorandum on National Education, in Arabic, Aug. 1966, p. 47. The same unpublished study mentioned on p. 301 estimates that in the period 1967–74 there will be 21,000 new university-level students, 23,000 new *bacheliers*, and 103,000 students will be awarded the secondary school certificate (CES). In the period 1972–7, c. 22,000 students annually will be awarded the CES, and 10,000 annually will pass the *baccalauréat*.

[7] Nor el-Ghorfi, *op. cit.*, p. 33. On Moroccan agricultural development, one might also consult Jacques Dubois, 'Pour une réforme de l'administration agricole au Maroc', *Institutions et Développement Agricole du Maghreb*, Etudes Tiers Monde, Paris, 1965, pp. 77–184.

[8] These production figures were taken from *L'Avant-Garde*, 18 June 1966, p. 3. The population figures may be found in Saidi Salama and Abdullah Berrada, 'Démographie marocaine', *Confluent*, no. 50, April, May, June, 1965, pp. 200–17, esp. p. 204.

[9] Figures extracted from *The Economic Development of Morocco, op. cit.*, pp. 11–14; Kingdom of Morocco, Ministry of National Economy, *Tableaux Economiques*, Service Centrale de Statistiques, Rabat, 1960, p. 285; *CEDIES Informations*, Bulletin no. 386, 15 Feb. 1964, 7 pp.; Kingdom of Morocco, Délégation Générale à la Promotion Nationale et au Plan, *Plan Triennial 1965–1967*, Division de la Coordination Economique et du Plan, Rabat, 1965, pp. 75–120.

[10] There is no space here to discuss Moroccan planning. For those interested, the following would be usefully consulted: D.E.Ashford, *Morocco-Tunisia:*

Politics and Planning, Syracuse, 1965; Jane and Andrew Carey, 'The Two Developing Worlds of Morocco: A Case Study in Economic Development and Planning', *M.E.J.*, Autumn 1962, pp. 457–75; Albert Waterston, *Planning in Morocco*, Economic Development Institute, Johns Hopkins Press, 1962; treating post-1956 planning in relation to more general problems of development are: Samir Amin, *op. cit.*, vol. 2, pp. 105–76; and Pierre-Henry Dupuy, *Le Trésor, La Croissance, et la Monnaie au Maroc*, Rabat, 1965.

[11] For a detailed analysis, see Meynaud, *op. cit.*, *passim*, but especially p. 57.

[12] See for instance 'Projections de population', p. 2.

[13] See André Adam, 'Chronique sociale et culturelle', *A.A.N.*, 1964, pp. 206–8.

[14] See *Royal Memorandum on National Education*, p. 10; also 'Pour un enseignement national et démocratique', *L'Avant-Garde*, 18 April 1967, pp. 1, 3.

[15] *Royal Memorandum on National Education*, p. 18.

[16] See 'Doctrine de l'enseignement', press conference of the minister of education, Muhammed Benhima, in *Le Petit Marocain*, 7 April 1966, pp. 2–3; cf. Sahlain Marate, 'Après les hécatombes: les examens', *Lamalif*, no. 5, July–Aug. 1966, pp. 46–8; and Ashford, 'Second and Third Generation Elites', p. 14.

[17] The Istiqlal has drawn up an unrealistic plan to meet the crisis: see Istiqlal Party, *The Battle of Destiny: Toward the Reform and Arabization of Education* (in Arabic), Rabat, 1967.

[18] *Royal Memorandum on National Education*, p. 24.

[19] Experts of the IBRD recommended heavy budgetary cutbacks in educational outlays for the period 1965–70 and beyond. See the *Economic Development of Morocco*, pp. 40–1.

[20] Ashford found these characteristics to prevail among secondary school students and graduates in the Istiqlal. See his *Perspectives of a Moroccan Nationalist*, Totowa, New Jersey, 1964, p. 142.

[21] Apter, *op. cit.*, p. 341; see also Ashford, 'Second and Third Generation Elites', p. 37; the content of political religion in the Arab world has been perceptively discussed by Malcolm Kerr in 'Arab Radical Notions of Democracy', *St. Antony's Papers*, no. 16, Middle Eastern Affairs, no. 3, London, 1963, pp. 9–40.

[22] See André Adam, *Une Enquête auprès de la Jeunesse Musulmane du Maroc*, Série: Travaux et Mémoires, no. 28, Aix-en-Provence, 1963, p. 132.

[23] James Coleman warns against jumping to conclusions in regard to the challenge of presumptive elites and cites 'the capacity of elite survival in seemingly hopeless circumstances . . .'. See his 'Introduction to Part III', in *Education and Political Development*, p. 361.

[24] On the riots, see 'Les émeutes de Casablanca et la situation politique au Maroc', *Maghreb*, no. 9, May–June 1965, pp. 15–18; Jean Lacouture, 'Le pouvoir royal et les étudiants', *Le Monde*, 26 March 1965; and *Jeune Afrique*, 11 April 1965, pp. 14–15.

[25] For the unofficial estimates, see *Le Monde*, 31 March 1965, p. 6.

[26] Text of speech, in *Le Maroc en marche*, pp. 488–94.

[27] See *Le Monde*, 10 July 1968.

CONCLUSION

[1] Cf. Samuel P. Huntington, 'The Political Modernization of Traditional Monarchies', *Daedalus*, Summer 1966, p. 783; who sees the shah's ability to 'innovate' policies in an entirely different light.

[2] See Lucian W. Pye, *Politics, Personality, and Nation Building: Burma's Search for Identity* (5th imp.), Yale, 1968, pp. 18–19.

INDEX

'Ababou family, 95
Abarkash, Haddou (Haddou 'Rifi'),
238, 245, 252–3
'Abdarrahman, Sultan Moulay, 22,
329
'Abderrazak, Muhammed, 173,
184, 186, 187, 221, 226
'Abdi, 'Aissa Ben 'Omar-al, 36
'Abdesslam, Moulay, 209
'Abdjellil, 'Omar, education, 101;
agricultural engineer, 190; leader
in National Party, 49, 104;
president Banque du Crédit Populaire, 105, 107; in Istiqlal, 105,
118, 173, 181, 187; member
Private Economic Council (1967),
290
'Abduh, Muhammed, 44
'Abdullah, Prince Moulay, 151
'Abdullah, Said behlaj, 208
Abu Sitta, xiv, see Boucetta
Adam, André, 134, 202, 324, 332,
337, 343, 344, 352
Afghani, Jamal ad-Din al-, 44, 192
Agadir, 41, 91, 207
Aqjuj, Mess'ud, 242, 243
agnatic descent, 159
agriculture, the main occupation,
304; subsistence, 121; commercial, 33, 129, 140, 141; modern
methods, 40, 43; laborers, 135,
198; present depression, 304–5;
reform a political issue, 5; see
also labor unions, khammas agur-
ram, 147
Ahardan, Lahidi, 237
Ahardan, Mahjoubi, born Ait
Sgougou tribal federation, 90–1;
'Berberism', 123, 245, 247;
Azrou graduate, 116; early
nationalist career, 209, 237, 257;

leader in Mouvement Populaire,
90, 237–53; conflict with Khatib,
247–8, 251–2; electoral defeat,
1963, 91; Minister of Defence,
1963, 90, 248
'Aisha, Princess Lalla, 125
Ait Attab tribe, 20
Ait Mzal tribe, 134
Ait Sgougou tribal confederation,
90–1
Ait Swab tribe, 134
Aith Waryaghar tribe, 205, 206,
239, 240, 242
Aix-les-Bains conference (1955),
170, 204
Aknoul, 204
'Alami, the family, 97; 'Abd al-
Aziz, 105, 290; Hassan, 97
Alawi dynasty/family, history, 15,
20, 27, 28, 37, 44, 52; land-
holdings, 151–2; female mem-
bers, 151; present family, 144,
153–4; Alawi pashas, 153; Alawi
shurfa, 139
'Alawi, Moulay Ahmad, 153, 249,
263, 289, 290; Moulay al-
Arabi (Shaykh al-Islam), 44, 92;
Muhammed Ben Moulay 'Arafa
(Sultan 1953–5), 52, 53, 96, 139;
Moulay Hafidh, 153; Moulay
Larbi, 259, 263; see also Aisha,
Princess Lalla; Abdullah, Prince
Moulay; Ali, Prince Moulay;
Hassan II; Muhammed v
Algeria, French occupation, 24,
33; uprisings against French,
54, 174, 180, 183; situation cf.
Morocco, 3, 81, 317, 321; Algeria-
Morocco border conflict, 215,
264, 294; labor migration to, 205,
241

353

INDEX

'Ali, Prince Moulay, 151
alliance-building, -groups, 75–8,
  83, 88–90, 100, 132, 149, 194
Almohades dynasty, 69, 71, 89
Almoravids dynasty, 89
Alport, E. A., 337
Amar, David, 337
amghar (tribal leader), 79, 89, 91,
  112
Amharoq, 122, 139, 235
amil (local governor), 19, 95, 277
Amin, Samir, 324, 338, 348, 352
'Ammar, Tihami, 118, 119
Ammeln tribal group, 134
Ammoun, André, 336
Annegai, 'Abderrahman, 240, 289
Anti-Atlas, pacification, 35
Apter, D., 310, 352
Arabic, language, 11, 12, 28, 307;
  schools, 85, 113; tribes, 70
Arabization, 192, 307, 308
arbitration commissions, 89
Army, Moroccan, 146–7, 155, 161,
  180, 206, 287–9; Moroccan
  troops in French Army, 207; *see
  also* Forces Armés Royales
Arnaud, A. L., 73, 323, 334, 336
Aron, Raymond, 82, 334
Arslan, Shakib, 45
artisans, 193
Ashford, Douglas, 9, 137, 177, 302,
  325, 327, 331, 332, 340, 342, 343,
  344, 346, 348, 351, 352
as-saddad (courts), 236
assassination plots, 1959, 91; 1963,
  see plot arrests
*Association des Anciens Elèves
  d'Azrou*, 115, 116–9
Association of Veterans and War
  Victims, 243
'Attabi, Belhaj, 209
Aubin, Eugène, 23, 323, 328, 329,
  335, 336
Aubin, Jules and Jim, 325, 338,
  339, 348
'Awad, Abdul, 192, 341; Muh-
  ammed, 289, 290
Ayache, Albert, 111, 112, 127, 303,
  324, 330, 335, 336, 337, 338
'Ayyadi family, 95, 139
'azibs (feudal estates), 28
'Aziz, Sultan Moulay 'abdat, 15, 18
'Aziza, Lalla, 70

Azrou, 113; the College, 113–16,
  119, 309; graduates, 237, 282,
  287

Ba-Amran tribe, 208
Bahaism, 292–3
Bahnini, Ahmad, Prime Minister
  1963–5, 84, 249; president of
  PSD, 263
Bahnini, Muhammed, 269, 289
Balafrej, Ahmad, a Rabati, 255;
  National Party leader, 49, 104;
  Istiqlal, 173, 255; eclipse by
  Al-Fassi, 191; minister in Bekkai
  government, 181, 182; Prime
  Minister 1958, 136, 184–7; later
  inactivity, 194
baniqas, 39–40
Banque du Crédit Populaire, 105
baraka, 19, 35, 92, 97, 98, 144
Bargach, brothers, 256; family, 95,
  96, 97; Muhammed, 107
Barrou, Muhammed, 123
Barth, Frederick, 333
Basri, Fqih (Muhammed), resistance leader, 203, 205, 209, 343;
  in Istiqlal, 173, 184, 203; a
  'young turk', 136, 181; in UNFP,
  102, 203, 211; arrest (1959),
  211, 212, 218, 294; release (1960),
  212
bay'a, 19, 20
Bekkai, M'Barrek, a notable from
  the Beni Iznassen, 238; early
  career, 238; political inde-
  pendant, 238; president Association of Veterans..., 243; Prime
  Minister (1955–58), 56, 83–4,
  234, 238; resignation, 181; Minister of Interior (1960), 282
Bekkai, Muhammed, 142, 251
Bekkali, Abdullah, 190
Bel 'Abbas, Yussuf, 187, 246,
  249, 263, 264, 311
Bel 'Arbi; General, 210; Si
  Naceur, 107; Tayyib, 245, 290
Belgnaoui, Muhammed, 256
Beling, Willard, 342, 347
Bel Miloudi, Colonel, 205, 208,
  239, 240
Belqid, Hussein, 209
Ben 'Abboud, Mehdi, 203, 209
Ben Abderrazik, Muhammed, 290

354

Hassar family, 109
Hassoun, Hussein, 240, 245, 249, 263
Hiba, Al-, 36, 76
Hirschberg, H.Z., 337
Hoceima, al- (province), 246
hotels, 134
Hottinger, Arnold, 335
'Houses of Thought', 158, 314
Huntington, Samuel P., 352

Ibn Khaldun, 17
Ibrahim, Abdullah, release from prison, 174; in resistance, 174; a southerner, 136; a 'young turk' in Istiqlal, 136, 181, 182, 183, 184, 185, 186, 228–9; and split in Istiqlal, 186–94; and UNFP, 217–218; Prime Minister (1958), 187; dismissal (May 1960), 219; relations with king, 218
Ida ou Gnidif tribe, 134
Idriss, Moulay (founder of Fez), 27
Igzinnayan tribe, 204, 206, 239, 242
illiteracy, 84
independence of Morocco (1956), 54; first government, 56
industry, 33; industrial workers, 32, 35, 198; employment, 198; output, 305; development, 100
Institut des Hautes Etudes Marocaines, 102
intellectuals, intelligentsia, 35, 42, 196, 198, 213–16; emigration, 314; the 'intellectual proletariat', 300, 314, 321
Iran, 2–3, 151, 318
irrigation, 43, 140
Islah (Reform) Party, Tetouan, 257
Islam, 26, 43–6, 70, 71; Islamic reform, 317; Islamic socialism, 192, 244, 246; *see also* religion, shari'a
Isly, Battle of (1844), 16, 21, 22
Ismail, Sultan Moulay (1672–1727), 22, 30, 54, 95, 328
Israel, 11, 127
Istiqlal party, founding (Jan. 1944), 50, 104; components, organisation, leadership, 51, 177, 192–3; decapitation at exile of sultan (1953), 52–3; attitude to urban terrorists, 53; to rural resistance,

54; extent of Berber support, 57; of Sussi support, 136–8; bourgeois support, 103–4, 105, 192; opposition of rural notability, 235–7; association with Fassis, 104; feminist wing, 125; relations with Muhammed v, 56, 146–7, 149, 179–80, 182–3, 233–234; with UMT, 55, 228; with students, 214; predominance in 1956, 254; internal conflicts (1958–9), 76, 106, 169–85; position since the split, 47, 192–3; *see also* old turbans, young turks
Al-Istiqlal (Arabic daily), 176, 181, 184, 191
Italians, 33

jama'a (council of elders), 22, 41, 244
Jama'i family, 96, 100
Jazouli, Al-, 26
Jebli, Abdesslan, 209, 212
Jews, 11–12, 56, 71, 72, 94, 125–8, 194
Joannet, G.P., 342
Jordan, 3
judicial organization, judiciary, 236, 291–5
Juin, Resident-General, 51, 52, 53
Julien, C.-A., 323, 324, 328, 330
June War (1967), 149, 230
Justinard, Colonel, 7, 327, 329

Kebbaj, 'Abbas, 136, 206
Kenitra, 11
Kerr, Malcolm, 351, 352
khalifa (governor), 19, 20, 24, 41, 281
khammas (sharecroppers), 121, 135, 139, 160
Khattabi, al-, 'Abdulkrim, 37; Muhammed, 332
khatib (mosque official), 297
Khatib, family, 108; Abdellatif, 290; Abderrahman, 109, 248; Omar, 109
Khatib, Dr Abdulkrim, from al-Jadida, 206; political strength in the Rif, 206; leader in resistance, 174, 203, 205, 208; in MP (President till 1966), 109, 238, 239–53; conflict with Ahardan, 251–2;